580 Home-Style Recipes Right at Your Fingertips

WHEN we published the first edition of our *Taste of Home Annual Recipes* in late 1996, we suspected it would be popular. After all, many of our magazine readers had been asking us to gather an entire year's worth of *Taste of Home* recipes into one convenient, thoroughly indexed book.

But we were surprised—and pleasantly delighted—when that *1997 Taste of Home Annual Recipes* book became our *best-selling book* ever!

Like that first edition, we think this *1998 Taste of Home Annual Recipes* cookbook will become a valued reference in your kitchen for a number of reasons:

1. Its 324 pages are organized into 16 handy chapters for easy reference. Between its covers you have at hand every single *Taste of Home* recipe we published in 1997.

2. Plus we've included *dozens* of bonus recipes never before published in *Taste of Home*. So you'll have a whole group of new down-home recipes to try.

3. We've listed all 580 of these recipes in *three different indexes* to make any of them easy to find—one indexes them by food category, one tells you which issue of *Taste of Home* it originally appeared in, and one designates every recipe that meets diabetic and restricted diet needs. These handy indexes can be found on pages 306-318.

4. The full-color pictures in this cookbook are *bigger* than ever so you can plainly see what many of these dishes will look like before you begin preparing them.

5. We've used larger print for easy reading while cooking. And each recipe is presented "all-on-a-page", so you never have to turn back and forth while cooking.

6. This volume is printed on the highest-quality coated paper to make the foods more attractive and appealing. More importantly, it lets you wipe away spatters easily.

7. The book lies open and *stays open* as you cook. Its durable hard cover will give you *years* of use (you'll never have to worry about dog-earring your magazine collection again).

But the real proof of this volume's value is in the tasting. Your family will *rave* at the results of these recipes, all of which are favorites of other families.

Tight on time? The 55 fast-to-fix recipes in our "Meals in Minutes" chapter offer you complete menus (including dessert) that you can take from start to finish in 30 minutes or less.

On a budget? The frugal yet flavorful feast on page 280—featuring "Hearty Bean Soup", "Cornmeal Rolls" and "Hot Water Gingerbread"—costs just 99¢ a plate!

Family picnic? Or need a dish for a potluck or other group gathering? Try one of the 42 "Potluck Pleasers" recipes.

Planning a special supper? Turn to the "My Mom's Best Meal" and "Editors' Meals" chapters for 12 delectable meals that come straight from the kitchens of fellow country cooks.

With 580 delicious dishes to choose from, you're sure to refer to this treasury of recipes again and again for years to come!

1998 Taste of Home Annual Recipes

Editor: Julie Schnittka
Art Director: Linda Dzik
Food Editor: Coleen Martin
Associate Editor: Kristine Krueger
Production: Ellen Lloyd, Claudia Wardius
Cover Design: Vicky Marie Moseley
Cover Photography: Glenn Thiesenhusen

Taste of Home®

Executive Editor: Kathy Pohl
Food Editor: Coleen Martin
Associate Food Editor: Sue A. Jurack
Assistant Food Editor: Corinne Willkomm
Senior Editor: Bob Ottum
Managing Editor: Ann Kaiser
Assistant Managing Editor: Faithann Stoner
Associate Editors: Henry de Fiebre, Kristine Krueger, Sharon Selz
Test Kitchen Home Economist: Julie Seguin
Test Kitchen Assistants: Judith Scholovich, Sherry Smalley
Editorial Assistants: Mary Ann Koebernik, Barb Czysz, Heather Kuenzi
Design Director: Jim Sibilski
Art Director: Vicky Marie Moseley
Food Photography: Scott Anderson, Glenn Thiesenhusen
Food Photography Artist: Stephanie Marchese
Photo Studio Coordinator: Anne Schimmel
Production: Ellen Lloyd, Judy Pope, Claudia Wardius
Publisher: Roy Reiman

Taste of Home Books
©1997 Reiman Publications, L.P.
5400 S. 60th St., Greendale WI 53129

International Standard Book Number:
0-89821-216-2
International Standard Serial Number:
1094-3463

PICTURED AT RIGHT. Clockwise from upper right: Stars and Stripes Parfaits (p. 151), Marble Squares (p. 125), Cheesy Potato Bake, Mom's Meat Loaf, Cucumbers with Dressing and Purple Plum Pie (pp. 202 and 203); Yogurt Yeast Rolls (p. 167) and Chicken Provencale (p. 70).

Taste of Home 1998 Annual Recipes

PICTURED ON THE FRONT COVER. Clockwise from upper left: Roasted Chicken and Potatoes (p. 190), Cornmeal Rolls (p. 280), Cranberry Orange Sundaes (p. 149) and Dilled Corn and Peas (p. 65).

PICTURED ON THE BACK COVER. Clockwise from top: Peanut Butter Chocolate Chip Cookies (p. 118), Chocolate Cherry Pie (p. 146) and Chocolate Tea Bread (p. 107).

Photo Contributor: p. 201—Bray Photography, St. Joseph, MO.

FOR ADDITIONAL COPIES of this book or information on other books, write: *Taste of Home* Books, P.O. Box 990, Greendale WI 53129. **Credit card orders call toll-free 1-800/558-1013.**

Snacks & Beverages

For great beginnings to any meal—or as special treats throughout the day—you can rely on these hearty appetizers, satisfying snacks and refreshing beverages.

—— 🍸 🍸 🍸 ——

LOVE THOSE SNACKS! Clockwise from upper right: Twice-Baked New Potatoes (p. 18), Spinach Turnovers (p. 20), Festive Sausage Cups (p. 19), Appetizer Roll-Ups (p. 21), Holiday Wassail (p. 11), Percolator Punch (p. 11) and Homemade Eggnog (p. 10).

Asparagus Ham Swirls

(Pictured above)

I came across the recipe for this hot appetizer years ago and have made it many times to share with friends and co-workers. Asparagus, ham and cheese combine into a fun finger food.
—Nancy Ingersol
Midlothian, Illinois

  16 fresh asparagus spears, trimmed
   3 tablespoons Dijon mustard
  16 thin slices fully cooked ham
  16 slices process Swiss cheese
   2 eggs, beaten
   1 cup dry bread crumbs
Cooking oil

In a skillet, cook asparagus in a small amount of water until crisp-tender, about 6-8 minutes; drain well. Spread about 1 teaspoon of mustard on each ham slice. Top with one slice of cheese. Place an asparagus spear at one end (trim to fit if needed). Roll up each ham slice tightly; secure with three toothpicks. Dip ham rolls in egg, then roll in bread crumbs. In an electric skillet, heat 1 in. of oil to 350°. Fry rolls, a few at a time, until golden brown, about 3-4 minutes. Drain on paper towels; keep warm. Cut each roll between the toothpicks into three pieces. **Yield:** 4 dozen.

Fruity Summer Cooler

When the melons first come in, we make this delightful thirst-quenching cooler. People are sure to comment on the fabulous flavor.
—Ruth Andrewson
Leavenworth, Washington

   6 to 8 ice cubes
  1/2 cup cubed cantaloupe
  1/2 cup pineapple chunks
  1/2 cup cranberry juice
  1/3 cup sliced banana
  1/4 cup pineapple juice
   1 tablespoon honey
  3/4 teaspoon lemon juice
  1/4 teaspoon grated lemon peel

Place all ingredients in a blender or food processor; cover and blend until smooth. **Yield:** 2-3 servings.

— ♟ ♟ ♟ —

Dilly Vegetable Spread

My family enjoys this snack throughout the day. Packed with vegetables, ham and cheese, it's also good as a sandwich spread or stuffed in a tomato.
—Donna Jandreau, Lincoln, Maine

   2 packages (one 8 ounces, one 3 ounces)
       cream cheese, softened
   1 tablespoon dill pickle juice
   1 teaspoon Worcestershire sauce
   1 teaspoon garlic powder
  1/2 teaspoon pepper
  1/4 teaspoon salt
   1 large tomato, seeded and diced
   4 medium dill pickles, diced
   1 medium green pepper, chopped
   1 medium onion, chopped
  1/2 pound fully cooked ham, diced
  1/2 pound American cheese, diced
Crackers

In a mixing bowl, beat cream cheese until smooth. Add the next five ingredients and mix well. Stir in tomato, pickles, green pepper, onion, ham and cheese. Chill. Serve with crackers. **Yield:** 6 cups.

— ♟ ♟ ♟ —

Cinnamon Maple Granola

When I get a craving for a light, wholesome snack, I mix up a batch of this granola. I love the sweetness of the coconut and maple syrup and the crunchy nuts.
—Erin Phillips, Akron, Ohio

   1 cup old-fashioned oats
  1/2 cup chopped walnuts

1/4 cup flaked coconut
1/4 cup pure maple syrup
1 tablespoon corn syrup
1 teaspoon ground cinnamon
1 teaspoon vanilla extract

Combine oats, walnuts and coconut in a greased 13-in. x 9-in. x 2-in. baking pan; set aside. In a saucepan over medium heat, combine syrups and cinnamon; bring to a boil. Cook and stir for 1 minute. Remove from the heat; stir in vanilla. Pour over oat mixture and toss to coat. Bake at 275° for 30-40 minutes or until golden brown, stirring every 10 minutes. Cool, stirring occasionally. Store in an airtight container. **Yield:** about 2 cups.

— 🥄 🥄 🥄 —

Pinto Bean Dip

(Pictured below right)

Whenever there's a gathering, friends tell me, "Be sure to bring your bean dip!" With several delightful layers, this is more than a snack—some guests practically make a meal out of it. You'll need big chips to pick up all the scrumptious ingredients.
—Claire Rademacher, Whittier, California

1 can (29 ounces) pinto beans, rinsed and drained
1-1/4 teaspoons salt, *divided*
1/4 teaspoon pepper
1/8 to 1/4 teaspoon hot pepper sauce
3 large ripe avocados, peeled and pitted
4 teaspoons lemon juice
1 cup (8 ounces) sour cream
1/2 cup mayonnaise
1 envelope taco seasoning mix
1 cup sliced green onions
2 medium tomatoes, chopped
1-1/2 cups (6 ounces) shredded cheddar cheese
1 can (2-1/4 ounces) sliced ripe olives, drained
Tortilla chips

In a bowl, mash beans with a fork; stir in 3/4 teaspoon salt, pepper and hot pepper sauce. Spread onto a 12-in. serving plate. Mash avocados with lemon juice and remaining salt; spread over bean

mixture. Combine sour cream, mayonnaise and taco seasoning; spread over avocado layer. Sprinkle with onions, tomatoes, cheese and olives. Serve with tortilla chips. **Yield:** 25-30 servings.

— 🥄 🥄 🥄 —

Chili Con Queso

My husband created this thick, cheesy Southwestern dip by adapting a recipe he found in a cookbook. Everyone agrees it's excellent. —Patricia Leinheiser
Albuquerque, New Mexico

1 medium onion, chopped
1 to 2 garlic cloves, minced
2 tablespoons butter *or* margarine
1 can (4 ounces) chopped green chilies
2-1/2 cups (10 ounces) shredded cheddar cheese
2 cups (8 ounces) shredded Monterey Jack cheese
1 cup milk
Tortilla chips

In a saucepan, saute onion and garlic in butter until tender. Add chilies; cook and stir for 5 minutes. Reduce heat to low. Gradually add small amounts of cheeses and milk; stir until melted after each addition. Serve warm with tortilla chips. **Yield:** 3 cups.

Skinned in a Snap

To easily remove the skin from a clove of garlic, place the clove on a flat rubber jar opener, fold one side of the opener over and roll the garlic a few times on a flat surface with the palm of your hand. Presto—clean garlic!

Toast the Holidays!

CHEERS...but be cautious as you clink glasses or mugs in a holiday toast—you won't want to spill a drop of these festive beverages! Crowd-pleasers served by some of the country's best cooks, they are sure to garner compliments.

— 🍷 🍷 🍷 —

Homemade Eggnog

(Pictured below)

This holiday treat is well worth the time it takes to make it. After just one taste, folks will know it's home-made, not some store-bought variety.
—*Pat Waymire, Yellow Springs, Ohio*

12 eggs
1-1/2 cups sugar
1/2 teaspoon salt
2 quarts milk, *divided*
2 tablespoons vanilla extract
1 teaspoon ground nutmeg
2 cups whipping cream
Additional nutmeg, optional

In a heavy 4-qt. saucepan, whisk together eggs, sugar and salt. Gradually add 1 qt. of milk. Cook and stir over low heat until a thermometer reads 160°-170°, about 30-35 minutes. Pour into a large heatproof bowl; stir in the vanilla, nutmeg and remaining milk. Place the bowl in an ice-water bath, stirring frequently until mixture is cool. If

SWEET SIPPING. Homemade Eggnog (shown in the punch bowl above), Holiday Wassail (in mugs) and Percolator Punch are bright beverages to serve for Yuletide gatherings.

the mixture separates, process in a blender until smooth. Cover and refrigerate for at least 3 hours. When ready to serve, beat the cream in a mixing bowl on high until soft peaks form; whisk gently into the cooled milk mixture. Pour into a chilled 5-qt. punch bowl. Sprinkle with nutmeg if desired. **Yield:** 3-1/2 quarts. **Editor's Note:** Eggnog may be stored, covered, in the refrigerator for several days. Whisk before serving.

— ☕ ☕ ☕ —

Holiday Wassail

(Pictured below left)

Apricots lend golden color and goodness to this fruity beverage. It's so delicious you'll want to make it for parties year-round. —*Ruth Seitz*
Columbus Junction, Iowa

> 1 can (16 ounces) apricot halves, undrained
> 4 cups unsweetened pineapple juice
> 2 cups apple cider
> 1 cup orange juice
> 18 whole cloves
> 6 cinnamon sticks (3-1/2 inches), broken
> **Additional cinnamon sticks, optional**

In a blender or food processor, blend apricots and liquid until smooth. Pour into a large saucepan. Add pineapple juice, cider and orange juice. Place the cloves and cinnamon sticks in a double thickness of cheesecloth; bring up corners of cloth and tie with a string to form a bag. Add to saucepan. (Or place loose spices directly in the saucepan and strain before serving.) Bring to a boil. Reduce heat; cover and simmer for 15-20 minutes. Serve hot in mugs. Garnish each with a cinnamon stick if desired. **Yield:** 2 quarts.

— ☕ ☕ ☕ —

Percolator Punch

(Pictured at left)

I serve this simple punch for club and group activities. Because it calls for just two ingredients and is "brewed" in a coffeepot, it couldn't be easier!
—*Margaret Allen, Abingdon, Virginia*

> 9 cups apple cider
> 1/2 cup cinnamon red-hot candies

Pour apple cider into percolator; place candies in percolator basket. Cover and begin the perking cycle. When cycle is complete, remove the basket and leave punch in the pot to keep warm. **Yield:** 2-1/4 quarts.

White Hot Chocolate

Once you sample this smooth drink with a hint of spice, you'll never want ordinary hot chocolate again.
—*Debbi Smith, Crossett, Arkansas*

> 3 cups half-and-half cream, *divided*
> 2/3 cup vanilla baking chips
> 1 cinnamon stick (3 inches)
> 1/8 teaspoon ground nutmeg
> 1 teaspoon vanilla extract
> 1/4 teaspoon almond extract
> **Ground cinnamon, optional**

In a saucepan, combine 1/4 cup of cream, vanilla chips, cinnamon stick and nutmeg. Stir over low heat until chips are melted; discard cinnamon. Add remaining cream; stir until heated through. Remove from the heat; add extracts. Sprinkle each serving with ground cinnamon if desired. **Yield:** 4 servings.

— ☕ ☕ ☕ —

Slow Cooker Cider

I like to welcome family and friends into our home during the holidays with the wonderful aroma of this cider. Best of all, slow cooking means no last-minute rush.
—*Alpha Wilson, Roswell, New Mexico*

> 2 cinnamon sticks (4 inches)
> 1 teaspoon whole cloves
> 1 teaspoon whole allspice
> 2 quarts apple cider
> 1/2 cup packed brown sugar
> 1 medium orange, sliced

Place cinnamon, cloves and allspice in a double thickness of cheesecloth; bring up the corners of cloth and tie with a string to form a bag. Place cider and brown sugar in a slow cooker; stir until sugar dissolves. Add spice bag. Place orange slices on top. Cover and cook on low for 2-5 hours. Remove spice bag before serving. **Yield:** 2 quarts.

— ☕ ☕ ☕ —

Sherbet Punch

Lime is my favorite flavor for Christmas, but I make this same recipe with raspberry sherbet, too.
—*Jeanne Bunders, Wauzeka, Wisconsin*

> 1/2 gallon lime *or* raspberry sherbet, softened
> 1 liter ginger ale
> 2 cups lemon-lime soda
> 2 cups grapefruit *or* citrus soda

Just before serving, place the sherbet in a punch bowl. Add ginger ale and soda; stir until sherbet is almost dissolved. **Yield:** 4-1/2 quarts.

Cheesy Asparagus Bites

(Pictured below)

When I managed a cafeteria, I would cook up different snacks for the staff. These tiny squares with a big asparagus flavor disappeared fast. —Lois McAtee
Oceanside, California

- 1/2 cup diced onion
- 1 garlic clove, minced
- 2 tablespoons cooking oil
- 2 cups (8 ounces) shredded sharp cheddar cheese
- 1/4 cup dry bread crumbs
- 2 tablespoons minced fresh parsley
- 1/4 teaspoon salt
- 1/4 teaspoon pepper
- 1/8 to 1/4 teaspoon dried oregano
- 1/8 teaspoon hot pepper sauce
- 4 eggs, beaten
- 1 pound fresh asparagus, trimmed and cut into 1/2-inch pieces

In a skillet, saute onion and garlic in oil until tender. Combine cheese, bread crumbs, parsley, salt, pepper, oregano and hot pepper sauce. Stir in the onion mixture and eggs. Cook asparagus in a small amount of water until crisp-tender, about 3-4 minutes; drain well. Stir into cheese mixture. Pour into a greased 9-in. square baking pan. Bake at 350° for 30 minutes or until a knife inserted near the center comes out clean. Let stand for 15 minutes. Cut into small squares; serve warm. **Yield:** 5 dozen.

Nutty Caramel Corn

Sweet, crunchy and chewy, this irresistible snack never lasts very long around our house. I make multiple batches for gatherings and to give as gifts.
—Lois Davis, Clarkson, New York

- 6 quarts popped popcorn
- 1-1/2 cups walnut halves
- 1 cup sliced almonds
- 1-1/3 cups sugar
- 1 cup butter *or* margarine
- 1/2 cup light corn syrup
- 1 teaspoon vanilla extract

Remove all unpopped kernels from popcorn. Place popcorn and nuts in a large bowl; mix well. In a saucepan, combine sugar, butter and corn syrup; bring to a boil. Boil for 5 minutes, stirring occasionally. Remove from the heat; add vanilla. Pour over popcorn mixture; stir to coat. Place on two greased baking sheets to dry, about 1 hour. Store in an airtight container. **Yield:** about 6-1/2 quarts.

Yogurt Fruit Dip

This creamy dip is super for warm weather and nice enough for a special brunch. —Sandy Szwarc
Albuquerque, New Mexico

✓ This tasty dish uses less sugar, salt and fat. Recipe includes *Diabetic Exchanges.*

- 1 carton (16 ounces) plain yogurt
- 2 tablespoons brown sugar
- 1 tablespoon orange juice concentrate

Dash ground cinnamon

Line a strainer with a paper coffee filter or cheesecloth; place over a bowl. Put yogurt in strainer; refrigerate for 8 hours. Discard liquid in bowl. Combine yogurt, brown sugar, orange juice concentrate and cinnamon; mix well. Serve with fresh fruit. **Yield:** 1-1/4 cups. **Diabetic Exchanges:** One 2-tablespoon serving (prepared with nonfat yogurt) equals 1/2 skim milk; also, 35 calories, 35 mg sodium, 1 mg cholesterol, 6 gm carbohydrate, 3 gm protein, trace fat.

Zucchini Picadillo

This savory snack served in homemade tortilla cups or with chips is fun and filling. —Mary Livengood
Indianapolis, Indiana

- 1/2 pound ground beef
- 1/4 pound bulk Italian sausage

1/4 cup chopped onion
2 garlic cloves, minced
1 can (14-1/2 ounces) diced tomatoes, undrained
1 medium zucchini, diced
1 cup uncooked instant rice
3/4 cup water
1/2 teaspoon dried basil
1/2 teaspoon salt
8 flour tortillas (8 inches)

In a large skillet over medium heat, brown beef, sausage, onion and garlic; drain. Add tomatoes, zucchini, rice, water, basil and salt; cook until zucchini and rice are tender, about 10 minutes. Meanwhile, form eight 3-in. balls from aluminum foil; place on a baking sheet. Drape a flour tortilla over the top of each ball; secure sides with toothpicks to form a shell. Bake at 400° for 8-10 minutes or until firm. Remove the toothpicks; place shells on plates. Fill with zucchini mixture; serve warm. Zucchini mixture can also be served as a dip with tortilla chips. **Yield:** 8 servings.

— 🏆 🏆 🏆 —

Chocolate Quivers

These smooth, cool snacks are more fun than chocolate pudding. They're a nice make-ahead treat that I keep on hand for guests. —Shirley Kidd
New London, Minnesota

2 envelopes unflavored gelatin
2 cups milk, *divided*
1/2 cup instant chocolate drink mix
1/4 cup sugar

In a bowl, dissolve gelatin in 1 cup milk. In a small saucepan over medium-high heat, combine drink mix, sugar and remaining milk; bring to a boil, stirring until chocolate and sugar are dissolved. Add to gelatin mixture and mix well. Pour into an 8-in. square pan. Cool at room temperature for 30 minutes. Cover and refrigerate until firm, about 5 hours (do not freeze). Cut with a knife or cookie cutter. **Yield:** about 1 dozen.

— 🏆 🏆 🏆 —

Lo-Cal Apple Snack

This quick and easy snack is often requested as a treat for the office. It's a simple and harvest-fresh way to serve autumn's best apples—kids love it. —Nancy Horan, Sioux Falls, South Dakota

✓ This tasty dish uses less sugar, salt and fat. Recipe includes *Diabetic Exchanges.*

4 medium Golden Delicious apples, peeled, cored and sliced into rounds
1/2 cup apple juice
1/4 teaspoon ground cinnamon
1 tablespoon grated lemon peel

In an ungreased 11-in. x 7-in. x 2-in. microwave-safe baking dish, arrange the apples in two rows. Pour apple juice over apples. Sprinkle with cinnamon and lemon peel. Cover and microwave on high for 7 minutes or until apples are tender, turning after 3-1/2 minutes. **Yield:** 4 servings. **Diabetic Exchanges:** One serving equals 1-1/2 fruit; also, 88 calories, 1 mg sodium, 0 cholesterol, 23 gm carbohydrate, trace protein, trace fat. **Editor's Note:** This recipe was tested in a 700-watt microwave.

Mozzarella Dip

(Pictured above)

For a great party snack that inspires munching on raw vegetables, give this creamy dip a try. —Faye Hintz, Springfield, Missouri

2 cups mayonnaise
1 cup (8 ounces) sour cream
1 cup (4 ounces) shredded mozzarella cheese
2 tablespoons grated Parmesan cheese
1 tablespoon dried minced onion
1 teaspoon sugar
Dash *each* garlic salt and seasoned salt

In a bowl, combine all ingredients and mix well. Cover and chill for at least 1 hour. Serve with raw vegetables or tortilla chips. **Yield:** 3-1/2 cups.

SUPER SNACKS like Layered Shrimp Dip, Festive Ham 'n' Cheese Spread and Bandito Chicken Wings (shown above, clockwise from top) flavor the holidays...or any occasion.

Bandito Chicken Wings

(Pictured above)

These golden wings make a mouth-watering appetizer. If you like foods extra-spicy, you can add more hot pepper sauce to suit your tastes. —Gloria Jarrett
Loveland, Ohio

- **12 whole chicken wings (about 2 pounds)**
- **1/2 teaspoon salt**
- **1/8 teaspoon pepper**
- **1/2 cup butter *or* margarine, *divided***
- **2 tablespoons cooking oil**
- **1/2 cup taco sauce**
- **1/4 cup barbecue sauce**
- **1/4 cup French salad dressing**
- **1 teaspoon Worcestershire sauce**
- **1/8 teaspoon hot pepper sauce**

Cut chicken wings into three sections; discard wing tips. Sprinkle with salt and pepper. In a skillet over medium heat, combine 2 tablespoons butter and oil. Fry chicken until brown, about 6-8 minutes on each side. Place in a greased 13-in. x 9-in. x 2-in. baking dish. In a saucepan, combine taco sauce, barbecue sauce, French dressing, Worcestershire sauce, hot pepper sauce and remaining butter; cook and stir over medium heat until the butter is melted and sauce is blended. Pour 1/2 cup over the chicken wings. Bake, uncovered, at 300° for 15-20 minutes or until chicken juices run clear. Serve with the remaining sauce. **Yield:** 6-8 servings.

Layered Shrimp Dip

(Pictured above)

People's eyes light up when I set this special snack on the table. It has a terrific combination of flavors and looks so pretty. Once folks start dipping, they can't seem to stop! I think you'll like it, too. —Sue Broyles
Cherokee, Texas

- **1 package (3 ounces) cream cheese, softened**
- **6 tablespoons salsa, *divided***
- **1/2 cup cocktail sauce**
- **3 cans (6 ounces *each*) small shrimp, rinsed and drained**

1 can (2-1/4 ounces) sliced ripe olives,
   drained
1 cup (4 ounces) shredded cheddar cheese
1 cup (4 ounces) shredded Monterey Jack
   cheese
Sliced green onions
Tortilla chips

Combine cream cheese and 3 tablespoons of salsa; spread into an ungreased 9-in. pie plate. Combine cocktail sauce and remaining salsa; spread over cream cheese. Place shrimp evenly over top. Sprinkle with olives. Combine cheeses; sprinkle over olives. Top with onions. Chill. Serve with tortilla chips. **Yield:** 12-16 servings.

———— 🍷 🍷 🍷 ————

Festive Ham 'n' Cheese Spread

(Pictured at left)

My family goes wild over this mild-tasting yet hearty cheese spread. Now they turn their noses up if I offer any store-bought varieties. —Cara Flora
Olathe, Colorado

2 packages (8 ounces *each*) cream cheese,
   softened
1/2 cup sour cream
2 tablespoons dry onion soup mix
1 cup finely chopped fully cooked ham
1 cup (4 ounces) shredded Swiss *or* cheddar
   cheese
1/4 cup chopped fresh parsley

In a mixing bowl, beat cream cheese, sour cream and soup mix until smooth. Stir in ham and cheese. Form into a ball or spoon into a plastic wrap-lined mold. Roll in parsley or sprinkle parsley on top. Refrigerate. **Yield:** 12-14 servings (about 4 cups).

———— 🍷 🍷 🍷 ————

Hot Beef-Mushroom Appetizer

This creamy, savory snack smells wonderful while it is baking. It's a mushroom lover's delight that folks will look forward to time and again. —Mary Jo O'Brien
Hastings, Minnesota

2 medium onions, chopped
1/4 cup butter *or* margarine
1 package (8 ounces) cream cheese,
   softened
1/2 pound fresh mushrooms, chopped
1 package (4-1/2 ounces) dried beef,
   chopped
1/2 teaspoon Worcestershire sauce
1/4 teaspoon garlic powder
Crackers *or* party rye bread

In a skillet, saute onions in butter until tender. Stir in cream cheese until smooth. Add mushrooms, beef, Worcestershire sauce and garlic powder; mix well. Spoon into an ungreased 9-in. pie plate. Bake at 375° for 15-20 minutes. Serve warm with crackers or rye bread. **Yield:** 12-16 servings (3 cups).

———— 🍷 🍷 🍷 ————

New Year's Punch

Our family toasts to the New Year with this sparkling beverage. I've also prepared it for spring luncheons and bridal showers. —Audrey Thibodeau
Mesa, Arizona

1 can (46 ounces) pineapple juice
4 cups brewed tea
3 cups apple juice
1/2 cup lemon juice
2 cups ginger ale

In a gallon container, combine pineapple juice, tea, apple juice and lemon juice; mix well. Store in the refrigerator. Add the ginger ale just before serving. **Yield:** about 30 servings.

———— 🍷 🍷 🍷 ————

Fried Cinnamon Strips

I first made these crispy Mexican-style strips for a special family night at our church. Most of them were snapped up before dinner! —Nancy Johnson
Laverne, Oklahoma

1 cup sugar
1 teaspoon ground cinnamon
1/4 teaspoon ground nutmeg
10 flour tortillas (8 inches)
Cooking oil

In a large resealable plastic bag, combine sugar, cinnamon and nutmeg; set aside. Cut tortillas into 3-in. x 2-in. strips. Heat 1 in. of oil in a skillet or electric fry pan to 375°; fry 4-5 strips at a time for 30 seconds on each side or until golden brown. Drain on paper towels. While still warm, place strips in bag with sugar mixture; shake gently to coat. Serve immediately or store in an airtight container. **Yield:** 5 dozen.

Party Pleasures

Iced tea or lemonade looks lovely and tastes great when served with special cubes. Freeze a sprig of mint or slivers of lemon peel in each cube and drop a few in each glass.

Tex-Mex Dip

For a cool, creamy snack with a bit of a kick, try this recipe. It goes fast at weddings, card parties or any gathering. You'll be amazed that this flavorful dip has only three ingredients! —Carol Battle
Heathsville, Virginia

✓ This tasty dish uses less sugar, salt and fat. Recipe includes *Diabetic Exchanges*.

2 cups (16 ounces) sour cream
1 cup salsa
4 pita breads (6 inches)

In a bowl, combine sour cream and salsa. Cover and chill for at least 2 hours. Cut each pita into six wedges; separate each wedge into two pieces. Place on an ungreased baking sheet. Bake at 275° for 5-10 minutes or until crisp. Serve with the dip. **Yield:** 3 cups. **Diabetic Exchanges:** 2 pieces of pita bread and 2 tablespoons of dip (prepared with nonfat sour cream) equals 1 vegetable, 1/2 starch; also, 52 calories, 175 mg sodium, 1 mg cholesterol, 10 gm carbohydrate, 2 gm protein, trace fat.

Hot Macadamia Spread

(Pictured above)

While my husband was in the Army, I'd get together with the other wives for snacks and to exchange favorite recipes. I enjoy serving this rich spread because most guests can't quite put their finger on the zippy ingredient—horseradish. —Naomi Francis
Waukesha, Wisconsin

1 package (8 ounces) cream cheese, softened
2 tablespoons milk
1/2 cup sour cream
2 teaspoons prepared horseradish
1/4 cup finely chopped green pepper
1 green onion, chopped
1/2 teaspoon garlic salt
1/4 teaspoon pepper
1/2 cup chopped macadamia nuts *or* almonds
2 teaspoons butter *or* margarine
Assorted crackers

In a mixing bowl, beat cream cheese and milk until smooth. Stir in sour cream, horseradish, green pepper, onion, garlic salt and pepper. Spoon into an ungreased shallow 2-cup baking dish; set aside. In a skillet, saute nuts in butter for 3-4 minutes or until lightly browned. Sprinkle over cream cheese mixture. Bake, uncovered, at 350° for 20 minutes. Serve with crackers. **Yield:** 6-8 servings.

Stuffed Mushroom Caps

Our state is well-known for wonderful fresh mushrooms. A cheesy filling stuffed in the caps makes a scrumptious snack. —Cherie Sechrist
Red Lion, Pennsylvania

24 large fresh mushrooms
6 tablespoons butter *or* margarine
3/4 cup plain dry bread crumbs
1 envelope dry onion soup mix
1/2 cup sliced almonds
1/4 cup shredded Parmesan cheese

Remove stems from mushrooms and finely chop; set caps aside. In a skillet, saute chopped mushrooms in butter until tender, about 6-8 minutes. Remove from the heat; stir in bread crumbs, soup mix and almonds. Stuff firmly into mushroom caps. Place in a greased 15-in. x 10-in. x 1-in. baking pan; sprinkle with cheese. Bake, uncovered, at 425° for 12-15 minutes or until tender. **Yield:** 2 dozen.

Glazed Sausage Bites

These tangy meatballs have a great flavor because they're made with sausage instead of the traditional ground beef. Everyone loves the zesty sauce. —Sue Broyles, Cherokee, Texas

1 pound bulk pork sausage
1 egg
1/2 cup saltine *or* butter-flavored cracker crumbs
2 tablespoons milk
1/2 teaspoon rubbed sage
1/2 cup water
1/4 cup ketchup
2 tablespoons brown sugar
1 tablespoon soy sauce
1 tablespoon vinegar

In a bowl, combine the sausage, egg, crumbs, milk and sage; mix well. Shape into 1-in. balls. In a skillet over medium heat, brown meatballs; drain. Combine remaining ingredients; mix well. Add to skillet; bring to a boil. Reduce heat; cover and simmer for 15-20 minutes or until centers of meatballs are no longer pink. **Yield:** 2 dozen.

Caramel Peanut Butter Dip

When crisp autumn apples are available, I make this quick delicious dip. My family loves the combination of caramel and peanut butter—the consistency is perfect for dipping.
—Sandra McKenzie
Braham, Minnesota

30 caramels
1 to 2 tablespoons water
1/4 cup plus 2 tablespoons creamy peanut butter
1/4 cup finely crushed peanuts, optional
Sliced apples

In a microwave-safe bowl, microwave caramels and water on high for 1 minute; stir. Microwave 1 minute more or until smooth. Add peanut butter and mix well; microwave for 30 seconds or until smooth. Stir in peanuts if desired. Serve warm with apples. **Yield:** 1 cup. **Editor's Note:** This recipe was tested in a 700-watt microwave.

Rye Party Puffs

(Pictured at right)

These puffs are pretty enough for a wedding reception yet hearty enough to snack on while watching football on television.
—Kelly Thornberry
LaPorte, Indiana

1 cup water
1/2 cup butter *or* margarine
1/2 cup all-purpose flour
1/2 cup rye flour

2 teaspoons dried parsley flakes
1/2 teaspoon garlic powder
1/4 teaspoon salt
4 eggs
Caraway seeds
CORNED BEEF FILLING:
2 packages (8 ounces *each*) cream cheese, softened
2 packages (2-1/2 ounces *each*) cooked corned beef, finely chopped
1/2 cup mayonnaise
1/4 cup sour cream
2 tablespoons minced chives
2 tablespoons finely chopped onion
1 teaspoon spicy brown *or* horseradish mustard
1/8 teaspoon garlic powder
10 small stuffed olives, chopped

In a saucepan over medium heat, bring water and butter to a boil. Add flours, parsley, garlic powder and salt all at once; stir until a smooth ball forms. Remove from the heat; let stand for 5 minutes. Beat in eggs, one at time. Beat until smooth. Drop the batter by rounded teaspoonfuls 2 in. apart onto greased baking sheets. Sprinkle with caraway seeds. Bake at 400° for 18-20 minutes or until golden. Remove to wire racks. Immediately cut a slit in each puff to allow steam to escape; cool. In a mixing bowl, combine the first eight filling ingredients; mix well. Stir in olives. Split puffs; add filling. Refrigerate until serving. **Yield:** 4-1/2 dozen.

Apricot Wraps

(Pictured below)

I accumulated a large recipe collection from around the world while my husband served in the Air Force for 25 years. This appetizer is one of our favorites.
—Jane Ashworth, Beavercreek, Ohio

 1 **package (14 ounces) dried apricots**
1/2 **cup whole almonds**
 1 **pound sliced bacon**
1/4 **cup plum *or* apple jelly**
 2 **tablespoons soy sauce**

Fold each apricot around an almond. Cut bacon strips into thirds; wrap a strip around each apricot and secure with a toothpick. Place on two ungreased 15-in. x 10-in. x 1-in. baking pans. Bake, uncovered, at 375° for 25 minutes or until bacon is crisp, turning once. Meanwhile, in a small saucepan, combine jelly and soy sauce; cook and stir over low heat for 5 minutes or until warmed and smooth. Remove apricots to paper towels; drain. Serve with sauce for dipping. **Yield:** about 4-1/2 dozen.

Festive Pumpkin Dip

An unexpected use for pumpkin is in this creamy, zippy snack dip. It's a chunky, satisfying dip perfect for any time. —Evelyn Kennell, Roanoke, Illinois

 12 **ounces cream cheese, softened**
3/4 **cup cooked *or* canned pumpkin**
 2 **tablespoons taco seasoning mix**
1/8 **teaspoon garlic powder**
1/3 **cup chopped dried beef**
1/3 **cup chopped green pepper**

1/3 **cup chopped sweet red pepper**
 1 **can (2-1/4 ounces) sliced ripe olives, drained**
 1 **round loaf (1 pound) Italian *or* pumpernickel bread**
Raw vegetables, crackers *or* corn chips

In a mixing bowl, beat cream cheese, pumpkin, taco seasoning and garlic powder until smooth. Stir in beef, peppers and olives. Cover and refrigerate until ready to serve. Just before serving, cut top off bread; scoop out the bread from inside, leaving a 1/2-in. shell (save the bread from inside to make croutons or bread crumbs or for another use). Fill shell with cream cheese mixture. Serve with vegetables, crackers or corn chips. **Yield:** 3 cups.

Creamy Sourdough Snack

I received many compliments on this rich, creamy dip when I served it at a special party for my mother's 50th birthday. I know you will, too! —Darelyn Payes
Hayward, California

1-1/2 **cups (12 ounces) sour cream**
 2 **packages (3 ounces *each*) cream cheese**
1/2 **cup chopped green onions**
 1 **teaspoon Worcestershire sauce**
 2 **cups (8 ounces) shredded sharp cheddar cheese**
1-1/2 **cups cubed fully cooked ham**
 1 **round loaf (1 pound) sourdough bread**
Chopped fresh parsley, optional

In a saucepan, combine sour cream, cream cheese, onions and Worcestershire sauce; cook and stir over low heat until blended. Add cheese and ham; cook and stir until the cheese is melted and ham is heated through. Cut top off bread; carefully hollow out top and bottom of loaf, leaving a 1/2-in. shell. Cut bread into cubes. Pour dip into shell; sprinkle with parsley if desired. Serve with bread cubes. **Yield:** 3-1/2 cups.

Twice-Baked New Potatoes

(Pictured on page 6)

These satisfying mouthfuls are perfect for a late afternoon or evening get-together when something a little heartier is needed. —Susan Herbert
Aurora, Illinois

1-1/2 **pounds small red potatoes**
 2 **to 3 tablespoons vegetable oil**
1/2 **cup sour cream**

1 cup (4 ounces) shredded Monterey Jack
   cheese
1 package (3 ounces) cream cheese,
   softened
1/3 cup minced green onions
1 teaspoon dried basil
1 garlic clove, minced
1/2 teaspoon salt
1/4 to 1/2 teaspoon pepper
1/2 pound sliced bacon, cooked and
   crumbled

Pierce potatoes; rub skins with oil. Place in a baking pan. Bake, uncovered, at 400° for 50 minutes or until tender. Allow to cool to the touch. In a mixing bowl, combine sour cream, Monterey Jack, cream cheese, onions, basil, garlic, salt and pepper. Cut potatoes in half; carefully scoop out pulp, leaving a thin shell. Add pulp to the cheese mixture and mash; stir in bacon. Stuff potato shells. Broil for 7-8 minutes or until heated through. **Yield:** about 2 dozen.

— 🍵 🍵 🍵 —

Festive Sausage Cups

(Pictured on page 6)

Since this recipe uses prepared pie crust, it's a snap to form and fill these individual sausage cups. They're a savory and filling snack. —Gail Watkins
South Bend, Indiana

Pastry for double-crust pie (9 inches)
1 pound bulk hot pork sausage
6 green onions, chopped
1 tablespoon butter *or* margarine
1/2 cup chopped canned mushrooms
1/4 cup thinly sliced stuffed olives
3/4 teaspoon salt
1/4 teaspoon pepper
1/4 cup all-purpose flour
2 cups whipping cream
1 cup (4 ounces) shredded Swiss cheese
Chopped stuffed olives

On a lightly floured surface, roll pastry to 1/8-in. thickness. Cut with a 2-1/2-in. round cookie cutter. Press onto the bottom and up the sides of greased miniature muffin cups. Bake at 400° for 6-8 minutes or until lightly browned. Remove from pans to cool on wire racks. In a skillet, brown sausage; drain well and set aside. In the same skillet, saute onions in butter until tender. Add mushrooms, sliced olives, salt and pepper. Sprinkle with flour. Add cream; bring to a boil, stirring constantly. Stir in sausage. Reduce heat; simmer until thickened, about 5-10 minutes, stirring constantly. Spoon into pastry cups; sprinkle with cheese. Place on ungreased baking sheets. Bake at 350° for 10 minutes or until cheese is melted. Garnish with chopped olives. Serve hot. **Yield:** 4 dozen.

Spiced Nut Mix

(Pictured above)

Many Christmases ago, a good friend gave me a special gift—this recipe and a sack of ingredients. I think of her every time I stir up this mix. —Patti Holland
Parker, Colorado

3 egg whites
2 teaspoons water
2 cans (12 ounces *each*) salted peanuts
1 cup whole blanched almonds
1 cup walnut halves
1-3/4 cups sugar
3 tablespoons pumpkin pie spice
3/4 teaspoon salt
1 cup raisins

In a mixing bowl, beat egg whites and water until frothy. Add nuts; stir gently to coat. Combine sugar, pie spice and salt; add to the nut mixture and stir gently to coat. Fold in raisins. Spread into two greased 15-in. x 10-in. x 1-in. baking pans. Bake, uncovered, at 300° for 20-25 minutes or until lightly browned, stirring every 10 minutes. Cool. Store in an airtight container. **Yield:** about 10 cups.

Savory Bread Strips

(Pictured above)

For a friend's surprise party, I decided to try a new recipe and came up with this crispy bread topped with ham, olives and more. The savory ingredients in this irresistible appetizer blend so well that I'm always asked for the recipe.
—Mary Nichols
Dover, New Hampshire

    1 **package (1/4 ounce) active dry yeast**
6-1/2 **teaspoons sugar, *divided***
  1/2 **cup warm water (110° to 115°)**
    3 **tablespoons olive *or* vegetable oil**
    2 **tablespoons dried minced onion**
    2 **teaspoons dried basil**
    1 **teaspoon dried oregano**
    1 **teaspoon rubbed sage**
    1 **teaspoon garlic powder**
  1/2 **cup cold water**
    3 **cups all-purpose flour**
TOPPING:
  1/4 **cup olive *or* vegetable oil**
    2 **garlic cloves, minced**
  1/2 **cup chopped ripe olives**
1-1/2 **cups chopped fully cooked ham**
    1 **cup shredded Parmesan cheese**
  1/2 **cup chopped onion**
  1/2 **cup minced fresh parsley**

In a small bowl, dissolve yeast and 1/2 teaspoon of sugar in the warm water; set aside. In a small saucepan, combine oil, onion, basil, oregano, sage and garlic powder; cook over medium heat for 1 minute. Remove from the heat; stir in cold water. In a mixing bowl, combine flour and remaining sugar. Stir in oil and yeast mixtures. Turn onto a lightly floured surface; knead for 3 minutes. Place dough on a greased 15-in. x 10-in. x 1-in. baking pan. Cover and let stand for 15 minutes. Pat dough evenly into baking pan. Combine topping ingredients; sprinkle evenly over dough. Bake at 375° for 25-30 minutes or until well browned. Cut into 2-in. x 1-in. strips. Serve warm or cold. **Yield:** about 6 dozen.

— ▼ ▼ ▼ —

Spinach Turnovers

(Pictured on page 6)

The flaky cream cheese pastry adds sensational texture to these hot appetizers...and just wait until you taste the wonderful filling.
—Jean von Bereghy
Oconomowoc, Wisconsin

    2 **packages (8 ounces *each*) cream cheese, softened**
  3/4 **cup butter *or* margarine, softened**
2-1/2 **cups all-purpose flour**
  1/2 **teaspoon salt**
FILLING:
    5 **bacon strips, diced**
  1/4 **cup finely chopped onion**
    2 **garlic cloves, minced**
    1 **package (10 ounces) frozen chopped spinach, thawed and well drained**
    1 **cup small-curd cottage cheese, undrained**
  1/4 **teaspoon salt**
  1/4 **teaspoon pepper**
  1/8 **teaspoon ground nutmeg**
    1 **egg, beaten**
Salsa, optional

In a mixing bowl, beat cream cheese and butter until smooth. Combine flour and salt; gradually add to creamed mixture (dough will be stiff). Turn onto a floured surface; gently knead 10 times. Cover and refrigerate for at least 2 hours. Meanwhile, in a skillet, cook bacon until crisp. Remove bacon; drain, reserving 1 tablespoon of drippings. Saute onion and garlic in the drippings until tender. Remove from the heat; stir in bacon, spinach, cottage cheese, salt, pepper and nutmeg. Cool. On a lightly floured surface, roll dough to 1/8-in. thickness. Cut into 3-in. circles. Lightly brush edges of circles with egg. Place 1 heaping teaspoon of filling in the center of each circle. Fold over; seal edges and prick tops with a fork. Brush with egg. Bake at 400° for 10-12 minutes or until golden brown. Serve with salsa if desired. **Yield:** about 4 dozen. **Editor's Note:** Turnovers may be frozen after baking. To reheat, place unthawed turnovers on a baking sheet. Bake at 400° for 10 minutes.

— 🥤 🥤 🥤 —

Appetizer Roll-Ups

(Pictured on page 6)

Cream cheese and a variety of herbs and vegetables make even deli cold cuts a fancy, filling appetizer. Bite-size pieces look so pretty set on a platter in a circle. But the arrangement never stays complete very long once this snack is served. —*Marcella Funk*
Salem, Oregon

ROAST BEEF:
    4 ounces cream cheese, softened
1/4 cup minced fresh cilantro *or* parsley
    2 to 3 tablespoons minced banana peppers
    1 garlic clove, minced
1/2 pound thinly sliced cooked roast beef
HAM AND TURKEY:
  12 ounces cream cheese, softened
1/2 cup shredded carrot
1/2 cup shredded zucchini
    4 teaspoons dill weed
1/2 pound thinly sliced fully cooked ham
1/2 pound thinly sliced cooked turkey

In a bowl, combine cream cheese, cilantro, peppers and garlic. Spread about 2 tablespoons on each slice of beef. Roll up tightly; wrap in plastic wrap. In another bowl, combine cream cheese, carrot, zucchini and dill. Spread about 2 tablespoons on each slice of ham and turkey. Roll up tightly; wrap in plastic wrap. Refrigerate overnight. Slice into 1-1/2-in. pieces. **Yield:** 6-7 dozen.

— 🥤 🥤 🥤 —

Avocado Salsa

(Pictured at right)

When I found this recipe, I was planning a party and thought it might be a fun, different salsa to set out with chips. It was an absolute success. People loved the corn and avocado combination.
—*Susan Vandermeer, Ogden, Utah*

    1 package (16 ounces) frozen corn, thawed
    2 cans (2-1/4 ounces *each*) sliced ripe
       olives, drained
    1 medium sweet red pepper, chopped
    1 small onion, chopped
    5 garlic cloves, minced

1/3 cup olive *or* vegetable oil
1/4 cup lemon juice
    3 tablespoons cider *or* white wine vinegar
    1 teaspoon dried oregano
1/2 teaspoon salt
1/2 teaspoon pepper
    4 medium ripe avocados
Tortilla chips

In a large bowl, combine corn, olives, red pepper and onion. In a small bowl, combine garlic, oil, lemon juice, vinegar, oregano, salt and pepper; mix well. Pour over corn mixture; toss to coat. Cover and refrigerate overnight. Just before serving, chop avocados and stir into salsa. Serve with tortilla chips. **Yield:** about 7 cups.

Ripe for Recipes

To speed the ripening of an avocado, place it in a paper bag along with an apple. Pierce the bag in several places and keep at room temperature for 1 to 3 days.

Four-Cheese Pate

(Pictured below)

This impressive and festive-looking cheese spread is simple to put together. —Jeanne Messina
Darien, Connecticut

    3 packages (8 ounces *each*) cream cheese,
        softened, *divided*
    2 tablespoons milk
    2 tablespoons sour cream
    3/4 cup chopped pecans
    4 ounces Brie *or* Camembert, rind removed,
        softened
    1 cup (4 ounces) shredded Swiss cheese
    4 ounces crumbled blue cheese
    1/2 cup pecan halves
Red and green apple slices *or* crackers

In a mixing bowl, beat one package of cream cheese with milk and sour cream until smooth. Spread into a 9-in. pie plate lined with plastic wrap. Sprinkle with chopped pecans. In a mixing bowl, beat Brie, Swiss, blue cheese and remaining cream cheese until thoroughly combined. Gently spread over chopped pecans, smoothing the top to form a flat surface. Cover and chill overnight or up to 3-4 days. Before serving, invert onto a serving tray and remove plastic wrap. Arrange pecan halves on top. Serve with apples or crackers. **Yield:** 16-20 servings.

Chocolate-Covered Prunes

We harvest prunes here on our farm, so that delicious fruit is a staple in our kitchen. While our grandchildren enjoy all the dishes I prepare, these little treats are their favorite. —Alcy Thorne
Los Molinos, California

    48 dried pitted prunes (about 1 pound)
    48 whole almonds *or* walnut halves
     2 cups (12 ounces) semisweet chocolate
        chips
     2 tablespoons creamy peanut butter

Stuff each prune with an almond or walnut half. Melt chocolate chips in a microwave-safe bowl or double boiler. Add peanut butter; mix well. Dip prunes and place on waxed paper to harden. Store in the refrigerator. **Yield:** 4 dozen.

———— 🏺 🏺 🏺 ————

Kookie Cookies

You won't be able to stop eating this snack, which is sweet, salty, crunchy and chewy all at the same time! It's a quick way to dress up plain corn chips.
—Helen Bachman, Champaign, Illinois

    1 package (10-1/2 ounces) corn chips
    1 cup light corn syrup
    1 cup sugar
    1 cup creamy peanut butter

Spread corn chips in a greased 15-in. x 10-in. x 1-in. baking pan. In a saucepan over medium heat, bring corn syrup and sugar to a boil. Remove from the heat; stir in peanut butter until smooth. Pour over corn chips. Cool. Break into pieces. **Yield:** about 3 dozen.

———— 🏺 🏺 🏺 ————

Corn Salsa

I grow my own tomatoes, peppers, garlic and herbs to use in all of my cooking. Fresh ingredients make this salsa special. My recipe ideas come from combining foods I've enjoyed. —Dave Fisher
Ten Mile, Tennessee

    1 can (15-1/4 ounces) whole kernel corn,
        drained
    1/2 cup chopped green pepper
    1/2 cup chopped sweet red pepper
    1/2 cup chopped red onion
     1 medium tomato, chopped
    1/4 cup sliced ripe olives
     2 tablespoons chopped pickled jalapeno
        peppers

1 teaspoon pickled jalapeno pepper juice
2 tablespoons vinegar
2 tablespoons cider *or* red wine vinegar
1/2 teaspoon garlic salt
1/2 teaspoon pepper

Combine all ingredients in a large bowl. Cover and chill for several hours. **Yield:** 4 cups.

— 🍷 🍷 🍷 —

Honey Fruit Dip

One Mother's Day, my husband surprised me with an unusual gift—a beehive! Before long, we had more honey than we could eat. So we decided to go into business. This recipe shows how versatile honey can be. We serve it with fresh fruit for dipping or as a topping for cake or pancakes.
—Joann Olstrom
Reedsport, Oregon

1 carton (6 ounces) lemon custard-style yogurt
1 package (3 ounces) cream cheese, softened
1 tablespoon honey
2 medium apples, sliced
2 medium pears, sliced

In a food processor or blender, combine yogurt, cream cheese and honey; cover and process until smooth. Serve with apples and pears. Store in the refrigerator. **Yield:** about 1 cup.

— 🍷 🍷 🍷 —

Tomato Cheese Pinwheels

(Pictured above right)

These cheesy pinwheels are our favorite for Mother's Day. No matter how many of these pinwheels we bake, there are never any leftovers. Their light cheddar tang complements the tomato flavor beautifully. They look complicated but are easy to prepare.
—Maggie Gassett, Hillsborough, New Hampshire

4 to 4-1/2 cups all-purpose flour, *divided*
2 tablespoons sugar
1 package (1/4 ounce) active dry yeast
1-1/4 teaspoons salt
3/4 cup warm tomato juice (120° to 130°)
1/2 cup warm water (120° to 130°)
1/4 cup butter *or* margarine
1 egg
2 cups (8 ounces) finely shredded sharp cheddar cheese
2 tablespoons snipped chives

In a mixing bowl, combine 1 cup flour, sugar, yeast and salt. Add tomato juice, water and butter; beat

for 2 minutes on medium speed. Add the egg and enough remaining flour to form a soft dough. Place in a greased bowl, turning once to grease top. Cover and refrigerate for 2 hours or until doubled. Punch dough down. Divide in half; roll each half into a 15-in. x 12-in. rectangle approximately 1/8 in. thick. Cut into 3-in. squares. Place 2 in. apart on greased baking sheets. Make 1-in. slits in each corner of each square. Combine the cheese and chives; place 1 heaping teaspoon in the center of each square. Bring every other corner up to center, overlapping slightly to form a pinwheel; press firmly. Bake at 400° for 8-10 minutes. Remove to a wire rack to cool. **Yield:** 40 appetizers.

Chili Pepper Pointers

Choose chili peppers with vivid color and tight glossy skin. Avoid those that are bruised or shriveled or have spots. Taste the peppers first before adding them to recipes, since two that look alike can be radically different in heat. Red peppers aren't necessarily hotter than green ones.

Frosty Chocolate Treat

Kids of all ages love to cool off with this simple creamy beverage. It's a much-requested treat in the summer.
—Gloria Jarrett, Loveland, Ohio

1 quart chocolate milk
1/2 cup sweetened condensed milk
1-3/4 cups whipped topping

In a bowl, combine chocolate milk and condensed milk. Fold in whipped topping. Freeze in an ice cream maker according to manufacturer's directions. **Yield:** about 5 cups.

Tomato Chili Dip

This fresh-tasting dip is perfect for summer barbecues and picnics. Canned green chilies and a fresh jalapeno pepper give just the right amount of "zip".
—Rachael Santarsiero, Orange City, Iowa

✓ This tasty dish uses less sugar, salt and fat. Recipe includes *Diabetic Exchanges*.

4 large tomatoes
8 green onions
2 cans (4 ounces *each*) chopped green chilies
1 can (4-1/4 ounces) chopped ripe olives, drained
6 tablespoons cider *or* red wine vinegar
1 tablespoon olive *or* vegetable oil
1-1/2 to 2 teaspoons garlic powder
1 fresh jalapeno pepper, seeded and chopped, optional
Tortilla chips

Chop tomatoes and onions into 1/4-in. pieces; place in a large bowl. Stir in the next five ingredients. Add jalapeno if desired. Cover and refrigerate overnight. Serve with tortilla chips. **Yield:** 8 cups.
Diabetic Exchanges: One 1/4-cup serving (calculated without chips) equals 1 starch; also, 25 calories, 65 mg sodium, 0 cholesterol, 4 gm carbohydrate, 1 gm protein, 1 gm fat.

Chocolate Mousse Balls

I love working with my grandkids in the kitchen. The key is using recipes like this that really let them get involved and have yummy results. —Laura Young Nevada, Ohio

6 milk chocolate candy bars (1.55 ounces *each*)

Toasted Zucchini Snacks

(Pictured above)

I added green pepper to this recipe I got years ago from a friend. I prepare this rich snack for company when zucchini is plentiful. Everyone seems to enjoy it.
—Jane Bone, Cape Coral, Florida

2 cups shredded zucchini
1 teaspoon salt
1/2 cup mayonnaise *or* salad dressing
1/2 cup plain yogurt
1/4 cup grated Parmesan cheese
1/4 cup finely chopped green pepper
4 green onions, thinly sliced
1 garlic clove, minced
1 teaspoon Worcestershire sauce
1/4 teaspoon hot pepper sauce
36 slices snack rye bread

In a bowl, toss the zucchini and salt; let stand for 1 hour. Rinse and drain, pressing out excess liquid. Add the next eight ingredients; stir until combined. Spread a rounded teaspoonful on each slice of bread; place on a baking sheet. Bake at 375° for 10-12 minutes or until bubbly. Serve hot. **Yield:** 3 dozen.

1 container (12 ounces) frozen whipped
    topping, thawed
1 cup crushed vanilla wafers

In a saucepan over low heat, melt candy bars. Cool for 10 minutes. Place whipped topping in a bowl; fold in melted chocolate. Cover and chill for 3 hours. Shape into 1-in. balls and roll in the wafer crumbs. Refrigerate or freeze. **Yield:** about 3 dozen.

— 🍷 🍷 🍷 —

Fresh Salsa

After my mild green chilies are roasted, I peel, dice and freeze them to use all year. This colorful zesty salsa is great with chips or served with other dishes.
—*Terry Thompson, Albuquerque, New Mexico*

✓ This tasty dish uses less sugar, salt and fat. Recipe includes *Diabetic Exchanges.*

6 Anaheim chilies, roasted, peeled and
    diced *or* 2 cans (4 ounces *each*) chopped
    green chilies
4 large tomatoes, chopped
3 green onions, sliced
2 tablespoons minced fresh cilantro *or*
    parsley
1/2 to 1 jalapeno pepper, seeded and minced
1 garlic clove, minced
1/3 cup cider *or* red wine vinegar
1/3 cup olive *or* vegetable oil
1/2 teaspoon pepper
1 teaspoon salt, optional

In a bowl, combine chilies, tomatoes, onions, cilantro, jalapeno and garlic. In another bowl, combine vinegar, oil, pepper and salt if desired; stir into vegetable mixture. Cover and chill for at least 2 hours. **Yield:** 4-1/2 cups. **Diabetic Exchanges:** One 2-tablespoon serving (prepared with fresh chilies and without salt) equals 1/2 fat; also, 27 calories, 3 mg sodium, 0 cholesterol, 2 gm carbohydrate, trace protein, 2 gm fat.

— 🍷 🍷 🍷 —

Simple Tuna Spread

Salsa is the new and different ingredient in this creamy tuna spread. It gives a surprising spark we enjoy.
—*Peggy Burdick, Burlington, Michigan*

1 package (8 ounces) cream cheese,
    softened
3 tablespoons salsa
2 teaspoons dried parsley flakes
1 teaspoon dried minced onion
1 can (6 ounces) tuna, drained and flaked

In a bowl, combine cream cheese and salsa; stir in parsley and onion. Fold in tuna. Refrigerate until serving. Serve on bread, snack rye or crackers. **Yield:** 1-1/2 cups.

— 🍷 🍷 🍷 —

Oyster Mushroom Spread

Oyster mushrooms are a popular wild food in our area. Since they're expensive if you can find them in the grocery store, this appetizer is a real treat.
—*Judie Anglen, Riverton, Wyoming*

1 pound fresh oyster mushrooms, cut into
    bite-size pieces
2 pints whipping cream
1/2 teaspoon seasoned salt
1/4 teaspoon garlic salt
Assorted crackers

In a saucepan, combine the first four ingredients; bring to a boil over medium heat. Reduce heat; simmer, uncovered, for 4 hours or until sauce is thickened to desired consistency, stirring occasionally. Serve warm on crackers. **Yield:** about 2-1/2 cups.

— 🍷 🍷 🍷 —

Pecan Cheddar Crisps

These crispy snacks are super as a party appetizer. They're also nice to nibble on anytime. They look like cookies, so folks are surprised by the cheesy taste when they take their first bite.
—*Ozela Haynes
Emerson, Arkansas*

1/2 cup butter *or* margarine, softened
1/2 cup finely shredded cheddar cheese
1 cup all-purpose flour
1/4 teaspoon paprika
1/4 teaspoon salt
1/2 cup pecan halves

In a mixing bowl, cream the butter and cheese. Combine flour, paprika and salt; add to creamed mixture. Shape dough into 1-in. balls. Place 2 in. apart on ungreased baking sheets. Top each with a pecan; press down to flatten. Bake at 350° for 15-20 minutes or until golden brown. Remove to a wire rack to cool. **Yield:** about 2 dozen.

Grate Idea!

When a recipe calls for minced onion, use your cabbage grater. It also works well on hard-cooked eggs for egg salad or potato salad.

Salads

Folks will eagerly pile hearty portions of these salads on their plates—whether they're the main course or an appetizing accompaniment.

—— 🍴 🍴 🍴 ——

TOSSED-TOGETHER TREASURES. Clockwise from upper left: Apple Pineapple Salad (p. 38), Asparagus, Apple and Chicken Salad (p. 39), Crazy Quilt Salad (p. 28) and Springtime Pasta Salad (p. 33).

Garden Spaghetti Salad

(Pictured above)

This refreshing salad is very popular with my family, especially in summer when crisp sweet corn is fresh. It is particularly good alongside a grilled meat entree.
—Gloria O'Bryan, Boulder, Colorado

    8 ounces spaghetti, broken into 2-inch pieces
    1 tablespoon olive *or* vegetable oil
    2 cups cooked fresh *or* frozen corn
    2 cups cooked fresh *or* frozen lima beans
    2 medium tomatoes, peeled, seeded and chopped
  3/4 cup thinly sliced green onions
  1/3 cup minced fresh parsley
    6 bacon strips, cooked and crumbled, *divided*
DRESSING:
  1/3 cup olive *or* vegetable oil
    3 tablespoons cider *or* red wine vinegar
    2 tablespoons lemon juice
    1 teaspoon sugar
    1 teaspoon salt
  1/4 teaspoon paprika
Dash pepper

Cook spaghetti according to package directions; rinse in cold water and drain. Place in a large bowl; toss with oil. Add the next five ingredients; stir in three-fourths of the bacon. In a small bowl, whisk all dressing ingredients. Pour over spaghetti mixture; toss gently. Garnish with remaining bacon. Serve immediately or chill. **Yield:** 10-12 servings.

Crazy Quilt Salad

(Pictured on page 27)

This sensational bean salad started out with my mother's recipe, which I changed a bit to suit our tastes. The thyme and mustard give it such zest. It's a staple menu item every time our family gets together.
—Roseanne Martyniuk, Red Deer, Alberta

    1 can (16 ounces) kidney beans, rinsed and drained
    1 can (15 ounces) lima beans, rinsed and drained
    1 can (14-1/2 ounces) green beans, drained
    1 can (14-1/2 ounces) wax beans, drained
    1 cup thinly sliced celery
    1 large green pepper, chopped
  1/2 cup thinly sliced onion
DRESSING:
  1/3 cup vinegar
  1/4 cup vegetable oil
1-1/2 teaspoons ground mustard
    1 teaspoon dried thyme
  1/2 teaspoon salt
  1/4 teaspoon pepper
  1/4 teaspoon garlic powder

Place the first seven ingredients in a large bowl. Combine dressing ingredients; mix well. Pour over bean mixture and toss gently. Cover and refrigerate for 6 hours or overnight, stirring occasionally. **Yield:** 10-12 servings.

———— 🛒 🛒 🛒 ————

Celebration Antipasto

In this simple recipe, a colorful combination of vegetables is tossed with a specially seasoned dressing. It makes a nice accompaniment to many meals.
—Audrey Thibodeau, Mesa, Arizona

✓ This tasty dish uses less sugar, salt and fat. Recipe includes *Diabetic Exchanges.*

    1 medium cucumber, halved and sliced
    1 medium zucchini, julienned
    1 medium carrot, julienned
    1 medium red onion, sliced
    1 cup fresh broccoli florets
    1 cup fresh cauliflowerets
    1 can (2-1/4 ounces) sliced ripe olives, drained, optional
  1/2 cup olive *or* vegetable oil
  1/4 cup white wine vinegar
    1 teaspoon dried oregano
  1/2 teaspoon ground mustard
  1/4 teaspoon garlic powder
  1/4 teaspoon salt, optional

1/8 teaspoon pepper
1/8 teaspoon celery salt
Lettuce leaves

In a bowl, combine the vegetables and olives if desired. In a small bowl, whisk oil, vinegar and seasonings. Pour over vegetables and toss. Chill for 3 hours. Serve in a lettuce-lined bowl with a slotted spoon. **Yield:** 16 servings. **Diabetic Exchanges:** One 1/2-cup serving (prepared without olives and salt) equals 1 vegetable, 1 fat; also, 72 calories, 10 mg sodium, 0 cholesterol, 2 gm carbohydrate, 1 gm protein, 7 gm fat.

Orange Gelatin Salad

Our six kids love helping me peel, measure, pour and stir in the kitchen. With sweet orange segments, tangy pineapple and crunchy carrots, this is one of their favorites to make—and eat! —Joan Parker
Charlotte, North Carolina

1 package (3 ounces) orange gelatin
1 cup boiling water
1 can (8 ounces) crushed pineapple in juice
1 can (11 ounces) mandarin oranges, drained
1 cup grated carrots

In a bowl, dissolve gelatin in water. Drain pineapple, reserving juice; set the pineapple aside. Add enough water to the juice to make 1 cup; stir into gelatin. Chill until partially set. Fold in oranges, carrots and pineapple. Pour into a 5-cup serving bowl. Chill until firm. **Yield:** 4-6 servings.

Wild Rice Salad

Mom harvested her own wild rice when we were kids. So wild rice dishes were a special treat for us. This is still one of my favorite foods. I assure you you'll enjoy this hearty, satisfying salad anytime of year. —Jean Halldorson, Mozart, Saskatchewan

2 cups cooked wild rice
4 hard-cooked eggs, chopped
1 cup cubed cheddar cheese
1/2 cup mayonnaise
1/4 cup sliced stuffed olives
1/2 cup chopped pecans

In a bowl, combine rice, eggs, cheese, mayonnaise and olives; mix well. Cover and chill for at least 2 hours. Just before serving, add the pecans and toss. **Yield:** 6 servings.

Chicken and Black Bean Salad

(Pictured below)

Here in California, we cook out year-round. I grill extra chicken specifically for this quick meal. It's so colorful and fresh-tasting that even our kids love it. —Cindie Ekstrand, Duarte, California

✓ This tasty dish uses less sugar, salt and fat. Recipe includes *Diabetic Exchanges.*

1/3 cup olive *or* vegetable oil
2 tablespoons lime juice
2 tablespoons chopped fresh cilantro *or* parsley
1-1/2 teaspoons sugar
1 garlic clove, minced
1/2 teaspoon chili powder
1/2 teaspoon salt, optional
1/4 teaspoon pepper
1 can (15 ounces) black beans, rinsed and drained
1 can (11 ounces) Mexicorn, drained
1 medium sweet red pepper, julienned
1/3 cup sliced green onions
6 cups torn romaine
1-1/2 cups cooked chicken strips
Additional cilantro *or* parsley, optional

In a jar with a tight-fitting lid, combine the first eight ingredients; shake well and set aside. In a bowl, toss beans, corn, red pepper and onions; set aside. Arrange romaine on individual plates; top with bean mixture and chicken. Drizzle with dressing; garnish with cilantro if desired. **Yield:** 6 servings. **Diabetic Exchanges:** One serving (prepared without salt) equals 2 fat, 1 lean meat, 1 starch, 1 vegetable; also, 259 calories, 519 mg sodium, 21 mg cholesterol, 23 gm carbohydrate, 12 gm protein, 14 gm fat.

Melons Make Summer Super

SWEET, juicy melons are among the season's tastiest treats. You can make them an appetizing addition to your warm-weather menus with these recipes.

— 🍷 🍷 🍷 —

Superstar Spinach Salad

(Pictured below)

Cantaloupe really "stars" in this delicious salad—especially if you cut pieces into that shape. But no mat- *ter how you present this dish, it's always festive, filling and wonderful.* —Kathy Crow, Payson, Arizona

    1 **cantaloupe half, seeded and peeled**
    7 **cups torn fresh spinach**
1-1/2 **cups cubed fully cooked ham**
    1 **cup thinly sliced red onion**
1/2 **cup halved green grapes**
DRESSING:
    3 **tablespoons sugar**
    2 **tablespoons orange juice**

MARVELOUS MELON shines in dishes like Watermelon Boat, Superstar Spinach Salad and Chicken Salad on Cantaloupe Rings (shown above, clockwise from top). Family and friends will dig into these refreshing salads.

2 tablespoons vinegar
1 tablespoon chopped onion
1-1/2 teaspoons grated orange peel
Dash pepper
1/3 cup vegetable oil
1 teaspoon poppy seeds
1/3 cup chopped pecans, toasted

Cut melon half into 1/2-in. rings. Cut rings with a 1-1/2-in. star-shaped cookie cutter or into 1-in. pieces; place in a bowl. Add the spinach, ham, onion and grapes. Chill for at least 2 hours. Place sugar, orange juice, vinegar, onion, orange peel and pepper in a blender; cover and blend until smooth. With the blender running, gradually add oil until slightly thickened. Stir in poppy seeds. Cover and chill. Just before serving, pour dressing over salad and toss. Top with pecans. **Yield:** 6 servings.

Watermelon Boat

(Pictured at left)

"Wow!" is what folks will say when they first see this lovely fruit salad piled high in an eye-catching watermelon boat. The light dressing really lets the fresh flavor of fruit shine through. —Ruth Seitz
Columbus Junction, Iowa

1 cup lemon juice
1 cup sugar
2 teaspoons all-purpose flour
2 eggs, beaten
1 cup whipping cream, whipped
1 large watermelon
1 large honeydew, cut into cubes _or_ balls
1 large cantaloupe, cut into cubes _or_ balls
2 pints fresh strawberries, sliced
1/2 pound green grapes

Combine the lemon juice, sugar and flour in a saucepan; bring to a boil. Reduce heat to low. Stir 1/4 cup into eggs; return all to pan. Cook and stir for 15 minutes or until the mixture coats a spoon (do not boil). Cool. Fold in whipped cream; cover and chill until serving. For watermelon boat, cut a thin slice from bottom of melon with a sharp knife to allow it to sit flat (see diagram above right). Mark a horizontal cutting line 2 in. above center of melon. With a long sharp knife, cut into melon along cutting line, making sure to cut all the way through. Gently pull off top section of rind. Remove fruit from both sections and cut into cubes or balls; set aside. To cut decorative edge, place melon on its side. Position a 2-1/2-in. 8-point star cookie cutter against inside edge of melon, allowing only half of star to cut through rind (see diagram below). Use

a mallet if necessary to help push cookie cutter through melon. Insert a toothpick into flat edge of removed piece. Attach piece onto melon edge where last cut ends. Repeat cutting and attaching pieces until the entire melon edge is completed. Combine honeydew, cantaloupe, strawberries, grapes and watermelon; spoon into boat. Serve dressing on the side. **Yield:** 32-36 servings (about 2 cups dressing). **Editor's Note:** Any star or petal cutter with an even number of points may be used. Or serve this salad in an 8-qt. serving bowl.

Chicken Salad on Cantaloupe Rings

(Pictured at far left)

A hearty chicken salad on a cantaloupe ring is a fun and flavorful way to perk up a summer luncheon.
—Sharon Bickett, Chester, South Carolina

2-1/2 cups cubed cooked chicken
1 cup thinly sliced celery
1 cup halved green grapes
2 tablespoons minced fresh parsley
1/2 cup mayonnaise
1 tablespoon lemon juice
1 tablespoon cider vinegar
1-1/2 teaspoons prepared mustard
1/2 teaspoon salt
1/2 teaspoon sugar
1/8 teaspoon pepper
4 cantaloupe rings
Toasted sliced almonds

In a large bowl, combine chicken, celery, grapes and parsley. Combine the next seven ingredients; mix well. Pour over chicken mixture and toss. Chill for at least 1 hour. To serve, place 1 cup of chicken salad on each cantaloupe ring; sprinkle with almonds. **Yield:** 4 servings.

A Splash of Citrus

Make a delicious ham salad by mixing in 1 teaspoon of orange juice for every tablespoon of mayonnaise. It adds a light fruity touch.

Deli-Style Pasta Salad

(Pictured below)

Pasta provides a base for this tongue-tingling make-ahead salad. It has lots of fresh and satisfying ingredients topped with a flavorful dressing. It's terrific to serve to company or take to a potluck.
—Joyce McLennan, Algonac, Michigan

  1 package (7 ounces) tricolor spiral pasta
  6 ounces thinly sliced hard salami, julienned
  6 ounces provolone cheese, cubed
  1 can (2-1/4 ounces) sliced ripe olives, drained
  1 small red onion, thinly sliced
  1 small zucchini, halved and thinly sliced
1/2 cup chopped green pepper
1/2 cup chopped sweet red pepper
1/4 cup minced fresh parsley
1/4 cup grated Parmesan cheese
1/2 cup olive *or* vegetable oil
1/4 cup cider *or* red wine vinegar
  1 garlic clove, minced
1-1/2 teaspoons ground mustard
  1 teaspoon dried basil
  1 teaspoon dried oregano
1/4 teaspoon salt
Dash pepper
  2 medium tomatoes, cut into wedges

Cook the pasta according to package directions; rinse in cold water and drain. Place in a large bowl; add the next nine ingredients. In a jar with tight-fitting lid, combine oil, vinegar, garlic, mustard, basil, oregano, salt and pepper; shake well. Pour over salad and toss to coat. Cover and chill for 8 hours or overnight. Toss before serving. Garnish with tomatoes. **Yield:** 10-12 servings.

Molded Cranberry Fruit Salad

Instead of putting a bowl of plain cranberry sauce on the holiday table, I like to whip up this festive fruity salad. It adds pretty color to the meal.
—Virginia Rexroat, Jenks, Oklahoma

✓ This tasty dish uses less sugar, salt and fat. Recipe includes *Diabetic Exchanges.*

  2 packages (3 ounces *each*) cherry gelatin
  2 cups boiling water
  1 package (12 ounces) fresh *or* frozen cranberries
  1 large apple, peeled and chopped
  1 large orange, peeled, chopped and seeded
  1 piece of orange peel (1 inch)
  1 can (20 ounces) crushed pineapple, undrained

In a bowl, dissolve gelatin in water. Stir in all remaining ingredients. Process in small batches in a blender until coarsely chopped. Pour into a 13-in. x 9-in. x 2-in. dish or a 3-qt. serving bowl. Chill until set, about 2-3 hours. **Yield:** 16 servings. **Diabetic Exchanges:** One 1/2-cup serving (prepared with sugar-free gelatin and unsweetened pineapple) equals 1 fruit; also, 47 calories, 46 mg sodium, 0 cholesterol, 11 gm carbohydrate, 2 gm protein, trace fat.

Basil Garden Salad

Basil is one of the easiest herbs to grow and adds flavor to many foods. In summer, I like to use it fresh in tossed salads like this.
—Bobbie Talbott, Veneta, Oregon

✓ This tasty dish uses less sugar, salt and fat. Recipe includes *Diabetic Exchanges.*

  2 cups torn leaf lettuce
  1 cup torn Bibb lettuce
  3 green onions with tops, sliced
  1 medium tomato, peeled and diced
  6 fresh mushrooms, sliced
  9 fresh basil leaves, thinly sliced
  3 tablespoons olive *or* vegetable oil
  2 tablespoons red wine vinegar
1/4 teaspoon pepper
1/2 teaspoon salt, optional
1/2 teaspoon sugar, optional

Toss the lettuce, onions, tomato, mushrooms and basil in a large salad bowl. Combine remaining ingredients in a jar with tight-fitting lid; shake well. Pour over the salad and toss. Serve immediately. **Yield:** 6 servings. **Diabetic Exchanges:** One 1-cup serving (prepared without salt and sugar) equals

1-1/2 fat, 1/2 vegetable; also, 78 calories, 6 mg sodium, 0 cholesterol, 3 gm carbohydrate, 1 gm protein, 7 gm fat.

— 🏆 🏆 🏆 —

Springtime Pasta Salad

(Pictured on page 26)

The dill in the dressing makes this salad unique. It's a perfect make-ahead dish for a picnic or party.
—Vicki Schrupp, Little Falls, Minnesota

  2 cups spiral pasta
  1 medium zucchini, cubed
  1/2 cup sliced ripe olives
  1/2 cup chopped sweet red pepper
  1/4 cup chopped onion
  1/2 cup mayonnaise _or_ salad dressing
  1/4 cup sour cream
1-1/4 teaspoons dill weed
  1/2 teaspoon salt
  1/2 teaspoon ground mustard
  1/4 teaspoon pepper
  1/4 teaspoon garlic salt

Cook pasta according to package directions; drain and rinse with cold water. Place in a large bowl. Add zucchini, olives, red pepper and onion. Combine remaining ingredients; pour over salad and toss to coat. Cover and chill for 2 hours. **Yield:** 6-8 servings.

— 🏆 🏆 🏆 —

Zippy Tuna Salad

With crunchy pecans and sweet pineapple, this tuna salad is my favorite—and anything but boring!
—Tammy Toups, Beaumont, Texas

  1 can (8 ounces) crushed pineapple
  1 can (12 ounces) tuna, drained and flaked
  2 hard-cooked eggs, chopped
  1/2 cup chopped celery
  1/4 cup chopped onion
  6 tablespoons mayonnaise
  1/2 teaspoon Dijon mustard
  1/4 teaspoon Creole seasoning
  1/8 teaspoon minced garlic
Dash celery salt
Dash cayenne pepper
  1/4 cup chopped pecans

Drain pineapple, reserving 2 tablespoons of juice. Combine pineapple, tuna, eggs, celery and onion. In a small bowl, combine mayonnaise, mustard, seasonings and reserved pineapple juice. Add to tuna mixture; mix well. Chill. Add pecans just before serving. **Yield:** 3 cups.

Orange Salad with Honey Dressing

(Pictured above)

This light, refreshing salad is perfect for a ladies' luncheon. The delicate, flavorful dressing goes so well with the orange slices. On a bed of green lettuce, it looks as good as it tastes.
—Diane Hixon
Niceville, Florida

1/4 cup sugar
  8 teaspoons lemon juice
  2 tablespoons vinegar
  5 teaspoons honey
1/2 teaspoon ground mustard
1/2 teaspoon paprika
1/8 teaspoon salt
1/8 teaspoon celery seed
1/2 cup vegetable oil
Boston lettuce
  6 oranges, peeled and sliced

In a blender or food processor, combine the first nine ingredients; blend until slightly thickened. Pour into a jar or airtight container; chill. Line a serving platter or individual salad plates with lettuce. Arrange orange slices on top. Shake dressing; drizzle over oranges. **Yield:** 6-8 servings.

German Hot Noodle Salad

(Pictured above)

Here's a tasty takeoff on German potato salad. It's flavored like the traditional side dish but uses noodles in place of potatoes. —Gordon Kremer
Sacramento, California

    2 cups wide egg noodles
    3 bacon strips
1/4 cup chopped onion
    1 tablespoon sugar
    1 tablespoon all-purpose flour
1/4 teaspoon salt
1/8 teaspoon ground mustard
1/2 cup water
1/4 cup cider vinegar
    1 cup sliced celery
    2 tablespoons chopped fresh parsley

Cook noodles according to package directions. Meanwhile, in a skillet, cook the bacon until crisp. Crumble and set aside. Reserve 1 tablespoon of drippings in the skillet; saute onion until tender. Stir in sugar, flour, salt and mustard; add water and vinegar. Cook and stir until thickened and bubbly, about 2-3 minutes. Rinse and drain noodles; add to skillet. Stir in celery and parsley; heat through. Transfer to a serving bowl; sprinkle with bacon. **Yield:** 4 servings.

Chicken Salad Supreme

To give your chicken pasta salad even greater taste, simmer the chicken until tender, then use the broth and additional water to cook the noodles.

Cool Cucumber Pasta

Looking for a new food idea for your next picnic? People say this salad is crispy, sweet and unique. It's fine summertime fare. —Jeanette Fuehring
Concordia, Missouri

    8 ounces tube pasta
    1 tablespoon vegetable oil
    2 medium cucumbers, thinly sliced
    1 medium onion, thinly sliced
1-1/2 cups sugar
    1 cup water
  3/4 cup vinegar
    1 tablespoon prepared mustard
    1 tablespoon dried parsley flakes
    1 teaspoon salt
    1 teaspoon pepper
1/2 teaspoon garlic salt

Cook the pasta according to package directions; drain and rinse in cold water. Place in a large bowl; stir in oil, cucumbers and onion. Combine the remaining ingredients; pour over salad and toss. Cover and chill for 3-4 hours, stirring occasionally. Serve with a slotted spoon. **Yield:** 8-10 servings.

———— 🍷 🍷 🍷 ————

Marinated Bean Salad

Parsley is a pretty accent to a colorful combination of beans, black-eyed peas and onion. The sweet and tangy dressing is unbeatable. —Iola Egle
McCook, Nebraska

    1 can (16 ounces) kidney beans, rinsed
      and drained
    1 can (14-1/2 ounces) cut green beans,
      drained
    1 can (14-1/2 ounces) cut wax beans,
      drained
    1 can (15-1/2 ounces) black-eyed peas,
      rinsed and drained
1/2 cup vegetable oil
1/2 cup vinegar
1/2 cup sugar
1/4 cup minced fresh parsley
    1 teaspoon salt
1/2 teaspoon pepper
1/2 teaspoon ground mustard
1/2 teaspoon dried basil
1/2 teaspoon dried tarragon
    1 medium onion, thinly sliced into rings

Combine beans and peas in a large bowl. In a small bowl, combine the next nine ingredients; mix well. Pour over bean mixture and stir well. Cover and chill for at least 2 hours. Add onion rings just before serving. Serve with a slotted spoon. **Yield:** 12-14 servings.

— 🥄 🥄 🥄 —

Tomatoes with Parsley Dressing

The perfect balance of herbs and seasonings brings out the fabulous flavor of vine-ripened tomatoes. This dish always appeals to everyone who tries it.
—Helen Morgenroth, Port Lavaca, Texas

  6 medium tomatoes, sliced
2/3 cup vegetable oil
1/4 cup vinegar
1/4 cup sliced green onions
1/4 cup minced fresh parsley
  1 tablespoon sugar
  2 teaspoons minced fresh marjoram *or* 3/4
    teaspoon dried marjoram
  1 teaspoon salt
1/4 teaspoon pepper
  1 garlic clove, minced

Place tomatoes in a large bowl. Combine remaining ingredients in a container with a tight-fitting lid; shake well. Pour over tomatoes. Chill for several hours or overnight, spooning dressing over tomatoes at least twice. **Yield:** 6 servings.

— 🥄 🥄 🥄 —

Rainbow Gelatin

Our kids love this salad's array of colors. The cool cream cheese layers complement the layers of gelatin.
—Steve Mirro, Cape Coral, Florida

  6 packages (3 ounces *each*) assorted
    flavored gelatin
  6 cups boiling water, *divided*
  3 cups cold water, *divided*
  1 package (8 ounces) cream cheese, cut
    into six cubes

In a bowl, dissolve one package of gelatin in 1 cup boiling water. Add 1/2 cup cold water; stir. Spoon half into an oiled 10-in. fluted tube pan. Chill until almost set, about 40 minutes. Cool the other half of gelatin mixture; pour into a blender. Add one cube of cream cheese and blend until smooth. Spoon over the first layer. Chill until set. Repeat five times, alternating plain gelatin layer with creamed gelatin layer, and chilling between each step. Just before serving, unmold onto a serving platter. **Yield:** 16-20 servings. **Editor's Note:** This salad takes time to prepare since each layer must be set before the next layer is added. Also remember that the pan will be inverted when unmolded, so put the flavor of gelatin you want on top in the pan first.

Tuna-Stuffed Jumbo Shells

(Pictured below)

These light, fresh-tasting stuffed shells really star as part of a luncheon menu. I came up with this distinctive combination of ingredients by accident one day using leftovers from other recipes. It's a cool summer main dish.
—Phy Bresse
Lumberton, North Carolina

  10 jumbo pasta shells
1/2 cup mayonnaise
  2 tablespoons sugar
  1 can (12 ounces) tuna, drained and flaked
  1 cup diced celery
1/2 cup diced green onions
1/2 cup diced green pepper
1/2 cup shredded carrot
  2 tablespoons minced fresh parsley
CREAMY CELERY DRESSING:
1/4 cup sour cream
1/4 cup sugar
1/4 cup cider vinegar
  2 tablespoons mayonnaise
  1 teaspoon celery seed
  1 teaspoon onion powder
Lettuce leaves and red onion rings, optional

Cook pasta according to package directions; rinse in cold water and drain. In a bowl, combine mayonnaise and sugar. Stir in the tuna, celery, onions, green pepper, carrot and parsley. Spoon into pasta shells; cover and refrigerate. For the dressing, combine sour cream, sugar, vinegar, mayonnaise, celery seed and onion powder. Arrange lettuce, onion rings and shells on a serving platter; drizzle with dressing. **Yield:** 5 servings.

Hot Five-Bean Salad

(Pictured below)

This crowd-pleaser is like a German potato salad made with colorful beans. My mom's been preparing this salad for years—it's so simple to create and great to take to church suppers.
—Angela Leinenbach
Newport News, Virginia

 8 bacon strips, diced
 2/3 cup sugar
 2 tablespoons cornstarch
 1-1/2 teaspoons salt
 Pinch pepper
 3/4 cup vinegar
 1/2 cup water
 1 can (16 ounces) kidney beans, rinsed and drained
 1 can (15 ounces) lima beans, rinsed and drained
 1 can (15 ounces) garbanzo beans, rinsed and drained
 1 can (14-1/2 ounces) green beans, drained
 1 can (14-1/2 ounces) wax beans, drained

In a skillet, cook the bacon until crisp; reserve 1/4 cup of drippings. Set the bacon aside. Add sugar, cornstarch, salt and pepper to drippings. Stir in vinegar and water; bring to a boil, stirring constantly. Cook and stir for 2 minutes. Add the beans; reduce heat. Cover and simmer for 15 minutes or until beans are heated through. Place in a serving bowl; top with bacon. **Yield:** 10-12 servings.

Anytime Cucumber Slices

I received this recipe from a friend at church who would make a large batch for picnics and potlucks.
—Jeanne Bunders, Wauzeka, Wisconsin

 3 to 4 large cucumbers, sliced
 2 medium onions, thinly sliced
 3 tablespoons minced fresh dill *or* 1 tablespoon dill weed
 1 cup sugar
 1/2 cup vinegar
 1/2 cup water
 1 teaspoon salt

In a bowl, combine cucumbers, onions and dill. In a saucepan, combine sugar, vinegar, water and salt; bring to a boil. Pour over cucumber mixture. Cover and refrigerate for 3 hours or overnight. **Yield:** 6 cups.

Summertime Main-Dish Salad

This salad has all the spark of Cajun jambalaya. Family and friends agree it's cool and satisfying.
—Ruby Williams, Bogalusa, Louisiana

✓ This tasty dish uses less sugar, salt and fat. Recipe includes *Diabetic Exchanges.*

 2-1/2 cups cubed fully cooked ham
 1/3 cup chopped onion
 2 garlic cloves, minced
 1 teaspoon dried oregano
 1 teaspoon dried thyme
 1/4 teaspoon cayenne pepper
 1/4 teaspoon pepper
 1 tablespoon cooking oil
 1/3 cup cider *or* red wine vinegar
 4 cups cooked rice
 3 cups diced cooked chicken
 2 celery ribs, thinly sliced
 1/2 cup julienned green pepper
 1/2 cup julienned sweet red pepper
 2 green onions with tops, sliced
 1 pint cherry tomatoes

In a skillet over medium heat, saute the first seven ingredients in oil until vegetables are tender. Remove from the heat; stir in vinegar. Cool for 5 minutes. In a bowl, toss the rice, chicken, celery, peppers and onions. Stir in the ham mixture. Cover and chill for at least 2 hours. Garnish with tomatoes. **Yield:** 9 servings. **Diabetic Exchanges:** One 1-cup serving (prepared with low-fat ham) equals 2 lean meat, 1-1/2 starch, 1 vegetable; also, 251 calories, 576 mg sodium, 47 mg cholesterol, 31 gm carbohydrate, 18 gm protein, 5 gm fat.

Mandarin Orange Tossed Salad

This quick and easy salad never misses with dinner guests. Once in a while, I'll add avocado and blue cheese for a more interesting flavor. —David Collin Martinez, California

>   1 **can (15 ounces) mandarin oranges**
>   1/4 **cup olive *or* vegetable oil**
>   1/4 **cup tarragon wine vinegar**
>   1/4 **teaspoon sugar**
>   1/4 **teaspoon salt**
>   1/8 **teaspoon pepper**
>   1/8 **teaspoon dried basil**
>   1/8 **teaspoon ground savory**
>   8 **cups torn leaf lettuce**
>   1 **medium red onion, sliced**
>   1/2 **cup sliced almonds, toasted**

Drain oranges, reserving 1/4 cup syrup; set oranges aside. In a jar with tight-fitting lid, combine syrup, oil, vinegar, sugar, salt, pepper, basil and savory; shake well. In a salad bowl, toss lettuce, oranges and onion. Add the dressing and toss. Top with almonds; serve immediately. **Yield:** 10-12 servings.

Seven-Vegetable Salad

With this fun, no-lettuce salad, you can mix and match vegetables to suit your tastes.
—Kim Wiehe-Kaylor, Sidney, Ohio

✓ This tasty dish uses less sugar, salt and fat. Recipe includes *Diabetic Exchanges.*

1-3/4 cups cauliflowerets
1-1/4 cups chopped cucumber
>   1 **cup sliced celery**
>   1/2 **cup quartered cherry tomatoes**
>   1/4 **cup julienned green pepper**
>   1/4 **cup julienned sweet red pepper**
>   2 **tablespoons sliced green onions**
>   1/4 **cup salad dressing**

In a large bowl, combine all vegetables. Pour dressing over; toss to coat. **Yield:** 5 servings. **Diabetic Exchanges:** One 1-cup serving (prepared with fat-free salad dressing) equals 1-1/2 vegetable; also, 37 calories, 131 mg sodium, 0 cholesterol, 8 gm carbohydrate, 1 gm protein, trace fat.

Spaghetti Fruit Salad
(Pictured above)

My great-aunt gave me the recipe for this rich, fruity salad, which goes especially well with a ham dinner. Before I even tasted it, I knew it would be good. I've never walked away from her kitchen disappointed.
—Carolyn Shepherd, O'Neill, Nebraska

>   1 **cup confectioners' sugar**
>   2 **eggs**
>   1/2 **cup lemon juice**
>   1/2 **teaspoon salt**
>   8 **ounces spaghetti, broken into 2-inch pieces**
>   1 **can (20 ounces) pineapple tidbits**
>   3 **medium tart apples, diced**
>   1 **carton (8 ounces) frozen whipped topping, thawed**
>   1/4 **cup chopped walnuts**
Maraschino cherries, halved

In a saucepan, combine sugar, eggs, lemon juice and salt; cook and stir over medium heat until temperature reaches 160° and mixture is thickened, about 4 minutes. Cool completely. Cook spaghetti according to the package directions; drain and rinse in cold water. Place in a large bowl. Drain pineapple, reserving juice. Pour juice over the spaghetti; stir in apples. Toss gently; drain. Stir in the egg mixture and pineapple. Cover and refrigerate overnight. Fold in whipped topping just before serving. Garnish with walnuts and cherries. **Yield:** 12-14 servings.

fruit, 1 fat; also, 105 calories, 34 mg sodium, 0 cholesterol, 14 gm carbohydrate, 1 gm protein, 6 gm fat.

— 🍵 🍵 🍵 —

Molded Rhubarb Salad

This bright red salad sets fresh tart rhubarb in a fruity-sweet gelatin blend.   *—Sue Seymour*
Valatie, New York

    3 **cups diced rhubarb**
    2 **cups water**
1-2/3 **cups sugar**
    1 **package (6 ounces) strawberry gelatin**
    1 **can (20 ounces) crushed pineapple, drained**
 1/2 **cup chopped walnuts**

In a saucepan over medium heat, cook rhubarb in water until tender, about 5 minutes. Remove from the heat; stir in sugar and gelatin until dissolved. Add pineapple and nuts. Pour into a 6-cup mold that has been coated with nonstick cooking spray. Chill until set. **Yield:** 10-12 servings.

— 🍵 🍵 🍵 —

Orange and Onion Salad

I've relied on this recipe for years. I first prepared it for a ladies' luncheon where it was met with raves.
—Ruth Peterson, Jenison, Michigan

    6 **tablespoons olive *or* vegetable oil**
    2 **tablespoons orange juice**
    4 **teaspoons vinegar**
    1 **tablespoon minced fresh rosemary *or* 1 teaspoon dried rosemary, crushed**
 1/2 **teaspoon salt**
 1/4 **teaspoon pepper**
    1 **small red onion**
    4 **medium oranges, peeled and sectioned**
    8 **cups torn romaine**

In a large salad bowl, whisk oil, orange juice, vinegar, rosemary, salt and pepper. Cut onion into thin slices, then into 1-in. pieces; add to dressing. Add oranges and romaine; toss gently. **Yield:** 8 servings.

— 🍵 🍵 🍵 —

Sunshine Salad

We especially like this salad with barbecue. I've been making this dish for years...it never goes out of style.
—Page Alexander, Baldwin City, Kansas

    1 **package (3 ounces) lemon gelatin**
    1 **cup boiling water**

Apple Pineapple Salad

(Pictured above)

I came up with the recipe for this fun fruit salad years ago. It's a refreshing change-of-pace for me and my husband, who's diabetic.   *—Jessie Craven*
Odessa, Missouri

✓ This tasty dish uses less sugar, salt and fat. Recipe includes *Diabetic Exchanges.*

    1 **can (20 ounces) pineapple chunks**
 1/4 **cup butter *or* margarine**
    2 **tablespoons lemon juice**
    1 **tablespoon cornstarch**
    2 **tablespoons water**
    2 **tablespoons sugar *or* artificial sweetener equivalent**
    3 **cups chopped unpeeled red apples**
    2 **cups green grapes**
    2 **teaspoons poppy seeds**
 3/4 **cup chopped pecans, toasted**

Drain pineapple juice into a saucepan; set the pineapple aside. Add butter and lemon juice; cook over medium heat until butter is melted. In a small bowl, combine cornstarch and water until smooth; stir into juice mixture. Bring to a boil; boil and stir for 2 minutes. Reduce heat; add sugar. Cool to room temperature, about 30 minutes. In a large bowl, combine pineapple, apples, grapes and poppy seeds. Add dressing; toss to coat. Cover and chill for at least 1 hour. Just before serving, gently toss in pecans. **Yield:** 16 servings. **Diabetic Exchanges:** One 1/2-cup serving (prepared with unsweetened pineapple, reduced-fat margarine and artificial sweetener) equals 1

1 can (8 ounces) crushed pineapple
1/3 cup orange juice concentrate
1 can (11 ounces) mandarin oranges, drained

In a bowl, dissolve gelatin in boiling water. Drain pineapple, reserving juice. Set pineapple aside. Add enough water to the juice to equal 1 cup; stir into gelatin. Add orange juice concentrate. Chill until partially set. Fold in the pineapple and oranges. Pour into a 4-cup mold or glass bowl. Chill until set. **Yield:** 6 servings.

— 🛒 🛒 🛒 —

Asparagus, Apple and Chicken Salad
(Pictured on page 27)

This cool, colorful salad is a palate-pleaser. Apples and asparagus seem an unlikely match, but they form a terrific trio with chicken. I make this salad quite often while asparagus is in season. —Nancy Horsburgh Everett, Ontario

1 cup cut fresh asparagus (1-inch pieces)
2 tablespoons cider vinegar
2 tablespoons vegetable oil
2 teaspoons honey
2 teaspoons minced fresh parsley
1/2 teaspoon salt
1/4 teaspoon pepper
1 cup cubed cooked chicken
1/2 cup diced red apple
2 cups torn mixed greens
Alfalfa sprouts, optional

Cook asparagus in a small amount of water until crisp-tender, about 3-4 minutes; drain and cool. In a bowl, combine the next six ingredients. Stir in the chicken, apple and asparagus; toss. Serve over greens. Garnish with alfalfa sprouts if desired. **Yield:** 3 servings.

— 🛒 🛒 🛒 —

Raggedy Ann and Andy Salads

When "faced" with a boring salad, my granddaughter suggests making these fruity salads instead. She likes making them as much as eating them.
—Lee Hill-Nelson, Waco, Texas

2 cups torn lettuce
4 canned peach *or* apricot halves
8 raisins
4 maraschino cherries, halved
1 cup grated carrots* *or* shredded cheddar cheese

Place 1/2 cup lettuce each on four plates. Place peach halves, cut side down, on lettuce. On each peach, place two raisins for eyes and two cherry halves for mouth. Arrange carrots around peach for hair. **Yield:** 4 servings. ***Editor's Note:** Grate carrots crosswise for boy's hair and lengthwise for girl's hair.

— 🛒 🛒 🛒 —

Zesty Gazpacho Salad
(Pictured below)

This refreshing salad is excellent for a summer cookout. Since you mix it ahead, the flavors have time to blend and there's no last-minute fussing.
—Teresa Fischer, Munster, Indiana

2 medium zucchini, chopped
2 medium tomatoes, chopped
1 small ripe avocado, chopped
1 cup fresh *or* frozen corn, thawed
1/2 cup thinly sliced green onions
1/2 cup picante sauce
2 tablespoons minced fresh parsley
2 tablespoons lemon juice
1 tablespoon vegetable oil
3/4 teaspoon garlic salt
1/4 teaspoon ground cumin

In a bowl, combine the first five ingredients. In a small bowl, combine remaining ingredients; mix well. Pour over zucchini mixture; toss to coat. Cover and refrigerate for at least 4 hours. **Yield:** 8-10 servings.

Soups & Sandwiches

You won't want to restrict this spread of kettle creations and piled-high sandwiches to your lunchtime menus. These hearty recipes make filling dinners as well.

CLASSIC COMBINATION. Clockwise from upper left: Butternut Bisque (p. 53), Meatball Sub Sandwiches (p. 44), Hearty Chicken Noodle Soup (p. 42) and Bean 'n' Burger Pockets (p. 47).

Hearty Chicken Noodle Soup

(Pictured above)

I'm grateful that my mother taught me to make these wonderful old-fashioned noodles, which were a big favorite of mine when I was growing up. They give the chicken soup a delightful down-home flavor.
—*Cindy Renfrow, Sussex, New Jersey*

    1 stewing chicken (about 6 pounds), cut up
    2 quarts water
    1 large onion, quartered
    1 cup chopped fresh parsley
    1 celery rib, sliced
    5 chicken bouillon cubes
    5 whole peppercorns
    4 whole cloves
    1 bay leaf
    2 teaspoons salt
 1/2 teaspoon pepper
Dash dried thyme
    2 medium carrots, thinly sliced
NOODLES:
1-1/4 cups all-purpose flour
 1/2 teaspoon salt
    1 egg
    2 tablespoons milk

In a large kettle, combine the first 12 ingredients; bring to a boil. Reduce heat; cover and simmer for 2-1/2 hours or until the chicken is tender. Remove chicken from broth; cool. Debone chicken and cut into chunks. Strain broth and skim fat; return to kettle. Add chicken and carrots. For noodles, mix flour and salt in a medium bowl. Make a well in the center. Beat egg and milk; pour into the well. Stir together, forming a dough. Turn dough onto a floured surface; knead 8-10 times. Roll into a 12-in. x 9-in. rectangle. Cut into 1/2-in. strips; cut the strips into 1-in. pieces. Bring soup to a simmer; add the noodles. Cover and cook for 12-15 minutes or until noodles are tender. **Yield:** 10-12 servings.

Pizza Bread

When I was growing up, my parents worked. So I learned basic cooking skills in Boy Scouts to prepare meals at home. These days, my wife, Diane, and I share the kitchen responsibilities.
—*Steve Mirro*
Cape Coral, Florida

    1 pound lean ground beef
    2 cans (6 ounces *each*) tomato paste
    2 cans (2-1/4 ounces *each*) sliced ripe
      olives, drained
 1/2 cup grated Parmesan cheese
    1 tablespoon snipped chives
    1 teaspoon salt
 1/2 teaspoon dried oregano
 1/4 teaspoon pepper
    1 loaf (20 inches) French bread, halved
      lengthwise
    8 ounces sliced mozzarella cheese

Combine the uncooked beef, tomato paste, olives, Parmesan cheese, chives, salt, oregano and pepper. Spread to the edges of the cut surface of the bread. Place on a greased 15-in. x 10-in. x 1-in. baking pan. Bake at 350° for 25 minutes. Top with mozzarella cheese; return to the oven for 5 minutes or until cheese melts. **Yield:** 4-6 servings.

Black Bean Soup

I know you'll come to rely on this recipe like I have. It's loaded with beans, meat and flavor for a real stick-to-the-ribs meal.
—*Joy Rackham*
Chimacum, Washington

    4 cups (2 pounds) dry black beans
    7 cups water
    1 medium onion, chopped
 1/2 cup chopped green pepper
    2 celery ribs, chopped

3 garlic cloves, minced
1 tablespoon cooking oil
2 smoked ham hocks
2 cans (4 ounces *each*) chopped green
    chilies
2 teaspoons chicken bouillon granules
3 bay leaves
1 teaspoon chili powder
1 teaspoon ground cumin
1/2 teaspoon sugar
Pinch pepper
1 pound fresh kielbasa
1 can (14-1/2 ounces) diced tomatoes,
    undrained

Rinse beans; place in a large kettle or Dutch oven. Add water and bring to a boil. Reduce heat; cover and simmer for 1-1/2 hours. In a skillet over medium heat, saute onion, green pepper, celery and garlic in oil until tender. Add to the beans. Add ham hocks, chilies, bouillon and seasonings. Cover and simmer for 1-1/2 to 2 hours or until the beans are tender. Meanwhile, in a skillet, cook kielbasa until juices are no longer pink. Cut in half lengthwise; slice into 1/4-in. pieces. Add kielbasa and tomatoes to soup. Remove ham hocks; cut meat from bones and return to the soup. Cover and simmer for 30 minutes. Remove bay leaves. **Yield:** 10-12 servings (3 quarts).

— ♎ ♎ ♎ —

Surprise Sandwich Spread

When our kids were young, this was their favorite sandwich. I also like to serve the spread on party rye bread for a special snack. —Audrey Thibodeau
Mesa, Arizona

2 cups ground fully cooked ham, roast beef
    or chicken
2 hard-cooked eggs, chopped
1/4 cup mayonnaise, ketchup *or* chili sauce
1 teaspoon prepared mustard
1/2 teaspoon Worcestershire sauce
1/4 teaspoon celery salt
1/8 teaspoon onion powder
1/8 teaspoon pepper
2 tablespoons chopped celery, onion *or*
    olives, optional
1 tablespoon sweet pickle relish, optional
8 slices bread

In a medium bowl, combine the first eight ingredients. If desired, add celery, onion or olives and/or relish. Spread 1/2 cup on four slices of bread; top with remaining bread. **Yield:** 4 servings.

Spicy Sausage Sandwiches

(Pictured below)

These hearty sandwiches are packed with flavor and very versatile. They're terrific for breakfast, lunch or a light supper. The pretty corn and pepper salsa is a garden-fresh topper for the browned sausage patties.
—Eileen Sullivan, Lady Lake, Florida

SALSA:
2 jalapeno peppers
1 large fresh banana pepper
1/2 cup diced sweet red pepper
1/2 cup diced Vidalia *or* sweet onion
1/2 cup fresh *or* frozen corn
1 tablespoon chopped fresh cilantro *or*
    parsley
SANDWICH:
1 pound bulk pork sausage
6 English muffins, split and toasted
6 slices Colby/Jack cheese

Remove seeds and membranes from jalapeno and banana peppers if desired (for a less spicy salsa). Dice peppers and place in a bowl; add remaining salsa ingredients and mix well. Cover and refrigerate until ready to serve. Form the sausage into six patties; cook in a skillet over medium heat until meat is no longer pink. Place each on an English muffin half; top with 1 tablespoon salsa and a slice of cheese. Cover with other muffin half. Serve remaining salsa on the side. **Yield:** 6 servings.

Meatball Sub Sandwiches

(Pictured below)

These hot, meaty sandwiches have a tangy barbecue-style sauce rather than the more traditional Italian tomato sauce. Onion and pepper slices make each bite twice as nice. —Kim Marie Van Rheenen
Mendota, Illinois

    9 submarine sandwich buns
1-1/2 pounds lean ground beef
    1 egg
  1/4 cup milk
    1 tablespoon diced onion
    1 teaspoon salt
  1/4 teaspoon pepper
    2 tablespoons cooking oil, *divided*
    2 medium green peppers, julienned
    1 medium onion, sliced
    1 tablespoon all-purpose flour
    1 bottle (12 ounces) chili sauce
    1 cup water
    1 tablespoon brown sugar
    1 teaspoon ground mustard

Cut a thin slice off the top of each roll; scoop out bread from inside. Crumble 1-1/4 cups of the bread and place in a large bowl. Cover rolls and tops with plastic wrap; set aside. To the crumbled bread, add the beef, egg, milk, diced onion, salt and pepper. Shape into 27 meatballs, about 1-1/2 in. each. In a large skillet, cook meatballs in 1 tablespoon of oil for 20-25 minutes or until no longer pink. Remove with a slotted spoon; set aside. Add remaining oil to skillet; saute green peppers and sliced onion until tender. Remove with a slotted spoon; set aside. Stir flour into the skillet. Add chili sauce and water; bring to a boil. Cook and stir for 1-2 minutes. Stir in brown sugar and mustard. Add meatballs, peppers and onion; cover and simmer

for 20 minutes. Meanwhile, warm rolls in a 325° oven for 8-10 minutes. Spoon three meatballs and sauce into each roll; replace tops. **Yield:** 9 servings.

— 🥦 🥦 🥦 —

Dandelion Soup

This creamy soup is a great way to celebrate the end of winter. Fix a batch soon...I guarantee you'll have compliments cropping up like weeds!
—Mary Ellen Dycus, Leland, Mississippi

    1 package (6.9 ounces) chicken-flavored
      rice mix
    3 cans (10-3/4 ounces *each*) condensed
      cream of chicken soup, undiluted
    5 cups water
    2 cups cubed cooked chicken
    4 cups dandelion greens, torn

Prepare rice according to package directions; set aside. In a large saucepan or Dutch oven over medium heat, combine soup and water. Add rice and chicken; heat through. Add dandelion greens; cook until tender, about 6-8 minutes. **Yield:** 10-12 servings. **Editor's Note:** When dandelions aren't in season, you may substitute fresh spinach for the dandelion greens.

— 🥦 🥦 🥦 —

Jim's Potato Soup

Our kids claimed they didn't like potato soup. But after one taste of my version, they came clamoring for seconds! The secret is adding cayenne pepper to give it a little kick, plus topping it with cheese and bacon bits. —Jim Wick, Orlando, Florida

  1/3 cup diced celery
  1/3 cup diced carrot
  1/4 cup diced onion
    2 tablespoons butter *or* margarine
    2 tablespoons all-purpose flour
    1 quart milk
    2 chicken bouillon cubes
    2 tablespoons minced fresh parsley
  1/2 teaspoon salt
  1/2 teaspoon seasoned salt
  1/4 teaspoon cayenne pepper
    6 medium potatoes, peeled and cooked
Chives, shredded cheddar cheese and bacon
  bits, optional

In a 3-qt. Dutch oven or kettle, saute the celery, carrot and onion in butter until tender. Stir in flour until smooth. Gradually add milk; cook and stir until thickened and bubbly. Add bouillon, parsley, salt, seasoned salt and cayenne. Simmer for 20 minutes, stirring occasionally. Cube half of the potatoes and

mash the other half; add all to the soup. Simmer for 20-25 minutes or until heated through. Garnish individual servings with chives, cheese and bacon bits if desired. **Yield:** 8 servings (2 quarts).

Turkey Tortilla Roll-Ups

To keep lunches new and exciting for my family, I like to prepare these roll-ups. They can be prepared ahead, so they're great for brown-bag lunches.
—*Darlene Markel, Sublimity, Oregon*

  3/4 **cup sour cream**
    6 **flour tortillas (8 inches)**
1-1/2 **cups diced cooked turkey**
    1 **cup (4 ounces) finely shredded cheddar**
      cheese
    1 **cup shredded lettuce**
  1/2 **cup chopped ripe olives**
  1/2 **cup chunky salsa**

Spread 2 tablespoons sour cream over each tortilla. Top with turkey, cheese, lettuce, olives and salsa. Roll up each tortilla tightly; wrap in plastic wrap. Refrigerate until serving. **Yield:** 6 servings.

Cream of Carrot Soup

This soup, packed with vitamin-rich and wholesome ingredients, is both beautiful and delicious.
—*LaVonne Hegland, St. Michael, Minnesota*

  6 **to 8 medium carrots (1 pound), coarsely**
    chopped
  2 **medium potatoes, peeled and diced**
  1 **cup water**
  2 **medium onions, chopped**
  2 **to 3 garlic cloves, minced**
1/4 **cup butter *or* margarine**
1/3 **cup all-purpose flour**
  2 **teaspoons salt**
  1 **teaspoon sugar**
  6 **cups milk**
  1 **cup half-and-half cream**
Pinch cayenne pepper
Paprika

Place carrots, potatoes and water in a saucepan; cover and cook over medium heat until the vegetables are tender. Drain, reserving cooking liquid. In a skillet, saute onions and garlic in butter for 10 minutes. Add flour; cook and stir for 2 minutes. Place carrots, potatoes, onion mixture, salt and sugar in a blender or food processor; cover and puree until smooth, adding reserved cooking liquid as needed. Pour into a 3-qt. saucepan or Dutch oven.

Stir in milk and heat through. Add cream and cayenne; heat through (do not boil). Garnish with paprika. **Yield:** 10-12 servings.

Cream of Asparagus Soup
(Pictured above)

It's not difficult to fix a batch of this smooth, comforting soup. It has wonderful homemade goodness. A single steaming bowl really warms me up...but I usually can't resist going back for seconds. —*Veva Hepler*
Walla Walla, Washington

  1/2 **cup chopped onion**
    1 **tablespoon cooking oil**
    2 **cans (14-1/2 ounces *each*) chicken broth**
2-1/2 **pounds fresh asparagus, trimmed and cut**
    into 1-inch pieces
  1/4 **teaspoon dried tarragon**
  1/4 **cup butter *or* margarine**
  1/4 **cup all-purpose flour**
  1/2 **teaspoon salt**
  1/4 **teaspoon white pepper**
    3 **cups half-and-half cream**
1-1/2 **teaspoons lemon juice**
Shredded Swiss cheese

In a large saucepan over medium heat, saute onion in oil until tender. Add broth, asparagus and tarragon; simmer until the asparagus is tender, about 8-10 minutes. In a blender or food processor, puree the asparagus, a third at a time; set aside. In a Dutch oven or soup kettle, melt the butter; stir in flour, salt and pepper. Cook and stir for 2 minutes or until golden. Gradually add cream. Stir in the pureed asparagus and lemon juice; heat through. Garnish with cheese if desired. **Yield:** 8 servings (about 2 quarts).

Slow-Cooker Vegetable Soup

(Pictured above)

What a treat to come home from work and have this savory soup ready to eat. I like to pair it with crusty rolls topped with melted mozzarella cheese.
—Heather Thurmeier, Pense, Saskatchewan

✓ This tasty dish uses less sugar, salt and fat. Recipe includes *Diabetic Exchanges.*

> 1 pound boneless round steak, cut into 1/2-inch cubes
> 1 can (14-1/2 ounces) diced tomatoes, undrained
> 3 cups water
> 2 medium potatoes, peeled and cubed
> 2 medium onions, diced
> 3 celery ribs, sliced
> 2 carrots, sliced
> 3 beef bouillon cubes
> 1/2 teaspoon dried basil
> 1/2 teaspoon dried oregano
> 1/2 teaspoon salt, optional
> 1/4 teaspoon pepper
> 1-1/2 cups frozen mixed vegetables

In a slow cooker, combine the first 12 ingredients. Cover and cook on high for 6 hours. Add vegetables; cover and cook on high 2 hours longer or until the meat and vegetables are tender. **Yield:** 8-10 servings (about 2-1/2 quarts). **Diabetic Exchanges:** One 1-cup serving (prepared without salt) equals 1 starch, 1 lean meat, 1 vegetable; also, 143 calories, 464 mg sodium, 31 mg cholesterol, 15 gm carbohydrate, 13 gm protein, 3 gm fat.

Curried Pumpkin Soup

This comforting soup is wonderfully warming on an autumn day, and the subtle curry flavor lets the pumpkin star. My family really enjoys dishes like this that have a delightful down-home flavor.
—Eleanor Dunbar
Peoria, Illinois

✓ This tasty dish uses less sugar, salt and fat. Recipe includes *Diabetic Exchanges.*

> 1 small onion, chopped
> 1 teaspoon cooking oil
> 2 cups chicken broth
> 1-1/2 cups cooked *or* canned pumpkin
> 1 tablespoon lemon juice
> 1 teaspoon curry powder
> 1 teaspoon sugar
> 1/2 teaspoon salt, optional
> Dash pepper
> 1/2 cup half-and-half cream *or* evaporated milk
> Chopped fresh parsley, optional

In a saucepan over medium heat, saute onion in oil until tender. Add broth, pumpkin, lemon juice, curry powder, sugar, salt if desired and pepper; bring to a boil. Reduce heat; cover and simmer for 15 minutes. Stir in cream; heat through. Garnish with parsley if desired. **Yield:** 4 servings. **Diabetic Exchanges:** One 1-cup serving (prepared with low-sodium broth and evaporated skim milk and without salt) equals 1/2 starch, 1/2 fat; also, 67 calories, 60 mg sodium, 3 mg cholesterol, 11 gm carbohydrate, 3 gm protein, 2 gm fat.

Stuffed Pork Burgers

Having raised hogs in the past, I've served pork often and in a variety of ways. Everyone who has sampled these burgers agrees that they're the best.
—Jean Smith, Monona, Iowa

> 1/2 cup chopped fresh mushrooms
> 1/4 cup sliced green onions
> 1/4 teaspoon garlic powder
> 1 tablespoon butter *or* margarine
> 1-1/2 pounds ground pork
> 2 tablespoons Worcestershire sauce
> 1 teaspoon ground mustard
> 1/2 teaspoon salt
> 1/2 teaspoon pepper
> 4 kaiser rolls, split
> 4 lettuce leaves
> 4 slices red onion
> 8 thin slices tomato
> Prepared mustard

In a skillet, saute the mushrooms and onions with garlic powder in butter until vegetables are tender. Remove from the heat. In a bowl, combine pork, Worcestershire sauce, mustard, salt and pepper. Shape into eight patties. Spoon mushroom mixture into the center of four patties to within 1/2 in. of edges. Top with remaining patties and pinch edges to seal. Grill, uncovered, over medium coals for 10-15 minutes, turning once, or until juices run clear. Serve on rolls with lettuce, onion, tomato and mustard. **Yield:** 4 servings.

Minute Minestrone

This recipe came about by accident when I combined a week's worth of family leftovers. Everyone gobbled it up without knowing my secret!   —Lyn Robitaille
East Hartland, Connecticut

      4 **cups water**
      1 **package (1.7 ounces) vegetable soup mix**
      1 **can (16 ounces) kidney beans, rinsed and drained**
      1 **can (15-1/2 ounces) corn, drained**
      1 **can (8 ounces) tomato sauce**
      2 **cups cubed cooked beef, chicken _or_ turkey**
      1 **cup cooked leftover vegetables**
      1 **cup sliced celery**
      1 **cup chopped onion**
   3/4 **teaspoon salt**
   1/8 **teaspoon pepper**
      2 **cups cooked elbow macaroni**

In a large saucepan, bring water and soup mix to a boil over medium heat. Add beans, corn, tomato sauce, meat, vegetables, celery, onion, salt and pepper; bring to a boil. Reduce heat; cover and simmer for 10 minutes. Add macaroni and heat through. **Yield:** 10-12 servings.

Bean 'n' Burger Pockets

(Pictured at right)

This recipe started out as an alternative to baked beans. One day I decided to add ground beef and stuff the mixture into pita bread, and now it's a sandwich we enjoy often.
      —Gwen Parsons
Boring, Oregon

1-1/4 **pounds ground beef**
      1 **can (8 ounces) tomato sauce**

      1 **can (14-1/2 ounces) diced tomatoes, undrained**
   1/2 **cup chopped onion**
      1 **garlic clove, minced**
      1 **tablespoon brown sugar**
      1 **teaspoon seasoned salt**
      1 **teaspoon chili powder**
   1/2 **teaspoon ground cumin**
   1/8 **teaspoon _each_ dried thyme, savory, marjoram, oregano and parsley flakes**
      1 **can (8-3/4 ounces) navy beans, rinsed and drained**
      1 **can (8-3/4 ounces) kidney beans, rinsed and drained**
      1 **can (8-3/4 ounces) lima beans, rinsed and drained**
      5 **pita breads, halved**
   1/2 **cup shredded cheddar cheese, optional**

In a heavy saucepan or Dutch oven, brown beef; drain. Add tomato sauce, tomatoes, onion, garlic, brown sugar and seasonings. Cover and simmer for 1 hour, stirring occasionally. Stir in beans; heat through. Spoon about 1/2 cup into each pita half. Top with cheese if desired. **Yield:** 5 servings.

Vegetable Chili

(Pictured below)

This chili, packed with beans and vegetables, has an appealing red color and fabulous flavor. I always make a large batch so that everyone can have seconds.
—Charlene Martorana, Madison, Ohio

✓ This tasty dish uses less sugar, salt and fat. Recipe includes *Diabetic Exchanges.*

   2 large onions, chopped
   1 medium green pepper, chopped
   3 garlic cloves, minced
   1 tablespoon cooking oil
1/2 cup water
   2 medium carrots, cut into chunks
   2 medium potatoes, peeled and cubed
   1 can (14-1/2 ounces) chicken broth
   1 to 2 tablespoons chili powder
   2 tablespoons sugar
   1 teaspoon ground cumin
3/4 teaspoon dried oregano
   1 small zucchini, sliced 1/4 inch thick
   1 small yellow squash, sliced 1/4 inch thick
   2 cans (28 ounces *each*) crushed tomatoes
1/3 cup ketchup
   1 can (16 ounces) kidney beans, rinsed and drained
   1 can (15 ounces) garbanzo beans, rinsed and drained
   1 can (15 ounces) black beans, rinsed and drained
   1 can (15-1/2 ounces) black-eyed peas, rinsed and drained

In a Dutch oven or soup kettle, saute onions, green pepper and garlic in oil until tender. Add water and carrots; cover and cook over medium-low heat for 5 minutes. Add potatoes, broth, chili powder, sugar, cumin and oregano; cover and cook for 10 minutes. Add zucchini, squash, tomatoes and ketchup; bring to a boil. Reduce heat; cover and simmer for 15 minutes. Stir in beans and peas; simmer for 10 minutes. **Yield:** 12-16 servings. **Diabetic Exchanges:** One 1-cup serving (prepared with low-sodium broth) equals 1-1/2 starch, 1 vegetable, 1/2 fat; also, 160 calories, 390 mg sodium, 1 mg cholesterol, 29 gm carbohydrate, 7 gm protein, 2 gm fat.

———— 🛒 🛒 🛒 ————

Roasted Tomato Soup

Served warm or cold, this soup makes a savory first course or light lunch. People always comment on its big fresh tomato taste.
—Kriss Erickson
Haena, Hawaii

   3 pounds tomatoes, cored
1/3 cup olive *or* vegetable oil, *divided*
   6 garlic cloves, minced
   2 tablespoons chopped fresh thyme *or* 2 teaspoons dried thyme
   2 cups chopped onion
1/4 cup minced fresh basil *or* 1 tablespoon dried basil
   1 can (14-1/2 ounces) chicken broth
1/2 cup half-and-half cream
Salt and pepper to taste

Place tomatoes in a roasting pan; drizzle with 1/4 cup oil. Sprinkle with garlic and thyme. Bake, uncovered, at 350° for 1 hour, turning occasionally. In a large saucepan, saute onion in remaining oil until softened. Add roasted tomatoes and basil; cook for 5 minutes. Add broth; bring to a boil. Cook and stir for 5 minutes. Put through a sieve or food mill; return puree to pan. In a small saucepan over medium-low heat, warm cream (do not boil). Stir cream, salt and pepper into soup. **Yield:** 4-6 servings.

———— 🛒 🛒 🛒 ————

Beef 'n' Bean Pockets

These tasty pockets have bread, meat, vegetables and cheese all wrapped up in one. The recipe came from an aunt in Montana who worked in a school cafeteria and fixed these for the children.
—Arlene Zerbst
Newcastle, Wyoming

   2 pounds ground beef
   1 small onion, chopped
   1 can (16 ounces) refried beans
   1 can (8 ounces) tomato sauce
   2 teaspoons chili powder

> 1 teaspoon garlic powder
> 1 teaspoon salt
> 1/2 teaspoon pepper
> 1/2 teaspoon paprika
> Dash cayenne pepper
> 2 loaves (1 pound *each*) frozen white bread dough, thawed
> 1 cup (4 ounces) shredded cheddar cheese

In a skillet, brown beef and onion; drain. Add the next eight ingredients; bring to a boil. Reduce heat; cover and simmer for 15 minutes, stirring occasionally. Cool. Roll each loaf of dough into a 16-in. x 8-in. rectangle, about 1/4 in. thick. Cut into eight 4-in. squares. Spoon 1/4 cup filling into the center of each square; top with 1 tablespoon of cheese. Bring the four corners together up over filling; pinch seams to seal. Place on greased baking sheets. Cover and let rise for 15 minutes. Bake at 350° for 20-25 minutes or until browned. Serve immediately, or freeze and reheat in the microwave at 50% power for 1-1/2 minutes each. **Yield:** 16 servings.

Carrot Apple Soup

On a brisk fall day, I don't think anything is more appealing than a steaming bowl of this carrot soup. It picks up a hint of sweetness from the apples.
—*Ruby Williams, Bogalusa, Louisiana*

✓ This tasty dish uses less sugar, salt and fat. Recipe includes *Diabetic Exchanges.*

> 1 tablespoon butter *or* margarine
> 8 medium carrots, thinly sliced
> 2 medium tart apples, peeled and chopped
> 1 medium onion, chopped
> 1 celery rib, thinly sliced
> 5 cups chicken broth
> 1/2 teaspoon rubbed sage
> 1/4 teaspoon pepper
> 1 bay leaf

In a large saucepan, melt butter. Add carrots, apples, onion and celery; cook and stir until onion is tender, about 5 minutes. Add broth, sage, pepper and bay leaf; bring to a boil. Reduce heat; cover and simmer for 20 minutes or until the carrots are tender. Remove bay leaf. Cool soup for 5 minutes. Puree one-third at a time in a blender or food processor. Return to pan; cover and cook over medium until heated through. **Yield:** 7 servings. **Diabetic Exchanges:** One 1-cup serving (prepared with reduced-fat margarine and low-sodium broth) equals 1 vegetable, 1/2 fruit, 1/2 fat; also, 90 calories, 131 mg sodium, 4 mg cholesterol, 16 gm carbohydrate, 3 gm protein, 3 gm fat.

Lemon Asparagus Soup

(Pictured above)

We have a small asparagus patch, and my husband and I wait eagerly for this tasty vegetable to appear every spring. We're pleased to use our precious harvest in this soup. Lemon and nutmeg give it a surprising spark.
—*Darlene Swille, Green Bay, Wisconsin*

✓ This tasty dish uses less sugar, salt and fat. Recipe includes *Diabetic Exchanges.*

> 1 medium onion, chopped
> 1/2 cup chopped celery
> 1/4 cup butter *or* margarine
> 2 tablespoons cornstarch
> 1 cup water
> 2 chicken bouillon cubes
> 3/4 pound fresh asparagus, trimmed and cut into 1-inch pieces
> 2 cups milk
> 1/4 to 1/2 teaspoon grated lemon peel
> 1/8 teaspoon ground nutmeg
> Dash seasoned salt

In a 2-qt. saucepan, saute the onion and celery in butter until tender. Dissolve cornstarch in water; add to the saucepan with bouillon. Bring to a boil over medium heat; cook and stir for 2 minutes. Add asparagus. Reduce heat; cover and simmer until asparagus is crisp-tender, about 3-4 minutes. Stir in the milk, lemon peel, nutmeg and seasoned salt. Cover and simmer for 25 minutes, stirring occasionally. **Yield:** 4 servings. **Diabetic Exchanges:** One 1-cup serving (prepared with margarine, low-sodium bouillon and skim milk) equals 2 fat, 1 starch, 1 vegetable; also, 182 calories, 248 mg sodium, 2 mg cholesterol, 14 gm carbohydrate, 5 gm protein, 12 gm fat.

Cabbage Patch Soup

My family is always glad to see this slightly sweet and mildly zippy soup as part of the menu. The cabbage is shredded, so the kids never notice it!
—*Fran Strother, Wasilla, Alaska*

> 1/2 **pound ground beef**
> 1-1/2 **cups chopped onion**
> 1/2 **cup sliced celery**
> 2 **cups water**
> 1 **can (16 ounces) kidney beans, rinsed and drained**
> 1 **can (14-1/2 ounces) stewed tomatoes**
> 1 **cup shredded cabbage**
> 1 **teaspoon chili powder**
> 1/2 **teaspoon salt**
> **Hot mashed potatoes, optional**

In a saucepan over medium heat, brown the beef; drain. Add onion and celery; cook until tender. Add water, beans, tomatoes, cabbage, chili powder and salt; bring to a boil. Reduce heat; cover and simmer for 20-30 minutes or until cabbage is tender. Top each bowl with mashed potatoes if desired. **Yield:** 4-6 servings.

Creamy Onion Soup

My husband works at a grain elevator and is outside in all kinds of weather. He appreciates having a big bowl of this soup waiting when he comes home.
—*Naomi Giddis, Two Buttes, Colorado*

✓ This tasty dish uses less sugar, salt and fat. Recipe includes *Diabetic Exchanges.*

> 1 **pound yellow onions (about 3 medium), sliced**
> 2 **tablespoons butter *or* margarine**
> 4 **cups chicken broth**
> **Dash *each* pepper and dried thyme**
> 1/4 **teaspoon salt, optional**
> 2 **cups milk, *divided***
> 1/3 **cup all-purpose flour**

In a 3-qt. saucepan over medium heat, saute the onions in butter until tender. Add broth, pepper, thyme and salt if desired; bring to a boil. Reduce heat; cover and simmer for 20 minutes. Add 1-2/3 cups milk. Stir flour into the remaining milk until smooth; add to soup. Bring to a boil; boil and stir for 2 minutes or until thickened. **Yield:** 6 servings (1-1/2 quarts). **Diabetic Exchanges:** One 1-cup serving (prepared with margarine, low-sodium broth and skim milk and without salt) equals 1 vegetable, 1 starch, 1 fat; also, 133 calories, 162 mg sodium, 5 mg cholesterol, 17 gm carbohydrate, 6 gm protein, 5 gm fat.

Venison Tenderloin Sandwiches

(Pictured above)

My son-in-law supplies me with venison for these savory sandwiches. Prepared this way, the meat is very tender. —*Patricia El-Zoghbi, Wells, New York*

✓ This tasty dish uses less sugar, salt and fat. Recipe includes *Diabetic Exchanges.*

> 2 **large onions, sliced**
> 2 **cans (4 ounces *each*) sliced mushrooms, drained**
> 1/4 **cup butter *or* margarine**
> 1/4 **cup Worcestershire sauce**
> 8 **venison tenderloin steaks (12 ounces), about 3/4 inch thick**
> 1/2 **teaspoon garlic powder**
> 1/4 **teaspoon pepper**
> 1/2 **teaspoon salt, optional**
> 4 **hard rolls, split**

In a skillet, saute the onions and mushrooms in butter and Worcestershire sauce until onions are tender. Flatten steaks to 1/2 in. thick; add to the skillet. Cook over medium heat until meat is done as desired, about 3 minutes on each side. Sprinkle with garlic powder, pepper and salt if desired. Place two steaks on each roll; top with onions and mushrooms. **Yield:** 4 servings. **Diabetic Exchanges:** One serving (prepared with margarine and without salt) equals 3 lean meat, 2 starch, 1-1/2 fat, 1 vegetable; also, 423 calories, 819 mg sodium, 85 mg cholesterol, 39 gm carbohydrate, 30 gm protein, 16 gm fat.

Tortellini Soup

This soup is filling and easy to prepare. It makes a fresh-tasting and satisfying first course or light meal in itself. —Karen Rago, Bristol, Pennsylvania

✓ This tasty dish uses less sugar, salt and fat. Recipe includes *Diabetic Exchanges*.

- **1 medium onion, chopped**
- **1 garlic clove, minced**
- **2 cans (14-1/2 ounces *each*) chicken broth**
- **1 package (8 ounces) cheese tortellini**
- **1 can (14-1/2 ounces) Italian stewed tomatoes**
- **1 package (10 ounces) frozen chopped spinach, thawed and drained**

In a large saucepan coated with nonstick cooking spray, saute the onion and garlic until tender. Add broth; bring to a boil. Add tortellini; reduce heat. Simmer for 10 minutes or until the tortellini is tender. Stir in the tomatoes and spinach; heat through. Serve immediately. **Yield:** 7 servings. **Diabetic Exchanges:** One 1-cup serving (prepared with low-sodium broth and no-salt-added tomatoes) equals 1 starch, 1 vegetable, 1 fat; also, 147 calories, 186 mg sodium, 14 mg cholesterol, 22 gm carbohydrate, 8 gm protein, 4 gm fat.

Hearty Cauliflower Soup

Our three young children aren't big cauliflower fans. But in this soup, the cauliflower can be mistaken for potatoes, and the rich sausage flavor helps disguise it even more. Hope you enjoy it as much as we do! —Sarah Root, Twelve Mile, Indiana

- **4 cups cauliflowerets**
- **1 cup thinly sliced carrots**
- **2 cups water**
- **1 pound fully cooked smoked sausage, cubed**
- **1/2 cup chopped onion**
- **1/3 cup all-purpose flour**
- **3/4 teaspoon salt**
- **1/8 teaspoon pepper**
- **2 cups milk**
- **8 ounces process American cheese, cubed**

In a saucepan, cook the cauliflower and carrots in water until tender; set aside (do not drain). In a skillet over medium heat, brown the sausage and onion; drain. Add flour, salt and pepper. Gradually add the milk; bring to a boil. Cook and stir for 2 minutes. Add cauliflower and carrots with cooking liquid; heat through. Stir in the cheese until melted. **Yield:** 6-8 servings.

Lima Bean Soup

(Pictured below)

Each fall there's a Lima Bean Festival in nearby West Cape May to honor the many growers there and showcase different recipes using their crop. This comforting chowder was a festival recipe contest winner. —Kathleen Olsack, North Cape May, New Jersey

- **3 cans (14-1/2 ounces *each*) chicken broth**
- **2 cans (15 ounces *each*) lima beans, rinsed and drained**
- **3 medium carrots, thinly sliced**
- **2 medium potatoes, peeled and diced**
- **2 small sweet red peppers, chopped**
- **2 small onions, chopped**
- **2 celery ribs, thinly sliced**
- **1/4 cup butter *or* margarine**
- **1-1/2 teaspoons dried marjoram**
- **1/2 teaspoon salt**
- **1/2 teaspoon pepper**
- **1/2 teaspoon dried oregano**
- **1 cup half-and-half cream**
- **3 bacon strips, cooked and crumbled**

In a Dutch oven or soup kettle, combine the first 12 ingredients; bring to a boil over medium heat. Reduce heat; cover and simmer for 25-35 minutes or until the vegetables are tender. Add cream; heat through but do not boil. Sprinkle with bacon just before serving. **Yield:** 10-12 servings (3 quarts).

Onion Hints

Slice or chop onions just before using, since their flavor deteriorates the longer they stay cut.

Zucchini Garden Chowder

(Pictured below)

Years ago, when my husband and I put in our first garden, a neighbor suggested zucchini since it's easy to grow. Our kids were reluctant to try new things, so I used our squash in this cheesy chowder—it met with solid approval from all of us!
—Nanette Jordan
Canton, Michigan

        2 medium zucchini, chopped
        1 medium onion, chopped
        2 tablespoons minced fresh parsley
        1 teaspoon dried basil
    1/3 cup butter *or* margarine
    1/3 cup all-purpose flour
        1 teaspoon salt
    1/4 teaspoon pepper
        3 cups water
        3 chicken bouillon cubes
        1 teaspoon lemon juice
        1 can (14-1/2 ounces) diced tomatoes, undrained
        1 can (12 ounces) evaporated milk
        1 package (10 ounces) frozen corn
        2 cups (8 ounces) shredded cheddar cheese
    1/4 cup grated Parmesan cheese
Pinch sugar, optional
Additional chopped parsley, optional

In a Dutch oven or soup kettle over medium heat, saute the zucchini, onion, parsley and basil in butter until the vegetables are tender. Stir in flour, salt and pepper. Gradually stir in water. Add the bouillon and lemon juice; mix well. Bring to a boil; cook and stir for 2 minutes. Add the tomatoes, milk and corn; bring to a boil. Reduce heat; cover and simmer for 5 minutes or until corn is tender. Just before serving, stir in cheeses until melted. Add sugar and garnish with parsley if desired. **Yield:** 8-10 servings (about 2-1/2 quarts).

Tasty Tomato Soup

Spicing up your tomato soup is a snap! Just before serving, stir in some Worcestershire sauce and prepared mustard, and top with any flavor of seasoned salad croutons. Everyone will comment on the terrific taste…and the fun crunch from the croutons.

Cream of Tomato Soup

This fresh-tasting soup is the first recipe I learned in my high-school home economics class. I've fixed it quite often since then. It's a wonderful way to use your ripe garden tomatoes.
—Gail Harris
Ramer, Tennessee

✓ This tasty dish uses less sugar, salt and fat. Recipe includes *Diabetic Exchanges*.

2-1/2 cups diced peeled tomatoes
    1/4 cup diced celery
    1/4 cup diced onion
        1 tablespoon vegetable oil
        2 tablespoons all-purpose flour
        1 cup evaporated milk
        1 teaspoon salt, optional
    1/8 teaspoon pepper
        3 tablespoons sour cream
        3 teaspoons minced fresh parsley

In a saucepan, combine the tomatoes, celery and onion; bring to a boil. Reduce heat; cover and simmer for 15 minutes, stirring often. Cool for 10 minutes; pour into a blender. Cover and process until smooth. In a large saucepan, heat oil; stir in flour until smooth. Gradually add milk; bring to a boil. Cook and stir for 2 minutes. Gradually stir in tomato mixture. Add salt if desired and pepper; heat through. Top individual servings with sour cream and parsley. **Yield:** 3 servings (3-1/2 cups). **Diabetic Exchanges:** One serving (prepared with evaporated skim milk and nonfat sour cream and without salt) equals 1-1/2 vegetable, 1 starch, 1 fat; also, 164 calories, 121 mg sodium, 3 mg cholesterol, 22 gm carbohydrate, 9 gm protein, 5 gm fat.

Butternut Bisque

(Pictured on page 40)

A delicious dinner is even more memorable when I start with this creamy soup. It has a bit of zip and super squash flavor. I like serving things that disappear like this soup does. I always get empty bowls back.
—Marion Tipton, Phoenix, Arizona

 2 **medium carrots, sliced**
 2 **celery ribs with leaves, chopped**
 2 **medium leeks (white portion only), sliced**
 1 **jalapeno pepper, seeded and minced**
1/4 **cup butter *or* margarine**
 2 **pounds butternut squash, peeled, seeded**
  and cubed (about 6 cups)
 2 **cans (14-1/2 ounces *each*) chicken broth**
1/2 **teaspoon ground ginger**
1/2 **cup half-and-half cream**
1/2 **teaspoon salt**
1/4 **teaspoon white pepper**
1/2 **cup chopped pecans, toasted**

In a large saucepan, saute carrots, celery, leeks and jalapeno in butter for 10 minutes, stirring occasionally. Add the squash, broth and ginger; bring to a boil. Reduce heat; cover and simmer until the squash is tender, about 25 minutes. Cool until lukewarm. In a blender or food processor, puree squash mixture in small batches until smooth; return to the pan. Add cream, salt and pepper; mix well. Heat through but do not boil. Garnish with pecans. **Yield:** 8 servings (2 quarts).

— 🌿 🌿 🌿 —

Hamburger Salad Sandwiches

My mother used to fix these hearty sandwiches for family birthdays. Everyone enjoys their unique flavor.
—Joyce Boriack, Georgetown, Texas

 1 **pound ground beef**
 1 **medium onion, chopped**
 1 **garlic clove, minced**
 1 **medium tomato, chopped**
1/2 **cup mayonnaise**
1/3 **cup chopped dill pickles**
 2 **tablespoons prepared mustard**
1/2 **teaspoon salt**
1/2 **teaspoon pepper**
 6 **hamburger buns, split**
Lettuce leaves

In a skillet, cook beef, onion and garlic until meat is browned and onion is tender; drain. Cool. Add tomato, mayonnaise, pickles, mustard, salt and pepper. Spoon about 1/2 cup onto each bun; top with lettuce. **Yield:** 6 servings.

Grilled Burgers

(Pictured above)

Sour cream makes these burgers delightfully moist, and thyme and black pepper give them zip. These sandwiches are a terrific taste of summer.
—Jesse and Anne Foust, Bluefield, West Virginia

 1/4 **cup sour cream**
  2 **teaspoons dried parsley flakes**
  1 **teaspoon dried thyme**
  1 **teaspoon salt**
 1/2 **teaspoon pepper**
2-1/2 **pounds ground beef**
 10 **hamburger buns, split**
Lettuce leaves, sliced tomato and onion, optional

In a large bowl, combine the first five ingredients; add beef and mix gently. Shape into 10 patties. Grill, uncovered, over medium coals for 4-5 minutes on each side or until meat is no longer pink. Serve on buns with lettuce, tomato and onion if desired. **Yield:** 10 servings.

No More Soggy Sandwiches

When making sandwiches to be eaten later, pack toppings like tomatoes, lettuce, pickles, etc. in separate plastic bags. Add them to the sandwiches just before serving.

Side Dishes

These country-style side dishes will take top billing when you present them at everyday dinners and special-occasion meals.

SPLENDID SIDE SHOW. Clockwise from upper left: Corn-Stuffed Tomatoes (p. 56), Winter Root Vegetables (p. 62), Cranberry Baked Beans (p. 58) and Never-Fail Egg Noodles (p. 60).

Corn-Stuffed Tomatoes

(Pictured above)

My husband and I look forward to this easy, fresh-tasting side dish in summer when tomatoes are at their best. I love to invite friends over for dinner and serve these colorful tomatoes. —Mrs. Patrick Dore
Burlington, Ontario

✓ This tasty dish uses less sugar, salt and fat. Recipe includes *Diabetic Exchanges.*

> **6 large tomatoes**
> **1/2 teaspoon salt, optional**
> **1/2 cup plain *or* Italian-seasoned bread crumbs**
> **2 cups frozen corn, thawed**
> **2 tablespoons *each* chopped green pepper, celery and onion**
> **2 tablespoons half-and-half cream**
> **1 tablespoon butter *or* margarine, melted**
> **2 tablespoons shredded mozzarella cheese**
> **1/4 cup water**

Cut a thin slice off the top of each tomato; scoop out and discard pulp. Sprinkle salt inside tomatoes if desired. Invert on paper towel to drain. Combine bread crumbs, corn, green pepper, celery, onion, cream and butter; spoon into the tomatoes. Place in an ungreased 13-in. x 9-in. x 2-in. baking dish. Sprinkle with cheese. Pour water into the baking dish. Bake, uncovered, at 350° for 30 minutes or until the tomatoes are tender. **Yield:** 6 servings. **Diabetic Exchanges:** One serving (prepared with plain bread crumbs, margarine and low-fat mozzarella and without salt) equals 1 starch,

1 vegetable, 1/2 fat; also, 131 calories, 108 mg sodium, 3 mg cholesterol, 27 gm carbohydrate, 5 gm protein, 2 gm fat.

Stuffed Onions

My husband, a pastor, was once paid in onions and potatoes by a little community. That's when I discovered this recipe. Baked with a tasty stuffing, the onions are mellow and tender. —Cathy Gilpin
Alamosa, Colorado

> **6 medium yellow onions (about 2 pounds)**
> **2 bacon strips, cut into 1-inch pieces**
> **1/4 cup dry bread crumbs**
> **2 tablespoons chopped fresh parsley *or* 2 teaspoons dried parsley flakes**
> **1 tablespoon butter *or* margarine**
> **1-1/2 cups sliced fresh mushrooms**
> **1/4 teaspoon salt**
> **Dash *each* pepper and ground nutmeg**
> **1/2 cup beef broth**
> **Additional parsley, optional**

In a Dutch oven, bring a small amount of water to a boil. Peel onions; using a slotted spoon, place onions in boiling water. Cook for 4-6 minutes or until softened; remove and let stand until cool enough to handle. Cut a 1/4-in. slice off the top of each onion. Remove center, leaving a 1/2-in. shell. Chop centers and tops of onions; set aside. In a skillet, cook bacon until crisp; remove to paper towel to drain. In the drippings, saute chopped onion until tender. Stir in bread crumbs and parsley. Add the butter and mushrooms; cook until mushrooms are tender. Add bacon, salt, pepper and nutmeg. Stuff onion shells; place in an ungreased shallow 1-qt. baking dish. Pour broth around onions. Bake, uncovered, at 375° for 45 minutes or until tender, basting frequently during the first 15 minutes. Sprinkle with parsley if desired. **Yield:** 6 servings.

Herbed Wild Rice

Like many other cooking enthusiasts, I've discovered that good food pleases the palate and soothes the soul! This rice has a nice nutty flavor and the wonderful aroma of sage. —David Collin
Martinez, California

✓ This tasty dish uses less sugar, salt and fat. Recipe includes *Diabetic Exchanges.*

> **1 cup sliced green onions**
> **2 tablespoons butter *or* margarine**

1 cup uncooked wild rice
3 cups chicken broth
1 teaspoon rubbed sage
3/4 teaspoon dried thyme
1/2 teaspoon salt, optional

In a saucepan over medium heat, saute the onions in butter until tender, about 5 minutes. Add rice; cook for 8-10 minutes. Add broth, sage, thyme and salt if desired. Pour into an ungreased 1-1/2-qt. baking dish. Cover and bake at 350° for 70-80 minutes or until rice is tender and liquid is absorbed. **Yield:** 8 servings. **Diabetic Exchanges:** One serving (prepared with margarine and low-sodium broth and without salt) equals 1 starch, 1 fat; also, 120 calories, 70 mg sodium, 2 mg cholesterol, 18 gm carbohydrate, 5 gm protein, 4 gm fat.

Mushroom Potatoes

I frequently prepare this side dish as a change from mashed potatoes. Our son is a real meat-and-potatoes man, and he thinks they're great. —Skip Dolliver
South Hamilton, Massachusetts

✓ This tasty dish uses less sugar, salt and fat. Recipe includes *Diabetic Exchanges.*

1 can (10-3/4 ounces) condensed cream of mushroom soup, undiluted
1/2 cup milk
1 large onion, chopped
4 medium potatoes, peeled, diced and cooked
Paprika

In a bowl, combine soup, milk and onion. Stir in the potatoes. Pour into a 1-1/2-qt. baking dish that has been coated with nonstick cooking spray. Sprinkle with paprika. Bake, uncovered, at 350° for 30 minutes or until bubbly. **Yield:** 8 servings. **Diabetic Exchanges:** One 1/2-cup serving (prepared with low-fat soup and skim milk) equals 1 starch; also, 80 calories, 159 mg sodium, 3 mg cholesterol, 16 gm carbohydrate, 2 gm protein, 1 gm fat.

Asparagus Mornay

(Pictured at right)

When I was growing up on my parents' dairy farm, we always had a large asparagus patch. I still love asparagus, but my husband and two children weren't that eager to eat it until I found this recipe. Now even my toughest vegetable critic, our son Aaron, enjoys these savory spears.
—Linda McKee
Big Prairie, Ohio

1-1/2 pounds fresh asparagus, trimmed
1 tablespoon butter *or* margarine
1 tablespoon all-purpose flour
1 cup half-and-half cream
1/2 teaspoon chicken bouillon granules
1/8 teaspoon ground nutmeg
1/8 teaspoon salt
1/2 cup shredded Swiss cheese
2 tablespoons crushed butter-flavored crackers

In a skillet, cook asparagus in a small amount of water until crisp-tender, about 6-8 minutes; drain. Arrange spears in the bottom of a greased 1-1/2-qt. baking dish; set aside and keep warm. In a small saucepan, melt butter over low heat. Add flour; cook and stir for 1 minute. Whisk in the cream, bouillon, nutmeg and salt; bring to a boil over medium heat. Cook and stir for 2 minutes. Remove from the heat; stir in cheese until melted. Pour over the asparagus. Sprinkle with cracker crumbs. Broil 6 in. from the heat for 3-5 minutes or until lightly browned. **Yield:** 4-6 servings.

Hot Potato

When making mashed potatoes, heat up the butter and milk before adding them. The potatoes stay hot this way.

Cranberry Baked Beans

(Pictured below)

I knew I'd found a winner when I got the idea to simmer beans in cranberry juice. The tartness of the juice is a nice subtle contrast to the sweet brown sugar and molasses in these baked beans. They're wonderful warm or cold.
—Wendie Osipowicz
New Britain, Connecticut

> 3 cups dry navy beans
> 5 cups cranberry juice
> 1/2 pound lean salt pork *or* bacon, diced
> 3/4 cup chopped onion
> 1/2 cup ketchup
> 1/4 cup molasses
> 5 teaspoons dark brown sugar
> 1-1/2 teaspoons ground mustard
> 1-1/2 teaspoons salt
> 1/8 teaspoon ground ginger

Place beans in a Dutch oven or soup kettle; add water to cover by 2 in. Bring to a boil; boil for 2 minutes. Remove from the heat; cover and let stand for 1 hour. Drain beans and discard liquid. Return beans to Dutch oven. Add cranberry juice; bring to a boil. Reduce heat; cover and simmer for 1 hour or until the beans are almost tender. Drain, reserving cranberry liquid. Place beans in a 2-1/2-qt. casserole or bean pot; add remaining ingredients and 1-1/2 cups of cranberry liquid. Cover and bake at 350° for 3 hours or until beans are tender and have reached desired consistency, stirring every 30 minutes. Add reserved cranberry liquid as needed. **Yield:** 10-12 servings.

Baked Vidalia Onion

Served alongside a variety of fish and meat, this tender onion is a nice change of pace. Folks find it a fun and flavorful side dish.
—Norma Durham
Rogersville, Tennessee

✓ This tasty dish uses less sugar, salt and fat. Recipe includes *Diabetic Exchanges.*

> 1 medium Vidalia *or* sweet onion
> 2 teaspoons butter *or* margarine
> 1/4 teaspoon salt, optional
> **Pepper to taste**
> **Garlic salt to taste, optional**

Quarter onion halfway through and open slightly. Place on an 18-in. x 12-in. piece of heavy-duty foil. Place butter in center of onion; sprinkle with seasonings. Fold foil to seal tightly. Bake at 350° for 60-70 minutes or until the onion is tender. Open foil carefully to allow steam to escape. **Yield:** 1 serving. **Diabetic Exchanges:** One serving (prepared with margarine and without salt and garlic salt) equals 1-1/2 vegetable, 1-1/2 fat; also, 116 calories, 93 mg sodium, 0 cholesterol, 10 gm carbohydrate, 1 gm protein, 8 gm fat.

Mixed Vegetables

This comforting skillet side dish was a huge hit with my family the first time I served it. It's now a regular menu item at our house.
—Anna Mary Beiler
Strasburg, Pennsylvania

✓ This tasty dish uses less sugar, salt and fat. Recipe includes *Diabetic Exchanges.*

> 1 cup sliced celery
> 1/2 cup chopped onion
> 2 garlic cloves, minced
> 3 tablespoons butter *or* margarine
> 1-1/2 cups chicken broth
> 4 cups cubed peeled potatoes
> 1 cup julienned carrots

1/4 teaspoon pepper
1 tablespoon chopped fresh parsley

In a skillet, saute celery, onion and garlic in butter until tender. Add broth, potatoes, carrots and pepper; bring to a boil. Reduce heat; cover and simmer for 15-20 minutes or until potatoes are tender. Uncover and simmer for 5 minutes or until broth has thickened slightly, stirring occasionally. Sprinkle with parsley; serve with a slotted spoon. **Yield:** 11 servings. **Diabetic Exchanges:** One 1/2-cup serving (prepared with low-fat margarine and low-sodium chicken broth) equals 1 vegetable, 1/2 starch, 1/2 fat; also, 79 calories, 66 mg sodium, 1 mg cholesterol, 14 gm carbohydrate, 2 gm protein, 2 gm fat.

Red Potato Bundles

As a basketball player in college, I was always hungry. My mother began supplying me with recipes, and I haven't stopped cooking since! —*Kriss Erickson*
Haena, Hawaii

6 small red potatoes, quartered
1 small onion, thinly sliced
6 whole garlic cloves, peeled
2 sprigs fresh rosemary *or* 1 to 2 teaspoons dried rosemary, crushed
1/2 teaspoon salt
Dash pepper
2 tablespoons grated Parmesan cheese
1/4 cup olive *or* vegetable oil

Place potatoes, onion and garlic on two pieces of heavy-duty aluminum foil, about 12 in. x 12 in.; top with rosemary, salt, pepper and cheese. Drizzle with oil. Fold foil in half diagonally; tightly seal edges of foil and shape each packet into a semicircle. Grill, covered, over medium coals for 40-45 minutes or until the potatoes are tender. Open foil carefully to allow steam to escape. **Yield:** 2 servings. **Editor's Note:** An oven may be used instead of a grill to prepare this recipe. Bake at 350° for 45 minutes.

Perfect Scalloped Potatoes

For extra nutrition and flavor, try adding some grated carrot and shredded cabbage to your scalloped potatoes.

Dried minced onion and canned sliced mushrooms can really enhance your favorite scalloped potato recipe as well.

Sesame Broccoli
(Pictured above)

With a tongue-tingling sauce and a topping of crunchy sesame seeds, broccoli makes a fancy but fuss-free side dish. This vegetable is so nutritious that it's great to have a special way to serve it. —*Doris Heath*
Bryson City, North Carolina

✓ This tasty dish uses less sugar, salt and fat. Recipe includes *Diabetic Exchanges.*

1 package (10 ounces) frozen broccoli spears
1 tablespoon vegetable oil
1 tablespoon soy sauce
1 tablespoon sugar
2 teaspoons vinegar
2 teaspoons sesame seeds, toasted

Cook the broccoli according to package directions. Meanwhile, in a small saucepan, combine oil, soy sauce, sugar and vinegar; heat on medium until sugar is dissolved and mixture is hot. Drain broccoli; place in a serving bowl. Drizzle with soy sauce mixture and sprinkle with sesame seeds. **Yield:** 4 servings. **Diabetic Exchanges:** One serving (prepared with light soy sauce) equals 2 vegetable, 1/2 fat; also, 81 calories, 143 mg sodium, trace cholesterol, 9 gm carbohydrate, 2 gm protein, 3 gm fat.

Fried Onions and Apples

Since a lot of delicious onions are grown in our state, they are always part of my menu. This tangy side dish is good with pork and beef. The inspiration for this unusual combination was a prolific apple tree!
—Janice Mitchell, Aurora, Colorado

3 large yellow onions, sliced
3 tablespoons butter *or* margarine
6 large tart red apples, sliced
1/2 cup packed brown sugar
1 teaspoon salt
1/2 teaspoon paprika
1/8 teaspoon ground nutmeg

In a large saucepan over medium heat, saute the onions in butter until tender. Place apples on top of onions. Combine remaining ingredients; sprinkle over apples. Cover and simmer for 10 minutes. Uncover and simmer 5 minutes longer or until the apples are tender. Serve with a slotted spoon. **Yield:** 12 servings.

Never-Fail Egg Noodles

(Pictured above)

Some 30 years ago, the small church I attended held a chicken and noodle fund-raiser supper. I was put in charge of noodles for 200 people! A lady shared this recipe and said it had been tried and tested by countless cooks. These noodles are just plain good eating!
—Kathryn Roach, Greers Ferry, Arkansas

1 egg plus 3 egg yolks
3 tablespoons cold water
1 teaspoon salt
2 cups all-purpose flour
Chopped fresh parsley, optional

In a mixing bowl, beat egg and yolks until light and fluffy. Add water and salt; mix well. Stir in flour. Turn onto a floured surface; knead until smooth. Divide into thirds. Roll out each portion to 1/8-in. thickness. Cut noodles to desired width (noodles shown in the photo were cut 2 in. x 1/2 in.). Cook immediately in boiling salted water or chicken broth for 7-9 minutes or until tender. Drain; sprinkle with parsley if desired. **Yield:** about 5-1/2 cups. **Editor's Note:** Uncooked noodles may be stored in the refrigerator for 2-3 days or frozen for up to 1 month.

No-Stick Noodles

If you rinse leftover noodles or macaroni with cold water before putting them in the refrigerator, they won't stick together the next time you use them.

Rice Medley

In this easy recipe, ordinary rice is dressed up with peas, shredded carrot and seasonings. This fresh-tasting and colorful side dish goes great with a variety of meaty main courses.
—Doyle Rounds
Bridgewater, Virginia

✓ This tasty dish uses less sugar, salt and fat. Recipe includes *Diabetic Exchanges.*

1 cup uncooked long grain rice
2-1/4 cups water
2 cups frozen peas, thawed
1 medium carrot, shredded
1-1/2 teaspoons salt-free herb seasoning
1 teaspoon chicken bouillon granules
1 teaspoon lemon juice

In a large saucepan, combine the first six ingredients; bring to a boil. Reduce heat; cover and simmer for 15 minutes or until the rice is tender. Remove from the heat; add lemon juice. Fluff with a fork. **Yield:** 10 servings. **Diabetic Exchanges:** One 1/2-cup serving (prepared with low-sodium bouillon) equals 1-1/2 starch; also, 103 calories, 33 mg sodium, 0 cholesterol, 22 gm carbohydrate, 3 gm protein, trace fat.

Carrot Mushroom Stir-Fry

When carrots are spruced up as a side dish, they're

usually mixed with sweet ingredients. But this savory combination with mushrooms is irresistible.
—*Jacqueline Thompson Graves*
Lawrenceville, Georgia

✓ This tasty dish uses less sugar, salt and fat. Recipe includes *Diabetic Exchanges.*

    6 to 8 medium carrots (1 pound), thinly sliced
    2 tablespoons butter *or* margarine, optional
    2 teaspoons olive *or* vegetable oil
    1 jar (6 ounces) sliced mushrooms, drained
    5 green onions with tops, thinly sliced
    1 tablespoon lemon juice
    1/2 teaspoon salt, optional
    1/4 teaspoon pepper

In a skillet over medium heat, stir-fry carrots in butter if desired and oil for 7 minutes. Add mushrooms and onions; cook and stir for 4-6 minutes or until vegetables are tender. Stir in lemon juice, salt if desired and pepper. **Yield:** 7 servings. **Diabetic Exchanges:** One 1/2-cup serving (prepared without butter, margarine or salt) equals 1-1/2 vegetable; also, 42 calories, 98 mg sodium, 0 cholesterol, 7 gm carbohydrate, 1 gm protein, 1 gm fat.

———— 🍵 🍵 🍵 ————

Squash Puffs

Getting our son and daughter to eat squash was out of the question until a friend suggested I try this recipe. These puffs are similar to hush puppies, which my kids love. Now they love these! —*Constance Ellenburg*
Southaven, Mississippi

    1 cup mashed cooked acorn squash
    1 egg
    1/4 cup diced onion
    1/2 cup self-rising flour*
    1/2 cup self-rising cornmeal*
    1 teaspoon sugar
    1/2 teaspoon salt
Cooking oil

In a bowl, combine squash, egg and onion. Combine flour, cornmeal, sugar and salt; add to squash mixture and mix well. In an electric skillet, heat 1/4 in. of oil to 365°. Drop batter by tablespoonfuls into oil. Fry, a few at a time, for 2-3 minutes or until crisp and golden, turning often. Drain on paper towels. **Yield:** 4-6 servings. ***Editor's Note:** As a substitute for self-rising flour, place 3/4 teaspoon baking powder and 1/4 teaspoon salt in a 1/2-cup measuring cup. Add all-purpose flour to measure 1/2 cup. There is no substitute for self-rising cornmeal.

———— 🍵 🍵 🍵 ————

'I Wish I Had That Recipe...'

"PINEAPPLE AU GRATIN served at Back Home in Elizabethtown, Kentucky is mouth-watering!" raves Bedelia Wilmoth from nearby Cecilia.

Restaurant owner Linda Fulkerson was delighted to share the makings of this old-fashioned side dish, which is often featured on the menu. "My mother, Lola Allen, has made Pineapple Au Gratin for as long as I can remember," says Linda. "Most all of the recipes we serve came from Mom—a terrific cook who raised nine children.

"Just like home, we change our menu daily. But you can always expect hearty entrees, homemade soups and desserts that include my husband Tom's special cobblers."

Back Home is located at 251 W. Dixie in Elizabethtown. The restaurant is open Tuesday through Saturday from 11 a.m. to 9 p.m., Sunday and Monday from 11 a.m. to 3 p.m.; 1-502/769-2800.

Pineapple Au Gratin

    2 cups self-rising flour*
    2 cups sugar
    3 cans (20 ounces *each*) unsweetened pineapple chunks
    1 cup (4 ounces) shredded cheddar cheese
    1/2 cup butter *or* margarine, melted
    70 butter-flavored crackers, crushed

In a bowl, combine flour and sugar. Drain the pineapple, reserving 1-1/2 cups of juice. Add juice to flour mixture; mix well. Stir in the pineapple and cheese. Pour into a greased 13-in. x 9-in. x 2-in. baking pan. Cover and bake at 350° for 30 minutes. Uncover and stir; bake 10 minutes longer. Combine melted butter and cracker crumbs; sprinkle over the pineapple mixture. Return to the oven for 10-15 minutes or until a knife inserted near the center comes out clean. **Yield:** 16-20 servings. ***Editor's Note:** As a substitute for *each* cup of self-rising flour, place 1-1/2 teaspoons baking powder and 1/2 teaspoon salt in a measuring cup; add all-purpose flour to equal 1 cup.

———— 🍵 🍵 🍵 ————

Winter Root Vegetables

(Pictured below)

Christmas dinner wouldn't be the same without this colorful side dish. We love the interesting combination of red potatoes, brussels sprouts and parsnips covered with a zippy sauce. —Mary Jane Jones
Williamstown, West Virginia

✓ This tasty dish uses less sugar, salt and fat. Recipe includes *Diabetic Exchanges.*

 2 **pounds small red potatoes, quartered**
 1 **pound brussels sprouts, halved**
 1/2 **pound parsnips, peeled and julienned**
 1/2 **pound carrots, cut into chunks**
 1/2 **pound turnips, peeled and cut into chunks**
 1/2 **cup butter *or* margarine**
 2 **tablespoons prepared horseradish**
 2 **tablespoons cider vinegar**
 2 **tablespoons snipped fresh dill *or* 2 teaspoons dill weed**
 1/2 **teaspoon salt, optional**
 1/4 **teaspoon pepper**

Cook vegetables separately in water until tender; drain. Melt butter; stir in remaining ingredients. Combine the vegetables and butter mixture; toss to coat. **Yield:** 10-12 servings. **Diabetic Exchanges:** One 1-cup serving (prepared with margarine and without salt) equals 1 vegetable, 1/2 starch, 1 fat; also, 97 calories, 72 mg sodium, 0 cholesterol, 12 gm carbohydrate, 2 gm protein, 5 gm fat.

—— 🛒 🛒 🛒 ——

Herbed Potatoes and Onions

We're trying to cut out fried foods in our diet. So I came up with this recipe. With the addition of onion, my family prefers these to regular fried potatoes. It's a quick and easy side dish. —Rosadene Herold
Lakeville, Indiana

✓ This tasty dish uses less sugar, salt and fat. Recipe includes *Diabetic Exchanges.*

 3 **medium red potatoes, thinly sliced**
 1 **medium onion, thinly sliced**
 1/2 **teaspoon Italian seasoning**
 1/8 **teaspoon pepper**
 2 **tablespoons butter *or* margarine, melted**

In an ungreased 2-qt. microwave-safe baking dish, layer half of the potato and onion slices. Combine Italian seasoning and pepper; sprinkle half over the onion and potato layer. Drizzle with 1 tablespoon of butter. Repeat layers. Cover with vented plastic wrap. Microwave on high for 12 minutes or until the potatoes are tender, turning the dish after 6 minutes. **Yield:** 4 servings. **Editor's Note:** This recipe was tested in a 700-watt microwave. **Diabetic Exchanges:** One serving (prepared with reduced-fat margarine) equals 1-1/2 starch, 1/2 fat; also, 127 calories, 71 mg sodium, 0 cholesterol, 22 gm carbohydrate, 2 gm protein, 4 gm fat.

—— 🛒 🛒 🛒 ——

Zucchini with Dill

This is a much-requested recipe. Everyone loves the creamy sour cream sauce enhanced with dill. —Diane Glowinski, Chicago, Illinois

✓ This tasty dish uses less sugar, salt and fat. Recipe includes *Diabetic Exchanges.*

 2 **pounds zucchini, julienned**
 2 **tablespoons butter *or* margarine**
 1 **tablespoon all-purpose flour**
 1/3 **cup cold water**
 1 **tablespoon lemon juice**
 1 **tablespoon sugar**
 1/2 **teaspoon salt, optional**
 1 **cup (8 ounces) sour cream**
 2 **tablespoons chopped fresh dill *or* 2 teaspoons dill weed**

In a large skillet, saute zucchini in butter until crisp-tender. Stir in flour. Add water, lemon juice, sugar

and salt if desired; bring to a boil. Cook and stir for 2 minutes. Reduce heat; simmer, uncovered, for 5 minutes. Remove from the heat; stir in sour cream and dill. **Yield:** 6 servings. **Diabetic Exchanges:** One serving (prepared with margarine and nonfat sour cream and without salt) equals 3 vegetable, 1/2 fat; also, 111 calories, 79 mg sodium, 3 mg cholesterol, 15 gm carbohydrate, 4 gm protein, 4 gm fat.

Onions Au Gratin

Most everyone cooks with onions, but few think of serving them as a vegetable side dish. My family really loves this recipe.
—*Christine Halandras*
Meeker, Colorado

  6 medium yellow onions
1/4 cup butter *or* margarine
1/2 cup beef broth
1/2 cup whipping cream
  2 tablespoons all-purpose flour
1/4 teaspoon salt
1/8 teaspoon pepper
1/2 cup shredded Swiss cheese
1/2 cup grated Parmesan cheese

Slice the onions into 1/2-in.-thick rings; saute in butter until tender. Place in a greased 8-in. square baking dish. In a bowl, stir broth, cream, flour, salt and pepper until smooth; pour over onions. Sprinkle with cheeses. Bake, uncovered, at 350° for 25-30 minutes or until cheese is golden brown and mixture is bubbly. **Yield:** 8 servings.

Hot Vegetable Plate

(Pictured above right)

A creamy mustard sauce adds spark to an interesting lineup of vegetables in this perfect fall side dish. I always receive compliments regarding the special presentation.
—*Julie Polakowski*
West Allis, Wisconsin

✓ This tasty dish uses less sugar, salt and fat. Recipe includes *Diabetic Exchanges*.

  1 medium kohlrabi
  1 medium turnip
  1 small rutabaga
  4 medium carrots, halved crosswise
  4 medium leeks (white portion only), sliced
12 fresh cauliflowerets
MUSTARD SAUCE:
1/4 cup butter *or* margarine
  2 tablespoons all-purpose flour

1/4 teaspoon salt, optional
Pinch pepper
  1 cup milk
  1 to 2 teaspoons Dijon mustard

Peel kohlrabi, turnip and rutabaga; cut into 1/4-in. slices. Halve the kohlrabi and turnip slices; quarter the rutabaga slices. Place all vegetables in a large saucepan and cover with water; cook until crisp-tender. Meanwhile, melt butter in a small saucepan; stir in flour. Bring to a boil; cook and stir for 2 minutes. Add salt if desired and pepper. Gradually add milk; cook and stir until mixture boils. Reduce heat; cook and stir for 1 minute or until thickened. Remove from the heat; stir in mustard. Drain vegetables; serve with warm mustard sauce. **Yield:** 8 servings. **Diabetic Exchanges:** One serving with 2 tablespoons sauce (prepared with margarine and skim milk and without salt) equals 1 starch, 1 vegetable, 1 fat; also, 152 calories, 146 mg sodium, 1 mg cholesterol, 22 gm carbohydrate, 4 gm protein, 6 gm fat.

Seasoned Fries

For french fries without a lot of added fat, season them with an equal amount of salt and chili powder and bake instead of deep-frying.

the syrup. Garnish with lemon and mint if desired. **Yield:** 6 servings.

— ❦ ❦ ❦ —

Garden Saute

I love to serve this side dish when we are hosting a dinner party. It's fun, colorful and nicely seasoned with a variety of herbs. —Nena Williams, Dallas, Texas

✓ This tasty dish uses less sugar, salt and fat. Recipe includes *Diabetic Exchanges.*

- 1/4 **cup chopped red onion**
- 1 **garlic clove, minced**
- 1 **medium yellow summer squash, sliced**
- 1 **medium zucchini, sliced**
- 1/2 **cup sliced fresh mushrooms**
- 1 **small tomato, cut into wedges**
- 1/4 **cup chopped celery**
- 1/2 **teaspoon lemon juice**
- 1/4 **teaspoon dried rosemary, crushed**
- 1/4 **teaspoon dill weed**
- 1/4 **teaspoon Italian seasoning**
- 1/8 **teaspoon fennel seed**
- 1/8 **teaspoon pepper**

In a large skillet coated with nonstick cooking spray, saute onion and garlic until softened. Add remaining ingredients; mix well. Cover and cook over medium heat for 5-7 minutes or until vegetables are tender, stirring occasionally. **Yield:** 6 servings. **Diabetic Exchanges:** One 1/2-cup serving equals 1 vegetable; also, 19 calories, 8 mg sodium, 0 cholesterol, 4 gm carbohydrate, 1 gm protein, trace fat.

— ❦ ❦ ❦ —

Honey Grapefruit Halves

I like to experiment with quick, economical meals using citrus from our own groves. Our packinghouse crew tells me this slightly sweet side dish is one of my best. It's a real eye-opener at breakfast! —Fred Peterson, Vero Beach, Florida

- 2 **large red grapefruit, halved**
- 4 **teaspoons honey**
- 4 **teaspoons brown sugar**
- 4 **maraschino cherries *or* whole fresh strawberries, optional**

Place grapefruit halves, cut side up, in an ovenproof pan. Loosen grapefruit sections. Drizzle with honey; sprinkle with brown sugar. Broil 5 in. from the heat for 2-3 minutes or until bubbly. Garnish each with a cherry or strawberry if desired. Serve warm. **Yield:** 4 servings.

Lemony Acorn Slices

(Pictured above)

I discovered this recipe a long time ago and have used it often. This preparation is a nice change from simple baked acorn squash. With the skins on the slices and a lemony syrup drizzled over them, this side dish looks as good as it tastes. —Nell Fletcher Sedalia, Colorado

- 2 **large acorn squash (about 2-1/4 pounds *each*)**
- 1 **cup plus 2 tablespoons water, *divided***
- 1/2 **cup sugar**
- 2 **tablespoons lemon juice**
- 1 **tablespoon butter *or* margarine**
- 1/4 **teaspoon salt**
- 1/8 **teaspoon pepper**
- **Lemon wedges and fresh mint, optional**

Wash squash. Cut in half lengthwise; remove and discard the seeds and membrane. Cut each half crosswise into 1/2-in. slices; discard ends. Place slices in a large skillet. Add 1 cup of water; bring to a boil. Reduce heat; cover and simmer for 20 minutes or until tender. Meanwhile, in a heavy saucepan, combine sugar and remaining water. Cook over medium heat until sugar melts and syrup is golden, stirring occasionally. Remove from the heat; carefully add lemon juice, butter, salt and pepper. Cook and stir over low heat until butter melts. Place squash on a serving plate; top with

Almond-Stuffed Pears

Pears make a comforting side dish in this special recipe. My family enjoys this hot fruit with a traditional ham dinner. I receive compliments every time I present this dish. —Margaret Allen, Abingdon, Virginia

6 medium pears, peeled, halved and cored
1-1/2 cups water
1/3 cup white grape juice
1/2 cup finely chopped toasted almonds
2 tablespoons brown sugar
1/8 teaspoon almond extract

Place pears, cut side down, in an ungreased 13-in. x 9-in. x 2-in. baking dish. Combine water and grape juice; pour over pears. Cover and bake at 350° for 35-45 minutes or until tender. Turn the pears over. Combine almonds, sugar and extract; mix well. Spoon into pear cavities. Bake, uncovered, for 5 minutes. Serve warm. **Yield:** 6 servings.

— 🍷 🍷 🍷 —

Oven-Roasted Potato Wedges

Rosemary lends a delicious, delicate flavor to these potato wedges. This recipe is perfect for company.
—Ellen Benninger, Stoneboro, Pennsylvania

✓ This tasty dish uses less sugar, salt and fat. Recipe includes *Diabetic Exchanges.*

4 unpeeled baking potatoes (2 pounds)
2 tablespoons olive *or* vegetable oil
1 medium onion, chopped
2 garlic cloves, minced
1 tablespoon minced fresh rosemary *or* 1 teaspoon dried rosemary, crushed
1/2 teaspoon salt, optional
1/4 teaspoon pepper

Cut potatoes lengthwise into wedges; place in a greased 13-in. x 9-in. x 2-in. baking pan. Drizzle with oil. Sprinkle with onion, garlic, rosemary, salt if desired and pepper; stir to coat. Bake, uncovered, at 400° for 45-50 minutes or until tender, turning once. **Yield:** 8 servings. **Diabetic Exchanges:** One serving (prepared without salt) equals 1 starch, 1 fat; also, 114 calories, 5 mg sodium, 0 cholesterol, 19 gm carbohydrate, 2 gm protein, 4 gm fat.

Better Baked Beans

For a rich autumn flavor, peel and slice an apple and fold it into baked beans. To make beans with a thick sauce, stir in a few teaspoons of quick-cooking tapioca before baking.

Dilled Corn and Peas

(Pictured below and on front cover)

Celebrate the harvest season with this striking combination of crisp colorful vegetables. Seasoned with dill, butter, salt and pepper, it's an easy but impressive addition to any meal. —Marlene Muckenhirn Delano, Minnesota

✓ This tasty dish uses less sugar, salt and fat. Recipe includes *Diabetic Exchanges.*

2-1/2 cups fresh *or* frozen sugar snap peas
2 cups fresh *or* frozen corn
1 small sweet red pepper, julienned
1/4 cup water
1 tablespoon butter *or* margarine
1 teaspoon minced fresh dill *or* 1/4 teaspoon dill weed
1/8 teaspoon salt, optional
1/8 teaspoon pepper

Place the peas, corn, red pepper and water in a saucepan; cover and cook over high heat for 2-4 minutes or until vegetables are crisp-tender. Drain. Add butter, dill, salt if desired and pepper; toss to coat. **Yield:** 8 servings. **Diabetic Exchanges:** One 1/2-cup serving (prepared with margarine and without salt) equals 1 vegetable, 1/2 starch, 1/2 fat; also, 84 calories, 20 mg sodium, 0 cholesterol, 16 gm carbohydrate, 4 gm protein, 2 gm fat.

Calico Squash Casserole

(Pictured below)

I have a thriving country garden and try a lot of recipes using my squash. It's a pleasure to present this beautiful and delicious casserole as part of a holiday menu or anytime. —Lucille Terry
Frankfort, Kentucky

2 cups sliced yellow summer squash (1/4 inch thick)
1 cup sliced zucchini (1/4 inch thick)
1 medium onion, chopped
1/4 cup sliced green onions
1 cup water
1 teaspoon salt, *divided*
2 cups crushed butter-flavored crackers
1/2 cup butter *or* margarine, melted
1 can (10-3/4 ounces) condensed cream of chicken soup, undiluted
1 can (8 ounces) sliced water chestnuts, drained
1 large carrot, shredded
1/2 cup mayonnaise
1 jar (2 ounces) diced pimientos, drained
1 teaspoon rubbed sage
1/2 teaspoon white pepper
1 cup (4 ounces) shredded sharp cheddar cheese

In a saucepan, combine the first five ingredients; add 1/2 teaspoon salt. Cover and cook until squash is tender, about 6 minutes. Drain well; set aside. Combine cracker crumbs and butter; spoon half into a greased shallow 1-1/2-qt. baking dish. Combine soup, water chestnuts, carrot, mayonnaise, pimientos, sage, pepper and remaining salt; fold into squash mixture. Spoon over crumbs. Sprinkle with cheese and the remaining crumb mixture. Bake, uncovered, at 350° for 30 minutes or until lightly browned. **Yield:** 8 servings.

—— 🥄 🥄 🥄 ——

Tangy Potato Cubes

A large collection of cookbooks is handy for reference, but I never follow a recipe exactly. I have more fun modifying them to suit my tastes. —Dave Fisher
Ten Mile, Tennessee

7 medium potatoes (about 2-3/4 pounds)
7 bacon strips, diced
4 green onions, diced
1/2 cup beef broth
1/4 cup cider vinegar
1/2 teaspoon dried oregano
1/2 teaspoon garlic salt
1/4 teaspoon dried thyme
1/4 teaspoon pepper
1/4 teaspoon sugar

In a large saucepan, cook potatoes in boiling water until tender; drain. Cool and cut into cubes. In a large skillet, cook bacon until crisp. Remove bacon; drain, reserving 2 tablespoons drippings. Saute onions in the drippings until tender. Add potatoes, bacon, broth, vinegar and seasonings; stir gently. Cover and simmer until heated through, about 5 minutes. **Yield:** 10-12 servings.

—— 🥄 🥄 🥄 ——

Green Rice

Don't turn away from this recipe because of its name. It's a creamy, comforting dish I know your family will come to love as much as mine does. —Ruth Glabe
Oronoco, Minnesota

2 cups uncooked long grain rice
1-1/2 cups milk
1 pound shredded process American cheese
1 cup chopped green pepper
1 cup minced fresh parsley
1/4 cup vegetable oil
1 to 2 garlic cloves, minced
Salt and pepper to taste

Cook rice according to package directions. Add remaining ingredients. Transfer to a greased 2-1/2-qt. baking dish. Bake, uncovered, at 350° for 55-60 minutes or until the green pepper is tender. **Yield:** 10-12 servings.

Apricot Carrots

My mother loved both apricots and carrots, so when I found this recipe, I knew I had to make it for her. It has become a family favorite.
—Latressa Allen
Fort Worth, Texas

> 1 pound carrots, sliced
> 1/4 cup apricot preserves
> 1 tablespoon butter *or* margarine
> 1 teaspoon lemon juice
> 1/4 teaspoon grated orange peel
> 1/8 teaspoon ground nutmeg

Place carrots in a saucepan with enough water to cover; bring to a boil. Cover and cook for 8 minutes or until crisp-tender; drain. Add remaining ingredients; cook and stir over medium heat for 3 minutes or until preserves are melted and carrots are coated. **Yield:** 4 servings.

Down-Home Succotash

If you grow corn, you can have it be really fresh for this recipe if you make sure everything is ready before you pick the corn! That's the way I like it.
—Marian Platt, Sequim, Washington

> 1/4 pound sliced bacon, diced
> 2 cups fresh corn
> 1/2 pound lima beans
> 1 medium green pepper, chopped
> 1 medium onion, chopped
> 2 medium tomatoes, cut into wedges

In a large skillet, cook the bacon until crisp. Remove bacon to paper towels; drain, reserving 1 tablespoon of drippings. Add corn, beans, green pepper and onion to drippings; simmer for 10-15 minutes or until the vegetables are almost tender, adding water if necessary. Stir in tomatoes and bacon; cook just until tomatoes are heated through. **Yield:** 12-14 servings.

Sensational Side Dish

When preparing buttered carrots, stir in a pinch of celery seed. It makes this vegetable side dish a lot more exciting.

Two-Season Squash Medley

(Pictured above)

Both winter and summer squash star in this fun, colorful vegetable stir-fry. I've cooked in several restaurants and for many guests in my home, and this dish has been well-received for years.
—Mary Beth LaFlamme, Eagle Bridge, New York

> 2 tablespoons butter *or* margarine
> 2 tablespoons olive *or* vegetable oil
> 1 medium yellow summer squash, sliced
> 1 medium zucchini, sliced
> 3/4 pound butternut squash, peeled, seeded and julienned
> 1 medium onion, sliced
> 1 medium green pepper, julienned
> 1 medium sweet red pepper, julienned
> 3 to 4 garlic cloves, minced
> 1 tablespoon minced fresh thyme *or* 1 teaspoon dried thyme
> 1/4 teaspoon garlic salt
> 1/4 teaspoon pepper

In a large skillet, heat butter and oil over medium heat. Add vegetables, garlic and thyme. Cook and stir until tender, about 15 minutes. Add garlic salt and pepper. **Yield:** 6-8 servings.

Main Dishes

With these mouth-watering entrees featuring beef, poultry, pork, game and more, coming up with exciting weekly menus is a snap!

FARE WITH FLAIR. Clockwise from upper left: Hearty Red Beans and Rice (p. 70), Stuffed Chicken Breasts (p. 81), Curried Beef-Stuffed Squash (p. 94) and Gingered Pork and Asparagus (p. 77).

Hearty Red Beans and Rice

(Pictured on page 68)

I picked up this recipe while working for the Navy in New Orleans years ago. It's a mouth-watering combination of meats, beans and seasonings. I take this dish to many potlucks and never fail to bring home an empty pot.
—Kathy Jacques
Chesterfield, Michigan

    1 pound dry red kidney beans
    2 teaspoons garlic salt
    1 teaspoon Worcestershire sauce
1/4 teaspoon hot pepper sauce
    1 quart water
1/2 pound fully cooked ham, diced
1/2 pound fully cooked smoked sausage, diced
    1 cup chopped onion
1/2 cup chopped celery
    3 garlic cloves, minced
    1 can (8 ounces) tomato sauce
    2 bay leaves
1/4 cup minced fresh parsley
1/2 teaspoon salt
1/2 teaspoon pepper
Hot cooked rice
Additional parsley, optional

Place beans in a Dutch oven or kettle; add water to cover by 2 in. Bring to a boil; boil for 2 minutes. Remove from the heat; cover and let stand for 1 hour. Drain beans and discard liquid. Add garlic salt, Worcestershire sauce, hot pepper sauce and water; bring to a boil. Reduce heat; cover and simmer for 1-1/2 hours. Meanwhile, in a skillet, saute ham and sausage until lightly browned. Remove with a slotted spoon to bean mixture. Saute onion, celery and garlic in drippings until tender; add to bean mixture. Stir in tomato sauce and bay leaves. Cover and simmer for 30 minutes or until beans are tender. Discard bay leaves. Measure 2 cups of beans; mash and return to the bean mixture. Stir in parsley, salt and pepper. Serve over rice. Garnish with parsley if desired. **Yield:** 8-10 servings.

Chicken Provencale

(Pictured above)

When I serve this entree at a dinner party, people always comment on the tender chicken and flavorfully seasoned beans. I sometimes fix it a day ahead—it's as good as it is the first day it's made.
—Barbara Zeilinger, Columbus, Indiana

    1 broiler-fryer chicken (3 to 4 pounds), cut up
    1 tablespoon cooking oil
1-1/2 cups chopped onion
    3 garlic cloves, minced
    2 cans (15-1/2 ounces *each*) great northern beans, rinsed and drained
    1 can (29 ounces) diced tomatoes, undrained
    3 medium carrots, sliced 1/4 inch thick
    1 tablespoon instant chicken bouillon
    1 teaspoon dried thyme
1/2 teaspoon dried oregano
1/2 teaspoon pepper

In a skillet, brown the chicken in oil; remove and set aside. Saute onion and garlic in drippings until tender. Stir in remaining ingredients. Spoon into a 3-qt. baking dish; arrange chicken pieces on top. Cover and bake at 350° for 65-75 minutes or until chicken juices run clear. **Yield:** 4 servings.

Turkey Tetrazzini

This is the traditional main course on our New Year's Eve buffet. It uses up lots of leftover holiday turkey and always gets rave reviews. —Audrey Thibodeau
Mesa, Arizona

    6 tablespoons butter
    6 tablespoons all-purpose flour
1/2 teaspoon salt
1/4 teaspoon pepper

1/8 teaspoon cayenne pepper
3 cups chicken broth
1 cup whipping cream
1 package (1 pound) linguine, cooked and
   drained
4 cups cubed cooked turkey
1 cup sliced fresh mushrooms
1 jar (4 ounces) diced pimientos, drained
1/4 cup chopped fresh parsley
4 to 5 drops hot pepper sauce
1/3 cup grated Parmesan cheese

In a saucepan over medium heat, melt the butter. Add the flour, salt, pepper and cayenne; stir until smooth. Gradually add broth; bring to a boil. Cook and stir for 2 minutes or until thickened. Remove from the heat; stir in cream. Mix 2 cups of sauce with linguine; pour into a greased 13-in. x 9-in. x 2-in. baking dish. Make a well in center of noodles, leaving about a 6-in. x 4-in. space. To the remaining sauce, add turkey, mushrooms, pimientos, parsley and hot pepper sauce; mix well. Pour into the center of dish. Sprinkle with Parmesan cheese. Cover and bake at 350° for 30 minutes. Uncover and bake 20-30 minutes more or until bubbly and heated through. **Yield:** 8-10 servings.

Spicy Bean and Beef Pie
(Pictured at right)

My daughter helped me come up with this recipe when we wanted a one-dish meal that was different than a casserole. This pie slices nicely and is a fun and filling dish. —*Debra Dohy, Massillon, Ohio*

1 pound ground beef
2 to 3 garlic cloves, minced
1 can (11-1/2 ounces) condensed bean with
   bacon soup, undiluted
1 jar (16 ounces) thick and chunky picante
   sauce, *divided*
1/4 cup cornstarch
1 tablespoon chopped fresh parsley
1 teaspoon paprika
1 teaspoon salt
1/4 teaspoon pepper
1 can (16 ounces) kidney beans, rinsed and
   drained
1 can (15 ounces) black beans, rinsed and
   drained
2 cups (8 ounces) shredded cheddar cheese,
   divided
3/4 cup sliced green onions, *divided*
Pastry for double-crust pie (10 inches)
1 cup (8 ounces) sour cream
1 can (2-1/4 ounces) sliced ripe olives, drained

In a skillet, cook beef and garlic until the beef is browned; drain. In a large bowl, combine soup, 1 cup of picante sauce, cornstarch, parsley, paprika, salt and pepper; mix well. Fold in beans, 1-1/4 cups of cheese, 1/2 cup onions and the beef mixture. Line pie plate with bottom pastry; fill with bean mixture. Top with remaining pastry; seal and flute edges. Cut slits in the top crust. Bake at 425° for 30-35 minutes or until lightly browned. Let stand for 5 minutes before cutting. Garnish with sour cream, olives and remaining picante sauce, cheese and onions. **Yield:** 8 servings.

Dilled Pork Roast

I'm always looking for different ways to dress up ordinary foods. Here dill nicely complements pork roast. —*Clara Sever, Vandling, Pennsylvania*

1 boneless pork shoulder roast (3 to 4
   pounds), trimmed
1 tablespoon salt
1-1/2 teaspoons coarsely ground pepper
1-1/2 teaspoons garlic powder
6 tablespoons minced fresh dill *or* 2
   tablespoons dill weed

Cut about five deep slits across top of roast. Combine seasonings; stuff some into the slits. Tie meat securely. Rub roast with the remaining seasonings. Place in a large resealable plastic bag and refrigerate overnight. Remove roast from bag and place in a greased roasting pan. Bake, uncovered, at 325° for 2-1/2 to 3 hours or until a meat thermometer reads 160°-170°. Let stand 10 minutes before slicing. **Yield:** 8-10 servings.

Best-Ever Beans and Sausage

(Pictured below)

My wife devised this dish, which is extremely popular with our friends and family. When she asks, "What can I share?" the reply is always, "Bring your beans and sausage...and a couple copies of the recipe." I hope you enjoy it as much as we do. —Robert Saulnier
Clarksburg, Massachusetts

1-1/2 pounds bulk hot pork sausage
1 medium green pepper, chopped
1 medium onion, chopped
1 can (31 ounces) pork and beans, undrained
1 can (16 ounces) kidney beans, rinsed and drained
1 can (15-1/2 ounces) great northern beans, rinsed and drained
1 can (15-1/2 ounces) black-eyed peas, rinsed and drained
1 can (15 ounces) pinto beans, rinsed and drained
1 can (15 ounces) garbanzo beans, rinsed and drained
1-1/2 cups ketchup
3/4 cup packed brown sugar
2 teaspoons ground mustard

In a skillet over medium heat, brown sausage; drain. Add green pepper and onion; saute until tender. Drain. Add remaining ingredients; mix well. Pour into a greased 13-in. x 9-in. x 2-in. baking dish. Cover and bake at 325° for 1 hour. Uncover and bake 20-30 minutes longer or until bubbly. **Yield:** 12-16 servings.

Green Chili Stew

Anaheim chilies are the top crop in New Mexico. I roast them to use in a variety of dishes. Peppers give this down-home stew a wonderful rich flavor my family loves. —Mary Spill
Tierra Amarilla, New Mexico

✓ This tasty dish uses less sugar, salt and fat. Recipe includes *Diabetic Exchanges.*

1 pound ground beef *or* chuck
1 pound ground pork
8 to 10 Anaheim chilies, roasted, peeled and chopped *or* 3 cans (4 ounces *each*) chopped green chilies
4 medium potatoes, peeled and diced
1 can (28 ounces) diced tomatoes, undrained
2 cups water
1 garlic clove, minced
1 teaspoon salt, optional
1/2 teaspoon dried oregano
1/4 teaspoon pepper
1/4 teaspoon dried coriander

In a large kettle or Dutch oven, brown beef and pork; drain. Add remaining ingredients. Cover and simmer for 45 minutes. **Yield:** 10 servings. **Diabetic Exchanges:** One 1-cup serving (prepared with ground chuck and low-sodium tomatoes and without salt) equals 2-1/2 meat, 1 vegetable, 1/2 starch; also, 247 calories, 58 mg sodium, 63 mg cholesterol, 16 gm carbohydrate, 20 gm protein, 12 gm fat.

— 🍷 🍷 🍷 —

Italian Flank Steak

Savory and satisfying, this steak is nice for entertaining or busy days because it marinates overnight and grills in minutes. Leftovers—if there are any—make super sandwiches! —Walajean Saglett
Canandaigua, New York

✓ This tasty dish uses less sugar, salt and fat. Recipe includes *Diabetic Exchanges.*

2 envelopes (.7 ounce *each*) fat-free Italian salad dressing mix
2 tablespoons vegetable oil
1 tablespoon lemon juice
1 flank steak (1 pound)

Combine salad dressing mix, oil and lemon juice. Brush onto both sides of steak; place in a shallow dish. Cover and refrigerate several hours or overnight. Grill over hot coals for 4 minutes per side for medium, 5 minutes per side for medium-well or until desired doneness is reached. **Yield:** 4 servings. **Diabetic Exchanges:** One serving equals 3 meat, 1/2 starch; also, 267 calories, 793 mg sodium, 59 mg cholesterol, 8 gm carbohydrate, 24 gm protein, 16 gm fat.

— ▼ ▼ ▼ —

Oriental Pork with Hot Mustard Sauce

You're not likely to have many leftovers when you serve this taste-bud-tingling pork dish. Does it ever go fast when I make it for a party!
—*Alice Hoffman*
Perry, Iowa

✓ This tasty dish uses less sugar, salt and fat. Recipe includes *Diabetic Exchanges*.

   1 tablespoon ground mustard
   1 teaspoon vegetable oil
   1 teaspoon vinegar
   1/8 teaspoon salt, optional
Dash ground turmeric
   1/4 cup milk
   1/4 cup soy sauce
   2 tablespoons ketchup
   1 tablespoon sugar
   1/4 teaspoon molasses
   1 garlic clove, crushed
   2 pork tenderloins (1 pound *each*)
   1 tablespoon sesame seeds, toasted, optional

In a bowl, combine mustard, oil, vinegar, salt if desired and turmeric; gradually stir in milk until smooth. Refrigerate. In a large resealable plastic bag or shallow glass dish, combine soy sauce, ketchup, sugar, molasses and garlic. Add pork; seal or cover and refrigerate for 4-6 hours, turning occasionally. Place the pork in a shallow roasting pan; discard marinade. Bake, uncovered, at 350° for 40 minutes or until a meat thermometer reads 160°-170°. Let stand for 5 minutes. Slice pork; sprinkle with sesame seeds if desired. Serve with the mustard sauce. **Yield:** 8 servings. **Diabetic Exchanges:** One serving (prepared with skim milk and reduced-sodium soy sauce, and without salt and sesame seeds) equals 3 lean meat; also, 168 calories, 201 mg sodium, 67 mg cholesterol, 3 gm carbohydrate, 25 gm protein, 5 gm fat.

Spice It Up!

In lasagna recipes that call for ground beef, substitute ground Italian sausage instead. You'll receive raves!

Asparagus Quiche
(Pictured above)

Once those first fresh asparagus spears sprout up, invite some special friends for a brunch and pull out this recipe. This lovely pie has a hint of Swiss cheese and beautiful green asparagus peeking out of every slice.
—*Ann Eastman, Greenville, California*

   1 pound fresh asparagus, trimmed
   1 unbaked pastry shell (9 inches)
   3 tablespoons butter *or* margarine
   3 tablespoons all-purpose flour
   1/2 teaspoon salt
1-1/2 cups milk
   4 eggs, beaten
   1/2 cup shredded Swiss cheese
   1/4 cup dry bread crumbs

Cut eight asparagus spears into 4-in. pieces; cut remaining spears into 1/2-in. pieces. Cook all of the asparagus in a small amount of water until crisp-tender; drain and set aside. Line the unpricked pastry shell with a double thickness of heavy-duty foil. Bake at 450° for 5 minutes. Remove foil; bake 5 minutes longer. Remove from the oven and set aside. In a saucepan over medium heat, melt butter; stir in flour and salt. Gradually add milk; cook and stir until thickened. Stir a small amount into eggs; return all to pan. Stir in cheese and the 1/2-in. asparagus pieces. Pour into crust. Sprinkle with bread crumbs. Bake at 400° for 35 minutes or until a knife inserted near the center comes out clean. Arrange the 4-in. asparagus pieces in a spoke pattern on top. **Yield:** 6-8 servings.

Meat Shell Potato Pie
(Pictured above)

Guests always comment on the unique presentation and taste of this delightfully different dish. Instead of a pastry shell, its base is made of ground beef.
—Julie Sterchi, Flora, Illinois

  1 pound ground chuck *or* lean ground beef
  1 can (10-3/4 ounces) condensed cream of mushroom soup, undiluted, *divided*
1/4 cup chopped onion
  1 egg
1/4 cup dry bread crumbs
  2 tablespoons chopped fresh parsley
1/4 teaspoon salt
Pinch pepper
  2 cups mashed potatoes
  4 bacon strips, cooked and crumbled
1/2 cup shredded cheddar cheese

In a large bowl, combine beef, 1/2 cup of soup, onion, egg, bread crumbs, parsley, salt and pepper; mix well. Press onto the bottom and up the sides of a 9-in. pie plate. Bake at 350° for 25 minutes; drain. Combine potatoes and remaining soup in a bowl; mix until fluffy. Spread over meat crust. Sprinkle with bacon and cheese. Bake at 350° for 15 minutes. Let stand for a few minutes. Cut into wedges. **Yield:** 6 servings.

Deep-Dish Ham Pie
(Pictured above)

Whenever I have leftover ham to use up, my family can expect to see this meaty pie on the table. It's loaded with ham and fabulous flavor.
—Lucinda Walker, Somerset, Pennsylvania

1/4 cup butter *or* margarine
1/4 cup all-purpose flour
1/2 teaspoon salt
1/4 teaspoon ground mustard
1/8 teaspoon pepper
  1 cup milk
  1 teaspoon dried minced onion
2-1/2 cups cubed fully cooked ham
  1 cup frozen peas
  2 hard-cooked eggs, chopped
Pastry for single-crust pie (8 inches)

Melt butter in a saucepan; stir in flour, salt, mustard and pepper until smooth. Gradually add milk and onion; bring to a boil. Cook and stir for 2 minutes or until thickened. Stir in ham, peas and eggs. Pour into an ungreased 8-in. square or 11-in. x 7-in. x 2-in. baking dish. On a floured surface, roll pastry to fit top of dish; place over filling. Seal and flute the edges; cut slits in the top. Bake at 425° for 25 minutes or until crust is golden brown and filling is bubbly. **Yield:** 6 servings.

MMM-MEMORABLE MEALS are made of Meat Shell Potato Pie, Special Chicken Potpie and Deep-Dish Ham Pie (shown at left, top to bottom).

Special Chicken Potpie

(Pictured at left)

This one-dish meal topped with homemade biscuits is oh-so-comforting. My family prefers it to any other potpie recipes I've tried. —Marcy Schewe
Danube, Minnesota

      1 broiler-fryer chicken (3 to 3-1/2 pounds), quartered
      4 cups water
      4 teaspoons chicken bouillon granules
      3 medium carrots, halved crosswise
      2 medium onions
      1 bay leaf
   1/2 pound fresh mushrooms, quartered
      2 celery ribs, halved crosswise
      3 tablespoons butter *or* margarine
      5 tablespoons all-purpose flour
   1/2 cup whipping cream
      1 teaspoon poultry seasoning
      1 teaspoon salt
   1/4 teaspoon pepper
      1 cup frozen peas
BISCUITS:
1-1/2 cups all-purpose flour
      2 teaspoons baking powder
1-1/4 teaspoons sugar
   1/4 teaspoon salt
      5 tablespoons shortening
   1/2 cup milk

In a Dutch oven or soup kettle, combine the first six ingredients; bring to a boil. Reduce heat; cover and simmer for 20 minutes. Add mushrooms and celery; cover and simmer for 15 minutes or until the chicken and vegetables are tender. Remove chicken and vegetables. Debone chicken; dice and set aside. Slice vegetables and set aside. Strain broth, reserving 2 cups. (Discard remaining broth or save for another use.) Melt butter in a saucepan; stir in flour until smooth. Cook and stir over medium heat until slightly thickened and bubbly. Gradually stir in cream and reserved broth; bring to a boil. Cook and stir for 2 minutes. Add poultry seasoning, salt, pepper, peas and reserved chicken and vegetables. Pour into a 2-qt. round baking dish. Set aside and keep warm. For biscuits, combine flour, baking powder, sugar and salt. Cut in shortening until mixture resembles coarse crumbs. Stir in milk just until mixed. On a floured surface, roll to 1/2-in. thickness. Cut with a 2-in. biscuit cutter. Place biscuits on top of chicken mixture. Bake at 400° for 20 minutes or until biscuits are golden brown. **Yield:** 6-8 servings.

Apricot-Glazed Chicken

With my husband's dietary restrictions, I feel as if I'm cooking "low everything". He likes good food, so I try to find recipes he can enjoy. We both agree this chicken is delicious. —Lois Collier
Vineland, New Jersey

✓ This tasty dish uses less sugar, salt and fat. Recipe includes *Diabetic Exchanges.*

      2 boneless skinless chicken breast halves (1/2 pound)
   1/4 cup apricot all-fruit spread
1-1/2 teaspoons soy sauce
      1 teaspoon Dijon mustard
      1 teaspoon honey
      1 teaspoon butter *or* margarine, melted

Coat a broiler pan with nonstick cooking spray; place chicken on pan. Broil 5 in. from the heat for 2 minutes on each side. Combine remaining ingredients; brush half over the chicken. Broil for 3 minutes. Turn chicken over; brush with remaining apricot mixture. Broil for 2-3 minutes or until juices run clear. **Yield:** 2 servings. **Diabetic Exchanges:** One serving (prepared with margarine and light soy sauce) equals 4 very lean meat, 1 fruit; also, 216 calories, 309 mg sodium, 73 mg cholesterol, 14 gm carbohydrate, 27 gm protein, 5 gm fat.

——— 🍴 🍴 🍴 ———

Herb-Rubbed Turkey

Rubs really have a way of locking in the flavor of meats. Here a wonderful blend of seasonings makes turkey extraordinary. —Twila Burkholder
Middleburg, Pennsylvania

      2 tablespoons rubbed sage
      1 tablespoon salt
      2 to 3 teaspoons pepper
      2 teaspoons curry powder
      2 teaspoons garlic powder
      2 teaspoons celery seed
      2 teaspoons dried parsley flakes
      1 teaspoon paprika
   1/2 teaspoon ground mustard
   1/4 teaspoon ground allspice
      3 bay leaves, crumbled
      1 turkey (14 to 16 pounds)

In a small bowl, combine all of the seasonings; mix well. Rub half the seasoning mixture in the cavity of the turkey. Rub remaining mixture over the turkey skin. Tie the drumsticks together and place turkey in a roasting pan. Roast using your favorite cooking method until a meat thermometer reads 185°. **Yield:** 12-14 servings.

Dijon Sirloin Tips

(Pictured below)

I received this recipe years ago. This beef and mushroom dish is such a hit with our family it's become a tradition for birthdays and Christmas.
—Janelle Lee, Lake Charles, Louisiana

1-1/4 pounds sirloin tips, cubed
2 tablespoons butter *or* margarine
1 tablespoon cooking oil
3 cups sliced fresh mushrooms
1 garlic clove, minced
1/2 cup beef broth
1/4 cup white wine vinegar
1-1/2 teaspoons soy sauce
2 teaspoons Dijon mustard
2 teaspoons cornstarch
1/2 cup whipping cream
Hot cooked noodles
Chopped fresh parsley, optional

In a large skillet, brown the meat in butter and oil; transfer to an ungreased 2-qt. baking dish. In the same skillet, saute mushrooms and garlic until mushrooms are tender, about 3 minutes. Pour mushrooms, garlic and drippings over meat. Cover and bake at 300° for 2 hours or until meat is tender. In a skillet, combine the broth, vinegar and soy sauce; bring to a boil. Boil for 2 minutes; set aside. Combine mustard, cornstarch and cream; stir into broth mixture. Bring to a boil; boil for 2 minutes, stirring constantly. Drain juices from baking dish into broth mixture. Cook over medium heat, stirring constantly, until thickened and bubbly. Add beef mixture. Serve over noodles. Garnish with parsley if desired. **Yield:** 4 servings.

Turkey Meat Loaf

I first made this different meat loaf when my husband and I had to start watching our diet. Since then, every time I serve it to family and friends, I'm asked for the recipe. The turkey is a nice change.
—Ruby Rath, New Haven, Indiana

✓ This tasty dish uses less sugar, salt and fat. Recipe includes *Diabetic Exchanges.*

2 pounds ground turkey breast
1 cup quick-cooking oats
1 medium onion, chopped
1/2 cup shredded carrot
1/2 cup milk
1 egg *or* egg substitute equivalent
2 tablespoons ketchup
1 teaspoon garlic powder
1/4 teaspoon pepper
TOPPING:
1/4 cup ketchup
1/4 cup quick-cooking oats

In a large bowl, combine the first nine ingredients; mix well. Press into a 9-in. x 5-in. x 3-in. loaf pan that has been coated with nonstick cooking spray. Combine topping ingredients; spread over loaf. Bake, uncovered, at 350° for 65 minutes or until juices run clear. **Yield:** 10 servings. **Diabetic Exchanges:** One serving (prepared with skim milk and egg substitute) equals 3 very lean meat, 1 starch; also, 154 calories, 186 mg sodium, 27 mg cholesterol, 11 gm carbohydrate, 23 gm protein, 2 gm fat.

Country Beef Patties

When my family wants a down-home dinner, this is the recipe they usually request. Bacon in the patties gives a subtle smoky flavor, while tomato gravy adds a little zip.
—Bernice Morris, Marshfield, Missouri

1 pound ground beef
2 uncooked bacon strips, diced
1 teaspoon diced onion
1/2 teaspoon salt
1/8 teaspoon pepper
TOMATO GRAVY:
2 tablespoons chopped green pepper
1 tablespoon chopped onion
1 can (14-1/2 ounces) diced tomatoes, undrained
1 to 2 bay leaves
1 teaspoon sugar
1/2 teaspoon celery salt
1/8 teaspoon salt
1/8 teaspoon pepper

1/2 cup water
2 tablespoons all-purpose flour

In a bowl, combine beef, bacon, onion, salt and pepper. Shape into four oval patties; brown in a skillet over medium heat. Remove patties and keep warm. Drain all but 1 tablespoon drippings; saute green pepper and onion in drippings until tender. Add tomatoes, bay leaves, sugar, celery salt, salt and pepper. Combine water and flour until smooth; add to tomato mixture, stirring constantly. Bring to a boil; cook and stir for 2 minutes. Return patties to gravy. Reduce heat; cover and simmer for 30 minutes. Uncover and simmer 10 minutes longer. Remove the bay leaves. **Yield:** 4 servings.

Gingered Pork and Asparagus

(Pictured on page 68)

My husband and I were thrilled when I found this recipe for asparagus and juicy pork slices smothered in a snappy ginger sauce. —Kathleen Purvis
Franklin, Tennessee

✓ This tasty dish uses less sugar, salt and fat. Recipe includes *Diabetic Exchanges.*

6 tablespoons apple juice
6 tablespoons soy sauce
4 garlic cloves, minced
1 tablespoon ground ginger
1 pound pork tenderloin, thinly sliced
2 tablespoons cooking oil, *divided*
1 pound fresh asparagus, cut into 1-inch pieces
1-1/2 teaspoons cornstarch
Hot cooked rice, optional

In a large resealable plastic bag or shallow glass container, combine the first four ingredients. Remove 1/3 cup and set aside. Add pork to remaining marinade; seal bag or cover container and turn to coat. Refrigerate for 1 hour. In a large skillet or wok over medium-high heat, stir-fry half of the pork in 1 tablespoon oil for 2-3 minutes or until no longer pink. Remove pork with a slotted spoon; set aside. Repeat with remaining pork and oil. In the same skillet, stir-fry the asparagus for 2-3 minutes or until crisp-tender. Stir cornstarch into reserved marinade; add to the skillet. Bring to a boil; cook and stir for 2 minutes or until thickened. Return pork to skillet and heat through. Serve over rice if desired. **Yield:** 4 servings. **Diabetic Exchanges:** One serving (prepared with light soy sauce and without rice) equals 3 lean meat, 2 vegetable, 1/2 fat; also, 258 calories, 557 mg sodium, 67 mg cholesterol, 11 gm carbohydrate, 28 gm protein, 11 gm fat.

Creamed Grouse on Toast

(Pictured above)

A bold-tasting game bird like grouse is so tempting made this way. The lemon juice gives the savory sauce a refreshing spark. This versatile main dish is just as good prepared with chicken or turkey.
—Philan Welsh, Spencer, Wisconsin

2 quarts water
1 bay leaf
4 grouse *or* squab (3/4 to 1 pound *each*)
1/2 cup chopped onion
1/2 cup sliced fresh mushrooms
2 tablespoons butter *or* margarine
2 tablespoons all-purpose flour
1 cup chicken broth
2 tablespoons lemon juice
1/2 teaspoon salt
1/8 teaspoon pepper
1/4 cup whipping cream
2 tablespoons minced fresh parsley
Toast *or* hot cooked rice
Chopped fresh parsley, optional

In a Dutch oven, bring water, bay leaf and grouse to a boil. Reduce heat; cover and simmer until the meat is tender. Remove grouse; cool. Debone and cut into pieces. In a skillet over medium heat, saute onion and mushrooms in butter until tender. Add flour. Stir in broth, lemon juice, salt and pepper; bring to a boil. Cook and stir for 2 minutes. Add grouse and heat through. Add cream and parsley; mix well. Heat through. Serve over toast or rice; garnish with parsley if desired. **Yield:** 4 servings.

Instead of Frying Fish

(Pictured above)

This quick recipe is one I discovered years ago in a fund-raiser cookbook. Since my husband is an avid fisherman, I've put it to good use over the years. The crispy potato chip coating bakes up toasty brown, and the fillets stay nice and moist. —Sharon Funfsinn
Mendota, Illinois

>   1 pound walleye, perch *or* pike fillets
> 1/4 cup milk
>   1 cup crushed potato chips
> 1/4 cup grated Parmesan cheese
> 1/4 teaspoon dried thyme
>   1 tablespoon dry bread crumbs
>   2 tablespoons butter *or* margarine, melted

Cut fish into serving-size pieces. Place milk in a shallow bowl. In another shallow bowl, combine potato chips, Parmesan cheese and thyme. Dip fish in milk, then coat with the potato chip mixture. Sprinkle a greased 8-in. square baking dish with bread crumbs. Place fish over crumbs; drizzle with butter. Bake, uncovered, at 500° for 12-14 minutes or until fish flakes easily with a fork. **Yield:** 4 servings.

———— 🍷 🍷 🍷 ————

Roast Pork with Spiced Cherry Sauce

This mouth-watering roast looks fancy, but it isn't difficult to fix. The pork slices topped with a delicious cherry sauce make an elegant main dish without a lot of fuss. —Mavis Diment, Marcus, Iowa

>   1 boneless pork loin roast (3 to 4 pounds)
>   1 teaspoon salt
>   1 teaspoon pepper
>   1 teaspoon rubbed sage
>   1 can (16 ounces) pitted tart red cherries
> 1-1/2 cups sugar
>   1/4 cup vinegar
>   12 whole cloves
>   1 cinnamon stick (3 inches)
>   1/3 cup cornstarch
>   1 tablespoon lemon juice
>   1 tablespoon butter *or* margarine
>   3 to 4 drops red food coloring, optional

Rub roast with salt, pepper and sage; place in an ungreased shallow baking pan. Bake, uncovered, at 325° for 1-1/2 to 2 hours or until a meat thermometer reads 160°-170°. Meanwhile, drain cherries, reserving liquid. Set cherries aside. Add water to cherry liquid to measure 3/4 cup. Pour 1/2 cup into a saucepan; add sugar, vinegar, cloves and cinnamon. Bring to a boil. Reduce heat; simmer, uncovered, for 10 minutes. Remove and discard the spices. In a small bowl, combine cornstarch and remaining cherry liquid until smooth; add to saucepan. Bring to a boil; cook for 2 minutes, stirring constantly. Stir in lemon juice, butter, cherries and food coloring if desired; heat through. Let roast stand for 10 minutes; slice and serve with the cherry sauce. **Yield:** 8-10 servings.

———— 🍷 🍷 🍷 ————

Asparagus Bacon Quiche

Lovely asparagus peeks out of every slice of this hearty quiche, which is delicious and a little different. I like to make it for special occasions—it's a welcome addition to any brunch buffet. —Suzanne McKinley
Lyons, Georgia

>   1 unbaked pastry shell (9 inches)
>   1 pound fresh asparagus, trimmed and cut
>   into 1-inch pieces
>   6 bacon strips, cooked and crumbled
>   3 eggs
> 1-1/2 cups half-and-half cream
>   1 cup grated Parmesan cheese, *divided*
>   1 tablespoon sliced green onions
>   1 teaspoon sugar
>   1/2 teaspoon salt
>   1/4 teaspoon pepper
> **Pinch ground nutmeg**

Line the unpricked pastry shell with a double thickness of heavy-duty foil. Bake at 450° for 5 minutes; remove foil. Bake 5 minutes more; remove from the oven and set aside. Cook the asparagus in a small amount of water until crisp-tender, about 3-4 minutes; drain well. Arrange the bacon and asparagus in the crust. In a bowl, beat eggs; add cream, 1/2 cup of cheese, onions, sugar, salt, pepper and nutmeg. Pour over asparagus. Sprinkle with remaining cheese. Bake at 400° for 10 minutes. Reduce heat to 350°; bake 23-25 minutes longer or until a knife inserted near the center comes out clean. **Yield:** 6-8 servings.

— 🍵 🍵 🍵 —

Peanut Butter Chicken Skewers

Most people associate peanut butter with snacks or desserts. This fantastic dish proves it also makes a mouth-watering sauce for chicken. —Jeanne Bennett
North Richland Hills, Texas

1/2 cup creamy peanut butter
1/2 cup water
1/4 cup soy sauce
  4 garlic cloves, minced
  3 tablespoons lemon juice
  2 tablespoons brown sugar
3/4 teaspoon ground ginger
1/2 teaspoon crushed red pepper flakes
  4 boneless skinless chicken breast halves
  2 cups shredded red cabbage
Sliced green onion tops

In a saucepan, combine the first eight ingredients; cook and stir over medium-high heat for 5 minutes or until smooth. Reserve half of the sauce. Slice chicken lengthwise into 1-in. strips; thread onto skewers (if using bamboo skewers, soak them in water for at least 20 minutes). Grill, uncovered, over medium-hot coals for 2 minutes; turn and brush with peanut butter sauce. Continue turning and basting for 4-6 minutes or until juices run clear. Place cabbage on a serving plate; top with chicken. Sprinkle with onion tops. Serve with reserved sauce. **Yield:** 4 servings.

— 🍵 🍵 🍵 —

Ham and Vegetable Linguine

(Pictured above right)

I've been pleasing dinner guests with this delicious pasta dish for years. The delicate cream sauce blends well with the colorful and hearty mix of vegetables. I chop the vegetables ahead of time and later prepare this dish in a snap.
—Kerry Kerr McAvoy
Rockford, Michigan

  1 package (8 ounces) linguine
1/2 pound fresh asparagus, cut into 1-inch pieces
1/2 pound fresh mushrooms, sliced
  1 medium carrot, thinly sliced
  1 medium zucchini, diced
  2 cups julienned fully cooked ham
1/4 cup butter *or* margarine
  1 cup whipping cream
1/2 cup frozen peas
  3 green onions, sliced
1/4 cup grated Parmesan cheese
  1 teaspoon dried basil
3/4 teaspoon salt
Dash *each* pepper and ground nutmeg
Additional Parmesan cheese, optional

Cook linguine according to package directions. Meanwhile, in a large skillet, saute asparagus, mushrooms, carrot, zucchini and ham in butter until the vegetables are tender. Add cream, peas, onions, Parmesan, basil, salt, pepper and nutmeg; bring to a boil. Reduce heat; simmer for 3 minutes, stirring frequently. Rinse and drain linguine; add to vegetable mixture and toss to coat. Sprinkle with Parmesan cheese if desired. **Yield:** 4 servings.

Choice Chili

For a nice thick pot of chili, mix in a can of refried beans. No one will notice the "secret", but they'll sure enjoy the extra hearty chili!

Asparagus Puff Ring

(Pictured below)

Every spring when I make this family-favorite entree, I'm struck by how impressive it looks. Ham and asparagus in a creamy sauce are piled high in a cheesy cream puff shell. It's delicious and deceivingly simple to prepare!
—Shirley De Lange
Byron Center, Michigan

3/4 cup water
6 tablespoons butter *or* margarine
3/4 cup all-purpose flour
1/2 teaspoon salt
3 eggs
1/4 cup grated Parmesan cheese, *divided*
FILLING:
1 pound fresh asparagus, cut into 1-inch pieces
1/4 cup diced onion
2 tablespoons butter *or* margarine
2 tablespoons all-purpose flour
1/2 teaspoon salt
1/4 teaspoon pepper
1-1/2 cups milk
1/2 cup shredded Swiss cheese
2 tablespoons grated Parmesan cheese
2 cups diced fully cooked ham

In a saucepan over medium heat, bring water and butter to a boil. Add flour and salt all at once; stir until a smooth ball forms. Remove from the heat; let stand for 5 minutes. Add eggs, one at a time, beating well after each; beat until smooth. Stir in 3 tablespoons Parmesan cheese. Using 1/4 cupfuls of dough, form a ring around the sides of a greased 10-in. quiche pan or pie plate (mounds should touch). Top with remaining cheese. Bake at 400° for 35 minutes. Meanwhile, cook asparagus until crisp-tender, about 3-4 minutes; drain. In a saucepan, saute onion in butter until tender. Stir in flour, salt and pepper. Gradually add milk; bring to a boil over medium heat, stirring constantly. Reduce heat; stir in cheeses until melted. Stir in ham and asparagus; spoon into ring. Serve immediately. **Yield:** 6 servings.

Italian-Style Beef Liver

My family loves liver, but I get tired of serving the standard liver and onions. Here a rich tomato sauce makes the liver nice and tender.
—Mina Dyck
Boissevain, Manitoba

1/3 cup all-purpose flour
1/4 teaspoon salt
1 pound beef liver, cut into bite-size pieces
4 teaspoons cooking oil, *divided*
1 cup thinly sliced onion
1/2 cup chopped celery
2 cans (14-1/2 ounces *each*) diced tomatoes, undrained
1 bay leaf
2 tablespoons chopped fresh parsley
1 tablespoon chopped fresh basil *or* 1 teaspoon dried basil
1 teaspoon salt
1/4 teaspoon pepper
Hot cooked spaghetti
Grated Parmesan cheese

Combine flour and salt; toss with liver. Heat 2 teaspoons oil in a skillet; cook liver until no longer pink. Remove and set aside. In the same skillet, saute onion and celery in remaining oil until tender, about 5 minutes. Stir in tomatoes, bay leaf, parsley, basil, salt and pepper. Cover and simmer for 20 minutes, stirring occasionally. Add the liver; cover and cook 5 minutes longer or until heated through. Remove bay leaf. Serve over spaghetti; sprinkle with cheese. **Yield:** 4 servings.

Chilies Rellenos Casserole

I love to cook with tasty green chilies and use recipes featuring them when I entertain. This hearty casserole has a big pepper taste in every bite.
—Nadine Estes, Alto, New Mexico

1 can (7 ounces) whole green chilies
1-1/2 cups (6 ounces) shredded Colby/
    Monterey Jack cheese
3/4 pound ground beef
1/4 cup chopped onion
1 cup milk
4 eggs
1/4 cup all-purpose flour
1/4 teaspoon salt
1/8 teaspoon pepper

Split chilies and remove seeds; dry on paper towels. Arrange chilies on the bottom of a greased 2-qt. baking dish. Top with cheese. In a skillet, brown beef and onion; drain. Spoon over the cheese. In a mixing bowl, beat milk, eggs, flour, salt and pepper until smooth; pour over beef mixture. Bake, uncovered, at 350° for 45-50 minutes or until a knife inserted near the center comes out clean. Let stand 5 minutes before serving. **Yield:** 6 servings.

Meatballs in Sweet Clove Sauce

The kitchen is the domain of my wife, Ruth, but she doesn't mind if I want to step in once in a while and prepare these savory meatballs.
         —Bill Cowan
         Hanover, Ontario

4 slices dry bread, diced
1/4 cup lemon juice
1 egg
1 small onion, diced
1 teaspoon seasoned salt
1-1/2 pounds ground beef
SAUCE:
1 cup tomato juice
1/2 cup chili sauce
1/2 cup packed brown sugar
1 teaspoon ground mustard
1/4 teaspoon ground cloves

In a bowl, soak bread in lemon juice for 2 minutes. Add egg, onion and salt; stir in beef. Shape into 1-1/2-in. balls; place in a greased 13-in. x 9-in. x 2-in. baking dish. Bake, uncovered, at 350° for 25 minutes; drain. Combine sauce ingredients; pour over meatballs. Bake 30 minutes longer or until hot and bubbly. **Yield:** 6 servings.

Well-Mixed Meat Loaf

When making meat loaf, first combine all ingredients except the ground beef. The seasonings will be more evenly distributed this way with little effort.

Stuffed Chicken Breasts
(Pictured above)

Mushroom and rice stuffing turns plain chicken breasts into a terrific main dish that your guests will remember. Pecans add a harvest taste to the moist chicken.
         —Pat Neu, Gainesville, Texas

1-1/2 cups sliced fresh mushrooms
1-1/3 cups uncooked instant rice
1/4 cup chopped onion
1/4 cup chopped celery leaves
1/4 cup butter *or* margarine
1-1/2 cups water
1-1/2 teaspoons salt
1/2 teaspoon dried oregano
1/2 teaspoon rubbed sage
1/2 teaspoon dried thyme
1/4 teaspoon pepper
1/3 cup chopped pecans, toasted
6 bone-in chicken breast halves

In a saucepan, saute mushrooms, rice, onion and celery leaves in butter until onion is tender. Add water and seasonings; bring to a boil. Reduce heat; cover and simmer for 5-7 minutes or until rice is tender and liquid is absorbed. Stir in pecans. Stuff 1/2 cup of rice mixture under the skin of each chicken breast. Place in a greased 13-in. x 9-in. x 2-in. baking dish. Bake, uncovered, at 350° for 1-1/2 hours or until juices run clear. **Yield:** 6 servings.

BIG FISH STORY has tasty ending with Catfish Jambalaya, Cracker-Coated Fried Perch and Italian-Style Walleye (shown above, clockwise from right).

Catfish Jambalaya

(Pictured above)

My family owns a catfish processing plant. This colorful, zippy main dish is a great favorite of ours.
—*Mrs. Bill Saul, Macon, Mississippi*

✓ This tasty dish uses less sugar, salt and fat. Recipe includes *Diabetic Exchanges.*

> **2 cups chopped onion**
> **1/2 cup chopped celery**
> **1/2 cup chopped green pepper**
> **2 garlic cloves, minced**
> **1/4 cup butter *or* margarine, optional**
> **1 can (10 ounces) diced tomatoes and green chilies, undrained**
> **1 cup sliced fresh mushrooms**
> **1/4 teaspoon cayenne pepper**
> **1/2 teaspoon salt, optional**
> **1 pound catfish fillets, cubed**
> **Hot cooked rice, optional**
> **Sliced green onions, optional**

In a saucepan over medium-high heat, saute onion, celery, green pepper and garlic in butter until tender, about 10 minutes. Add tomatoes, mushrooms, cayenne and salt if desired; bring to a boil. Add catfish. Reduce heat; cover and simmer until the fish flakes easily with a fork, about 10 minutes. If desired, serve with rice and top with green onions. **Yield:** 4 servings. **Diabetic Exchanges:** One serving (calculated without rice and green onions; prepared with nonstick cooking spray instead of butter or margarine and without salt) equals 3 very lean meat, 2 vegetable; also, 161 calories, 395 mg sodium, 66 mg cholesterol, 12 gm carbohydrate, 21 gm protein, 4 gm fat.

— ▰ ▰ ▰ —

Italian-Style Walleye

(Pictured above)

Herbs and melted cheese dress up fillets in this recipe. When I want a quick fish dinner, this is the recipe I turn to. —*Cathy Lueschen, Columbus, Nebraska*

> **4 to 6 walleye fillets (about 1-1/2 pounds)**
> **1 can (15 ounces) tomato sauce**

2 tablespoons chopped fresh parsley
1 teaspoon Italian seasoning
1/2 teaspoon dried basil
1/4 teaspoon salt
1/8 teaspoon pepper
1 cup (4 ounces) shredded mozzarella cheese

Place walleye in a greased shallow 3-qt. or 13-in. x 9-in. x 2-in. baking dish. Combine tomato sauce, parsley, Italian seasoning, basil, salt and pepper; pour over the fish. Bake, uncovered, at 350° for 15 minutes. Sprinkle with mozzarella cheese. Bake 5-10 minutes longer or until fish flakes easily with a fork. **Yield:** 4-6 servings.

— 🍴 🍴 🍴 —

Cracker-Coated Fried Perch

(Pictured at left)

Your favorite fisherman would be proud to find his catch fried with this golden coating. I've gotten raves each time I've made this fish. —Dennis Dornfeldt
Sheboygan, Wisconsin

2 eggs
1/2 cup milk
2 cups butter-flavored cracker crumbs
1/2 teaspoon garlic salt
1/4 teaspoon dried oregano
1/4 teaspoon dried tarragon
1/4 teaspoon pepper
1 pound perch fillets
Cooking oil

In a shallow bowl, beat eggs and milk. In another shallow bowl, combine cracker crumbs, garlic salt, oregano, tarragon and pepper. Dip the perch in egg mixture, then coat with crumbs. Heat oil in a skillet over medium heat. Fry fish for several minutes on each side or until it flakes easily with a fork. **Yield:** 4 servings.

— 🍴 🍴 🍴 —

Trout Amandine

I catch wonderful trout here and this is a simple yet delicious way to prepare it. —Bonnie Sue Greene
Mesa, Colorado

2 teaspoons salt
1/2 teaspoon pepper
4 pan-dressed trout (about 1 pound *each*)
2 eggs
1/2 cup half-and-half cream
1/2 cup all-purpose flour

1/2 cup slivered almonds
3 tablespoons butter *or* margarine, *divided*
3 to 4 tablespoons lemon juice
1/2 teaspoon dried tarragon
1/4 cup olive *or* vegetable oil

Sprinkle salt and pepper in the cavity of each trout. In a shallow bowl, beat eggs and cream. Dip trout in egg mixture, then roll in flour. In a small skillet over low heat, saute the almonds in 2 tablespoons butter until lightly browned. Add lemon juice and tarragon; heat through. Remove from the heat and keep warm. Meanwhile, in a skillet over medium heat, combine oil and remaining butter. Fry the trout for 8-10 minutes; carefully turn and fry 8 minutes longer or until it flakes easily with a fork. Top with almond mixture. **Yield:** 4 servings.

— 🍴 🍴 🍴 —

Grilled Game Hens

I love to cook and bake just about everything, but grilling is my specialty. These game hens pick up wonderful flavor from a sweet and refreshing marinade. —Kriss Erickson, Haena, Hawaii

2 Cornish game hens (1 to 1-1/2 pounds *each*), split lengthwise
1/4 cup olive *or* vegetable oil
1/3 cup white wine vinegar
4 garlic cloves, minced
3 tablespoons chopped fresh cilantro *or* parsley
3 tablespoons honey
3 tablespoons soy sauce
1 to 2 tablespoons ground ginger
1/4 teaspoon crushed red pepper flakes
Dash pepper

Place hens in a large resealable plastic bag or shallow glass container. Add remaining ingredients; seal or cover and refrigerate for at least 1 hour. Remove hens, reserving marinade. Place hens in a 13-in. x 9-in. x 2-in. disposable aluminum pan. Pour marinade over hens; cover pan. Grill, covered, over medium-hot coals, basting frequently, for 35-40 minutes or until juices run clear and a meat thermometer reads 170°. Place hens directly over coals for the last 3-4 minutes of cooking time, turning once. **Yield:** 4 servings.

Pan-Frying Pointers

To keep fried fish warm until all of it is cooked, place fish on a paper towel-lined baking sheet and put in a 275° oven for no more than 20 minutes.

Asparagus Shepherd's Pie

(Pictured below)

Shepherd's pie takes on a tasty twist with this version. Between the fluffy mashed potato topping and the savory ground beef base is a bed of tender, green asparagus. Even my kids ask for big helpings.
—*Steve Rowland, Fredericksburg, Virginia*

- 6 medium potatoes, peeled and quartered
- 1 pound ground beef
- 1 large onion, chopped
- 2 garlic cloves, minced
- 1 can (10-3/4 ounces) condensed cream of asparagus soup, undiluted
- 1/4 teaspoon pepper
- 1 pound fresh asparagus, trimmed and cut into 1-inch pieces
- 1/2 cup milk
- 1/4 cup butter *or* margarine
- 1 teaspoon rubbed sage
- 3/4 teaspoon salt
- 1/2 cup shredded mozzarella cheese
- Paprika

In a saucepan, cover potatoes with water; cook until very tender. Meanwhile, in a skillet, brown beef; drain. Add onion and garlic; cook until onion is tender. Stir in soup and pepper; pour into a greased 2-qt. baking dish. Cook the asparagus in a small amount of water until crisp-tender, about 3-4 minutes; drain and place over the beef mixture. Drain potatoes; mash with milk, butter, sage and salt. Spread over the asparagus. Sprinkle with cheese and paprika. Bake, uncovered, at 350° for 20 minutes. **Yield:** 6-8 servings.

———— 🍃 🍃 🍃 ————

Sour Cream Cardamom Waffles

Cardamom has such a delicate flavor. I've been making coffee cakes with this interesting spice for years, and now I found a use for it in waffles. More often than not, my family will request these waffles instead of plain ones.
—*Ruth Andrewson*
Leavenworth, Washington

- 1 cup all-purpose flour
- 1/4 cup sugar
- 1 teaspoon baking powder
- 1 teaspoon ground cardamom
- Dash salt
- 2/3 cup milk
- 2/3 cup sour cream
- 1/4 cup butter *or* margarine, melted
- 2 eggs, *separated*

In a bowl, combine flour, sugar, baking powder, cardamom and salt. Combine milk, sour cream, butter and egg yolks; stir into dry ingredients just until combined. Beat egg whites until stiff peaks form; fold into batter. Bake in a preheated waffle iron according to manufacturer's directions until golden brown (waffles will be soft). Serve with honey or syrup. **Yield:** 6 waffles (about 6-1/2 inches).

———— 🍃 🍃 🍃 ————

Easy Baked Chicken

This moist chicken has a rich herb flavor. It's a dish I prepared often for my mother, who was diabetic. Now I still make it for myself. —*Christine Richburg*
Brewton, Alabama

✓ This tasty dish uses less sugar, salt and fat. Recipe includes *Diabetic Exchanges*.

- 1 packet (1/2 ounce) butter flavored mix*
- 3/4 cup tomato juice
- 2 tablespoons cider *or* red wine vinegar
- 1 tablespoon soy sauce
- 1 teaspoon ground ginger
- 1 garlic clove, minced
- 1/2 teaspoon dried oregano

1 broiler-fryer chicken (3 pounds), cut up and skin removed

Prepare butter granules according to package directions. Stir in tomato juice, vinegar, soy sauce, ginger, garlic and oregano. Place chicken in a resealable plastic bag. Add marinade; seal and refrigerate 8 hours or overnight. Place chicken and marinade in a 13-in. x 9-in. x 2-in. baking pan coated with nonstick spray. Bake, uncovered, at 375° for 1 hour or until juices run clear, spooning marinade over chicken several times. **Yield:** 6 servings. **Diabetic Exchanges:** One serving equals 3 lean meat, 1 vegetable; also, 193 calories, 415 mg sodium, 61 mg cholesterol, 4 gm carbohydrate, 23 gm protein, 9 gm fat. ***Editor's Note:** This recipe was tested with Butter Buds butter flavored mix.

Lemon Herb Chicken

This recipe proves that some simple seasonings can really enhance the naturally terrific taste of chicken. I depend on this recipe often in summer.
—Janice Smith, Cynthiana, Kentucky

✓ This tasty dish uses less sugar, salt and fat. Recipe includes *Diabetic Exchanges*.

1/2 cup lemon juice
1/4 cup vegetable oil
1/4 cup minced fresh parsley
1 teaspoon dried tarragon
1/4 teaspoon pepper
8 boneless skinless chicken breast halves (2 pounds)

In a large resealable plastic bag or shallow glass dish, combine the first five ingredients. Add chicken. Seal or cover and refrigerate for 4 hours or overnight. Drain; discard marinade. Grill chicken, uncovered, over medium-low coals for 10-15 minutes or until juices run clear, turning several times. **Yield:** 8 servings. **Diabetic Exchanges:** One serving equals 4 very lean meat, 1/2 fat; also, 174 calories, 66 mg sodium, 73 mg cholesterol, 1 gm carbohydrate, 27 gm protein, 7 gm fat.

Easy Seasoning

Looking for a simple, light chicken recipe? Coat chicken breasts with a mixture of olive oil, rosemary and oregano before roasting them. Your family will come back for seconds!

Pheasant Stir-Fry

(Pictured above)

I learned creative ways to prepare game while cooking for hunters at a lodge in Alaska, where my husband was a guide. Everyone enjoyed this savory stir-fry.
—Darlene Kenning, Hutchinson, Minnesota

2 tablespoons soy sauce
2 tablespoons cornstarch
1 tablespoon minced fresh gingerroot *or* 3/4 teaspoon ground ginger
1 tablespoon chicken bouillon granules
1-1/3 cups water
1 boneless skinless pheasant breast (about 3/4 pound), cut into strips
2 tablespoons cooking oil, *divided*
1 cup broccoli florets
1 cup *each* julienned carrots, celery and onion
1 cup frozen snow peas
Hot cooked white *or* wild rice

In a small bowl, combine the soy sauce, cornstarch, ginger and bouillon. Add water; set aside. In a skillet or wok over medium-high heat, stir-fry pheasant in 1 tablespoon of oil until no longer pink, about 3-4 minutes. Remove and keep warm. Add remaining oil to pan. Stir-fry broccoli and carrots for 2 minutes. Add celery, onion and peas; stir-fry until the vegetables are crisp-tender, about 4-5 minutes. Stir soy sauce mixture and add to the skillet; bring to a boil. Cook and stir for 2 minutes. Return meat to pan and heat through. Serve over rice. **Yield:** 4 servings.

until meat is no longer pink and vegetables are tender; drain. Add the tomatoes, tomato paste, sugar, oregano, basil, 1/2 teaspoon pepper and salt; bring to a boil. Reduce heat; simmer, uncovered, for 45 minutes or until thick, stirring occasionally. Combine ricotta cheese, 1/2 cup Parmesan cheese, egg, parsley and remaining pepper. In a greased 13-in. x 9-in. x 2-in. baking dish, layer a fourth of the noodles, a third of the ricotta mixture, a fourth of the meat sauce and 1/2 cup mozzarella cheese. Repeat layers twice. Top with the remaining noodles, sauce and Parmesan. Cover and bake at 400° for 45 minutes. Sprinkle with remaining mozzarella; bake, uncovered, 10 minutes more. Let stand 15 minutes before serving. **Yield:** 12 servings.

Hearty Vegetable Casserole

This layered dinner is a handy one-dish meal with lots of fall vegetables. It's gone to many potluck meals at our church. —Bill Cowan, Hanover, Ontario

- **1 cup sliced turnips**
- **1 cup diced carrots**
- **1 cup diced potatoes**
- **1 cup frozen peas**
- **1 cup diced parsnips**
- **1 cup shredded cabbage**
- **Salt and pepper to taste**
- **1 can (8 ounces) cut green beans**
- **2 tablespoons chopped onion**
- **1 package (12 ounces) fresh pork sausage links**
- **1 can (10-3/4 ounces) condensed cream of mushroom soup, undiluted**

In a greased 13-in. x 9-in. x 2-in. glass baking dish, layer the first six vegetables in order given, seasoning with salt and pepper between layers. Drain beans, reserving liquid; set liquid aside. Place beans over cabbage; sprinkle with salt and pepper. Top with onion. Brown sausage; drain. Place over onion. Combine soup and bean liquid; pour over sausage. Cover and bake at 350° for 1 hour. Turn sausage over; bake, uncovered, 30 minutes longer or until vegetables are tender. **Yield:** 6 servings.

Classic Lasagna

(Pictured above)

A definite crowd-pleaser, this classic lasagna is thick, rich and meaty with lots of cheese—just the way I like it. Even though my parents were Hungarian, I have a weakness for savory Italian foods like this.
—Suzanne Barker, Bellingham, Washington

- **1/2 pound bulk Italian sausage**
- **1/2 pound ground beef**
- **1-1/2 cups diced onion**
- **1 cup diced carrot**
- **3 garlic cloves, minced**
- **1/4 teaspoon crushed red pepper flakes**
- **2 cans (28 ounces *each*) whole tomatoes, undrained**
- **2 tablespoons tomato paste**
- **1 teaspoon *each* sugar, dried oregano and basil**
- **1 teaspoon pepper, *divided***
- **1/2 teaspoon salt**
- **2 cartons (15 ounces *each*) ricotta cheese**
- **3/4 cup grated Parmesan cheese, *divided***
- **1 egg**
- **1/3 cup minced fresh parsley**
- **1 package (12 ounces) lasagna noodles, cooked, rinsed and drained**
- **2 cups (8 ounces) shredded mozzarella cheese**

In a large saucepan over medium heat, cook sausage, beef, onion, carrot, garlic and pepper flakes

---

Chicken Cordon Bleu

I came up with this recipe as a way to make something a little different. The bacon adds great flavor, and the chicken is dipped twice into an egg mixture for a nice crust.
—Jim Wick, Orlando, Florida

4 large boneless skinless chicken breast
   halves
2 tablespoons butter *or* margarine, softened
1 teaspoon dried thyme
4 thin slices fully cooked ham
4 thin slices Swiss cheese
8 bacon strips
2 eggs
1/2 cup milk
1/2 cup all-purpose flour
3/4 cup dry bread crumbs
1/2 teaspoon garlic powder
1 teaspoon dried oregano
1/4 cup shredded Parmesan cheese

Flatten chicken breasts; spread butter on the insides. Sprinkle with thyme. Top with a slice of ham and cheese; roll up tightly. Wrap each with two slices of bacon and secure with toothpicks. In a small bowl, beat eggs and milk; set aside. Place flour in another bowl. Combine the bread crumbs, garlic powder, oregano and cheese. Dip each chicken breast into egg mixture, then flour, again into egg mixture and then into crumbs. Place on a greased baking sheet. Bake, uncovered, at 350° for 40-45 minutes or until chicken juices run clear. **Yield:** 4 servings.

Quail with Rice

Quail is a family favorite every fall when my husband goes hunting. This recipe makes an elegant meal for family or guests. Since it uses only one skillet, there's hardly any cleanup or fuss.
       —Lenora Picolet
       Dwight, Kansas

4 bacon strips, halved
8 quail (about 2 pounds)
1 cup shredded carrots
1/2 cup sliced green onions
1/2 cup minced fresh parsley
2-1/2 cups chicken broth
1 cup uncooked long grain rice
1/2 teaspoon salt
1/4 teaspoon lemon-pepper seasoning

In a large skillet over medium heat, cook bacon until nearly crisp. Remove bacon; drain, reserving 2 tablespoons drippings. Brown quail in drippings. Remove and keep warm. Saute carrots, onions and parsley in drippings until tender. Add broth, rice, salt and lemon pepper; bring to a boil. Place quail over rice; place one bacon strip on each. Reduce heat; cover and simmer for 25-30 minutes or until rice is tender and quail is cooked. **Yield:** 4 servings.

Pork Kabobs

(Pictured below)

These delightful picnic kabobs are my daughter's favorite. My husband also enjoys them, even though he never cared much for pork. The refreshing sauce is a tempting topping for the sizzling grilled meat.
    —Louise Wetmore, Cottage Grove, Minnesota

1/2 cup vegetable oil
1/4 cup chopped onion
3 tablespoons lemon juice
1 tablespoon minced fresh parsley
1 garlic clove, minced
1/2 teaspoon salt
1/2 teaspoon dried marjoram
1/8 teaspoon pepper
2 pounds boneless pork, cut into 1-inch
   cubes
CUCUMBER YOGURT SAUCE:
1 carton (8 ounces) plain yogurt
1/2 cup chopped cucumber
1 tablespoon chopped onion
1 tablespoon minced fresh parsley
1 teaspoon lemon juice
1/8 teaspoon garlic salt
Pita bread

In a resealable plastic bag or shallow glass container, combine the first eight ingredients; add pork and toss to coat. Seal or cover and refrigerate overnight. Meanwhile, combine sauce ingredients; cover and refrigerate for several hours. Drain pork and discard marinade; thread pork on skewers, leaving a small space between pieces. Grill, uncovered, over medium coals for 8-10 minutes or until the meat is no longer pink, turning frequently. Serve in pita bread with sauce. **Yield:** 6-8 servings.

Sunny Asparagus Tart
(Pictured below)

This tart looks as good as it tastes. The distinctive caraway crust and rich, custard-like filling dotted with tender slices of asparagus make it a dish you'll be proud to serve time after time. —Susan Kuklinski
Delafield, Wisconsin

1-1/2 cups all-purpose flour
  1/2 teaspoon caraway seeds
  1/8 teaspoon salt
    5 tablespoons cold butter (no substitutes)
    2 tablespoons cold shortening
    3 to 5 tablespoons ice water
FILLING:
1-1/2 pounds fresh asparagus
    1 package (3 ounces) cream cheese, softened
    1 egg yolk
    1 cup whipping cream
    3 eggs
  3/4 teaspoon salt
  1/4 teaspoon white pepper
  1/4 pound thinly sliced fully cooked ham, julienned
  1/3 cup grated Parmesan cheese

In a bowl, combine flour, caraway and salt; cut in butter and shortening until the mixture resembles coarse crumbs. Sprinkle with water, 1 tablespoon at a time; stir with a fork until dough can be formed into a ball. On a floured surface, roll dough to fit a 10-in. tart pan. Place dough in pan. Freeze for 10 minutes. Cut the asparagus into 2-1/2-in. pieces. Set tips aside; cut remaining pieces in half. Cook all of the asparagus in a small amount of water until crisp-tender, about 3-4 minutes; drain. In a mixing bowl, combine the cream cheese and egg yolk; gradually add cream (mixture will be slightly lumpy). Beat in eggs, one at a time. Add salt and pepper. Place ham and asparagus pieces (not tips) over crust; pour half of the cream cheese mixture over the top. Bake at 425° for 15 minutes. Pour the remaining cream cheese mixture over top. Arrange asparagus tips on top of tart; sprinkle with cheese. Bake at 375° for 40 minutes or until a knife inserted near the center comes out clean. Let stand for 15 minutes before cutting. **Yield:** 6-8 servings.

Asparagus Tip
Asparagus is best cooked the day it is purchased, but it will keep in the refrigerator for up to 3 days.

Crispy Fried Chicken

Family and friends can't get enough of my version of "picnic chicken". This chicken is delicious hot or cold. —Jeanne Schnitzler, Lima, Montana

    4 cups all-purpose flour, *divided*
    2 tablespoons garlic salt
    1 tablespoon paprika
    1 tablespoon pepper, *divided*
2-1/2 teaspoons poultry seasoning
    2 eggs
1-1/2 cups water
    1 teaspoon salt
    2 broiler-fryer chickens (3-1/2 to 4 pounds *each*), cut up
Cooking oil for deep-fat frying

In a large resealable plastic bag or shallow bowl, combine 2-2/3 cups flour, garlic salt, paprika, 2-1/2 teaspoons pepper and poultry seasoning. In another bowl, beat eggs and water; add salt and remaining flour and pepper. Dip chicken in egg mixture, then shake or dredge in flour mixture. In a deep-fat fryer, heat oil to 365°. Fry chicken, several pieces at a time, turning once, for about 10 minutes or until the chicken is golden brown and crispy and the juices run clear. Drain on paper towels. **Yield:** 8 servings.

Spiced Pork Chops

This is one of my favorite creations that I'm happy to share with you. These pork chops cooked in cider are so tender you can cut them with a fork. —Jim Wick
Orlando, Florida

1/4 cup all-purpose flour
1/2 teaspoon ground mustard
1/4 teaspoon pepper
1/8 teaspoon ground allspice
  4 pork loin chops (1-1/2 inches thick)
  2 tablespoons cooking oil
1-1/2 cups apple cider
  2 tablespoons brown sugar
  2 medium tart apples, peeled and sliced
1/3 cup raisins
1/2 teaspoon ground cinnamon
Hot buttered noodles, optional
1/2 teaspoon caraway seeds, optional

Combine the flour, mustard, pepper and allspice; dredge the pork chops, reserving remaining flour mixture. In a skillet, brown chops in oil. Remove to a 2-qt. baking dish. To the drippings, add cider, brown sugar and remaining flour mixture; cook and stir until bubbly. Arrange apples and raisins around chops; sprinkle with cinnamon. Pour the cider mixture over all. Cover and bake at 350° for 70 minutes or until pork is no longer pink. If desired, combine noodles and caraway seeds; serve with pork. **Yield:** 4 servings.

—— 🍴 🍴 🍴 ——

Apple-Stuffed Pork Chops

I've been making these delicious extra-thick chops for over 30 years. It's a wonderful entree to serve company and is also savored by our family on special occasions. —Paula Disterhaupt, Glenwood, Iowa

  1 tablespoon chopped onion
1/4 cup butter *or* margarine
  3 cups soft bread cubes
  2 cups finely chopped apples
1/4 cup finely chopped celery
  2 teaspoons minced fresh parsley
3/4 teaspoon salt, *divided*
  6 pork loin chops (1-1/2 inches thick)
1/8 teaspoon pepper
  1 tablespoon cooking oil

In a skillet, saute onion in butter until tender. Remove from the heat; add bread, apples, celery, parsley and 1/4 teaspoon salt. Cut a large pocket in the side of each pork chop; sprinkle the inside and outside with pepper and remaining salt. Spoon stuffing loosely into pockets. In a large skillet, brown the chops on both sides in oil. Place in an ungreased large baking pan. Cover and bake at 350° for 30 minutes. Uncover and bake 30 minutes longer or until meat juices run clear. Make gravy from pan juices if desired. **Yield:** 6 servings.

Homemade Manicotti

(Pictured above)

These tender manicotti are much easier to stuff than the purchased variety. People are amazed when I say I made my own noodles. When my son fixed this recipe for friends, they were impressed with his cooking skills.
—SueAnn Bunt, Painted Post, New York

CREPE NOODLES:
1-1/2 cups all-purpose flour
  1 cup milk
  3 eggs
1/2 teaspoon salt
FILLING:
1-1/2 pounds ricotta cheese
1/4 cup grated Romano cheese
  1 egg
  1 tablespoon minced fresh parsley *or* 1 teaspoon dried parsley flakes
  1 jar (28 ounces) spaghetti sauce
Shredded Romano cheese, optional

Place flour in a bowl; whisk in milk, eggs and salt until smooth. Pour about 2 tablespoons onto a hot greased 8-in. skillet; spread to a 5-in. circle. Cook over medium heat until set; do not brown or turn. Repeat with remaining batter, making 18 crepes. Stack crepes between waxed paper; set aside. For filling, combine cheeses, egg and parsley. Spoon 3-4 tablespoons down the center of each crepe; roll up. Pour half of the spaghetti sauce into an ungreased 13-in. x 9-in. x 2-in. baking dish. Place crepes, seam side down, over the sauce; pour remaining sauce over top. Cover and bake at 350° for 20 minutes. Uncover and bake 20 minutes longer or until heated through. Sprinkle with Romano cheese if desired. **Yield:** 6 servings.

um heat, saute onion and garlic in 3 tablespoons of oil until onion is tender. Add squash; cook until tender. Add 1 teaspoon of salt and pepper; remove from the heat and keep warm. Add remaining oil to skillet; stir-fry chicken with herbs and remaining salt until juices run clear. Place pasta on a serving platter; top with chicken and squash. **Yield:** 8 servings.

Cajun Country Fried Chicken

I've perfected my own Cajun seasoning made from 11 herbs and spices. But in this recipe, a store-bought variety works just as well.
—Dave Fisher
Ten Mile, Tennessee

   2 cups milk
   2 tablespoons Cajun seasoning, *divided*
   8 boneless skinless chicken breast halves
   4 boneless skinless chicken thighs, halved
1-1/4 cups all-purpose flour
 1/2 teaspoon lemon-pepper seasoning
 1/2 teaspoon garlic salt
Cooking oil

In a large bowl, combine milk and 1 tablespoon Cajun seasoning; add chicken. Cover and refrigerate for at least 2 hours. In a large resealable plastic bag, combine flour, lemon pepper, garlic salt and remaining Cajun seasoning. Drain chicken and discard milk mixture. Place chicken in flour mixture and shake to coat. In a skillet, heat 1/4 in. of oil; fry chicken for 7-8 minutes or until juices run clear. **Yield:** 8-10 servings.

Oatmeal Waffles

Our grandkids visit for a week at a time during school breaks and summer vacations. This recipe gives our morning meals some variety and gets the kids to eat nutritious oatmeal. —Lee Hill-Nelson, Waco, Texas

1-1/2 cups quick-cooking oats
 1/2 cup whole wheat flour
   1 teaspoon baking soda
   1 teaspoon sugar
 1/2 teaspoon salt
   2 cups buttermilk
   2 eggs
   2 tablespoons butter *or* margarine, melted
Peanut butter *and/or* applesauce, optional

In a bowl, combine the first five ingredients. In another bowl, combine buttermilk, eggs and butter; stir into the dry ingredients until smooth. Bake

Pasta with Chicken and Squash

(Pictured above)

This is a special dish that we enjoy often. A bed of noodles is covered with a creamy cheese sauce, tender squash and strips of chicken that've been stir-fried with flavorful herbs. It's delicious and pretty, too!
—Pam Hall, Elizabeth City, North Carolina

   1 package (16 ounces) spiral pasta
   2 cups whipping cream
   1 tablespoon butter *or* margarine
   2 cups (8 ounces) shredded Mexican cheese blend *or* cheddar cheese
   1 small onion, chopped
   1 garlic clove, minced
   5 tablespoons olive *or* vegetable oil, *divided*
   2 medium zucchini, julienned
   2 medium yellow summer squash, julienned
1-1/4 teaspoons salt, *divided*
 1/8 teaspoon pepper
   1 pound boneless skinless chicken breasts, julienned
 1/4 teaspoon *each* dried basil, marjoram and savory
 1/4 teaspoon dried rosemary, crushed
 1/8 teaspoon rubbed sage

Cook pasta according to package directions. Meanwhile, heat cream and butter in a large saucepan until butter melts. Add cheese; cook and stir until melted. Rinse and drain pasta; add to cheese mixture. Cover and keep warm. In a skillet over medi-

in a preheated waffle iron according to manufacturer's directions until golden brown. Serve with peanut butter and/or applesauce if desired. **Yield:** 6-8 waffles (6-1/2 inches).

Low-Fat Fettuccine

This dish has a delightful combination of noodles, ham, cheese and vegetables in a creamy sauce. Best of all, since it's so quick to prepare, I can make it from scratch even on days when I get home from work close to dinnertime. —*Andrea Buchmann, Orlando, Florida*

✓ This tasty dish uses less sugar, salt and fat. Recipe includes *Diabetic Exchanges.*

   1 package (12 ounces) fettuccine
   1 cup chicken broth
   2 garlic cloves, minced
   1 cup quartered fresh mushrooms
1/2 cup thinly sliced green onions
   4 ounces cream cheese, cubed
   4 ounces fully cooked ham, cubed
   1 cup quartered cherry tomatoes
1/2 cup grated Parmesan cheese
1/4 teaspoon white pepper

Cook fettuccine according to package directions. Meanwhile, in a saucepan over medium heat, bring broth and garlic to a boil. Add mushrooms and onions; reduce heat. Simmer, uncovered, for 3-5 minutes or until mushrooms are tender. Add cream cheese and ham; cook and stir until cheese is melted. Add tomatoes; heat through. Remove from the heat; stir in Parmesan cheese and pepper. Rinse and drain fettuccine; top with sauce. **Yield:** 5 servings. **Diabetic Exchanges:** One 1/2-cup serving of sauce (prepared with low-sodium broth, fat-free cream cheese and low-fat ham, and calculated without fettuccine) equals 1-1/2 lean meat, 1 vegetable; also, 118 calories, 648 mg sodium, 22 mg cholesterol, 6 gm carbohydrate, 13 gm protein, 5 gm fat.

Asparagus Lasagna
(Pictured at right)

Our family had an asparagus farm during the Depression. My brother and I picked and sorted spears after school and on weekends...and, needless to say, we ate this vegetable quite often. This is one of the best ways Mother fixed it. —*Jane Galvin Englewood, Florida*

✓ This tasty dish uses less sugar, salt and fat. Recipe includes *Diabetic Exchanges.*

   1 pound fresh asparagus, trimmed
   2 garlic cloves, minced
1/2 teaspoon dried thyme
   2 tablespoons butter *or* margarine
   2 tablespoons all-purpose flour
1-1/3 cups milk
Pepper to taste
   5 lasagna noodles, cooked and drained
   1 cup (4 ounces) shredded mozzarella cheese
   1 cup julienned fully cooked ham

In a skillet, cook asparagus in a small amount of water until crisp-tender, about 6-8 minutes; drain and set aside. In a saucepan over medium heat, saute garlic and thyme in butter. Stir in flour. Gradually whisk in milk; cook and stir for 2 minutes or until thickened. Add pepper. Cut noodles in half; place four noodles in a greased 11-in. x 7-in. x 2-in. baking dish. Layer a third of the white sauce, mozzarella cheese, ham and asparagus over noodles. Top with three noodles and another layer of sauce, cheese, ham and asparagus. Repeat layers. Cover and bake at 350° for 30 minutes or until heated through. **Yield:** 4 servings. **Diabetic Exchanges:** One serving (prepared with margarine, skim milk, part-skim mozzarella and low-fat ham) equals 2 starch, 2 meat, 1 vegetable, 1 fat; also, 358 calories, 745 mg sodium, 34 mg cholesterol, 38 gm carbohydrate, 24 gm protein, 13 gm fat.

Roasts Have Real Appeal

ROASTS are at the heart of home cooking. A savory cut of meat seasoned and slowly cooked always makes a memorable meal…and the aroma can be almost as satisfying as that first delicious bite!

— 🍺 🍺 🍺 —

Autumn Pot Roast

(Pictured below)

Fork-tender and hearty, this beef pot roast is an old-fashioned stick-to-your-ribs main dish.
— *Shirley Kidd, New London, Minnesota*

   1 garlic clove, minced
   2 tablespoons cooking oil
   1 boneless rump roast (5 to 6 pounds)
   3 tablespoons cider *or* red wine vinegar
1/2 cup tomato juice
   2 tablespoons ketchup
   1 tablespoon sugar
   2 teaspoons salt
1/4 teaspoon pepper
   8 medium carrots, cut into thirds
1/2 pound small whole onions

1/2 cup all-purpose flour
   1 cup cold water
Salt and pepper to taste

In a Dutch oven over medium heat, saute garlic in oil for 1 minute. Add roast; brown on all sides. Combine vinegar, tomato juice, ketchup, sugar, salt and pepper; pour over roast. Cover and simmer for 2 hours. Add carrots and onions; cover and cook for 1 hour or until meat and vegetables are tender. Remove to a serving platter and keep warm. Skim fat from pan juices. Add water to juices to measure 3 cups. Mix flour and cold water until smooth; stir into pan juices. Bring to a boil; cook and stir for 2 minutes. Season with salt and pepper. Slice roast; serve with vegetables and gravy. **Yield:** 14-16 servings.

— 🍺 🍺 🍺 —

Roast Leg of Lamb

(Pictured below)

This lamb is perfect for a special dinner. A simple herb mixture provides an irresistible flavor.
— *Sharon Cusson, Augusta, Maine*

WHEN COMPANY'S COMING, treat them to hearty helpings of Roast Leg of Lamb, Autumn Pot Roast or Oktoberfest Roast Pork (shown above, top to bottom). Your family will rave about these roasts, too.

1 leg of lamb (6 to 9 pounds), trimmed
2 garlic cloves, minced
1/2 teaspoon dried thyme
1/2 teaspoon dried marjoram
1/2 teaspoon dried oregano
1/4 teaspoon salt
1/8 teaspoon pepper
1 teaspoon vegetable oil

Place roast on a rack in a shallow roasting pan. Cut 12-14 slits 1/2 in. deep in roast. Combine garlic, thyme, marjoram, oregano, salt and pepper; spoon 2 teaspoons into slits. Brush roast with oil; rub with remaining herb mixture. Bake, uncovered, at 325° for 2-3 hours or until meat reaches desired doneness (for rare, a meat thermometer should read 140°; medium, 160°; well-done, 170°). Let stand 10-15 minutes before slicing. **Yield:** 10-12 servings.

Oktoberfest Roast Pork

(Pictured below left)

We especially enjoy this roast at our own Oktoberfest dinner. There are never any leftovers. Everyone enjoys its authentic German flavor. —Carol Stevens
Basye, Virginia

✓ This tasty dish uses less sugar, salt and fat. Recipe includes *Diabetic Exchanges*.

1 pound dry navy beans
1 teaspoon rubbed sage
1 teaspoon salt, optional
1/2 teaspoon pepper
1/8 teaspoon ground allspice
Dash cayenne pepper
1 boneless rolled pork loin roast (3 pounds)
2 tablespoons cooking oil
2 tablespoons chopped fresh parsley
1/2 cup chicken broth
2 medium tart apples, cut into wedges
1 large red onion, cut into wedges

Place beans in a Dutch oven or soup kettle; add water to cover by 2 in. Bring to a boil; boil for 2 minutes. Remove from the heat; cover and let stand for 1 hour. Meanwhile, combine sage, salt if desired, pepper, allspice and cayenne; rub over roast. In a Dutch oven, brown roast in oil on all sides; drain. Drain beans and discard liquid; stir parsley into beans. Place beans around roast. Stir in broth. Cover and simmer for 2 hours or until a meat thermometer reads 150°. Place the apples and onions on top of beans; cover and simmer for 30 minutes or until beans are tender and meat thermometer reads 160°-170°. Let stand 10-15 minutes before slicing. **Yield:** 12 servings. **Diabetic Exchanges:**

One serving with 1/2 cup of cooked beans (prepared without salt) equals 3 meat, 1 starch; also, 304 calories, 83 mg sodium, 70 mg cholesterol, 14 gm carbohydrate, 27 gm protein, 15 gm fat.

Herbed Sirloin Tip

I count on this recipe for family feasts as well as company suppers. It's simple to prepare and delicious every time. —Janice Connelley, Mountain City, Nevada

2 teaspoons salt
1/2 teaspoon garlic salt
1/2 teaspoon celery salt
1/2 teaspoon dried rosemary, crushed
1/4 teaspoon *each* pepper, onion powder and paprika
1/8 teaspoon dill weed
1/8 teaspoon rubbed sage
1 sirloin tip roast (about 2 pounds)

Combine seasonings; rub over entire roast. Cover and refrigerate for at least 2 hours. Place roast on a rack in a roasting pan. Bake, uncovered, at 425° for 40-60 minutes or until meat reaches desired doneness (for rare, a meat thermometer should read 140°; medium-rare, 150°; well-done, 170°). Let stand for 10-15 minutes before slicing. **Yield:** 6-8 servings.

Smoky Chuck Roast

Most folks agree that roasts represent true country-style cooking. You get big outdoor barbecue flavor indoors with this version. —Myra Innes, Auburn, Kansas

1/4 cup water
1 tablespoon liquid smoke, optional
1 tablespoon brown sugar
1 teaspoon celery salt
1 teaspoon onion salt
1/2 teaspoon ground nutmeg
1/2 teaspoon mustard seed
1/4 teaspoon pepper
1 boneless chuck roast (2 to 3 pounds)
1/4 cup barbecue sauce

In a large resealable plastic bag or shallow container, combine the first eight ingredients. Add roast. Seal bag or cover container; refrigerate for 8 hours, turning once. Drain; discard marinade. Place roast in a greased 2-1/2-qt. baking pan. Cover and bake at 325° for 1-1/2 to 2 hours. Baste with barbecue sauce. Bake, uncovered, 10-20 minutes longer or until beef is fork-tender. **Yield:** 4-6 servings.

Curried Beef-Stuffed Squash

(Pictured below)

My husband and I look forward to this dinner. The savory beef tucked inside tender acorn squash halves is a satisfying autumn combination. Plus, it's a lighter entree and very flavorful. —Edna Lee
Greeley, Colorado

- 3 medium acorn squash (about 1 pound *each*), halved and seeded
- 1 pound ground beef
- 1/2 cup chopped onion
- 2 garlic cloves, minced
- 1 teaspoon beef bouillon granules
- 1/2 cup hot water
- 1/2 cup cooked rice
- 2 tablespoons chopped fresh parsley
- 1 tablespoon orange juice concentrate
- 1 teaspoon brown sugar
- 1 teaspoon curry powder
- 1/2 teaspoon ground ginger
- 1/4 teaspoon salt

Invert squash in a greased 15-in. x 10-in. x 1-in. baking pan. Bake, uncovered, at 350° for 35-45 minutes or until almost tender. Meanwhile, in a skillet, cook beef, onion and garlic until meat is browned and onion is tender; drain. Dissolve bouillon in water; add to skillet. Stir in remaining ingredients; mix well. Turn squash cut side up in pan and fill with meat mixture. Fill pan with hot water to a depth of 1/4 in.; cover loosely with foil. Bake at 350° for 20-30 minutes or until heated through. **Yield:** 6 servings.

— ☕ ☕ ☕ —

Chicken Rosemary

This chicken frequently appears on my dinner table. Leftovers—if there are any—are excellent for sandwiches the next day. Friends and family are always surprised to hear how a few everyday ingredients can liven up ordinary baked chicken. —Emily Chaney
Penobscot, Maine

- 4 boneless skinless chicken breast halves
- 2 to 3 tablespoons Dijon mustard
- 1/2 teaspoon garlic powder
- 2 tablespoons minced fresh rosemary *or* 2 teaspoons dried rosemary, crushed

Pepper to taste
- 1/2 cup grated Parmesan cheese

Place chicken in a greased 11-in. x 7-in. x 2-in. baking dish. Combine mustard and garlic powder; spread over the chicken. Sprinkle with rosemary and pepper. Top with cheese. Bake, uncovered, at 350° for 45 minutes or until juices run clear. **Yield:** 4 servings.

— ☕ ☕ ☕ —

Pizza Meat Loaf

Our two girls refused to eat meat loaf. But when I modified my recipe by adding pizza sauce to the meat mixture and covering the loaf with sauce and mozzarella cheese, they couldn't get enough! My husband and I enjoy it, too. —Loy Acerra Crane
Jackson, Tennessee

- 2 eggs, lightly beaten
- 1 can (8 ounces) pizza sauce, *divided*
- 1 cup saltine crumbs
- 1/2 cup grated Parmesan cheese
- 1/2 cup mozzarella cheese, *divided*
- 1/2 cup chopped onion
- 1/4 cup chopped green pepper
- 1 teaspoon seasoned salt
- 1 teaspoon dried oregano
- 1/4 teaspoon pepper
- 2 pounds ground beef

Additional pizza sauce, warmed, optional

In a bowl, combine eggs, 3/4 cup of pizza sauce, crumbs, Parmesan cheese, 1/4 cup of mozzarella

cheese, onion, green pepper, salt, oregano and pepper. Add beef; mix well. Pat into a greased 8-in. square baking dish. Bake at 350° for 50 minutes. Drain. Spread remaining pizza sauce over loaf; bake 10 minutes more. Sprinkle with remaining mozzarella; return to the oven for 3-4 minutes or until the cheese melts. Serve with additional pizza sauce if desired. **Yield:** 8-10 servings.

— 🍷 🍷 🍷 —

Steak with Creamy Peppercorn Sauce

My wife, Marilynn, and I both love spicy foods. This is one of her favorite dishes. I've been cooking it as a treat on her birthday for years. —David Collin
Martinez, California

2 to 3 tablespoons whole black peppercorns, crushed
1-1/2 teaspoons white pepper
4 New York strip steaks (about 12 ounces *each*)
1 teaspoon salt
1/4 cup butter *or* margarine, melted
1/4 cup Worcestershire sauce
1 teaspoon hot pepper sauce
1/4 cup half-and-half cream

Combine peppercorns and pepper; rub over both sides of steaks. Refrigerate for 1 hour. Sprinkle the salt in a large skillet; heat on high until salt begins to brown. Add steaks and sear on both sides. Add butter; reduce heat to medium-high. Cook steaks for 1-2 minutes on each side. Add Worcestershire and hot pepper sauce; cook each side 2-3 minutes longer or until meat is done as desired. Remove steaks and keep warm. Add cream to the skillet; cook and stir until smooth. Serve over steaks. **Yield:** 4 servings. **Editors' Note:** 1 tablespoon of whole green peppercorns can be substituted for 1 tablespoon of the black peppercorns; 1 tablespoon of whole white peppercorns (crushed) can be used in place of the white pepper.

— 🍷 🍷 🍷 —

Rabbit Breakfast Sausage

(Pictured above right)

As a palate-pleasing alternative to traditional pork sausage, my husband and I created this lower-fat version. It's moist, flavorful and delicious. We especially enjoy it for breakfast or brunch. —Carol Heuschkel
Winsted, Connecticut

1 dressed and boned rabbit (6 pounds), cut up
2 teaspoons salt

1-1/2 teaspoons rubbed sage
1-1/4 teaspoons white pepper
3/4 teaspoon ground nutmeg
1/2 teaspoon ground cinnamon
1 cup finely chopped peeled tart apple
2 tablespoons cooking oil

In a bowl, combine the first six ingredients; mix well. Cover and refrigerate overnight. In a meat grinder or food processor, process the mixture in small batches until coarsely ground. Stir in apple. Shape into 16 patties, 3 in. each. Heat the oil in a skillet; cook patties over medium heat for 5 minutes on each side or until sausage is browned and inside is no longer pink. **Yield:** 8 servings.

Trouble Grinding Meat?

Freeze cut-up meat in a single layer for about 45 minutes. You'll find the meat will go through the grinder perfectly.

cook beef, onion and green pepper until meat is browned and vegetables are tender; drain. Add mushrooms, garlic, basil, oregano, salt and pepper; cook and stir for 2 minutes. Add tomatoes; cook and stir for 2 minutes. Add squash; mix well. Cook, uncovered, until liquid has evaporated, about 10 minutes. Fill shells; place in a shallow baking dish. Bake, uncovered, at 350° for 15 minutes. Sprinkle with cheese; return to the oven for 5 minutes or until cheese is melted. **Yield:** 4-6 side-dish servings or 2 main-dish servings.

Spaghetti Squash Boats

(Pictured above)

Several fresh tasty ingredients go together in this recipe to make a spectacular summer supper. Spaghetti squash has an interesting texture that's lots of fun.
—*Vickey Lorenger, Detroit, Michigan*

> 1 medium spaghetti squash (2 to 2-1/2 pounds)
> 1/4 pound ground beef
> 1/2 cup chopped onion
> 1/2 cup chopped green pepper
> 1/2 cup sliced fresh mushrooms
> 1 garlic clove, minced
> 1/2 teaspoon dried basil
> 1/2 teaspoon dried oregano
> 1/4 teaspoon salt
> 1/8 teaspoon pepper
> 1 can (14-1/2 ounces) diced tomatoes, drained
> 1/3 cup shredded mozzarella cheese

Cut squash in half lengthwise; scoop out seeds. Place squash, cut side down, in a baking dish. Fill pan with hot water to a depth of 1/2 in. Bake, uncovered, at 375° for 30-40 minutes or until tender. When cool enough to handle, scoop out the squash, separating strands with a fork; set shells and squash aside. In a skillet over medium heat,

Pasta with Marinara Sauce

Why settle for typical marinara sauce when you can make this homemade marinara? It's quite simple to prepare, but folks will think you fussed all day.
—*Diane Hixon, Niceville, Florida*

> 2 garlic cloves, sliced
> 1/3 cup olive *or* vegetable oil
> 3 tablespoons minced fresh parsley
> 3 tablespoons minced onion
> 1 can (28 ounces) diced tomatoes, undrained
> 2 bay leaves
> Pinch salt and pepper
> 1 tablespoon chopped fresh basil
> Hot cooked pasta

In a large saucepan over medium heat, saute garlic in oil for 3 minutes. Add parsley, onion, tomatoes, bay leaves, salt and pepper; bring to a boil. Reduce heat; cover and simmer for 15 minutes. Add basil. Serve over pasta. **Yield:** 4 servings.

Hurray for Horseradish!

Next time you cook a pot roast, try spreading a thin layer of horseradish on top. This simple ingredient helps tenderize the meat and gives a little zip. Plus, it makes wonderful gravy.

Butternut Sausage Puff

(Pictured at far right)

Any brunch is extra-special when this hearty souffle is included. The thyme and sausage are perfect complements to the delicately sweet butternut squash.
—*Betty Humiston, Greenwich, New York*

> 2 cups hot mashed butternut squash
> 3 eggs, *separated*
> 1/4 cup all-purpose flour

'I Wish I Had That Recipe...'

"THE BEST-TASTING DISH I've ever eaten at any restaurant is Colonial Game Pie at Braddock's Tavern in Medford, New Jersey," notes Andrea Gray of Marlton Lakes, New Jersey.

Special events coordinator Kathleen Cooper shares the recipe. "It's from the early 1800's and was found in the attic of this historic hotel with the first innkeeper's registry," she reveals.

Located at 39 S. Main St. in Medford, Braddock's Tavern serves lunch Monday-Friday 11:30 a.m. to 2:30 p.m. and dinner 5:30 to 10 p.m.; Saturday dinner from 5 to 10 p.m.; Sunday brunch from 11 a.m. to 2:30 p.m. and dinner 4 to 9 p.m.; 1-609/654-1604.

Colonial Game Pie

1/2 **pound sliced bacon, diced**
2-1/2 **pounds beef stew meat, cubed**
2 **cans (14-1/2 ounces** *each***) beef broth**
1/2 **cup red currant jelly**
2 **dressed rabbits (about 3 pounds** *each***), cut up**
1 **can (14-1/2 ounces) chicken broth**
1/4 **cup Worcestershire sauce**
1 **bay leaf**
1 **teaspoon salt**
1/4 **teaspoon pepper**
1/4 **teaspoon cayenne pepper**
1/4 **pound pearl onions**
2 **medium carrots, diced**
2 **medium potatoes, diced**
1/2 **cup sliced fresh mushrooms**
1 **dressed duck (4-1/2 pounds), cut up**
6 **tablespoons all-purpose flour**
3/4 **cup cold water**
1 **package (17-1/4 ounces) frozen puff pastry, thawed**

In a kettle, cook bacon until crisp; drain, reserving bacon and 1/4 cup drippings in pan. Brown beef in drippings. Add beef broth and jelly; cover and simmer for 45 minutes. Meanwhile, cover rabbits with water in a stockpot; simmer for 1 hour or until meat falls from bones. Remove meat; set aside (discard bones). To beef mixture, add chicken broth, Worcestershire sauce, bay leaf, salt, pepper and cayenne; simmer for 20 minutes. Add onions, carrots, potatoes and mushrooms; simmer for 20 minutes or until tender. Remove bay leaf. In another pot, cover duck with water; simmer until the meat nearly falls from the bones. Remove meat; set aside (discard bones). Mix flour and water until smooth; stir into beef mixture. Cook until thickened and bubbly. Add rabbit and duck. Cut puff pastry into 3-in. squares; place on a greased baking sheet. Bake at 400° for 10-12 minutes or until puffed and golden. Place on individual servings of meat mixture. **Yield:** 16 servings.

1/4 **cup minced fresh parsley**
2 **tablespoons butter** *or* **margarine**
2 **teaspoons finely chopped onion**
2 **teaspoons lemon juice**
1/2 **teaspoon dried thyme**
1/4 **teaspoon salt**
1/2 **pound bulk pork sausage, cooked and drained**
Fresh thyme, optional

In a bowl, combine squash, egg yolks, flour, parsley, butter, onion, lemon juice, thyme and salt; mix until well blended. Stir in sausage. Cool for 10 minutes. In a small mixing bowl, beat egg whites until stiff peaks form; fold into squash mixture. Pour into a greased and floured 2-qt. baking dish. Bake, uncovered, at 375° for 45-50 minutes or until a knife inserted near the center comes out clean. Garnish with thyme if desired. **Yield:** 4-6 servings.

Breads, Coffee Cakes & Muffins

Welcome your family home with the enticing aroma of these homemade quick breads, coffee cakes, yeast breads and muffins.

OVEN-FRESH FAVORITES. Clockwise from upper left: Cinnamon Swirl Orange Bread (p. 102), Buttercup Squash Coffee Cake (p. 109), English Muffin Loaves (p. 103) and Cranberry Sweet Potato Muffins (p. 106).

Cranberry Nut Bread

(Pictured above)

I created this recipe 14 years ago by combining a couple of recipes from my collection. There's a big burst of tart cranberry and lots of crunchy nuts in every piece.
—*Dawn Lowenstein, Hatboro, Pennsylvania*

　　2　cups all-purpose flour
　　1　cup sugar
1-1/2　teaspoons baking powder
　　1　teaspoon salt
　1/2　teaspoon baking soda
　1/4　cup butter *or* margarine
　　1　egg
　3/4　cup orange juice
　　1　tablespoon grated orange peel
1-1/2　cups fresh *or* frozen cranberries
　1/2　cup chopped walnuts

In a bowl, combine flour, sugar, baking powder, salt and baking soda. Cut in butter until mixture resembles coarse crumbs. Beat egg, orange juice and peel; stir into dry ingredients just until blended. Add the cranberries and walnuts. Spoon into a greased and floured 8-in. x 4-in. x 2-in. loaf pan. Bake at 350° for 65-70 minutes or until a wooden pick inserted near the center comes out clean. Cool in pan 10 minutes before removing to a wire rack to cool completely. **Yield:** 1 loaf.

Garlic Bubble Loaf

This lovely golden loaf has great garlic flavor in every bite. People go wild over this bread whenever I serve it. —*Carol Shields, Summerville, Pennsylvania*

　1/4　cup butter *or* margarine, melted
　　1　tablespoon dried parsley flakes
　　1　teaspoon garlic powder
　1/4　teaspoon garlic salt
　　1　loaf (1 pound) frozen white bread dough, thawed

In a bowl, combine butter, parsley, garlic powder and garlic salt. Cut dough into 1-in. pieces; dip into butter mixture. Layer in a greased 9-in. x 5-in. x 3-in. loaf pan. Cover and let rise until doubled, about 1 hour. Bake at 350° for 30 minutes or until golden brown. **Yield:** 1 loaf.

Cinnamon Coffee Puffs

These muffins are good with breakfast, lunch or supper and are sure to become favorites of your entire family. —*Sharon Mensing, Greenfield, Iowa*

　1/3　cup butter *or* margarine, softened
　1/2　cup sugar
　　1　egg
　1/2　cup milk
1-1/2　cups all-purpose flour
1-1/2　teaspoons baking powder
　1/2　teaspoon salt
　1/4　teaspoon ground nutmeg
TOPPING:
　1/4　cup butter *or* margarine
　1/2　cup sugar
　　1　teaspoon ground cinnamon

In a mixing bowl, cream butter and sugar; beat in egg and milk. Combine flour, baking powder, salt and nutmeg; stir into creamed mixture (batter will be stiff). Fill greased or paper-lined muffin cups two-thirds full. Bake at 350° for 15-20 minutes or until muffins test done. Meanwhile, melt butter and combine sugar and cinnamon. Remove muffins from oven; immediately dip tops in butter, then in cinnamon-sugar. **Yield:** about 1 dozen.

Basil Dinner Rolls

People's taste buds are thrilled with the "surprise" inside each of these rolls—basil, Parmesan cheese and walnuts. —*Mary Kay Dixson, Decatur, Alabama*

　　7　to 7-1/2 cups all-purpose flour
　　1　tablespoon sugar
　　2　teaspoons salt
　　1　package (1/4 ounce) active dry yeast
2-1/2　cups warm water (120° to 130°)
　　1　cup chopped fresh basil
　1/4　cup finely chopped walnuts
　1/4　cup grated Parmesan cheese
Melted butter *or* margarine

In a mixing bowl, combine 6 cups of flour, sugar, salt and yeast. Add water; beat until smooth. Add enough remaining flour to form a soft dough. Turn onto a floured surface; knead until smooth and elastic, about 8-10 minutes. Place in a greased bowl, turning once to grease top. Cover and refrigerate overnight. Punch dough down; knead several times. Cover and let rest for 10 minutes. Meanwhile, combine the basil, walnuts and cheese; reserve 2 tablespoons for topping. Shape dough into 32 balls. On a floured surface, roll each ball into a 4-in. circle; place about 1-1/2 to 2 teaspoons of the basil mixture in the center of each. Pinch dough together over filling. Place 16 rolls each, seam side down, on two greased baking sheets with rolls touching. Cover and let rise until doubled, about 45 minutes. Brush tops with butter; sprinkle with reserved basil mixture. Bake at 375° for 25 minutes or until lightly browned. Serve warm. **Yield:** 32 rolls.

New Mexico Corn Bread

I've seen peppers used in a variety of ways, but this corn bread is one of the more traditional.
—*Nancy Hill, Edgewood, New Mexico*

      1 **cup yellow cornmeal**
      1 **tablespoon baking powder**
    3/4 **teaspoon salt**
      1 **cup cream-style corn**
      1 **cup (8 ounces) sour cream**
    2/3 **cup butter *or* margarine, melted**
      2 **eggs**
      1 **cup (4 ounces) shredded cheddar cheese**
      1 **can (4 ounces) chopped green chilies**

In a bowl, combine the cornmeal, baking powder and salt. Combine remaining ingredients. Add to dry ingredients and stir until blended. Pour into a greased 9-in. square baking pan. Bake at 350° for 1 hour or until bread tests done. **Yield:** 9 servings.

Blueberry Tea Bread

When you're looking for a "berry" impressive treat, turn to this recipe. —*Dorothy Simpson*
Blackwood, New Jersey

        2 **cups all-purpose flour**
        1 **cup sugar**
        1 **tablespoon baking powder.**
      1/4 **teaspoon salt**
    1-1/2 **cups fresh *or* frozen blueberries**
        1 **teaspoon grated orange peel**
        2 **eggs**
        1 **cup milk**
        3 **tablespoons vegetable oil**
Whipped cream cheese, optional

In a bowl, combine flour, sugar, baking powder and salt. Stir in blueberries and orange peel. In another bowl, beat the eggs; add milk and oil. Stir into dry ingredients just until moistened. Pour into a greased 9-in. x 5-in. x 3-in. loaf pan. Bake at 350° for 1 hour or until a toothpick inserted near the center comes out clean. Cool in pan for 10 minutes; remove to a wire rack to cool completely. Serve with cream cheese if desired. **Yield:** 1 loaf.

Poppy Seed Mini Muffins

(Pictured below)

These moist muffins may be small, but they're always a big hit on a brunch buffet or as a quick snack.
—*Kathryn Anderson, Casper, Wyoming*

      2 **cups all-purpose flour**
    3/4 **cup sugar**
      1 **teaspoon baking powder**
      1 **teaspoon baking soda**
    1/4 **teaspoon salt**
      1 **cup (8 ounces) sour cream**
    1/2 **cup vegetable oil**
      2 **eggs**
      2 **tablespoons poppy seeds**
      2 **tablespoons milk**
    1/2 **teaspoon vanilla extract**
    1/2 **teaspoon lemon extract**

In a large bowl, combine the flour, sugar, baking powder, baking soda and salt; set aside. Combine remaining ingredients; mix well. Stir into dry ingredients just until moistened. Fill greased or paper-lined mini-muffin cups two-thirds full. Bake at 400° for 12-15 minutes or until muffins test done. Cool in pan 10 minutes before removing to a wire rack. **Yield:** about 3-1/2 dozen.

Cinnamon Swirl Orange Bread

(Pictured below)

The tempting aroma as this bread's baking makes everybody eager for a thick slice of this yummy treat.
—Linda Eager, Harlan, Indiana

      1 package (1/4 ounce) active dry yeast
  1/4 cup warm water (110° to 115°)
      1 cup warm milk (110° to 115°)
  3/4 cup orange juice
  1/2 cup sugar
  1/4 cup shortening
      1 tablespoon grated orange peel
1-1/2 teaspoons salt
6-1/4 to 6-3/4 cups all-purpose flour
      1 egg, lightly beaten
FILLING:
  1/2 cup sugar
      2 to 3 teaspoons ground cinnamon
      2 teaspoons water
GLAZE:
      1 cup confectioners' sugar
      4 teaspoons orange juice
      1 teaspoon grated orange peel

Dissolve yeast in water. In a mixing bowl, combine milk, orange juice, sugar, shortening, peel and salt. Add 2 cups flour, yeast mixture and egg; mix well. Add enough remaining flour to form a soft dough. Turn onto a floured board and knead until smooth and elastic, about 8-10 minutes. Place in a greased bowl, turning once to grease top. Cover and let rise in a warm place until doubled, about 1-1/4 hours. Punch dough down and divide in half. Cover and let rest for 10 minutes. Roll each half into a 15-in. x 7-in. rectangle. For filling, combine sugar and cinnamon; sprinkle over each rectangle. Sprinkle each with 1 teaspoon water. Roll up, jelly-roll style, starting with a short end. Seal edges.

Place with sealed edge down in two greased 8-in. x 4-in. x 2-in. loaf pans. Cover and let rise until doubled, about 1 hour. Bake at 350° for 30-35 minutes or until golden brown. Remove from pan and cool on wire racks. Combine glaze ingredients; spread over loaves. **Yield:** 2 loaves.

— 🥄 🥄 🥄 —

Double Chocolate Banana Muffins

Combining two great flavors makes these moist muffins doubly good. I like to keep several batches in the freezer for drop-in guests.
—Donna Brockett
Kingfisher, Oklahoma

1-1/2 cups all-purpose flour
      1 cup sugar
  1/4 cup baking cocoa
      1 teaspoon baking soda
  1/2 teaspoon salt
  1/4 teaspoon baking powder
1-1/3 cups mashed ripe bananas (2 to 3 medium)
  1/3 cup vegetable oil
      1 egg
      1 cup (6 ounces) miniature semisweet chocolate chips

In a large bowl, combine the first six ingredients. In a small bowl, combine bananas, oil and egg; stir into dry ingredients just until moistened. Fold in chocolate chips. Fill greased or paper-lined muffin cups three-fourths full. Bake at 350° for 20-25 minutes or until muffins test done. **Yield:** about 1 dozen.

— 🥄 🥄 🥄 —

Corn Bread Muffins

I've worked in a cafeteria for over 20 years. I have come across quite a few corn bread recipes, and these muffins are some of the best I've ever tasted.
—Louise Rowe, Piqua, Ohio

✓ This tasty dish uses less sugar, salt and fat. Recipe includes *Diabetic Exchanges.*

1-1/2 cups yellow cornmeal
  1/2 cup all-purpose flour
      2 tablespoons sugar
      2 teaspoons baking powder
  1/2 teaspoon baking soda
  1/2 teaspoon salt
1-1/4 cups buttermilk
  1/4 cup unsweetened applesauce
      2 egg whites
      2 tablespoons vegetable oil

In a large bowl, combine the first six ingredients. Combine buttermilk, applesauce, egg whites and

oil; stir into the dry ingredients just until moistened. Fill greased or paper-lined muffin cups two-thirds full. Bake at 400° for 18-20 minutes or until muffins test done. Cool in pan 10 minutes before removing to a wire rack. **Yield:** 1 dozen. **Diabetic Exchanges:** One muffin equals 1 starch, 1 fat; also, 118 calories, 264 mg sodium, 1 mg cholesterol, 20 gm carbohydrate, 3 gm protein, 3 gm fat.

Easy Banana Bread

I watch several youngsters each day while their parents are at work. They come running when I announce it's time to cook. This bread is one of their favorite treats to help bake and eat. —*Sharon Ward*
King Ferry, New York

    1/3 cup shortening
    1/2 cup sugar
      2 eggs
  1-3/4 cups all-purpose flour
      1 teaspoon baking powder
    1/2 teaspoon baking soda
    1/2 teaspoon salt
      1 cup mashed ripe bananas (2 to 3 medium)

In a mixing bowl, cream shortening and sugar. Add eggs; mix well. Combine flour, baking powder, baking soda and salt; add to the creamed mixture alternately with bananas, beating well after each addition. Pour into a greased 8-in. x 4-in. x 2-in. loaf pan. Bake at 350° for 50-55 minutes or until a toothpick inserted near the center comes out clean. Let stand for 10 minutes before removing from pan; cool on a wire rack. **Yield:** 1 loaf.

Mini Elephant Ears

Our kids love to help stretch the pieces of convenient frozen dough to make these ears. After I fry them, the kids brush them with butter and sprinkle on the cinnamon-sugar. Then we all dig in! —*Malea Kruse*
Huntertown, Indiana

Frozen white dinner roll dough (10 rolls)
Cooking oil for deep-fat frying
    1/2 cup sugar
      1 tablespoon ground cinnamon
      3 tablespoons butter *or* margarine, melted

Cover the dough with plastic wrap and thaw at room temperature for about 2 hours. Heat oil in an electric skillet or deep-fat fryer to 375°. Combine the sugar and cinnamon; set aside. Stretch each piece of dough into a flat ear shape. Fry, a few at a time, for 1-1/2 minutes per side or until browned. Drain on paper towels. Brush with butter and sprinkle with cinnamon-sugar. **Yield:** 10 servings.

English Muffin Loaves
(Pictured above)

Slices of these festive fruit and nut loaves are a terrific breakfast on a cold morning. The best part is that no kneading is required. I serve one loaf right from the oven and freeze the other or give it as a gift.
—*Roberta Freedman, Mesilla Park, New Mexico*

      5 cups all-purpose flour, *divided*
      2 packages (1/4 ounce *each*) active dry yeast
      2 tablespoons sugar
      2 teaspoons ground cinnamon
      1 teaspoon salt
    1/4 teaspoon baking soda
  1-1/2 cups warm orange juice (120° to 130°)
    1/2 cup warm water (120° to 130°)
    1/4 cup vegetable oil
    1/2 cup chopped pecans
    1/2 cup chopped dried apricots
Cornmeal

In a mixing bowl, combine 2 cups flour, yeast, sugar, cinnamon, salt and baking soda. Add orange juice, water and oil; beat on low speed until moistened. Beat on high for 3 minutes. Stir in the pecans, apricots and remaining flour to form a stiff batter. Do not knead. Grease two 8-in. x 4-in. x 2-in. loaf pans; sprinkle with cornmeal. Spoon batter into pans; sprinkle with cornmeal. Cover and let rise in a warm place until doubled, about 45 minutes. Bake at 350° for 35-40 minutes or until golden brown. Immediately remove from pans to cool on wire racks. Slice and toast. **Yield:** 2 loaves.

Almond Apricot Coffee Cake

(Pictured above)

The nutty aroma and delicate fruit flavor make this cake special enough to serve for company.
—Sharon Mensing, Greenfield, Iowa

- 1 cup butter *or* margarine, softened
- 2 cups sugar
- 3 eggs
- 1 cup (8 ounces) sour cream
- 1 teaspoon almond extract
- 2 cups all-purpose flour
- 1 teaspoon baking powder
- 1/4 teaspoon salt
- 3/4 cup slivered almonds, *divided*
- 1 jar (10 to 12 ounces) apricot preserves, *divided*

In a mixing bowl, cream butter and sugar. Add the eggs, sour cream and extract; mix well. Combine flour, baking powder and salt; add to creamed mixture and mix well. Spread half of the batter in a greased and floured 12-cup fluted tube pan. Sprinkle with half of the almonds. Spread half of the preserves to within 1/2 in. of the edges. Cover with remaining batter. Spoon remaining preserves over batter to within 1/2 in. of edges. Sprinkle with remaining almonds. Bake at 350° for 55-60 minutes or until a toothpick inserted near the center comes out clean. Cool in pan for 15 minutes. Carefully invert onto a serving platter. **Yield:** 12-16 servings.

Graham Streusel Coffee Cake

(Pictured above)

If you're in a real hurry, you can omit the glaze and dust the cake with confectioners' sugar.
—Blanche Whytsell, Arnoldsburg, West Virginia

- 1-1/2 cups graham cracker crumbs
- 3/4 cup packed brown sugar
- 3/4 cup chopped pecans
- 1-1/2 teaspoons ground cinnamon
- 2/3 cup butter *or* margarine, melted
- 1 package (18-1/2 ounces) yellow cake mix
- 1/2 cup confectioners' sugar
- 1 tablespoon milk

Combine the first five ingredients; set aside. Prepare cake mix according to package directions. Pour half of the batter into a greased 13-in. x 9-in. x 2-in. baking pan. Sprinkle with half of the graham cracker mixture. Carefully spoon remaining batter on top. Sprinkle with remaining graham mixture. Bake at 350° for 40-45 minutes or until the cake tests done. Cool on a wire rack. Combine confectioners' sugar and milk; drizzle over cake. **Yield:** 12-16 servings.

PERK UP your mornings with a steaming cup of coffee or cocoa and healthy slices of Almond Apricot Coffee Cake, Cranberry Coffee Cake and Graham Streusel Coffee Cake (shown at left, clockwise from right).

Cranberry Coffee Cake

(Pictured at left)

This is one of the prettiest coffee cakes I've ever seen and also one of the best I've ever tasted.
—Darlene Markel, Sublimity, Oregon

  1 cup butter *or* margarine, softened
  1 cup sugar
  2 eggs
  2 cups all-purpose flour
  1 teaspoon baking powder
  1 teaspoon baking soda
1/2 teaspoon salt
  1 cup (8 ounces) sour cream
  1 teaspoon almond extract
  1 can (16 ounces) whole-berry cranberry
     sauce
1/2 cup chopped walnuts
GLAZE (optional):
1/3 cup confectioners' sugar
  2 to 4 teaspoons warm water
1/2 teaspoon almond extract

In a mixing bowl, cream butter and sugar. Add eggs; mix well. Combine flour, baking powder, baking soda and salt; add to creamed mixture alternately with sour cream. Add extract. Spoon a third of the batter into a greased 9-in. square baking pan. Top with a third of the cranberry sauce. Repeat layers twice. Sprinkle with walnuts. Bake at 350° for 60-65 minutes or until a toothpick inserted near the center comes out clean. If desired, combine glaze ingredients and drizzle over cake. **Yield:** 9 servings.

ꗖ ꗖ ꗖ

Praline Pull-Apart Coffee Cake

I developed this recipe for our church youth fund-raiser. We sold the cakes frozen and ready-to-bake.
—Carol Mead, Los Alamos, New Mexico

  1 package (1/4 ounce) active dry yeast
1/3 cup sugar, *divided*
1-1/2 cups warm water (110° to 115°), *divided*
1/4 cup instant nonfat dry milk powder
1/2 cup butter *or* margarine, softened
  1 teaspoon salt
  5 to 5-1/2 cups all-purpose flour
  2 eggs
TOPPING:
1/2 cup chopped pecans

  1 cup packed brown sugar
  3 tablespoons cornstarch
  2 teaspoons ground cinnamon
  1 teaspoon vanilla extract
1/4 teaspoon salt
3/4 cup butter *or* margarine, melted

In a small bowl, dissolve yeast and 1 teaspoon sugar in 1/4 cup water; set aside. In a mixing bowl, combine milk powder, butter, salt and remaining sugar and water; mix well. Add 2-1/2 cups flour, eggs and yeast mixture; mix well. Add enough remaining flour to form a soft dough. Turn onto a floured surface; knead until smooth and elastic, about 6-8 minutes. Place in a greased bowl, turning once to grease top. Cover and let rise in a warm place until doubled, about 1 hour. Meanwhile, sprinkle pecans in two greased 9-in. round cake pans. Combine brown sugar, cornstarch, cinnamon, vanilla and salt; sprinkle over pecans. Drizzle butter over top. Divide dough in half; shape each half into 16 balls. Place balls over topping. Cover and let rise in a warm place until nearly doubled, about 45 minutes. Bake at 375° for 30 minutes or until golden brown. Let cool for 1 minute; invert onto a serving platter. **Yield:** about 2-1/2 dozen. **Editor's Note:** Coffee cakes may be frozen before baking and thawed for 24 hours in the refrigerator. Place in a cold oven; set oven to 375°. Bake for 35-40 minutes or until browned.

ꗖ ꗖ ꗖ

Mother's Applesauce Muffins

The cinnamon and allspice are nice in these moist muffins. Sometimes I substitute mini chocolate chips for the raisins. —Peggy Burdick, Burlington, Michigan

  4 cups all-purpose flour
  1 tablespoon ground cinnamon
  1 tablespoon ground allspice
  2 teaspoons baking soda
  1 cup butter *or* margarine, softened
  2 cups sugar
  2 eggs
  2 cups applesauce
  2 tablespoons vanilla extract
  1 cup raisins

In a bowl, combine flour, cinnamon, allspice and baking soda; set aside. In a mixing bowl, cream butter and sugar. Beat in eggs, applesauce and vanilla; stir into dry ingredients just until moistened. Fold in raisins. Fill greased or paper-lined muffin cups three-fourths full. Bake at 350° for 20-25 minutes or until muffins test done. Cool in pan for 10 minutes; remove to a wire rack. **Yield:** 2 dozen.

Cranberry Sweet Potato Muffins

(Pictured below)

Bold autumn flavors of sweet potatoes, cranberries and cinnamon give seasonal appeal to these muffins. I recommend them for a change-of-pace treat with a meal, packed into a lunch box or eaten as a snack.
—Diane Musil, Lyons, Illinois

1-1/2 cups all-purpose flour
1/2 cup sugar
2 teaspoons baking powder
3/4 teaspoon salt
1/2 teaspoon ground cinnamon
1/2 teaspoon ground nutmeg
1 egg
1/2 cup milk
1/2 cup cold mashed sweet potatoes (without added butter or milk)
1/4 cup butter *or* margarine, melted
1 cup chopped fresh *or* frozen cranberries
Cinnamon-sugar

In a large bowl, combine flour, sugar, baking powder, salt, cinnamon and nutmeg. In a small bowl, combine egg, milk, sweet potatoes and butter; stir into dry ingredients just until moistened. Stir in cranberries. Fill greased or paper-lined muffin cups half full. Sprinkle with cinnamon-sugar. Bake at 375° for 18-22 minutes or until muffins test done. Cool in pan 10 minutes before removing to a wire rack. **Yield:** 1 dozen.

Carrot Pineapple Bread

Carrots paired with pineapple make a moist quick bread with a slightly tropical taste that's a delicious surprise. —Dorothy Bahlmann, Clarksville, Iowa

3 eggs
2 cups sugar
1 cup vegetable oil
1 cup finely shredded carrots
1 can (8 ounces) crushed pineapple, undrained
2 teaspoons vanilla extract
3 cups all-purpose flour
1-1/2 teaspoons ground cinnamon
1 teaspoon baking soda
1 teaspoon salt

In a mixing bowl, beat eggs, sugar and oil; add carrots, pineapple and vanilla. Combine dry ingredients; beat into the carrot mixture. Pour into two greased 8-in. x 4-in. x 2-in. loaf pans. Bake at 325° for 60-70 minutes or until a toothpick inserted near the center comes out clean. Cool in pans for 10 minutes; remove to a wire rack to cool completely. **Yield:** 2 loaves.

Dilly Parmesan Bread

This recipe originally called for chives. Over the years, I've substituted dill with wonderful results.
—Marian Bell, Cedar Grove, New Jersey

✓ This tasty dish uses less sugar, salt and fat. Recipe includes *Diabetic Exchanges.*

2 packages (1/4 ounce *each*) active dry yeast
2 cups warm water (110° to 115°)
4 to 4-1/2 cups all-purpose flour
1/2 cup grated Parmesan cheese
2 tablespoons sugar
2 tablespoons dill weed
2 tablespoons butter *or* margarine, softened
2 teaspoons salt
TOPPING:
2 tablespoons grated Parmesan cheese
1 teaspoon butter *or* margarine, melted

In a mixing bowl, dissolve yeast in water. Add 3 cups of flour, Parmesan cheese, sugar, dill, butter and salt; beat until smooth, about 2 minutes. Gradually beat in remaining flour (do not knead). Place in a greased bowl; turn once to grease top. Cover and let rise in a warm place until doubled, about 45 minutes. Stir batter down and beat 25 strokes with a spoon. Place in a greased 9-in. springform pan (do not allow to rise). Sprinkle with Parmesan cheese. Bake at 375° for 55-60 minutes or until golden brown. Brush with butter. Remove from pan and cool on a wire rack. **Yield:** 1 loaf (16 servings). **Diabetic Exchanges:** One slice (prepared with margarine) equals 2 starch, 1/2 fat; also, 156 calories,

361 mg sodium, 3 mg cholesterol, 26 gm carbohydrate, 5 gm protein, 3 gm fat.

— 🍵 🍵 🍵 —

Chocolate Tea Bread

Applesauce is the secret ingredient that makes this cake-like loaf so moist. It's always a success.
—Dorothy Bateman, Carver, Massachusetts

- 1/2 cup applesauce
- 1/3 cup shortening
- 2 eggs
- 1/3 cup water
- 1-1/4 cups sugar
- 1-1/2 cups all-purpose flour
- 1/3 cup baking cocoa
- 1 teaspoon baking soda
- 3/4 teaspoon salt
- 1/4 teaspoon baking powder
- 1 cup (6 ounces) semisweet chocolate chips
- 1/3 cup chopped walnuts

GLAZE:
- 1/2 cup confectioners' sugar
- 1 to 2 tablespoons milk
- 1/4 teaspoon vanilla extract
Pinch salt

In a mixing bowl, combine applesauce, shortening, eggs, water and sugar; beat on low speed for 30 seconds. Combine dry ingredients; add to applesauce mixture. Beat on low for 30 seconds. Beat on high for 2-1/2 minutes, scraping bowl occasionally. Fold in the chocolate chips and nuts. Pour into a greased and floured 9-in. x 5-in. x 3-in. loaf pan. Bake at 350° for 60-70 minutes or until a toothpick inserted in the center comes out clean. Cool in pan 10 minutes before removing to a wire rack to cool completely. Combine glaze ingredients; drizzle over bread. **Yield:** 1 loaf.

— 🍵 🍵 🍵 —

Toffee Coffee Cake

To make it even more delectable, I suggest topping this moist snack with a scoop of your favorite ice cream.
—Edie Despain, Logan, Utah

- 1/2 cup butter *or* margarine, softened
- 1 cup packed brown sugar
- 1/2 cup sugar
- 2 cups all-purpose flour
- 1 cup buttermilk
- 1 egg
- 1 teaspoon baking soda
- 1 teaspoon vanilla extract

- 3 chocolate English toffee candy bars (1.4 ounces *each*), chopped
- 1/4 cup chopped pecans

In a mixing bowl, blend butter, sugars and flour; set aside 1/2 cup. To the remaining butter mixture, add buttermilk, egg, baking soda and vanilla; mix well. Pour into a greased and floured 13-in. x 9-in. x 2-in. baking pan. Combine chopped candy bars and pecans with reserved butter mixture; sprinkle over coffee cake. Bake at 350° for 30-35 minutes or until a toothpick inserted near the center comes out clean. Cool on a wire rack. **Yield:** 12-16 servings.

— 🍵 🍵 🍵 —

'I Wish I Had That Recipe...'

"I WAKE UP mornings to the thought of the delicious Cinnamon Walnut Scones served by the Victorian Rose Tea Room in Port Orchard," says Rae Alexander of Bremerton, Washington.

Candace Stephenson, tea room baker, reveals, "I developed this recipe shortly after owner Sandy O'Donnell opened a few years ago."

The Victorian Rose Tea Room at 1130 Bethel Ave. in Port Orchard is open daily from 9 a.m. to 5 p.m. Call 1-360/876-5695.

Cinnamon Walnut Scones

- 1-3/4 cups all-purpose flour
- 1/4 cup finely chopped walnuts
- 4-1/2 teaspoons sugar
- 2-1/4 teaspoons baking powder
- 1/2 teaspoon salt
- 1/2 teaspoon ground cinnamon
- 1/4 cup cold butter *or* margarine
- 2 eggs
- 1/3 cup whipping cream
- 1/4 cup buttermilk

In a bowl, combine the first six ingredients; cut in butter until the mixture resembles coarse crumbs. Combine eggs and cream; stir into dry ingredients just until moistened. Turn onto a floured surface; gently pat into a 7-in. circle, 3/4-in. thick. Cut into eight wedges. Separate wedges; place on a lightly greased baking sheet. Brush tops with buttermilk. Let rest for 15 minutes. Bake at 450° for 14-16 minutes or until golden brown. **Yield:** 8 servings.

— —

Peanut-Chip Banana Bread

Bananas, peanut butter and chocolate chips make an irresistible combination in this moist quick bread.
—Nancy Fettig, Billings, Montana

2-1/2 cups all-purpose flour
1/2 cup sugar
1/2 cup packed brown sugar
1 tablespoon baking powder
3/4 teaspoon salt
1/4 teaspoon ground cinnamon
1 cup mashed ripe bananas (2 to 3 medium)
1 cup milk
3/4 cup chunky peanut butter
1 egg
3 tablespoons vegetable oil
1 teaspoon vanilla extract
1 cup (6 ounces) miniature semisweet
   chocolate chips
FROSTING:
3 tablespoons chunky peanut butter
2 tablespoons butter *or* margarine
1 cup confectioners' sugar
1 tablespoon milk
1 teaspoon vanilla extract
Chopped peanuts and additional miniature
   chocolate chips

In a mixing bowl, combine the first six ingredients. Combine bananas, milk, peanut butter, egg, oil and vanilla; mix well. Stir into dry ingredients just until combined. Add chocolate chips. Spoon into two greased 8-in. x 4-in. x 2-in. loaf pans. Bake at 350° for 50-55 minutes or until bread tests done. Cool in pans for 10 minutes before removing to a wire rack. When completely cooled, wrap each loaf in foil and refrigerate overnight. The next day, melt peanut butter and butter in a small saucepan; remove from the heat. Stir in confectioners' sugar, milk and vanilla. Frost loaves; sprinkle with nuts and chocolate chips. **Yield:** 2 loaves.

— ☕ ☕ ☕ —

Healthy Wheat Bread

I developed the recipe for this wonderful bread to suit my husband's diet. Even those who don't care for wheat bread will love these lightly sweet wholesome loaves.
—Betty Howell, Wichita, Kansas

✓ This tasty dish uses less sugar, salt and fat. Recipe includes *Diabetic Exchanges.*

3 to 4 cups all-purpose flour, *divided*
2 teaspoons salt
2 packages (1/4 ounce *each*) active dry
   yeast

1 cup water
1/2 cup honey
2 tablespoons vegetable oil
1 cup low-fat cottage cheese
4 egg whites
1-1/2 cups whole wheat flour
1/2 cup wheat germ
1/2 cup old-fashioned oats

In a large mixing bowl, combine 2 cups all-purpose flour, salt and yeast. In a saucepan, heat water, honey and oil to 120°-130°; stir in cottage cheese. Add to flour mixture with the egg whites; blend on low speed until moistened. Beat for 3 minutes on medium. Add whole wheat flour, wheat germ, oats and enough of the remaining all-purpose flour to form a soft dough. Turn onto a floured surface; knead until smooth and elastic, about 6-8 minutes. Place in a greased bowl, turning once to grease top. Cover and let rise in a warm place until doubled, about 1 hour. Punch dough down. Shape into two loaves. Place in two 8-in. x 4-in. x 2-in. loaf pans coated with nonstick cooking spray. Cover and let rise until doubled, about 1 hour. Bake at 375° for 35-40 minutes or until golden brown; cover with foil for the last 15 minutes to prevent overbrowning. Remove from pans; cool on wire racks. **Yield:** 2 loaves (32 slices). **Diabetic Exchanges:** One slice equals 1 starch, 1/2 fat; also, 100 calories, 170 mg sodium, trace cholesterol, 18 gm carbohydrate, 4 gm protein, 1 gm fat.

— ☕ ☕ ☕ —

Pear Zucchini Bread

Pretty pear pieces peek out of every slice of this moist bread. This recipe is a delightfully different way to use this mellow, sweet and juicy fruit. —Pat Habiger
Spearville, Kentucky

2 cups chopped peeled pears
1 cup shredded zucchini
1 cup sugar
1 cup packed brown sugar
3 eggs, beaten
1 cup vegetable oil
1 tablespoon vanilla extract
2 cups all-purpose flour
1 cup rye *or* whole wheat flour
2 teaspoons pumpkin pie spice
1 teaspoon baking soda
1/2 teaspoon baking powder
1/2 teaspoon salt
1/2 cup chopped pecans

In a large bowl, combine the first seven ingredients. Combine the flours, pie spice, baking soda, baking powder and salt; stir into pear mixture until blended. Fold in nuts. Pour into two greased 8-in. x 4-in. x 2-in. loaf pans. Bake at 350° for 55-65 minutes or until a toothpick inserted near the center comes out clean. Cool in pans for 10 minutes; remove to a wire rack to cool completely. **Yield:** 2 loaves.

Blueberry Buckle

This recipe has been passed around among the women of my church for years. Everyone loves the abundance of blueberries and the streusel topping.
—Anna Higbee, Absecon, New Jersey

- 1/4 cup butter *or* margarine, softened
- 3/4 cup sugar
- 2 eggs
- 1 teaspoon vanilla extract
- 2-1/4 cups all-purpose flour, *divided*
- 2 teaspoons baking powder
- 1/2 teaspoon salt
- 1/2 cup buttermilk
- 2-1/2 cups fresh *or* frozen blueberries

TOPPING:
- 1/4 cup all-purpose flour
- 1/4 cup packed brown sugar
- 1/4 cup sugar
- 1/2 teaspoon ground cinnamon
- 1/4 cup cold butter *or* margarine

In a mixing bowl, cream butter and sugar. Add eggs and vanilla; mix well. Combine 2 cups of flour, baking powder and salt; add to creamed mixture alternately with buttermilk. Mix well. Toss berries in remaining flour; fold into batter (discard any flour that doesn't stick to berries). Spread batter in a greased 9-in. square baking pan. For topping, combine flour, sugars and cinnamon; cut in butter until the mixture resembles coarse crumbs. Sprinkle over batter. Bake at 375° for 25-30 minutes or until a toothpick inserted near the center comes out clean. Cool on a wire rack. **Yield:** 9 servings.

Buttercup Squash Coffee Cake

(Pictured at top right)

My father grows a large squash patch, so each fall, I get an ample amount of his harvest. I make this treat to share with my co-workers. They rave about the moist cake, the crunchy streusel and the applesauce between the layers. —Mary Jones, Cumberland, Maine

STREUSEL:
- 1/4 cup packed brown sugar
- 1/4 cup sugar
- 1/4 cup all-purpose flour
- 1/4 cup quick-cooking oats
- 1/4 cup chopped nuts
- 1-1/2 teaspoons ground cinnamon
- 3 tablespoons cold butter *or* margarine

CAKE:
- 1/2 cup butter-flavored shortening
- 1 cup sugar
- 2 eggs
- 1 cup mashed cooked buttercup squash
- 1 teaspoon vanilla extract
- 2 cups all-purpose flour
- 2 teaspoons baking powder
- 1-1/2 teaspoons ground cinnamon
- 1/2 teaspoon baking soda
- 1/2 teaspoon salt
- 1/4 teaspoon ground ginger
- 1/4 teaspoon ground nutmeg
- Pinch ground cloves
- 1/2 cup unsweetened applesauce

GLAZE:
- 1/2 cup confectioners' sugar
- 1/4 teaspoon vanilla extract
- 1-1/2 teaspoons hot water

Combine the first six streusel ingredients. Cut in butter until crumbly; set aside. In a mixing bowl, cream shortening and sugar. Beat in eggs, one at a time. Beat in squash and vanilla. Combine dry ingredients; gradually add to the creamed mixture. Spoon half into a greased 9-in. springform pan. Spread applesauce over batter. Sprinkle with half of the streusel. Spoon remaining batter evenly over streusel. Top with the remaining streusel. Bake at 350° for 50-55 minutes or until cake tests done. Cool for 10 minutes; remove sides of pan. Combine glaze ingredients; drizzle over coffee cake. **Yield:** 10-12 servings.

Country-Style Condiments

Stocking up your pantry and refrigerator is easy with the sure-to-please recipes in this chapter. Family and friends will relish every bite of these homemade salad dressings, relishes, pickles, sauces and more.

TASTY TOPPINGS. Clockwise from upper right: Holiday Cranberry Chutney (p. 112), Tomato Relish (p. 113), Easy Freezer Pickles (p. 112), Pennsylvania Dutch Corn Relish (p. 113), Poppy Seed Dressing (p. 114), Versatile Salad Dressing (p. 115) and Zesty French Dressing (p. 114).

1 cup strawberries
1 cup blackberries
1 cup blueberries
4 cups sugar
1 pouch (3 ounces) **liquid fruit pectin**
1 tablespoon lemon juice

In a large bowl, crush all of the berries. Stir in sugar; let stand for 10 minutes. Combine pectin and lemon juice; add to fruit, stirring constantly until sugar is dissolved, about 3 minutes. Pour into jars or freezer containers, leaving 1/2-in. headspace. Cover tightly. Let stand at room temperature until set, up to 24 hours. Freeze or store in the refrigerator for up to 3 weeks. **Yield:** 6 half-pints. **Editor's Note:** If saskatoon berries are not available in your area, add an extra cup of one of the other berries.

Holiday Cranberry Chutney

(Pictured above)

A chunky chutney like this one makes a lovely gift in a decorated jar. It's great served as an appetizer or alongside a main dish. —Cheryl Lottman
Stillwater, Minnesota

1 bag (12 ounces) fresh *or* frozen cranberries
1-1/4 cups sugar
3/4 cup water
1 large tart apple, chopped
2 teaspoons ground cinnamon
1 teaspoon ground ginger
1/4 teaspoon ground cloves

In a saucepan, combine all ingredients; bring to a boil, stirring constantly. Reduce heat; simmer for 15-20 minutes or until apple is tender and mixture thickens. Cool completely. Store in the refrigerator. Serve over cream cheese with crackers or as a condiment with pork, ham or chicken. **Yield:** 3 cups.

Cardamom Yogurt Sauce

With a creamy texture and hint of spice, this delicious sauce really complements a variety of fruit.
—Geraldine Grisdale, Mt. Pleasant, Michigan

✓ This tasty dish uses less sugar, salt and fat. Recipe includes *Diabetic Exchanges.*

1 egg
1/4 cup orange juice
1 tablespoon honey
1 teaspoon ground cardamom
1 carton (8 ounces) plain yogurt

In a small saucepan, combine egg, orange juice, honey and cardamom. Cook over medium heat, stirring constantly until mixture thickens, about 5 minutes. Cook and stir 2 minutes longer. Cool for 20 minutes; fold in yogurt. Cover and chill for at least 1 hour. Serve over oranges, bananas and apples or fruit of your choice. **Yield:** 1-1/4 cups. **Diabetic Exchanges:** 1/4 cup of sauce (prepared with nonfat yogurt) equals 1/2 skim milk; also, 53 calories, 43 mg sodium, 44 mg cholesterol, 8 gm carbohydrate, 3 gm protein, trace fat.

Wild Berry Freezer Jam

One year, I decided I wanted to make a wild berry jam but couldn't find a recipe, so I invented my own.
—Barbara Hohmann, Petawawa, Ontario

1 cup saskatoon berries
1 cup raspberries

Easy Freezer Pickles

(Pictured on page 111)

These crisp, no-cook pickle slices are so simple to fix.
—Lucile Johnson, Red Oak, Iowa

8 pounds cucumbers, thinly sliced
1 cup thinly sliced onion
3 tablespoons salt
4 cups sugar
2 cups vinegar

1 teaspoon celery seed
1 teaspoon ground turmeric
1 teaspoon mustard seed
1/2 teaspoon alum

In a large container, combine cucumbers, onion and salt; mix well. Let stand for 3 hours, stirring occasionally. Drain and rinse. In a bowl, combine remaining ingredients; let stand for 2-3 hours, stirring often. Pour over the cucumber mixture and stir well. Pack into 1-pt. freezer containers, leaving 1-in. headspace. Cover and freeze up to 6 weeks. Thaw before serving. **Yield:** 6 pints.

— 🍶 🍶 🍶 —

Tomato Relish

(Pictured on page 111)

My mother made this favorite relish for years. It's especially good served with a pork roast.
—Carole Anhalt, Manitowoc, Wisconsin

18 medium tomatoes, peeled, cored, seeded
   and chopped (8 cups)
 2 cups minced celery
 1 cup minced green pepper
 1 cup finely chopped onion
1/3 cup salt
 2 cups vinegar
1-1/2 cups sugar
1-1/2 teaspoons mustard seed
 1 teaspoon pepper

Place the vegetables in a large bowl; sprinkle with salt and mix well. Let stand for 30 minutes. Drain; rinse and drain again. In a large kettle, bring vinegar, sugar, mustard seed and pepper to a boil; reduce heat. Simmer for 15 minutes. Add vegetables; return to a boil. Ladle hot relish into hot jars, leaving 1/4-in. headspace. Adjust caps. Process for 20 minutes in a boiling-water bath. **Yield:** 4 pints.

— 🍶 🍶 🍶 —

Pennsylvania Dutch Corn Relish

(Pictured on page 111)

Cabbage gives this blue-ribbon relish a unique twist.
—Helen Hassler, Denver, Pennsylvania

20 large ears fresh corn, cut (4 quarts)
 6 medium green peppers, chopped (5 cups)
 6 medium sweet red peppers, chopped
   (5 cups)
 4 large onions, chopped (3 cups)
 1 medium head cabbage, chopped
   (2 quarts)
 6 cups vinegar

4 cups sugar
1 cup water
2 tablespoons ground mustard
2 tablespoons celery seed
2 tablespoons salt
1 tablespoon ground turmeric

In a large kettle, combine all ingredients. Simmer, uncovered, for 20 minutes, stirring occasionally. Ladle hot relish into hot jars, leaving 1/4-in. headspace. Adjust caps. Process for 15 minutes in a boiling-water bath. **Yield:** about 16 pints.

— 🍶 🍶 🍶 —

Bread-and-Butter Pickles

My husband, Tom, grows lots of cucumbers so I can make plenty of these tangy pickles.
—Carolyn Moseley, Greenville, South Carolina

 8 pounds cucumbers, thinly sliced
 6 medium onions, thinly sliced
 2 medium green peppers, chopped
1/3 cup canning salt
 6 cups cider vinegar
 5 cups sugar
 2 tablespoons mustard seed
1-1/2 teaspoons ground turmeric
1-1/2 teaspoons celery seed

In a large container, combine cucumbers, onions, peppers and salt. Cover with crushed ice; mix well. Let stand for 3 hours. Drain; rinse and drain again. In a large kettle, combine remaining ingredients; bring to a boil. Add cucumber mixture; return to a boil. Ladle hot mixture into hot jars, leaving 1/4-in. headspace. Adjust caps. Process for 10 minutes in a boiling-water bath. **Yield:** 8 pints.

— 🍶 🍶 🍶 —

Spiced Prunes

I like to serve these special prunes with meats or a cottage cheese salad or as a breakfast fruit.
—Alcy Thorne, Los Molinos, California

 1 pound dried pitted prunes
 2 cups water
 1 teaspoon ground cinnamon
 1 teaspoon ground cloves
1/2 teaspoon ground ginger
 3 tablespoons lemon juice

In a saucepan over medium heat, combine prunes, water, cinnamon, cloves and ginger; bring to a boil. Remove from the heat; cover and let stand until cool. Stir in lemon juice. **Yield:** 8 servings.

Poppy Seed Dressing

(Pictured at right)

The best way to use up fruit all year long is with this tongue-tingling sweet and tangy topping. Why not treat your family with this tonight? —Patricia Staudt
Marble Rock, Iowa

3/4 cup sugar
1-1/2 teaspoons onion salt
1 teaspoon ground mustard
1/3 cup vinegar
1 cup vegetable oil
1 tablespoon poppy seeds

In a small mixing bowl, combine sugar, onion salt and mustard. Add vinegar; mix well. Gradually add oil while beating on medium speed; beat for 5 minutes or until very thick. Stir in poppy seeds. Cover and refrigerate. Serve over fresh fruit or salad greens. Refrigerate leftovers. **Yield:** 1-2/3 cups.

— ☕ ☕ ☕ —

Thousand Island Dressing

It's almost unbelievable that a dressing so easy to fix can be so good. My daughter shared this recipe with me years ago. —Darlis Wilfer, Phelps, Wisconsin

2 cups mayonnaise
1/4 cup chili sauce
1/4 cup pickle relish

In a bowl, combine all ingredients. Cover and refrigerate. **Yield:** 2-1/2 cups.

— ☕ ☕ ☕ —

Zesty French Dressing

(Pictured above right)

The ingredients in this special French dressing are ones I likely have on hand. So it's easy to whip up a batch whenever I need it. —LaVonne Hegland
St. Michael, Minnesota

1 small onion, chopped
2/3 cup vegetable oil
1/2 cup sugar
1/3 cup vinegar
2 tablespoons ketchup
1-1/2 teaspoons Worcestershire sauce
1-1/2 teaspoons salt
1 teaspoon prepared mustard
1 teaspoon paprika
1/2 teaspoon garlic powder
1/2 teaspoon celery seed

YOU CAN'T BOTTLE flavor like Zesty French Dressing (top), Versatile Salad Dressing (in the potato salad) and Poppy Seed Dressing (on the fruit salad).

In a blender or food processor, process all ingredients until smooth and thickened. Cover and refrigerate for at least 1 hour. Shake well before serving. **Yield:** about 1-1/2 cups.

— ☕ ☕ ☕ —

Low-Fat Blue Cheese Dressing

You'll never miss the fat in this full-flavored dressing. I was thrilled to receive this recipe from a terrific chef at a California resort. —Tracey Baysinger
Salem, Missouri

✓ This tasty dish uses less sugar, salt and fat. Recipe includes *Diabetic Exchanges.*

1 cup (8 ounces) fat-free cottage cheese
1 cup (8 ounces) nonfat plain yogurt
2 tablespoons chopped onion
1 garlic clove, minced
1 tablespoon crumbled blue cheese

In a blender or food processor, combine cottage cheese, yogurt, onion and garlic; process until smooth. Stir in blue cheese. Store, covered, in the refrigerator. **Yield:** 1-3/4 cups. **Diabetic Exchanges:** One serving (1 tablespoon) equals a free food; also, 11 calories, 34 mg sodium, 1 mg cholesterol, 1 gm carbohydrate, 2 gm protein, trace fat.

— 🥄 🥄 🥄 —

Hot Bacon Dressing

You get an explosion of flavor in this hot dressing that's perfect for strong-flavored greens like spinach.
—*Connie Simon, Reed City, Michigan*

> 3/4 pound sliced bacon, diced
> 1/2 cup chopped onion
> 1 cup cider vinegar
> 2 cups water
> 1-1/2 cups sugar
> 1 jar (2 ounces) diced pimientos, drained
> 2 tablespoons Dijon mustard
> 1 teaspoon salt
> 1/4 teaspoon pepper
> 3 tablespoons cornstarch
> 2 tablespoons cold water

In a large skillet, cook bacon until crisp; remove bacon and set aside. Drain, reserving 2 tablespoons drippings in the skillet. Add onion and saute until tender; remove from the heat. Add the vinegar, water, sugar, pimientos, mustard, salt, pepper and bacon; mix well. Combine cornstarch and cold water; stir into skillet. Cook and stir until mixture comes to a boil. Boil for 2 minutes, stirring constantly. Serve warm over fresh spinach or mixed greens. Refrigerate leftovers and reheat before serving. **Yield:** about 4 cups.

— 🥄 🥄 🥄 —

Versatile Salad Dressing

(Pictured above left)

This is my most-used dressing. It's so creamy, mild and versatile—it gives old-fashioned goodness to potato salad, coleslaw and even deviled eggs.
—*Erlene Cornelius, Spring City, Tennessee*

> 2 cups sugar
> 3 tablespoons all-purpose flour
> 1 teaspoon salt
> 1/2 teaspoon ground mustard
> 3 eggs, lightly beaten
> 1 cup vinegar
> 1 cup water

Mayonnaise

In a saucepan, combine sugar, flour, salt and mustard; stir in eggs. Gradually stir in vinegar and wa-

ter until smooth. Bring to a boil over medium heat, stirring constantly; cook and stir for 2 minutes. Cover and refrigerate. Just before serving, combine desired amount of base with an equal amount of mayonnaise. Serve as a dressing for potato salad, coleslaw or salad greens. Refrigerate leftovers. **Yield:** 3-3/4 cups base.

— 🥄 🥄 🥄 —

Blue Cheese Dressing

We always thought bottled dressings tasted just fine until I began making my own. It is amazing how much better this rich homemade version tastes.
—*Gladys DeBoer, Castleford, Idaho*

> 6 ounces blue cheese *or* Roquefort, crumbled
> 2 cups mayonnaise
> 1 cup (8 ounces) sour cream
> 2 tablespoons vegetable oil
> 2 tablespoons vinegar
> 1 teaspoon garlic salt
> 1 teaspoon onion salt
> 1 teaspoon salt
> 1/2 teaspoon pepper

Place all ingredients in a blender; cover and process on medium speed until smooth, about 1 minute. Cover and refrigerate. **Yield:** 3 cups.

— 🥄 🥄 🥄 —

Dill Pickle Spears

Harvest season at our home isn't complete without these spears. We eat them as snacks and alongside sandwiches. —*Polly Coumos, Mogadore, Ohio*

> 1 quart vinegar
> 1 quart water
> 3/4 cup sugar
> 3/4 cup canning salt
> 3 tablespoons mixed pickling spices
> 25 to 30 medium pickling cucumbers, cut into quarters lengthwise
> 8 fresh dill heads
> 8 garlic cloves, peeled

In a saucepan, combine vinegar, water, sugar and salt; bring to a boil. Tie pickling spices in a cheesecloth bag. Place in the hot liquid; bring to a boil. Boil for 10 minutes. Remove cheesecloth bag and discard. Place dill heads in the bottom of eight pint jars. Pack cucumbers into jars to within 1/2 in. of jar top. Place 1 garlic clove in each jar. Ladle the boiling liquid over cucumbers, leaving 1/4-in. headspace. Adjust caps. Process for 10 minutes in a boiling-water bath. **Yield:** 8 pints.

Cookies & Bars

These delectable cookies and tempting bars will make all your days sweeter!

CRAZY FOR COOKIES. Clockwise from upper left: Christmas Shortbread Wreaths (p. 120), Glazed Orange Date Squares (p. 128), Mountain Cookies (p. 121) and Chocolate Nut Cookies (p. 124).

Dipped Gingersnaps

(Pictured above)

I get a great deal of satisfaction making and giving time-tested Yuletide treats like these chewy cookies.
—Laura Kimball, West Jordan, Utah

        2 cups sugar
    1-1/2 cups vegetable oil
        2 eggs
      1/2 cup molasses
        4 cups all-purpose flour
        4 teaspoons baking soda
        1 tablespoon ground ginger
        2 teaspoons ground cinnamon
        1 teaspoon salt
Additional sugar
        2 packages (12 ounces *each*) vanilla
          baking chips
      1/4 cup shortening

In a mixing bowl, combine the sugar and oil; mix well. Add eggs, one at a time, beating well after each addition. Stir in molasses. Combine dry ingredients; gradually add to creamed mixture and mix well. Shape into 3/4-in. balls and roll in sugar. Place 2 in. apart on ungreased baking sheets. Bake at 350° for 10-12 minutes or until cookie springs back when touched lightly. Remove to wire racks to cool. Melt vanilla chips with shortening in a saucepan over low heat. Dip the cookies halfway; shake off excess. Place on waxed paper-lined baking sheets to harden. **Yield:** about 14-1/2 dozen

——— 🍴 🍴 🍴 ———

Norwegian Cookies

These soft sugar cookies are a favorite with our four young children.
—Karen Skowronek
Minot, North Dakota

      1 cup butter (no substitutes), softened
      1 cup sugar
      1 egg
    1/2 teaspoon vanilla extract

    1/2 teaspoon almond extract
      2 cups all-purpose flour
    1/2 cup finely chopped walnuts
Red *and/or* green colored sugar

In a mixing bowl, cream butter and sugar. Add the egg and extracts; beat until light and fluffy. Add flour and nuts; beat just until moistened. Cover and chill 1 hour or until firm enough to handle. Shape into 1-in. balls; place 2 in. apart on greased baking sheets. Flatten to 1/4-in. thickness with a glass dipped in colored sugar. Sprinkle with additional sugar if desired. Bake at 350° for 10-12 minutes or until cookies are set. **Yield:** 3 dozen.

——— 🍴 🍴 🍴 ———

Peanut Butter Chocolate Chip Cookies

A combination of chocolate chips, peanut butter and oats makes these treats especially good.
—Clarice Schweitzer, Sun City, Arizona

    1/2 cup butter *or* margarine, softened
    1/2 cup sugar
    1/3 cup packed brown sugar
    1/2 cup chunky peanut butter
      1 egg
      1 teaspoon vanilla extract
      1 cup all-purpose flour
    1/2 cup old-fashioned oats
      1 teaspoon baking soda
    1/4 teaspoon salt
      1 cup (6 ounces) semisweet chocolate chips

In a mixing bowl, cream butter and sugars; beat in peanut butter, egg and vanilla. Combine flour, oats, baking soda and salt; stir into the creamed mixture. Stir in the chocolate chips. Drop by rounded tablespoonfuls onto ungreased baking sheets. Bake at 350° for 10-12 minutes or until golden brown. Cool for 1 minute before removing to a wire rack. **Yield:** 2 dozen.

——— 🍴 🍴 🍴 ———

Low-Fat Oatmeal Cookies

These oatmeal cookies are chewy with old-fashioned goodness and are low in fat.
—Kathleen Nolan
Lawrenceville, Georgia

✓ This tasty dish uses less sugar, salt and fat. Recipe includes *Diabetic Exchanges.*

      1 cup all-purpose flour
      1 cup quick-cooking oats
    1/2 cup sugar
    1/2 teaspoon baking powder
    1/2 teaspoon baking soda
    1/2 teaspoon salt

1/2 teaspoon ground cinnamon
2 egg whites
1/3 cup corn syrup
1 teaspoon vanilla extract
1/3 cup raisins

In a medium bowl, combine the first 10 ingredients; mix well. Stir in raisins (dough will be stiff). Drop by tablespoonfuls onto baking sheets that have been coated with nonstick cooking spray. Bake at 375° for 8-10 minutes or until lightly browned. **Yield:** 2-1/2 dozen. **Diabetic Exchanges:** One serving (two cookies) equals 1-1/2 starch; also, 102 calories, 138 mg sodium, 0 cholesterol, 24 gm carbohydrate, 2 gm protein, trace fat.

Rosemary Honey Cookies

You'll be delighted with this unusual cookie's wonderful flavor. —Audrey Thibodeau, Mesa, Arizona

1/2 cup shortening
1/4 cup butter *or* margarine, softened
3/4 cup sugar
1 egg
1/4 cup honey
1 tablespoon lemon juice
2 cups all-purpose flour
2 teaspoons dried rosemary, crushed
1 teaspoon baking soda
1/2 teaspoon salt
1/2 teaspoon ground cinnamon
1/4 teaspoon ground nutmeg

In a mixing bowl, cream shortening, butter and sugar. Beat in egg, honey and lemon juice. Combine dry ingredients; add to creamed mixture. Drop by teaspoonfuls 2 in. apart onto greased baking sheets. Bake at 325° for 12-14 minutes or until lightly browned. **Yield:** about 4 dozen.

Fudgy Brownies

When I was growing up, I helped my mother make delicious desserts for our farm family of eight.
—Judy Cunningham, Max, North Dakota

1-1/3 cups butter *or* margarine, softened
2-2/3 cups sugar
4 eggs
1 tablespoon vanilla extract
2 cups all-purpose flour
1 cup baking cocoa
1/2 teaspoon salt
Confectioners' sugar, optional

In a mixing bowl, cream butter and sugar. Add eggs and vanilla; mix well. Combine flour, cocoa and salt; add to the creamed mixture and mix well. Spread into a greased 13-in. x 9-in. x 2-in. baking pan. Bake at 350° for 25-30 minutes or until the top is dry and the center is set. Cool completely. Dust with confectioners' sugar if desired. **Yield:** 2-1/2 dozen.

Scandinavian Almond Bars

(Pictured below)

Delicate and crisp with a rich butter and almond flavor, these cookies are irresistible—and they look so lovely on a cookie tray! —Melva Baumer
Millmont, Pennsylvania

1 cup sugar
1/2 cup butter (no substitutes), softened
1 egg
1/2 teaspoon almond extract
1-3/4 cups all-purpose flour
2 teaspoons baking powder
1/4 teaspoon salt
1 tablespoon milk
1/2 cup sliced almonds, chopped
ICING:
1 cup confectioners' sugar
1/4 teaspoon almond extract
1 to 2 tablespoons milk

In a mixing bowl, cream sugar and butter; beat in egg and extract. Combine dry ingredients; add to creamed mixture and mix well. Divide dough into fourths; roll into 12-in. x 3-in. rectangles 5 in. apart on greased baking sheets. Brush with milk; sprinkle with almonds. Bake at 325° for 18-20 minutes or until firm to the touch and edges are lightly browned. Cool on pans for 5 minutes, then cut diagonally into 1-in. slices. Remove to wire racks to cool completely. Combine icing ingredients; drizzle over bars. **Yield:** about 4 dozen.

Chocolate Pretzel Cookies

(Pictured below)

These pretzel-shaped buttery chocolate cookies are covered in a rich mocha glaze and drizzled with white chocolate. My family goes wild over their chocolaty crunch. —Priscilla Anderson, Salt Lake City, Utah

    1/2 cup butter (no substitutes), softened
    2/3 cup sugar
      1 egg
      2 squares (1 ounce *each*) unsweetened
        chocolate, melted and cooled
      2 teaspoons vanilla extract
1-3/4 cups all-purpose flour
    1/2 teaspoon salt
MOCHA GLAZE:
      1 cup (6 ounces) semisweet chocolate chips
      1 teaspoon light corn syrup
      1 teaspoon shortening
      1 cup confectioners' sugar
      4 to 5 tablespoons hot coffee
      2 squares (1 ounce *each*) white baking
        chocolate, melted

In a mixing bowl, cream butter and sugar. Add the egg, chocolate and vanilla; mix well. Combine flour and salt; gradually add to creamed mixture and mix well. Cover and chill for 1 hour or until firm. Divide dough into fourths; form each portion into a 6-in. log. Divide each log into 12 pieces and roll each piece into a 9-in. rope. Place ropes on greased baking sheets; form into pretzel shapes and space 2 in. apart. Bake at 400° for 5-7 minutes or until firm. Cool 1 minute before removing to wire racks. For glaze, heat the chocolate chips, corn syrup and shortening in a small saucepan over low heat until melted. Stir in sugar and enough coffee to make a smooth glaze. Dip pretzels; place on waxed paper or wire racks to harden. Drizzle with white chocolate; let stand until chocolate is completely set. Store in an airtight container. **Yield:** 4 dozen.

Christmas Shortbread Wreaths

(Pictured on page 116)

I adapted this recipe from plain shortbread to use for a cookie exchange. The wreaths are big sellers at bake sales. Since they're so quick and easy to prepare, I'm happy to share them at the holidays.
—Donna Gendre, Stettler, Alberta

      1 cup all-purpose flour
    1/2 cup cornstarch
    1/2 cup confectioners' sugar
    3/4 cup butter (no substitutes), softened
Red and green sprinkles

In a bowl, combine flour, cornstarch and sugar. Blend in butter with a wooden spoon until the dough is smooth. Form into two balls. Chill for 30 minutes or until firm. On a floured surface, roll one ball into a 9-in. circle; transfer to a greased baking sheet. Cut out center with a small round cookie cutter. If desired, scallop outer and inner edges of wreath with the edge of a cookie cutter or a knife. Cut wreath into 12 wedges. Separate the wedges, leaving 1/8 in. between. Decorate outer and inner edges with sprinkles. Repeat for remaining dough. Bake at 300° for 18-22 minutes or until golden brown. Cool on pan for 5 minutes. Recut wreath into wedges. Remove to a wire rack to cool completely. To serve, arrange as a wreath on a large flat serving plate. **Yield:** 2 dozen (2 wreaths).

White Velvet Cutouts

We make these cutouts every Christmas and give lots of them as gifts. They melt in your mouth!
—Kim Hinkle, Wauseon, Ohio

      2 cups butter (no substitutes), softened
      1 package (8 ounces) cream cheese, softened
      2 cups sugar
      2 egg yolks
      1 teaspoon vanilla extract
4-1/2 cups all-purpose flour
BUTTER CREAM FROSTING:
3-1/2 cups confectioners' sugar, *divided*
      3 tablespoons butter (no substitutes),
        softened
      1 tablespoon shortening
    1/2 teaspoon vanilla extract
      3 to 4 tablespoons milk, divided
Red *and/or* green food coloring*, optional

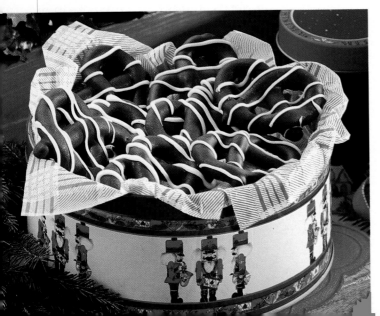

In a mixing bowl, cream butter and cream cheese until light and fluffy. Add sugar, egg yolks and vanilla; mix well. Gradually add flour. Cover and chill for 2 hours or until firm. Roll out on a floured surface to 1/4-in. thickness. Cut into 3-in. shapes; place 1 in. apart on greased baking sheets. Bake at 350° for 10-12 minutes or until set (not browned). Cool for 5 minutes; remove to wire racks to cool. For frosting, combine 1-1/2 cups sugar, butter, shortening, vanilla and 3 tablespoons milk in a mixing bowl; beat until smooth. Gradually add remaining sugar; beat until light and fluffy, about 3 minutes. Add enough remaining milk and food coloring until frosting reaches desired consistency. Frost cookies. **Yield:** about 7 dozen. ***Editor's Note:** For a deeper color of frosting, tint with food coloring paste available at kitchen and cake decorating supply stores.

—☕ ☕ ☕—

Mountain Cookies

(Pictured on page 117)

Wherever I take these cookies, people ask for the recipe. You'll be hard-pressed to eat just one!
—*Jeanne Adams, Richmond, Vermont*

   1 cup butter (no substitutes), softened
   1 cup confectioners' sugar
   2 teaspoons vanilla extract
   2 cups all-purpose flour
   1/2 teaspoon salt
FILLING:
   1 package (3 ounces) cream cheese, softened
   1 cup confectioners' sugar
   2 tablespoons all-purpose flour
   1 teaspoon vanilla extract
   1/2 cup finely chopped pecans
   1/2 cup flaked coconut
TOPPING:
   1/2 cup semisweet chocolate chips
   2 tablespoons butter *or* margarine
   2 tablespoons water
   1/2 cup confectioners' sugar

In a mixing bowl, cream the butter, sugar and vanilla. Combine flour and salt; gradually add to the creamed mixture and mix well. Shape into 1-in. balls; place 2 in. apart on ungreased baking sheets. Make a deep indentation in the center of each cookie. Bake at 350° for 10-12 minutes or until the edges just start to brown. Remove to wire racks to cool completely. For the filling, beat cream cheese, sugar, flour and vanilla in a mixing bowl. Add pecans and coconut; mix well. Spoon 1/2 teaspoon into each cookie. For topping, heat chocolate chips, butter and water in a small saucepan until melted. Stir in sugar. Drizzle over cookies. **Yield:** 4 dozen.

Butter Cookies

These cookies are favorites of my nephews, who love the creamy frosting. I like to shape the cookies into little hearts for Valentine's Day, but they're perfect throughout the year.
—*Ruth Griggs*
South Hill, Virginia

   1 cup butter (no substitutes), softened
   3/4 cup sugar
   1 egg
   1/2 teaspoon vanilla extract
2-1/2 cups all-purpose flour
   1 teaspoon baking powder
   1/4 teaspoon salt
FROSTING:
   1/2 cup butter (no substitutes), softened
   4 cups confectioners' sugar
   1 teaspoon vanilla extract
   3 to 4 tablespoons milk
Red food coloring, optional

In a mixing bowl, cream the butter and sugar. Add egg and vanilla; mix well. Combine flour, baking powder and salt; add to creamed mixture and mix well. Place the dough in a cookie press fitted with a heart plate; form cookies on ungreased baking sheets. Bake at 375° for 6-8 minutes or until set but not brown. Cool on wire racks. Beat butter, sugar and vanilla until smooth. Blend in enough milk until desired spreading consistency is reached. Add food coloring to a portion or all of the frosting if desired. Frost cookies. **Yield:** about 6-1/2 dozen.

—☕ ☕ ☕—

Almond Sandies

Buttery, rich and delicious, these are my husband's favorite cookie and very popular wherever I take them. They're a nice change from ordinary pecan sandies.
—*Joyce Pierce, Caledonia, Michigan*

   1 cup butter (no substitutes), softened
   1 cup sugar
   1 teaspoon almond extract
1-3/4 cups all-purpose flour
   1/2 teaspoon baking soda
   1/4 teaspoon baking powder
   1/4 teaspoon salt
   1/2 cup slivered almonds

In a mixing bowl, cream butter and sugar. Add extract; mix well. Combine flour, baking soda, baking powder and salt; gradually add to the creamed mixture. Fold in almonds. Drop by rounded teaspoonfuls onto ungreased baking sheets. Bake at 300° for 22-24 minutes or until lightly browned. Cool 1-2 minutes before removing to a wire rack. **Yield:** about 4 dozen.

3/4 cup butter *or* margarine, softened
1 cup sugar
1/4 cup molasses
1 egg
2 cups all-purpose flour
2 teaspoons baking powder
1/2 teaspoon baking soda
1 teaspoon ground cinnamon
1/2 teaspoon ground cloves
1/2 teaspoon ground ginger

In a mixing bowl, cream butter and sugar. Beat in molasses and egg. Combine dry ingredients; gradually add to creamed mixture. Chill for 1 hour or until firm. Shape into 1-in. balls; place on greased baking sheets. Press flat with a glass dipped in sugar. Bake at 375° for 8-10 minutes or until lightly browned. Cool on wire racks. **Yield:** 6 dozen.

Icebox Sugar Cookies

I've been making these old-fashioned cookies since I was a girl. No one can resist these light, buttery treats.
—*Louise Worsham, Kalamazoo, Michigan*

1 cup butter (no substitutes), softened
2 cups sugar
2 eggs
1 teaspoon vanilla extract
3-1/2 cups all-purpose flour
1 teaspoon baking soda
1/2 teaspoon salt

In a mixing bowl, cream butter and sugar. Beat in eggs and vanilla. Combine flour, baking soda and salt; gradually add to creamed mixture. On a lightly floured surface, shape dough into three 10-in.-long rolls. Tightly wrap each roll in waxed paper. Chill for 1 hour or until firm. Cut into 3/8-in. slices; place on greased baking sheets. Sprinkle with sugar. Bake at 375° for 8-10 minutes or until lightly browned. Cool on wire racks. **Yield:** about 8 dozen.

Crisp Graham Cookies

I was delighted to find the recipe for these fun cookies. The peanut butter makes them extra special.
—*Lori Daniels, Elkins, West Virginia*

1/2 cup butter-flavored shortening
1/2 cup packed brown sugar
1 egg
1-1/2 teaspoons vanilla extract
1 can (14 ounces) sweetened condensed milk

Chocolate Orange Cookies

(Pictured above)

My three sisters like the combination of chocolate and orange as much as I do, so we all savor these cookies.
—*Ruth Rumple, Rockford, Ohio*

1 cup butter (no substitutes), softened
3/4 cup sugar, *divided*
1 egg
1 teaspoon vanilla extract
2-1/2 cups all-purpose flour
1/2 teaspoon salt
1/4 cup finely grated orange peel
1 cup (6 ounces) semisweet chocolate chips, melted

In a mixing bowl, cream butter and 1/2 cup sugar. Add egg and vanilla. Gradually add flour and salt; mix well. Cover and chill for 15 minutes. Roll the dough on a floured surface to 1/4-in. thickness. Cut with a 2-in. cookie cutter or shape into 2-in. x 1-in. rectangles. Place 2 in. apart on ungreased baking sheets. Combine orange peel and remaining sugar; spread over cookies. Bake at 350° for 14-16 minutes or until the edges just begin to brown. Remove to wire racks to cool completely. Decorate cookies with melted chocolate. **Yield:** about 3 dozen.

Favorite Molasses Cookies

These cookies are sure to remind you of Grandma's kitchen. They're crispy outside and chewy inside.
—*Marjorie Jenkins, Lees Summit, Missouri*

3 tablespoons creamy peanut butter
1-1/2 cups all-purpose flour
1 cup graham cracker crumbs
1 teaspoon baking soda
1 teaspoon salt
2 cups (1 pound) plain M&M's
1/2 cup chopped pecans

In a mixing bowl, cream shortening and brown sugar; beat in egg. Add vanilla and milk. Blend in peanut butter. Combine dry ingredients; add to the creamed mixture. Stir in the M&M's and nuts. Drop by teaspoonfuls 1 in. apart onto ungreased baking sheets. Bake at 350° for 10-12 minutes or until golden brown. Cool on wire racks. **Yield:** 7 dozen (2-inch cookies).

— ☕ ☕ ☕ —

Chocolate Caramel Bars

Taking dessert or another treat to a church or school potluck is never a problem for me. I jump at the chance to offer these rich, chocolaty bars. —Steve Mirro
Cape Coral, Florida

1 package (14 ounces) caramels
1 can (5 ounces) evaporated milk, *divided*
3/4 cup butter *or* margarine, softened
1 package (18-1/4 ounces) German chocolate cake mix
2 cups (12 ounces) semisweet chocolate chips

In a small saucepan over low heat, melt caramels with 1/3 cup milk. Meanwhile, in a mixing bowl, cream the butter. Add dry cake mix and remaining milk; mix well. Spread half of the dough into a greased 13-in. x 9-in. x 2-in. baking pan. Bake at 350° for 6 minutes; sprinkle chocolate chips over dough. Gently spread caramel mixture over chips. Drop remaining dough by tablespoonfuls over caramel layer. Return to the oven for 15 minutes. **Yield:** 3 dozen.

— ☕ ☕ ☕ —

Holiday Hideaways

(Pictured at right)

People eagerly anticipate these tasty cookies as part of our "season's eatings" each year. The surprise cherry center surrounded by a fluffy cookie makes this treat especially fun.
—Marianne Blazowich
Jeannette, Pennsylvania

3/4 cup sugar
2/3 cup butter-flavored shortening
1 egg
1 tablespoon milk

1 teaspoon vanilla extract
1-3/4 cups all-purpose flour
1 teaspoon baking powder
1/2 teaspoon baking soda
1/2 teaspoon salt
2 jars (10 ounces *each*) maraschino cherries, well drained
10 ounces white confectionery coating*, *divided*
4 tablespoons butter-flavored shortening, *divided*
8 ounces dark chocolate confectionery coating*
Finely chopped pecans

In a mixing bowl, cream sugar and shortening. Add egg, milk and vanilla. Combine dry ingredients; gradually add to the creamed mixture and mix well. Form 2 teaspoonfuls of dough into a ball. Flatten ball and place a cherry in the center; shape dough around cherry. Repeat with remaining dough and cherries. Place balls 2 in. apart on ungreased baking sheets. Bake at 350° for 10-12 minutes or until set and the edges are lightly browned. Cool 1 minute before removing to wire racks to cool completely. Grate 2 oz. white confectionery coating; set aside. Melt remaining white coating with 2 tablespoons of shortening; melt dark coating with remaining shortening. Dip half the cookies into white coating; place on waxed paper. Sprinkle with pecans. Dip remaining cookies in dark coating; place on waxed paper. Sprinkle with grated white coating. Store in a covered container in the refrigerator. **Yield:** about 4-1/2 dozen. ***Editor's Note:** Confectionery coating is found in the baking section of most grocery stores. It is sometimes labeled "almond bark" or "candy coating" and is often sold in bulk packages of 1 to 1-1/2 pounds.

Chocolate Nut Cookies

(Pictured below)

Folks are quick to grab one of these cookies when they see they're chocolate. Once they discover the nuts and vanilla chips, they grab a second and sometimes a third. —Farralee Baldwin, Tucson, Arizona

    1 cup butter *or* margarine, softened
3/4 cup packed brown sugar
1/2 cup sugar
    1 egg
    1 teaspoon almond extract
    2 cups all-purpose flour
1/4 cup baking cocoa
    1 teaspoon baking soda
1/2 teaspoon salt
    1 cup (6 ounces) vanilla baking chips
    1 cup chopped almonds

In a mixing bowl, cream butter and sugars. Add egg and extract; mix well. Combine the flour, cocoa, baking soda and salt; add to creamed mixture and mix well. Stir in the chips and nuts. Drop by teaspoonfuls onto ungreased baking sheets. Bake at 375° for 7-9 minutes. Cool on pans for 1 minute before removing to wire racks; cool completely. **Yield:** about 5 dozen.

Raspberry Swirled Brownies

Chocolate and raspberries are an irresistible combination. When entertaining, I dress up these fruity brownies with a dollop of whipped cream, fresh berries and a sprig of mint. —Iola Egle, McCook, Nebraska

1/2 cup butter *or* margarine, softened
    1 cup sugar
    1 can (16 ounces) chocolate syrup
    4 eggs
1-1/2 cups all-purpose flour
    1 package (3 ounces) cream cheese, softened
2/3 cup raspberry preserves
    1 cup unsweetened raspberries
Whipped cream, fresh raspberries and mint, optional

In a mixing bowl, cream butter and sugar. Add chocolate syrup and eggs; mix well. Add flour and mix well. Beat cream cheese and preserves until smooth; gently stir in raspberries. Fold into the batter. Spread in a greased 15-in. x 10-in. x 1-in. baking pan. Bake at 350° for 30-35 minutes or until brownies test done. Cool. Cut into 2-1/2-in. diamonds. Garnish with whipped cream, raspberries and mint if desired. **Yield:** about 2-1/2 dozen.

— 🍷 🍷 🍷 —

Grandpa's Cookies

My grandpa, a widower, raised his three sons on his own and did all of the cooking and lots of baking. I can still picture him making these tasty cookies. —Karen Baker, Dover, Ohio

    2 cups butter *or* margarine, softened
    4 cups packed brown sugar
    4 eggs
1/2 cup water
    1 teaspoon vanilla extract
    7 cups all-purpose flour
    1 tablespoon cream of tartar
    1 tablespoon baking soda

In a mixing bowl, cream butter and brown sugar. Add eggs, water and vanilla; mix well. Combine remaining ingredients; add to the creamed mixture and mix well. Shape into three rolls; wrap with plastic wrap. Chill 4 hours or overnight. Cut rolls into 1/4-in. slices; place 2 in. apart on greased baking sheets. Bake at 375° for 8-10 minutes or until lightly browned. **Yield:** about 10 dozen.

— 🍷 🍷 🍷 —

Chocolate Chip Soybean Cookies

This super snack is crisp, sweet and nutritious. Our grandson Timothy is a big fan of these cookies. —Pat Waymire, Yellow Springs, Ohio

    1 cup margarine, softened
    3 cups packed brown sugar

4 **eggs**
2 **tablespoons milk**
1 **teaspoon vanilla extract**
3 **cups all-purpose flour**
1 **cup soy flour**
2 **teaspoons baking soda**
1 **teaspoon salt**
4 **cups (24 ounces) semisweet chocolate chips**
2 **cups roasted unsalted soybean nuts, chopped**

In a mixing bowl, cream the margarine and sugar. Add eggs, one at a time, beating well after each addition. Beat in milk and vanilla. Combine flours, baking soda and salt; add to creamed mixture and mix well. Stir in chocolate chips and soybean nuts. Drop by tablespoonfuls 2 in. apart onto greased baking sheets. Bake at 350° for 10 minutes or until lightly browned. **Yield:** 8 dozen.

— 🥄 🥄 🥄 —

Marble Squares

With cream cheese, sour cream and lots of chocolate, these bars are simply scrumptious. I'm sure you'll agree. —Pat Habiger, Spearville, Kansas

1 **package (8 ounces) cream cheese, softened**
2-1/3 **cups sugar, *divided***
3 **eggs**
3/4 **cup water**
1/2 **cup butter *or* margarine**
1-1/2 **squares (1-1/2 ounces) unsweetened baking chocolate**
2 **cups all-purpose flour**
1/2 **cup sour cream**
1 **teaspoon baking soda**
1/2 **teaspoon salt**
1 **cup (6 ounces) semisweet chocolate chips**

In a small mixing bowl, beat cream cheese and 1/3 cup sugar until light and fluffy. Beat in 1 egg; set aside. In a large saucepan, bring water, butter and chocolate to a boil, stirring occasionally. Remove from the heat. Add flour and remaining sugar; mix well. Stir in sour cream, baking soda, salt and remaining eggs until smooth. Pour into a greased and floured 15-in. x 10-in. x 1-in. baking pan. Dollop

It's a Wrap!

Cut a roll of clear plastic wrap in half to use for individually wrapping cookies and bars. You end up with two narrow rolls of the perfect size wrap.

cream cheese mixture over top; with a knife, cut through batter to create a marbled effect. Sprinkle with chocolate chips. Bake at 375° for 30-35 minutes or until a toothpick inserted near the center comes out clean. Cool before cutting. **Yield:** about 5 dozen.

Caramel Heavenlies

(Pictured above)

My mom made these dressy, sweet cookies for cookie exchanges when I was a little girl, letting me sprinkle on the almonds and coconut. —Dawn Burns
Troy, Ohio

12 **graham crackers (4-3/4 inches x 2-1/2 inches)**
2 **cups miniature marshmallows**
3/4 **cup butter *or* margarine**
3/4 **cup packed brown sugar**
1 **teaspoon ground cinnamon**
1 **teaspoon vanilla extract**
1 **cup sliced almonds**
1 **cup flaked coconut**

Line a 15-in. x 10-in. x 1-in. baking pan with foil. Place graham crackers in pan; cover with marshmallows. In a saucepan over medium heat, cook and stir butter, brown sugar and cinnamon until the butter is melted and the sugar is dissolved. Remove from the heat; stir in vanilla. Spoon over the marshmallows. Sprinkle with almonds and coconut. Bake at 350° for 14-16 minutes or until browned. Cool completely. Cut into 2-in. squares, then cut each square in half to form triangles. **Yield:** about 6 dozen.

Apricot Crescents

(Pictured above)

When I was in college, my roommate's mom sent these flaky horns in a holiday care package. I've been making them ever since. —Tamyra Vest, Scottsburg, Virginia

  1 cup butter (no substitutes)
  2 cups all-purpose flour
  1 egg yolk
1/2 cup sour cream
1/2 cup apricot preserves
1/2 cup flaked coconut
1/4 cup finely chopped pecans
Sugar

In a bowl, cut butter into flour until the mixture resembles coarse crumbs. Beat egg yolk and sour cream; add to crumb mixture and mix well. Chill for several hours or overnight. Divide dough into fourths. On a sugared surface, roll each portion into a 10-in. circle. Turn dough over to sugar top side. Combine preserves, coconut and pecans; spread over circles. Cut each circle into 12 wedges and roll each wedge into a crescent shape, starting at the wide end. Sprinkle with sugar. Place points down 1 in. apart on ungreased baking sheets. Bake at 350° for 15-17 minutes or until set and very lightly browned. Immediately remove to wire racks to cool. **Yield:** 4 dozen.

— 🍵 🍵 🍵 —

Marshmallow Brownies

Picnickers of all ages will love these yummy bars loaded with goodies. Fill your basket with these brownies when summertime fun beckons.
—Renee Schwebach, Dumont, Minnesota

  1 cup (6 ounces) butterscotch chips
1/2 cup butter *or* margarine
  2 eggs
2/3 cup packed brown sugar
  1 teaspoon vanilla extract
1-1/2 cups all-purpose flour
  2 teaspoons baking powder
1/2 teaspoon salt
  2 cups miniature marshmallows
  2 cups (12 ounces) semisweet chocolate chips
1/2 cup chopped walnuts

In a saucepan over low heat, melt butterscotch chips and butter; cool for 10 minutes. In a mixing bowl, beat eggs, brown sugar and vanilla. Add butterscotch mixture; mix well. Combine flour, baking powder and salt; add to batter and mix well. Stir in marshmallows, chocolate chips and nuts. Spread into a greased 13-in. x 9-in. x 2-in. baking pan. Bake at 325° for 25-30 minutes or until brownies test done with a toothpick. Cool before cutting. **Yield:** 3 dozen.

— 🍵 🍵 🍵 —

Chewy Peanut Butter Bars

These delectable bars are great for lunches and bake sales, yet use only ordinary kitchen staples.
—Beverly Swihart, Marion, Ohio

1/2 cup butter *or* margarine, softened
2/3 cup packed brown sugar
  2 egg yolks
  1 teaspoon vanilla extract
1-1/2 cups all-purpose flour
1/2 teaspoon baking powder
1/2 teaspoon salt
1/4 teaspoon baking soda
  3 cups miniature marshmallows
TOPPING:
2/3 cup light corn syrup
1/4 cup butter *or* margarine
  1 package (10 ounces) peanut butter chips
  2 teaspoons vanilla extract
  2 cups crisp rice cereal
  2 cups salted peanuts

In a mixing bowl, cream butter and sugar. Add egg yolks and vanilla; mix well. Combine flour, baking powder, salt and baking soda; add to the creamed mixture and mix well. Press into a greased 13-in. x 9-in. x 2-in. baking pan. Bake at 350° for 12-15 minutes or until golden. Sprinkle with marshmallows; return to oven just until marshmallows begin to puff, about 2 minutes. Cool. Meanwhile, combine corn syrup, butter, chips and vanilla in a large saucepan; cook and stir over low heat until chips are melted and mixture is smooth. Remove from the heat; stir in cereal and peanuts. Evenly spread warm topping over marshmallow layer. Refrigerate until set. **Yield:** 2 to 2-1/2 dozen.

— 🍂 🍂 🍂 —

Spiced Cutouts

Cardamom adds a nice subtle flavor to these spicy, crisp cookies. These treats are perfect for the holidays, but my family asks for them year-round.
—Delisa Narr, West Bend, Wisconsin

   1 **cup butter (no substitutes), softened**
1-1/2 **cups sugar**
   1 **tablespoon molasses**
   1 **egg**
3-1/4 **cups all-purpose flour**
   1 **tablespoon ground cinnamon**
   1 **tablespoon ground ginger**
   2 **teaspoons ground cardamom**
   2 **teaspoons ground cloves**
   2 **teaspoons baking soda**
 1/4 **cup orange juice**
   1 **tablespoon grated orange peel**

In a mixing bowl, cream butter and sugar; beat in molasses and egg. Combine flour, spices and baking soda; add to creamed mixture alternately with orange juice. Stir in peel. On a floured surface, roll the dough to 1/16-in. thickness. Cut with a 2-1/2-in. cookie cutter and place on ungreased baking sheets. Bake at 350° for 6-8 minutes or until edges are lightly browned. Cool on wire racks. **Yield:** about 9 dozen.

— 🍂 🍂 🍂 —

Golden Raisin Cookies

Since my children are grown, I make these buttery cookies for the neighborhood kids. They say they know when I'm baking since the aroma carries out to the street. —Isabel Podeszwa, Lakewood, New Jersey

   1 **cup butter (no substitutes), softened**
1-1/2 **cups sugar**
   1 **tablespoon lemon juice**
   2 **eggs**
3-1/2 **cups all-purpose flour**
1-1/2 **teaspoons cream of tartar**
1-1/2 **teaspoons baking soda**
   1 **package (15 ounces) golden raisins**
     (2-1/2 cups)

In a mixing bowl, cream butter and sugar. Add lemon juice and eggs. Combine dry ingredients; gradually add to creamed mixture. Stir in raisins. Roll into 1-in. balls. Place on greased baking sheets;

flatten with a floured fork. Bake at 400° for 8-10 minutes or until lightly browned. **Yield:** about 6 dozen.

— 🍂 🍂 🍂 —

Pinwheel Cookies
(Pictured below)

These pretty pinwheel cookies have tempting swirly layers of orange and chocolate. —Paulette Morgan
Moorhead, Minnesota

   1 **cup butter (no substitutes)**
   1 **package (3 ounces) cream cheese, softened**
   1 **cup sugar**
   1 **egg**
   1 **tablespoon grated orange peel**
   1 **teaspoon vanilla extract**
3-1/2 **cups all-purpose flour**
   1 **teaspoon salt**
FILLING:
   1 **cup (6 ounces) semisweet chocolate chips**
   1 **package (3 ounces) cream cheese, softened**
 1/2 **cup confectioners' sugar**
 1/4 **cup orange juice**

In a mixing bowl, cream the butter, cream cheese and sugar. Add egg, orange peel and vanilla; mix well. Combine flour and salt; add to the creamed mixture and mix well. Cover and chill for 4 hours or until firm. Meanwhile, combine all filling ingredients in a small saucepan. Cook and stir over low heat until smooth; set aside to cool. On a floured surface, divide dough in half; roll each half into a 12-in. x 10-in. rectangle. Spread with filling. Carefully roll up into a tight jelly roll and wrap in waxed paper. Chill overnight. Remove waxed paper; cut rolls into 1/4-in. slices. Place on ungreased baking sheets. Bake at 375° for 8-10 minutes or until lightly browned. Remove to wire racks to cool. **Yield:** about 8 dozen.

Chocolate Mint Wafers

(Pictured below)

When my family starts munching on these chocolaty treats with cool mint filling, a batch never stays around long. —Annette Esau, Durham, Ontario

   2/3 cup butter (no substitutes), softened
   1/2 cup sugar
   1/2 cup packed brown sugar
   1/4 cup milk
     1 egg
     2 cups all-purpose flour
   3/4 cup baking cocoa
     1 teaspoon baking powder
   1/2 teaspoon baking soda
   1/4 teaspoon salt
FILLING:
2-3/4 cups confectioners' sugar
   1/4 cup half-and-half cream
   1/4 teaspoon peppermint extract
   1/4 teaspoon salt
Green food coloring

In a mixing bowl, cream butter and sugars. Add milk and egg; mix well. Combine dry ingredients; gradually add to creamed mixture and mix well. Cover and chill 2 hours or until firm. Roll chilled dough on a floured surface to 1/8-in. thickness. Cut with a 1-1/2-in. cookie cutter and place 1 in. apart on greased baking sheets. Bake at 375° for 5-6 minutes or until edges are lightly browned. Remove to wire racks to cool completely. Combine filling ingredients; spread on half of the cookies and top with another cookie. **Yield:** about 7-1/2 dozen.

Glazed Orange Date Squares

(Pictured on page 117)

Orange, chocolate and chewy dates make a memorable combination. —Ruth Stoops, Cincinnati, Ohio

1-1/4 cups chopped dates
   3/4 cup packed brown sugar
   1/2 cup water
   1/2 cup butter *or* margarine
     1 cup (6 ounces) semisweet chocolate chips
     2 eggs
   1/2 cup milk
   1/2 cup orange juice
1-1/4 cups all-purpose flour
   3/4 teaspoon baking soda
   1/2 teaspoon salt
     1 cup chopped walnuts
ORANGE GLAZE:
     3 cups confectioners' sugar
   1/4 cup butter *or* margarine, softened
     1 to 2 teaspoons grated orange peel
   1/3 cup milk

In a saucepan, combine dates, brown sugar, water and butter. Simmer for 5 minutes, stirring occasionally, or until dates are softened. Remove from the heat; stir in chocolate chips. In a small bowl, beat eggs, milk and orange juice. Combine flour, baking soda and salt; add to chocolate mixture alternately with orange juice mixture, mixing well after each addition. Stir in the walnuts. Pour into a greased 15-in. x 10-in. x 1-in. baking pan. Bake at 350° for 25-30 minutes or until a toothpick inserted near the center comes out clean. Cool. In a bowl, combine confectioners' sugar, butter and orange peel. Stir in milk until glaze reaches desired spreading consistency. Spread over bars. **Yield:** 3 dozen.

Goblin Chewies

With candy orange slices and raisins or chocolate chips, these fun cookies are a perfect Halloween treat. —Bernice Morris, Marshfield, Missouri

     1 cup shortening
     1 cup packed brown sugar
     1 cup sugar
     2 eggs
     1 teaspoon vanilla extract
     2 cups all-purpose flour
     1 teaspoon baking soda
   1/2 teaspoon baking powder
   1/2 teaspoon salt
1-1/2 cups old-fashioned oats
     1 cup crisp rice cereal
     1 cup diced candy orange slices*

1 cup (6 ounces) semisweet chocolate chips
or raisins
**Additional raisins *or* chocolate chips and candy
orange slices**

In a mixing bowl, cream shortening and sugars. Add eggs and vanilla; mix well. Combine flour, baking soda, baking powder and salt; add to the creamed mixture. Stir in oats, cereal, orange slices and chips or raisins. Drop by tablespoonfuls 2 in. apart onto greased baking sheets. Flatten slightly with a fork. Decorate with raisin or chocolate chip eyes and orange slice mouths. Bake at 350° for 10-14 minutes. Cool on wire racks. **Yield:** about 6 dozen. ***Editor's Note:** Orange slices cut easier if microwaved for 5 seconds on high and cut with a sharp knife or kitchen scissors.

Oatmeal Pecan Cookies

It's hard to stop at one when nibbling on these delightful cookies. They're wholesome and travel well.
—*Debbi Smith, Crossett, Arkansas*

    1 cup shortening
    1 cup packed brown sugar
    1 cup sugar
    2 eggs
    1 teaspoon vanilla extract
1-1/2 cups all-purpose flour
    1 teaspoon baking soda
    1 teaspoon salt
    3 cups old-fashioned oats
    1 cup chopped pecans

In a mixing bowl, cream shortening and sugars. Add eggs and vanilla. Combine flour, baking soda and salt; gradually add to creamed mixture. Stir in oats and nuts. Chill for 30 minutes. Shape into 1-1/2-in. balls; place 2 in. apart on greased baking sheets. Bake at 350° for 10-12 minutes or until golden brown. Cool on wire racks. **Yield:** about 7 dozen.

Soft Gingersnaps

These cake-like cookies are delightfully old-fashioned, which makes it hard to believe they're low in fat.
—*Shonna Lee Leonard, Lower Sackville, Nova Scotia*

✓ This tasty dish uses less sugar, salt and fat. Recipe includes *Diabetic Exchanges.*

1-1/2 cups all-purpose flour
   1/2 cup whole wheat flour
     2 teaspoons baking soda

    1 teaspoon ground cinnamon
    1 teaspoon ground cloves
    1 teaspoon ground ginger
1/4 teaspoon salt
Egg substitute equivalent to 2 eggs
    1/2 cup sugar
    1/4 cup packed brown sugar
    1/4 cup vegetable oil
    1/4 cup molasses

In a mixing bowl, combine flours, baking soda, cinnamon, cloves, ginger and salt. Combine egg substitute, sugars, oil and molasses; mix well. Add to dry ingredients; mix well. Drop by teaspoonfuls 2 in. apart onto baking sheets coated with nonstick cooking spray. Bake at 350° for 8-10 minutes or until cookies spring back when lightly touched. Cool on pans 5 minutes before removing to wire racks to cool completely. **Yield:** 3 dozen. **Diabetic Exchanges:** One cookie equals 1/2 starch, 1/2 fat; also, 62 calories, 93 mg sodium, trace cholesterol, 11 gm carbohydrate, 1 gm protein, 2 gm fat.

Apple Nut Bars

For big apple taste packed into a tasty bar, give this recipe a try. It's extra nice since you don't have to peel the apples. —*Karen Nelson, Sullivan, Wisconsin*

✓ This tasty dish uses less sugar, salt and fat. Recipe includes *Diabetic Exchanges.*

    2 egg whites
2/3 cup sugar
1/2 teaspoon vanilla extract
1/2 cup all-purpose flour
    1 teaspoon baking powder
    2 cups chopped unpeeled tart apples
1/4 cup chopped pecans

In a bowl, whisk egg whites, sugar and vanilla for about 1-1/2 minutes. Add flour and baking powder; whisk for 1 minute. Fold in apples and pecans. Pour into an 8-in. square baking pan coated with nonstick cooking spray. Bake at 350° for 25-30 minutes or until bars test done. Cool. **Yield:** 1 dozen. **Diabetic Exchanges:** One bar equals 1 starch; also, 73 calories, 50 mg sodium, 0 cholesterol, 14 gm carbohydrate, 1 gm protein, 2 gm fat.

No More Mess

When making Rice Krispies treats, run your hands under cold water before pressing the mixture in a pan. The marshmallow won't stick to your fingers.

Cakes, Pies & Desserts

These moist cakes, sweet candies, palate-pleasing pies and tempting desserts make fantastic finales for all of your meals.

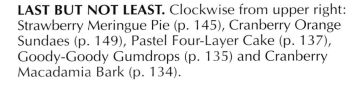

LAST BUT NOT LEAST. Clockwise from upper right: Strawberry Meringue Pie (p. 145), Cranberry Orange Sundaes (p. 149), Pastel Four-Layer Cake (p. 137), Goody-Goody Gumdrops (p. 135) and Cranberry Macadamia Bark (p. 134).

Apricot Cheese Kugel

(Pictured above)

This sweet noodle kugel is a fun dessert and a super addition to any brunch buffet. My family and friends scrape the pan clean. I got the recipe from my sister.
—Florence Palermo, Melrose Park, Illinois

- 1 package (16 ounces) wide egg noodles
- 1 package (8 ounces) cream cheese, softened
- 1 cup butter *or* margarine, softened
- 1-1/2 cups sugar
- 1/2 cup lemon juice
- 12 eggs
- 1 jar (18 ounces) apricot preserves
- 1/2 teaspoon ground cinnamon, *divided*

Cook noodles according to package directions. Meanwhile, in a mixing bowl, beat cream cheese, butter and sugar until smooth; add lemon juice and mix well. Beat in eggs, one at a time. Drain and rinse noodles; add to egg mixture. Spoon half into an ungreased 13-in. x 9-in. x 2-in. baking dish. Top with half of the preserves; sprinkle with half of the cinnamon. Repeat layers. Bake, uncovered, at 325° for 45 minutes or until golden brown and a knife inserted near the center comes out clean. Serve warm. **Yield:** 12-16 servings. **Editor's Note:** Kugel may be reheated in the oven or microwave.

------ 🍮 🍮 🍮 ------

Pine Nut Divinity

As a boy, I harvested pine nuts from nearby trees. Mom would then make this melt-in-your-mouth candy, which my sisters and I would sell at school fund-raisers. It was always a hit. —Ed Horkey
Ahwatukee, Arizona

- 3 cups sugar
- 2/3 cup water
- 1/2 cup light corn syrup
- 2 egg whites
- 1/8 teaspoon salt
- 1 teaspoon vanilla extract
- 1 cup pine nuts, toasted

In a large saucepan, combine sugar, water and corn syrup; bring to a boil over medium-high heat, stirring constantly. Cook over medium heat without stirring until a candy thermometer reads 260° (hard-ball stage), about 10-15 minutes. Remove from the heat. In a large mixing bowl, beat egg whites and salt until stiff peaks form. Beat on high while gradually pouring hot sugar mixture in a thin stream over egg whites; continue beating for about 3 minutes. Add vanilla; beat just until candy starts to lose its gloss, about 5 minutes. Stir in the pine nuts. Working quickly, drop by tablespoonfuls onto waxed paper; or pour into a buttered 9-in. square pan and cut into serving-size pieces. Store tightly covered. **Yield:** about 3 dozen. **Editor's Note:** It is not recommended to use a hand mixer for this recipe.

------ 🍮 🍮 🍮 ------

Mincemeat Apple Cake

For a festive holiday touch, I'll drizzle this cake with a glaze and decorate it with red and green candied cherries. —Priscilla Gilbert
Indian Harbour Beach, Florida

- 2 cups all-purpose flour
- 1/2 cup packed brown sugar
- 1 tablespoon baking powder
- 1/2 teaspoon ground cinnamon
- 1/2 teaspoon baking soda
- 1/4 teaspoon ground cloves
- 2 eggs
- 1 cup prepared mincemeat
- 1/3 cup applesauce
- 1/3 cup apple juice
- 3 tablespoons butter *or* margarine, melted

LEMON SAUCE:
- 1 cup sugar
- 3 tablespoons cornstarch
- 2 cups water
- 1/4 cup butter *or* margarine
- 1 tablespoon grated lemon peel
- 2 teaspoons lemon juice

In a bowl, combine the first six ingredients. In another bowl, beat eggs; add mincemeat, applesauce, juice and butter. Stir into dry ingredients. Pour into a greased 8-cup fluted tube pan. Bake at 350° for 35-40 minutes or until a toothpick inserted near the center comes out clean. Cool in pan for 10 minutes before removing to a wire rack. Meanwhile, for the sauce, combine sugar and cornstarch in a saucepan. Stir in water until smooth. Bring to a boil; cook and stir for 2 minutes. Remove from the heat; stir in butter until melted. Add lemon peel and juice. Serve warm with the cake. **Yield:** 10 servings. **Editor's Note:** An 11-in. x 7-in. x 2-in. baking pan can be used instead of the tube pan. Bake for 25-30 minutes or until cake tests done.

— 🝛 🝛 🝛 —

Huckleberry Cheese Pie

This pie has a cookie-like press-in crust, a fluffy cream filling and a layer of luscious huckleberries on top. I think it really shows off the lovely dark glossy berries.
—Dianne Doede, Trout Lake, Washington

1-1/4 cups all-purpose flour
    5 teaspoons confectioners' sugar
1/2 cup butter *or* margarine, melted
TOPPING:
    3/4 cup sugar
    1/4 cup cornstarch
    4 cups fresh *or* frozen huckleberries
    1/3 cup water
FILLING:
    1 package (8 ounces) cream cheese,
      softened
1/2 cup confectioners' sugar
    1 tablespoon lemon juice
    1 teaspoon grated lemon peel
    1 teaspoon vanilla extract
    1 cup whipping cream, whipped

In a bowl, combine flour and confectioners' sugar. Stir in butter. Press onto the bottom and sides of two greased 9-in. pie pans. Bake at 375° for 8-10 minutes or until golden brown. Cool on a wire rack. For the topping, combine sugar and cornstarch in a saucepan; stir in berries and water. Cook and stir over medium heat until mixture comes to a boil; boil for 2 minutes. Cool. In a mixing bowl, beat cream cheese, sugar, lemon juice, peel and vanilla until light and fluffy. Fold in whipped cream. Spoon half into each crust. Spoon topping over filling. Chill for 1 hour. **Yield:** 2 pies (12-16 servings).

Appealing Pie Crusts

A bit of grated orange or lemon peel mixed in with the flour makes pie crust special.

Raspberry Delight

(Pictured below)

I knew this cool, fruity and creamy dessert was a winner the first time I tasted it. I confirmed that fact a few summers ago when I entered the recipe in a contest at work—it won first place. Co-workers still call to request it.   *—Mary Olson, Albany, Oregon*

2-1/4 cups all-purpose flour
    2 tablespoons sugar
3/4 cup butter *or* margarine, softened
FILLING:
    1 package (8 ounces) cream cheese,
      softened
    1 cup confectioners' sugar
    1 teaspoon vanilla extract
1/4 teaspoon salt
    2 cups whipped topping
TOPPING:
    1 package (6 ounces) raspberry gelatin
    2 cups boiling water
    2 packages (10 ounces *each*) sweetened
      frozen raspberries
Additional whipped topping and fresh mint,
    optional

In a bowl, combine flour and sugar; blend in butter with a wooden spoon until smooth. Press into an ungreased 13-in. x 9-in. x 2-in. baking pan. Bake at 300° for 20-25 minutes or until set (crust will not brown). Cool. In a mixing bowl, beat cream cheese, confectioners' sugar, vanilla and salt until smooth. Fold in whipped topping. Spread over crust. For topping, dissolve gelatin in boiling water; stir in raspberries. Chill for 20 minutes or until mixture begins to thicken. Spoon over filling. Refrigerate until set. Cut into squares; garnish with whipped topping and mint if desired. **Yield:** 12-16 servings.

Christmas Candy...in a Wink!

THERE'S no need to be a veteran candy maker to turn out these melt-in-your-mouth confections. They're *simply* wonderful!

Cranberry Macadamia Bark

(Pictured below)

I fill Christmas tins with this special candy to give as gifts. Dried cranberries are a different taste twist.
—*Pamela Galiardi, San Jose, California*

1 pound white confectionery coating, cut into pieces
1 jar (3-1/2 ounces) macadamia nuts
1/2 cup dried cranberries

Melt coating in a saucepan over medium-low heat, stirring until smooth. Add nuts and cranberries; mix well. Spread onto a foil-lined baking sheet. Cool. Break into pieces. **Yield:** 1-1/4 pounds.

Peanut Butter Fudge

(Pictured below)

This is a favorite "never-fail" quickie recipe I've been depending on for years. The holidays wouldn't be the same without this luscious fudge!
—*Eleanore Peterson, Fort Atkinson, Wisconsin*

1 pound white confectionery coating, cut into pieces

SWEET TOOTH-TICKLING TREATS like Cranberry Macadamia Bark, Goody-Goody Gumdrops, Easy Chocolate Drops and Peanut Butter Fudge (shown above, clockwise from top) spread smiles.

1 cup creamy peanut butter
1 cup coarsely chopped walnuts

Melt coating in a saucepan over medium-low heat, stirring constantly until smooth. Remove from the heat; stir in peanut butter and walnuts. Spread into a greased 8-in. square pan. Chill until firm. Cut into squares. **Yield:** 1-3/4 pounds.

— 🍴 🍴 🍴 —

Easy Chocolate Drops

(Pictured below left)

Friends and family relish these crunchy goodies. I never knew that making candy could be so simple!
—Heather De Cal, Terrace Bay, Ontario

1 cup (6 ounces) semisweet chocolate chips
1 cup (6 ounces) butterscotch chips
1 cup shoestring potato sticks
1 cup salted peanuts

In a 2-qt. microwave-safe bowl, heat chips on high for 2 minutes or until melted, stirring once. Stir in potato sticks and peanuts. Drop by teaspoonfuls onto waxed paper-lined baking sheets. Chill until set, about 15 minutes. Store in airtight containers. **Yield:** 3-1/2 dozen. **Editor's Note:** This recipe was tested in a 700-watt microwave.

— 🍴 🍴 🍴 —

Goody-Goody Gumdrops

(Pictured at left)

These homemade jewel-toned squares are softer than store-bought gumdrops. But their fantastic flavor has true old-fashioned flair. *—SueAnn Bunt*
Painted Post, New York

3 envelopes unflavored gelatin
1-1/4 cups water, *divided*
1-1/2 cups sugar
1/4 to 1/2 teaspoon peppermint extract
Green and red food coloring
Additional sugar

In a small bowl, sprinkle gelatin over 1/2 cup water; let stand for 5 minutes. In a saucepan, bring sugar and remaining water to a boil over medium heat, stirring constantly. Add the gelatin; reduce heat. Simmer and stir for 5 minutes. Remove from the heat and stir in extract. Divide mixture into two bowls; add four drops green food coloring to one bowl and four drops red to the other. Pour into two greased 8-in. x 4-in. x 2-in. loaf pans. Chill 3 hours or until firm. Loosen edges from pan with a knife; turn onto a sugared board. Cut into 1/2-in. cubes; roll in sugar. Let stand at room temperature, un-

covered, for 3-4 hours, turning every hour so all sides dry. Cover and chill. **Yield:** about 1 pound.

— 🍴 🍴 🍴 —

Tiger Butter Candy

This candy is big on peanut butter flavor and fun to make. Best of all, it's made in the microwave for added convenience. *—Pamela Pogue, Mineola, Texas*

1 pound white confectionery coating, cut into pieces
1/2 cup chunky peanut butter
1/2 cup semisweet chocolate chips
4 teaspoons half-and-half cream

In a microwave-safe bowl, heat coating and peanut butter on medium for 3-4 minutes or until melted; mix well. Pour onto a foil-lined baking sheet coated with nonstick cooking spray; spread into a thin layer. In another microwave-safe bowl, heat chips and cream on high for about 30 seconds or until chips are soft; stir until smooth. Pour and swirl over peanut butter layer. Freeze for 5 minutes or until set. Break into small pieces. **Yield:** about 1-1/2 pounds. **Editor's Note:** This recipe was tested in a 700-watt microwave.

— 🍴 🍴 🍴 —

Pecan Logs

These logs slice into pretty rounds and are absolutely the best. Don't be surprised to see them quickly disappear from your holiday dessert tray.
—Suzanne McKinley, Lyons, Georgia

3 cups confectioners' sugar
1 jar (7 ounces) marshmallow creme
1 teaspoon vanilla extract
1 bag (14 ounces) caramels
3 tablespoons water
1-1/2 cups chopped pecans

In a bowl, combine the sugar, creme and vanilla; knead until smooth (mixture will be dry). Shape into six 4-1/2-in. x 1-1/4-in. logs. Cover and chill overnight. In the top of a double boiler over boiling water, cook and stir caramels and water until smooth. Dip logs into caramel; roll in pecans. Chill for 2 hours. Cut into 1/3-in. slices. **Yield:** about 6-1/2 dozen.

Looking for Confectionery Coating?

White confectionery coating is found in the baking section of most grocery stores. It is sometimes labeled "almond bark" or "candy coating" and is often sold in bulk packages of 1 to 1-1/2 pounds.

Butterfly Cake

(Pictured above)

This recipe starts out with an ordinary 13- x 9-inch pan. Then I cut the cake and pipe on some frosting. But you can simply decorate it with purchased candies and cake trims if you prefer. —Sue Gronholz
Columbus, Wisconsin

   1/2 cup shortening
1-1/2 cups sugar
     2 eggs
2-1/2 cups cake flour
    1 tablespoon baking powder
  1/2 teaspoon salt
    1 cup milk
    1 teaspoon vanilla extract
FROSTING/DECORATING:
    1 cup shortening
  1/2 cup butter *or* margarine, softened
4-1/2 cups confectioners' sugar, *divided*
  1/8 teaspoon salt
    1 teaspoon vanilla extract
    1 teaspoon almond extract
    3 to 5 tablespoons milk
Orange liquid *or* paste food coloring
Colored jimmies
Pastry bag *or* heavy-duty resealable plastic bag
Pastry tips—#98 shell and #5 round
Red shoestring licorice
Birthday candles

In a mixing bowl, cream shortening and sugar until light and fluffy. Add eggs, one at a time, beating well after each. Combine flour, baking pow-

der and salt; add alternately with milk to creamed mixture. Beat in vanilla. Pour into a waxed paper-lined 13-in. x 9-in. x 2-in. baking pan. Bake at 350° for 30-35 minutes or until cake tests done. Cool for 10 minutes; remove from pan to a wire rack to cool completely. Remove waxed paper. For frosting, cream shortening and butter until light and fluffy. Gradually beat in 2 cups confectioners' sugar; add salt, extracts and 3 tablespoons milk. Beat in remaining sugar. If necessary, add additional milk, 1 tablespoon at a time, until frosting reaches desired consistency. Remove 2 cups; set aside. Tint remaining frosting with orange food coloring.

To make butterfly, cut a 1-in.-wide strip of cake from the 9-in. side (see diagram below). Place a toothpick in the center of remaining cake. Using string, divide cake into four triangles, holding string at opposite corners. Depress string slightly into cake to mark cutting line; repeat for remaining corners. Cut cake along cutting lines. Place the 1-in. strip of cake (C) in the center of a 20-in. x 15-in. serving board to be the butterfly body. Frost top and sides of body with orange frosting. Place two smaller triangles (A) next to the body for bottom wings. Place two larger triangles (B) for top wings. Frost the sides and tops of wings with orange frosting. Smooth frosting with a warm spatula.

Decorate edges of cake with white frosting, using a pastry bag and shell tip. Mark circles on wings with the top of a 2-in. plastic cup. Sprinkle jimmies in circles; outline with white frosting, using round tip. Cut licorice into four small pieces; push ends into top of body for antennae. Place candles on the body. **Yield:** 12-14 servings.

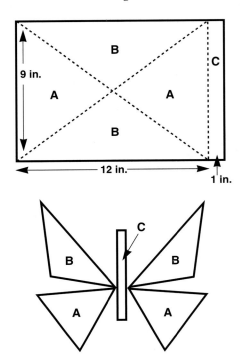

Sunflower Brittle

My mother made this candy for years using several kinds of nuts. Then I was married and my husband raised sunflowers, so it seemed natural to use those. People always comment on the unique delicious taste.
—_Trish Gehlhar, Ypsilanti, North Dakota_

   2 cups sugar
   1 cup light corn syrup
  1/2 cup water
1-1/2 cups raw _or_ roasted sunflower seeds
   1 tablespoon butter _or_ margarine
   1 teaspoon vanilla extract
   1 teaspoon baking soda

Butter the sides of a large heavy saucepan. Add sugar, corn syrup and water; bring to a boil, stirring constantly. Cook and stir over medium-low heat until a candy thermometer reads 260° (hard-ball stage). Stir in sunflower seeds and butter. Cook over medium heat to 300° (hard-crack stage). Remove from the heat; vigorously stir in vanilla and baking soda. Pour into a buttered 15-in. x 10-in. x 1-in. baking pan; spread evenly to fill pan. Cool completely. Break into pieces. Store in an airtight container with waxed paper between layers. **Yield:** about 1-1/2 pounds.

Soft 'n' Chewy Caramels

This candy is a "must" at our house for Christmas. We raised four children on nutritious meals made of simple ingredients. Now I enjoy making special treats like this for the grandkids. —_Darlene Edinger Turtle Lake, North Dakota_

2 cups sugar
1 cup light corn syrup
2 cups half-and-half cream, _divided_
1 cup butter _or_ margarine
1 teaspoon vanilla extract

Line a 13-in. x 9-in. x 2-in. pan with foil; butter the foil. Set aside. Combine sugar, corn syrup and 1 cup cream in a 5-qt. saucepan or Dutch oven; bring to a boil over medium heat, stirring constantly. Slowly stir in remaining cream. Cook over medium heat until a candy thermometer reads 250° (hard-ball stage), stirring frequently. Remove from the heat; stir in butter and vanilla until well mixed, about 5 minutes. Pour into prepared pan. Cool. Remove foil from pan; cut candy into 1-in. squares. Wrap individually in waxed paper; twist ends. **Yield:** 9-10 dozen (2 pounds).

Pastel Four-Layer Cake

(Pictured below)

My mother made this special birthday cake for me and my sister when we were growing up. It looks as good as it tastes and is easier to make than you'd think.
—_Bryan Anderson, Granite Falls, Minnesota_

1 package (18-1/4 ounces) chocolate cake mix
3 tablespoons all-purpose flour
Pinch salt
1-1/2 cups milk
3/4 cup butter _or_ margarine, softened
3/4 cup shortening
1-1/2 cups sugar
Yellow, red and green liquid food coloring
1/4 teaspoon _each_ lemon, peppermint, almond and vanilla extract
3 tablespoons baking cocoa

Prepare and bake cake according to the package directions, using two greased and floured 9-in. round cake pans. Cool for 10 minutes; remove from pans to wire racks to cool completely. In a saucepan, combine flour and salt. Gradually add milk; cook and stir over medium-high heat until thick, about 5-7 minutes. Remove from the heat; cover and refrigerate until completely cool. In a mixing bowl, beat butter, shortening and sugar until sugar dissolves. Add chilled milk mixture; beat for 7 minutes. Divide frosting equally among four bowls, with 1-1/4 cups in each. To the first bowl, add 2-3 drops yellow food coloring and lemon extract; mix well. To second bowl, add 2-3 drops red food coloring and peppermint extract. To third bowl, add 2-3 drops green food coloring and almond extract. To the last bowl, add the cocoa and vanilla. Split cake layers in half horizontally; spread each layer with a different frosting. Stack layers, using cocoa-frosted layer for the top. Do not frost sides of cake. **Yield:** 12 servings.

FRUIT-FILLED TREATS such as Apricot Layer Cake, Rhubarb Strawberry Crunch and Orange Bavarian (shown above, clockwise from top) are a refreshing finish to any meal.

Rhubarb Strawberry Crunch

(Pictured above)

Garden-fresh rhubarb takes a bow in this easy recipe. It's wonderful with ice cream. —Barbara Foss
Waukesha, Wisconsin

   1 cup all-purpose flour
   1 cup packed brown sugar
 3/4 cup quick-cooking oats
   1 teaspoon ground cinnamon
 1/2 cup butter *or* margarine
   4 cups sliced fresh *or* frozen rhubarb
   1 pint fresh strawberries, halved
   1 cup sugar
   2 tablespoons cornstarch
   1 cup water
   1 teaspoon vanilla extract
Vanilla ice cream, optional

In a bowl, combine the first four ingredients; cut in butter until crumbly. Press half into an ungreased 9-in. square baking pan. Combine rhubarb and strawberries; spoon over crust. In a saucepan, combine sugar and cornstarch. Stir in the water and vanilla; bring to a boil over medium heat. Cook and stir for 2 minutes. Pour over fruit. Sprinkle with remaining crumb mixture. Bake at 350° for 1 hour. Serve with ice cream if desired. **Yield:** 9 servings.

Orange Bavarian

(Pictured above)

This refreshing treat is perfect after a hearty meal. The old-fashioned flavor will take you back to Grandma's kitchen. —Adeline Piscitelli, Sayreville, New Jersey

    3 packages (3 ounces *each*) orange
      gelatin
2-1/4 cups boiling water
    1 cup (8 ounces) sour cream
    1 quart orange sherbet, softened
    1 can (11 ounces) mandarin oranges,
      drained and halved
Red and green grapes, optional

Dissolve gelatin in water. Stir in sour cream until smooth. Mix in sherbet until melted. Chill until partially set. Fold in oranges. Pour into a 7-cup ring mold coated with nonstick cooking spray. Cover and chill 8 hours or overnight. Just before serving, unmold onto a platter; fill the center with grapes if desired. **Yield:** 12-14 servings.

— 🍷 🍷 🍷 —

Apricot Layer Cake

(Pictured at left)

You don't have to tell anyone this tender fruity layer cake starts with a convenient mix. Of course, the cat will be out of the bag once folks request the recipe!
—Molly Knapp, Eureka, Illinois

    1 **package (18-1/2 ounces) white cake mix**
1-1/4 **cups water**
    3 **egg whites**
  1/3 **cup vegetable oil**
    1 **tablespoon grated orange peel**
    1 **teaspoon orange** *or* **lemon extract**
  2/3 **cup apricot preserves**
BROWN BUTTER FROSTING:
  1/2 **cup butter (no substitutes)**
3-1/2 **to 4 cups confectioners' sugar**
  1/3 **cup orange juice**
  1/4 **cup chopped pecans**

In a mixing bowl, combine the first six ingredients; beat on low speed for 30 seconds or until moistened. Beat on high for 2 minutes. Pour into two greased and floured 8-in. round cake pans. Bake at 350° for 30-35 minutes or until a toothpick inserted near the center comes out clean. Cool for 10 minutes; remove from pans to a wire rack to cool completely. Split each layer in half horizontally. Spread the cut side of each bottom layer with 1/3 cup apricot preserves; replace tops and set aside. For frosting, in a heavy saucepan, cook and stir butter over medium heat for 7-8 minutes or until golden brown. Pour into a mixing bowl; add 3 cups confectioners' sugar and orange juice. Beat until smooth. Add enough of the remaining sugar to reach spreading consistency. Spread frosting between filled cakes; frost top and sides of cake. Sprinkle with nuts. Store in the refrigerator. **Yield:** 12 servings.

— 🍷 🍷 🍷 —

Old-Fashioned Apple Cake

Everyone enjoys biting into this moist dark cake—they're greeted with an abundance of apples, nuts and chocolate chips! I hope you try this home-style dessert today.   *—Iola Egle, McCook, Nebraska*

    1 **cup butter** *or* **margarine, softened**
    2 **cups sugar**
    3 **eggs**

  1/2 **cup water**
    1 **tablespoon vanilla extract**
  1/4 **teaspoon almond extract**
2-1/2 **cups all-purpose flour**
    2 **tablespoons baking cocoa**
    1 **teaspoon baking powder**
  3/4 **teaspoon ground cardamom**
  3/4 **teaspoon ground cinnamon**
  1/2 **teaspoon ground allspice**
  1/2 **teaspoon baking soda**
  1/2 **teaspoon salt**
    2 **medium tart apples, peeled and shredded**
    1 **cup chopped walnuts**
  1/2 **cup semisweet chocolate chips**
CARDAMOM SUGAR:
  1/2 **cup sugar**
  1/4 **teaspoon ground cardamom**

In a mixing bowl, cream butter and sugar until fluffy. Add eggs, one at a time, beating well after each. Beat in water and extracts. Combine dry ingredients; add to creamed mixture. Stir in apples, nuts and chips. Pour into a greased and floured 10-in. fluted tube pan. Bake at 325° for 60-70 minutes or until a toothpick inserted near the center comes out clean. Cool for 10 minutes; remove from pan to a wire rack to cool completely. Combine sugar and cardamom in a blender; process for 1 minute. Sprinkle 3-5 tablespoons over cooled cake. Store remaining sugar in an airtight container for another use. **Yield:** 12-15 servings.

— 🍷 🍷 🍷 —

Chocolate Chip Pie

This dessert delights chocolate lovers. Best of all, it travels very well. So I often take it to potlucks and picnics. *—Ellen Benninger, Stoneboro, Pennsylvania*

    3 **eggs**
  3/4 **cup packed brown sugar**
  3/4 **cup sugar**
  3/4 **cup all-purpose flour**
  1/2 **cup butter** *or* **margarine, melted and**
      cooled
  1/4 **cup vegetable oil**
    1 **teaspoon vanilla extract**
1-1/2 **cups semisweet chocolate chips**
    1 **cup chopped pecans** *or* **walnuts**
    1 **unbaked pastry shell (9 inches)**

In a mixing bowl, beat eggs until foamy. Beat in sugars, flour, butter, oil and vanilla until well blended. Stir in chocolate chips and nuts. Pour into pie shell. Bake at 325° for 1-1/4 hours or until a knife inserted near the center comes out clean. Cool on a wire rack. Chill until serving. Refrigerate leftovers. **Yield:** 8 servings.

Cherry Berries on a Cloud

(Pictured below)

Whenever I serve this elegant dessert, I'm sure to be asked for the recipe. The base really is as light as air.
—*Darlene Alexander, Nekoosa, Wisconsin*

6 egg whites
1/2 teaspoon cream of tartar
1/4 teaspoon salt
1-3/4 cups sugar
FILLING:
2 packages (3 ounces *each*) cream cheese, softened
1 cup sugar
1 teaspoon vanilla extract
2 cups whipping cream, whipped
2 cups miniature marshmallows
TOPPING:
1 can (21 ounces) cherry pie filling
2 cups sliced fresh strawberries
1 teaspoon lemon juice

In a mixing bowl, beat egg whites, cream of tartar and salt until foamy. Gradually add the sugar, beating on high until stiff peaks form (do not underbeat). Spread evenly in a greased 13-in. x 9-in. x 2-in. baking pan. Bake at 275° for 1 hour; turn off oven (do not open door). Let cool in oven overnight or for at least 12 hours. Beat cream cheese, sugar and vanilla until smooth; gently fold in cream and marshmallows. Spread over meringue. Chill for 4 hours. Cut into 16 pieces. Combine topping ingredients; spoon 1/4 cup over each serving. **Yield:** 16 servings.

Raspberry Angel Food Cake

This angel food cake recipe proves that desserts don't have to be loaded with fat and calories to be delicious.
—*Kathy Kochan, Mendham, New Jersey*

✓ This tasty dish uses less sugar, salt and fat. Recipe includes *Diabetic Exchanges.*

10 egg whites
1-1/4 teaspoons cream of tartar
1 teaspoon vanilla extract
1/2 teaspoon almond extract
1/2 cup sugar
1 cup cake flour
2 cups fresh raspberries

In a mixing bowl, beat egg whites until frothy; beat in cream of tartar until soft peaks form. Add the extracts. Gradually beat in sugar until stiff, scraping bowl occasionally. Sift flour over beaten whites; sprinkle with berries. Gently fold flour and raspberries into batter until well mixed. Pour into an ungreased 10-in. tube pan. Bake at 325° for 40-45 minutes or until lightly browned and entire top appears dry. Immediately invert cake pan; cool completely, about 1 hour. **Yield:** 16 servings. **Diabetic Exchanges:** One serving equals 1 starch; also, 65 calories, 35 mg sodium, 0 cholesterol, 13 gm carbohydrate, 3 gm protein, trace fat.

Pioneer Bread Pudding

While traveling in Door County, Wisconsin, we stopped for lunch at a delightful cafe. The restaurant is famous for this bread pudding with lemon sauce.
—*Carol Parker, Eau Claire, Wisconsin*

2 cups cubed day-old bread (1/2-inch pieces), crusts removed
2 cups milk
1/4 cup sugar
3 tablespoons butter *or* margarine
Dash salt
2 eggs
1/2 teaspoon vanilla extract
LEMON SAUCE:
1/2 cup sugar
1 tablespoon cornstarch
Dash salt
1 cup water
1-1/2 teaspoons grated lemon peel
2 tablespoons butter *or* margarine
1 tablespoon lemon juice
1 drop yellow food coloring

Place bread cubes in a greased 1-qt. baking dish. In a saucepan, heat milk, sugar, butter and salt over low heat just until butter melts. In a bowl, beat eggs; whisk in warm milk mixture. Stir in vanilla. Pour over bread. Place the baking dish in a shallow pan of hot water. Bake, uncovered, at 350° for 40-45 minutes or until a knife inserted 1 in. from the edge comes out clean. For lemon sauce, combine sugar, cornstarch and salt in a saucepan. Stir in water and lemon peel; bring to a boil. Cook and stir for 2 minutes. Remove from the heat; stir in butter, lemon juice and food coloring. Serve warm or cold with the pudding. Refrigerate leftovers. **Yield:** 4-6 servings.

— 🍷 🍷 🍷 —

Sweetheart Fudge

Around our house, Valentine's Day just wouldn't be the same without this heavenly cocoa fudge. It makes a nice gift for those you love at any time of year.
—Dorothy Anderson, Ottawa, Kansas

    3 cups sugar
2/3 cup baking cocoa
1/8 teaspoon salt
1-1/2 cups milk
1/4 cup butter *or* margarine
    1 teaspoon vanilla extract

In a heavy saucepan, combine sugar, cocoa and salt. Stir in milk; bring to a rapid boil over medium heat, stirring constantly. Cook, without stirring, until candy thermometer reads 234° (soft-ball stage). Remove from the heat; add butter and vanilla (do not stir). Cool to 110°. Beat with a spoon until fudge thickens and just begins to lose its gloss. Immediately spread into a buttered 8-in. square pan. Cool. Cut into 1-in. squares. Store in an airtight container. **Yield:** about 5 dozen.

— 🍷 🍷 🍷 —

Banana Graham Dessert

My family loves this creamy pudding treat. I think you'll find this cool dessert especially appealing on hot summer days. *—Kathy Baker, Hamilton, Georgia*

✓ This tasty dish uses less sugar, salt and fat. Recipe includes *Diabetic Exchanges*.

    1 package (3.4 ounces) instant vanilla
      pudding mix
2-3/4 cups cold milk
    1 cup (8 ounces) sour cream
12 graham crackers
    2 large firm bananas, sliced

In a mixing bowl, beat pudding mix and milk on low speed for 2 minutes. Fold in sour cream. Let stand for 5 minutes. In a 3-qt. bowl, layer a third

of the graham crackers, bananas and pudding mixture. Repeat layers twice. Refrigerate. **Yield:** 9 servings. **Diabetic Exchanges:** One 1/2-cup serving (prepared with sugar-free pudding, skim milk, nonfat sour cream and reduced-fat graham crackers) equals 1-1/2 starch; also, 114 calories, 141 mg sodium, 4 mg cholesterol, 22 gm carbohydrate, 5 gm protein, 1 gm fat.

Peanut Butter Ice Cream Topping

(Pictured above)

Whenever there's an ice cream social at church, this scrumptious topping is requested. I don't mind, though, because it's so easy to make. *—Karen Buhr, Gasport, New York*

    1 cup packed brown sugar
1/2 cup light corn syrup
    3 tablespoons butter *or* margarine
Pinch salt
    1 cup creamy peanut butter
1/2 cup evaporated milk
Vanilla ice cream
Peanuts, optional

Combine brown sugar, corn syrup, butter and salt in a 1-1/2-qt. microwave-safe baking dish. Cover and microwave on high for 4 minutes or until mixture boils, stirring twice. Add peanut butter; stir until smooth. Stir in evaporated milk. Serve warm over ice cream. Sprinkle with peanuts if desired. Cover and store in the refrigerator. To reheat, microwave at 50% power for 1-2 minutes or until heated through. **Yield:** 2-3/4 cups. **Editor's Note:** This recipe was tested in a 700-watt microwave.

HOLIDAY DELIGHTS. Fruity Bundt Cake, Cherry Pecan Torte and Cranberry Graham Squares (clockwise from top) brighten a buffet.

Fruity Bundt Cake

(Pictured above)

Folks who typically don't care for traditional fruitcake will find this white bundt version irresistible. It has such wonderful color and flavor. —Blanche Whytsell
Arnoldsburg, West Virginia

       1 package (8 ounces) cream cheese, softened
       1 cup butter *or* margarine, softened
1-1/2 cups sugar
       4 eggs
1-1/2 teaspoons vanilla extract
2-1/4 cups cake flour, *divided*
1-1/2 teaspoons baking powder
       1 cup chopped pecans
1-1/2 cups chopped red and green candied cherries
GLAZE:
1-1/2 cups confectioners' sugar
       3 to 4 tablespoons milk
   1/2 teaspoon vanilla extract
Pinch salt
Additional candied cherries

In a mixing bowl, beat cream cheese, butter and sugar until fluffy. Add eggs, one at a time, beating well after each. Add vanilla. Combine 2 cups of flour and baking powder; gradually beat into batter. Combine pecans, cherries and remaining flour; fold into batter. Pour into a greased and floured 10-in. fluted tube pan. Bake at 325° for 1 hour or until cake tests done. Cool for 10 minutes; remove from pan to a wire rack to cool completely. Combine confectioners' sugar, milk, vanilla and salt; drizzle over cake. Garnish with cherries. **Yield:** 12-16 servings.

— 🛒 🛒 🛒 —

Cherry Pecan Torte

(Pictured above)

People I serve this dessert to are always surprised to hear that soda crackers are the "secret" ingredient in

this meringue. Topped with whipped cream and cherry pie filling, it can't be beat! —Dolores Lueken
Ferdinand, Indiana

6 egg whites
1/2 teaspoon cream of tartar
2 cups sugar
2 cups saltine crumbs
3/4 cup chopped pecans
2 teaspoons vanilla extract
2 cups whipping cream, whipped
1 can (21 ounces) cherry pie filling

In a mixing bowl, beat egg whites until foamy. Beat in cream of tartar. Gradually add sugar, beating on high until stiff peaks form. Fold in crumbs, pecans and vanilla. Spread into a greased 13-in. x 9-in. x 2-in. baking pan. Bake at 350° for 25 minutes. Cool completely. Spread whipped cream over top. Spoon pie filling over cream. Chill for at least 1 hour. **Yield:** 12-15 servings.

Cranberry Graham Squares

(Pictured at left)

This layered dessert is refreshingly creamy. Plus, it can be made in advance, so it's perfect for entertaining.
—*H. Stevenson, Davidson, Saskatchewan*

2 cups graham cracker crumbs
3/4 cup plus 2 tablespoons sugar, *divided*
1/8 teaspoon salt
1/2 cup plus 1 tablespoon butter *or* margarine, melted, *divided*
1 package (3 ounces) cook-and-serve vanilla pudding mix
1-1/2 cups cranberries
3/4 cup raisins
3/4 cup water
2 teaspoons cornstarch
1-1/2 teaspoons cold water
1 envelope whipped topping mix

In a bowl, combine cracker crumbs, 2 tablespoons sugar, salt and 1/2 cup butter; set 1/2 cup aside. Press remaining crumbs into an ungreased 9-in. square baking pan. Chill. Meanwhile, cook pudding according to package directions; cool for 5 minutes. Spread over crust. Chill. In a saucepan over medium heat, cook cranberries, raisins and water until berries pop, about 5-10 minutes. Stir in remaining sugar. Combine cornstarch and cold water until smooth; add to the cranberry mixture. Bring to a boil; cook and stir for 2 minutes. Remove from the heat; stir in remaining butter. Cool to room temperature. Spread over the pudding layer. Prepare whipped topping according to package directions; spread over cranberry layer. Sprinkle with reserved crumbs. Chill for at least 6 hours. Store in the refrigerator. **Yield:** 9 servings.

Double Peanut Butter Cake

My family loves peanut butter. So a cake that has it in the batter as well as in the frosting is a big hit around our house! —*Marie Hoyer, Hodgenville, Kentucky*

1/2 cup creamy peanut butter
1/4 cup butter *or* margarine, softened
3/4 cup sugar
2 eggs
1-1/2 cups all-purpose flour
2 teaspoons baking powder
1/4 teaspoon salt
3/4 cup milk
FROSTING:
1/3 cup chunky peanut butter
3 tablespoons butter *or* margarine, softened
3 cups confectioners' sugar
1/4 cup milk
1-1/2 teaspoons vanilla extract

In a mixing bowl, cream peanut butter, butter and sugar. Add eggs; mix well. Combine flour, baking powder and salt; add alternately with milk to the creamed mixture. Mix well. Pour into a greased 9-in. square baking pan. Bake at 350° for 30-35 minutes or until a toothpick inserted near the center comes out clean. Cool on a wire rack. For frosting, cream peanut butter and butter. Add sugar, milk and vanilla; mix until smooth. Frost cake. **Yield:** 9 servings.

Eggnog Rice Pudding

I find this pretty dessert particularly good for holiday entertaining. It makes good use of leftover eggnog.
—*Berdine Lilja, Elk River, Minnesota*

2-1/4 cups eggnog*
5 teaspoons cornstarch
2 cups cooked long grain rice
1/2 cup finely chopped red and green candied cherries
1 teaspoon vanilla extract
1/4 teaspoon salt

Place 2 cups of eggnog in a heavy saucepan. Combine the cornstarch and remaining eggnog until smooth; add to pan. Bring to a boil, stirring constantly; boil for 1-2 minutes. Remove from the heat; stir in rice, cherries, vanilla and salt. Spoon into dishes. Chill 2-3 hours. **Yield:** 4-6 servings. ***Editor's Note:** This recipe was tested with commercially prepared eggnog.

Orange Bliss Cheesecake

(Pictured below)

A subtle orange-flavored filling contrasts nicely with a chocolate-crumb crust. Family and friends always comment on the wonderful flavor and color.
—Audrey Thibodeau, Mesa, Arizona

  1 **cup chocolate wafer crumbs**
  3 **tablespoons butter *or* margarine, melted**
1/2 **cup orange juice**
  1 **envelope unflavored gelatin**
  3 **packages (8 ounces *each*) cream cheese, softened**
3/4 **cup sugar**
  1 **cup whipping cream, whipped**
  1 **tablespoon grated orange peel**
Mini chocolate chips and sliced orange wedges, optional

Combine crumbs and butter; press onto the bottom of an ungreased 9-in. springform pan. Bake at 350° for 10 minutes. Cool. In a saucepan, combine orange juice and gelatin; let stand for 5 minutes. Cook and stir over low heat until the gelatin dissolves. Cool for 10 minutes. Meanwhile, in a mixing bowl, beat cream cheese and sugar until light and fluffy; gradually add gelatin mixture. Beat on low until well mixed. Chill until partially set, about 3-5 minutes (watch carefully—mixture will set up quickly). Gently fold in whipped cream and orange peel. Spoon into the crust. Chill for 6 hours or overnight. Just before serving, run a knife around edge of pan to loosen. Remove sides of pan. Garnish with chocolate chips and oranges if desired. **Yield:** 8-10 servings.

Snack Cake

This cake packs and travels well since the topping bakes down into it—there's no messy frosting to contend with.
—Liz Raether, Algoma, Wisconsin

1/2 **cup butter *or* margarine, softened**
  1 **cup sugar**
  1 **egg**
  2 **cups all-purpose flour**
  2 **teaspoons baking powder**
1/2 **teaspoon salt**
3/4 **cup buttermilk**
  1 **teaspoon vanilla extract**
  1 **cup miniature marshmallows**
1/2 **cup semisweet chocolate chips**
TOPPING:
1/2 **cup chopped walnuts**
1/4 **cup packed brown sugar**
  2 **tablespoons butter *or* margarine, melted**

In a mixing bowl, cream butter and sugar; beat in egg until light and fluffy. Combine flour, baking powder and salt. In another bowl, combine buttermilk and vanilla. Add dry ingredients to the creamed mixture alternately with buttermilk mixture; mix well. Fold in marshmallows and chips. Pour into a greased and floured 13-in. x 9-in. x 2-in. baking pan. Combine all topping ingredients; sprinkle over batter. Bake at 350° for 30-35 minutes or until a toothpick inserted near the center comes out clean. **Yield:** 12-16 servings.

Oatmeal Banana Cupcakes

When you want a nutritious snack, reach for these cupcakes. They're so moist they don't need frosting.
—Louise Skinner, Hamilton, Ohio

   1/2 **cup butter *or* margarine, softened**
   1/2 **cup sugar**
    2 **eggs**
    1 **cup mashed ripe bananas**
   3/4 **cup honey**
1-1/2 **cups all-purpose flour**
    1 **cup quick-cooking oats**
    1 **teaspoon baking powder**
    1 **teaspoon baking soda**
   3/4 **teaspoon salt**

In a mixing bowl, cream butter and sugar. Add eggs, bananas and honey; mix well. Combine dry ingredients; stir into creamed mixture just until moistened. Fill paper-lined muffin cups two-thirds full. Bake at 350° for 18-20 minutes or until cupcakes test done. Cool in pan for 10 minutes before removing to a wire rack. **Yield:** 1-1/2 dozen.

Carrot Fruitcake

Start a new holiday tradition with this flavorful golden fruitcake. It's lighter and less sweet than many fruitcakes I've tried. —Judy Jungwirth
Athol, South Dakota

1-1/2 cups vegetable oil
   2 cups sugar
   4 eggs
   3 cups all-purpose flour
   2 teaspoons baking powder
   2 teaspoons baking soda
   2 teaspoons ground cinnamon
   1 teaspoon salt
   3 cups finely shredded carrots
1-1/2 cups coarsely chopped nuts
   1 cup *each* raisins, chopped dates and
      mixed candied fruit

In a mixing bowl, combine oil and sugar. Add eggs, one at a time, beating well after each addition. Combine flour, baking powder, baking soda, cinnamon and salt; add to egg mixture. Beat until smooth. Stir in remaining ingredients. Pour into two greased and floured 9-in. x 5-in. x 3-in. loaf pans. Bake at 350° for 1 hour or until a toothpick inserted near the center comes out clean. Cool in pans for 10 minutes; remove to a wire rack to cool completely. **Yield:** 2 loaves.

Joe's Ice Cream Dessert

I've been helping my mom in the kitchen since I was about 4 years old. But as a busy teen, I don't get to cook all that often. When I do, this is one of my favorite treats to fix. It's fun to make and great to eat.
—Joe McRoberts, Warren, Rhode Island

1/4 cup butter *or* margarine, melted
   1 pound chocolate cream-filled
      sandwich cookies, crushed, *divided*
1/2 gallon vanilla ice cream, softened
   4 chocolate toffee candy bars (1.4 ounces
      each), crushed, *divided*
1/2 gallon chocolate ice cream, softened

Combine butter and half of the cookie crumbs; press into a greased 13-in. x 9-in. x 2-in. pan. Carefully spread vanilla ice cream over crust. Combine half of the crushed candy bars and remaining cookie crumbs; sprinkle over vanilla ice cream. Carefully spread the chocolate ice cream over top. Sprinkle with the remaining crushed candy bars. Cover and freeze until firm, 6 hours or overnight. **Yield:** 12-16 servings.

Strawberry Meringue Pie

(Pictured above)

This dessert is simple, so don't be put off by the long directions. It's impressive-looking and perfect for any occasion. —Kathleen Mercier, Orrington, Maine

1/3 cup finely crushed saltines (about 12
      crackers), *divided*
   3 egg whites
1/4 teaspoon cream of tartar
1/8 teaspoon salt
   1 cup sugar
   1 teaspoon vanilla extract
1/2 cup chopped pecans, toasted
   1 package (4 ounces) German sweet
      chocolate
   2 tablespoons butter *or* margarine
   1 cup whipping cream
   2 tablespoons confectioners' sugar
   4 cups fresh strawberries, halved

Sprinkle 2 tablespoons of cracker crumbs into a greased 9-in. pie plate. In a mixing bowl, beat egg whites, cream of tartar and salt until soft peaks form. Gradually add sugar and continue beating until stiff peaks form. Fold in vanilla, pecans and remaining cracker crumbs. Spread meringue onto the bottom and up the sides of the prepared pan. Bake at 300° for 45 minutes. Turn off oven and do not open door; let cool in oven overnight. In a small saucepan over low heat, melt chocolate and butter, stirring constantly. Drizzle over shell. Let stand at least 15 minutes or until set. Top with berries. Whip cream and confectioners' sugar until soft peaks form; spoon over berries. **Yield:** 6-8 servings.

Chocolate Cherry Pie

(Pictured above)

This rich and creamy pie is sure to please any dyed-in-the-wool chocoholic! You'll find your family asking for this make-ahead dessert over and over.
—*Maxine Smith, Owanka, South Dakota*

    1 **cup all-purpose flour**
    2 **tablespoons sugar**
1/2 **teaspoon salt**
1/2 **cup cold butter *or* margarine**
FILLING:
    1 **can (14 ounces) sweetened condensed milk**
    1 **cup (6 ounces) semisweet chocolate chips**
1/2 **teaspoon salt**
    1 **can (21 ounces) cherry pie filling**
1/4 **to 1/2 teaspoon almond extract**
Whipped cream and maraschino cherries

In a bowl, mix flour, sugar and salt. Cut in butter until the mixture resembles coarse crumbs. Press firmly onto the bottom and sides of a 9-in. pie plate. Bake at 350° for 15-20 minutes or until golden brown. Cool completely. In a saucepan, combine milk, chocolate chips and salt; cook and stir over low heat until chocolate melts. Stir in pie filling and extract. Pour into crust. Chill for 2-3 hours or until firm. Garnish with whipped cream and cherries. **Yield:** 8 servings.

—— ☕ ☕ ☕ ——

Creamy Gelatin Dessert

*This yummy recipe was given to me by my husband's sister, Gloria, several years ago. It's the most re-*quested dessert when our five married children come for dinner.   —*Janis Garrett, Macon, Georgia*

    1 **package (6 ounces) lemon gelatin**
    2 **cups boiling water**
    2 **cups miniature marshmallows**
    4 **large ripe bananas, cut into 1/4-inch slices**
    1 **can (20 ounces) crushed pineapple**
    2 **cups cold water**
1/2 **cup sugar**
    2 **tablespoons all-purpose flour**
    2 **tablespoons butter *or* margarine**
    1 **cup whipping cream**
1/2 **cup chopped walnuts**

In a bowl, dissolve gelatin in boiling water. Stir in marshmallows until melted. Stir in bananas. Drain pineapple, reserving juice; set juice aside. Add pineapple and cold water to gelatin mixture; mix well. Pour into a 13-in. x 9-in. x 2-in. pan; chill until set. In a small saucepan, combine the sugar and flour. Gradually stir in reserved pineapple juice. Add butter; bring to a boil. Cook and stir for 2 minutes. Remove from the heat; cool to room temperature, about 35-40 minutes. Whip the cream; fold into pineapple juice mixture. Spread over gelatin. Sprinkle with nuts. Chill for 1-2 hours. **Yield:** 16-20 servings.

—— ☕ ☕ ☕ ——

Frozen Peanut Butter Torte

Whether you're entertaining special guests or seeking an everyday festive finale, you can't miss with this peanutty summer dessert.
—*Penney Kester*
Springville, New York

1/2 **cup all-purpose flour**
1/3 **cup quick-cooking oats**
1/4 **cup sugar**
1/4 **cup butter *or* margarine, softened**
1/4 **teaspoon baking soda**
FILLING:
1/2 **cup crunchy peanut butter**
1/3 **cup light corn syrup**
    2 **tablespoons honey**
1/2 **gallon vanilla ice cream, softened**
3/4 **cup chopped salted peanuts**

In a small mixing bowl, combine the first five ingredients and mix well. Pat onto the bottom of a greased 9-in. square baking pan. Bake at 350° for 15-17 minutes or until lightly browned. Cool to room temperature. In a bowl, combine peanut butter, corn syrup and honey; carefully spread half over crust. Spread half the ice cream over peanut butter layer. Drop remaining peanut butter mixture over ice cream. Sprinkle with half the nuts. Top with remaining ice cream and nuts. Freeze until firm, about 3-4 hours. Let stand for 5-10 minutes before serving. **Yield:** 9-12 servings.

— ☕ ☕ ☕ —

Pineapple Pecan Cake

A friend told me that this is the best cake he's ever eaten. My family agrees with him! —*Fern Eleson*
Whitney, Nebraska

  2 **cups sugar**
  2 **cups all-purpose flour**
  2 **teaspoons baking soda**
  2 **eggs**
  1 **can (20 ounces) crushed pineapple, undrained**
  1 **cup chopped pecans**
FROSTING:
  1/2 **cup butter** *or* **margarine, softened**
  1 **package (8 ounces) cream cheese, softened**
1-1/2 **cups confectioners' sugar**
  1 **teaspoon vanilla extract**

In a mixing bowl, combine the first five ingredients; mix well. Stir in pecans. Pour into an ungreased 13-in. x 9-in. x 2-in. baking pan. Bake at 350° for 40-45 minutes or until a toothpick inserted near the center comes out clean. Cool completely. In a mixing bowl, combine all frosting ingredients; beat until smooth. Frost cake. **Yield:** 16-20 servings.

— ☕ ☕ ☕ —

Apple Custard Pie

There's no need to pull out your rolling pin to make this sweet treat. It has an easy press-in crust under a mouthwatering apple and custard filling. —*Carol Adams*
Medina, Texas

1-1/2 **cups all-purpose flour**
  1/2 **teaspoon salt**
  1/2 **cup cold butter** *or* **margarine**
  3 **cups sliced peeled tart apples**
  1/3 **cup sugar**
  1 **teaspoon ground cinnamon**
CUSTARD:
  1 **cup evaporated milk**
  1 **egg**
  1/2 **cup sugar**

In a bowl, combine flour and salt; cut in butter until crumbly. Press onto the bottom and up the sides of a 9-in. pie plate. Arrange apples over crust. Combine sugar and cinnamon; sprinkle over the apples. Bake at 375° for 20 minutes. For custard, whisk milk, egg and sugar until smooth; pour over apples. Bake 25-30 minutes longer or until a knife

inserted near the center comes out clean. Cool on a wire rack. Refrigerate leftovers. **Yield:** 6-8 servings.

— ☕ ☕ ☕ —

'I Wish I Had That Recipe...'

ENJOYING LUNCH at a favorite local eatery, Wilsie Sherman of Eureka Springs, Arkansas never plays possum when it's time to order dessert.

"The Possum Pie at Myrtie Mae's is so delectable," raves Wilsie. "It's very pretty, topped with whipped cream and decorated with pecans. The texture is smooth and not heavy. I'd love to have the recipe."

From Myrtie Mae's Home Style Dining, associate manager David Heilemann shares the Possum Pie recipe.

"It was found in a box of recipes that were used in the cafe back in the early 1950's, when it was known as Mount Aire Camp," relates David. "Since then, the pie has been on our menu."

Myrtie Mae's Home Style Dining is in the Best Western Inn of the Ozarks on Highway 62 West in Eureka Springs. It's open daily from 6:30 a.m. to 9:30 p.m.

Possum Pie

  2 **packages (3 ounces** *each***) cream cheese, softened**
  3/4 **cup confectioners' sugar**
  1 **graham cracker crust (9 inches)**
  1/4 **cup chopped pecans**
  1/3 **cup instant chocolate pudding mix**
  1/4 **cup instant vanilla pudding mix**
1-3/4 **cups cold milk**
  3/4 **teaspoon vanilla extract**
  1/2 **cup whipping cream, whipped**
  12 **to 16 pecan halves**

In a mixing bowl, beat cream cheese and sugar until smooth. Spread onto bottom of crust. Sprinkle with chopped pecans. In another mixing bowl, combine pudding mixes. Add milk and vanilla; beat on low speed for 2 minutes. Spoon over the pecans. Refrigerate for at least 4 hours. Top with whipped cream and pecan halves. **Yield:** 8 servings.

— ☕ ☕ ☕ —

Broken Glass Dessert

(Pictured below)

Once you cut this dessert, you'll see how the recipe got its name...the pieces look like stained glass. People always comment on the pretty combination of colors.
—Kathy Crow, Cordova, Alaska

      1 envelope unflavored gelatin
  1/4 cup cold water
      1 cup pineapple juice
  1-1/2 cups graham cracker crumbs
  1/2 cup sugar
  1/2 cup butter *or* margarine, melted
      1 package (3 ounces) lime gelatin
  4-1/2 cups boiling water, *divided*
      1 package (3 ounces) strawberry gelatin
      1 package (3 ounces) orange gelatin
      1 carton (8 ounces) frozen whipped
         topping, thawed

Soften unflavored gelatin in cold water. Boil pineapple juice; stir into unflavored gelatin. Set aside until slightly thickened, about 3 hours. Meanwhile, combine crumbs, sugar and butter; press onto the bottom of a greased 13-in. x 9-in. x 2-in. pan. Chill. Combine lime gelatin and 1-1/2 cups boiling water; stir until gelatin is dissolved. Pour into an 8-in. x 4-in. x 2-in. loaf pan that has been coated with nonstick cooking spray; chill until very firm. Repeat for strawberry and orange gelatins. Place whipped topping in a large bowl; gently fold in pineapple juice mixture. When flavored gelatins are firm, cut into 1-in. cubes; gently fold into whipped topping mixture. Spoon over crust. Chill for at least 2 hours. **Yield:** 12-16 servings.

Pumpkin Apple Pie

The first time I made this for my family, they gobbled up this wonderful change-of-pace holiday dessert. It has a scrumptious layer of apples under the pumpkin.
—Elizabeth Montgomery, Taylorville, Illinois

  1/3 cup packed brown sugar
      1 tablespoon cornstarch
  1/2 teaspoon ground cinnamon
  1/4 teaspoon salt
  1/3 cup water
      2 tablespoons butter *or* margarine
      3 cups sliced peeled tart apples
Pastry for a single-crust pie (9 inches)
PUMPKIN LAYER:
  3/4 cup cooked *or* canned pumpkin
  3/4 cup evaporated milk
  1/3 cup sugar
      1 egg
  1/2 teaspoon ground cinnamon
  1/4 teaspoon salt
Whipped cream, optional

In a saucepan, combine brown sugar, cornstarch, cinnamon and salt. Add water and butter; bring to a boil. Add apples. Cook and stir for 4 minutes. Place pastry in a 9-in. pie pan; add apple mixture. In a bowl, whisk pumpkin, milk, sugar, egg, cinnamon and salt until smooth; pour over apple layer. Flute the edges of pastry. Bake at 375° for 50-55 minutes or until a knife inserted near the center comes out clean. If necessary, cover edges with foil toward the end of baking time to prevent overbrowning. Cool completely. Garnish with whipped cream if desired. Store in the refrigerator. **Yield:** 6-8 servings.

———— 🥄 🥄 🥄 ————

Blueberry-Peach Pound Cake

This recipe was a lucky experiment. I was going to make apple pound cake but found I had no apples. So, I used the blueberries and peaches I had on hand. It was a winning combination. *—Nancy Zimmerman Cape May Court House, New Jersey*

  1/2 cup butter *or* margarine, softened
  1-1/4 cups sugar
      3 eggs
  1/4 cup milk
  2-1/2 cups cake flour
      2 teaspoons baking powder
  1/4 teaspoon salt
  2-1/4 cups chopped peeled fresh peaches
         (1/2-inch pieces)
      2 cups fresh *or* frozen blueberries
Confectioners' sugar, optional

In a mixing bowl, cream butter and sugar. Add eggs, one at a time, beating well after each addition. Beat in milk. Combine the flour, baking powder and salt; add to creamed mixture. Stir in peaches and blueberries. Pour into a greased and floured 10-in. fluted tube pan. Bake at 350° for 60-70 minutes or until a toothpick inserted near the center comes out clean. Cool in pan for 15 minutes; remove to a wire rack to cool completely. Dust with confectioners' sugar if desired. **Yield:** 10-12 servings.

Slumber Party Pancakes

These fun chocolate pancakes—topped with ice cream and chocolate syrup—disappear fast when the kids have friends over for a slumber party. —Diane Hixon Niceville, Florida

    1/2 cup pancake mix
      2 tablespoons baking cocoa
      1 tablespoon sugar
      1 egg
    1/3 cup milk
      1 tablespoon vegetable oil
    1/4 cup miniature marshmallows
    1/4 cup pecan halves
Vanilla ice cream
Chocolate syrup *or* **ice cream topping**
Additional pecans, chopped, optional

In a bowl, combine pancake mix, cocoa and sugar. In another bowl, beat egg, milk and oil; stir into dry ingredients until almost smooth. Stir in marshmallows and pecans. Pour batter by 1/4 cupfuls onto a lightly greased hot griddle; turn when bubbles form on top of pancakes. Cook until second side is golden brown. Top with ice cream and syrup. Sprinkle with pecans if desired. **Yield:** 4 servings.

Pear Crumb Pie

*My guests find this pear filling and crumb topping a delectable change of pace from other fruit pies.
—Cathy Cremers, Pottstown, Pennsylvania*

1-1/3 cups all-purpose flour
    1/2 teaspoon salt
    1/2 cup shortening
      2 to 3 tablespoons cold water
FILLING:
    1/2 cup packed brown sugar
      2 tablespoons cornstarch
    1/2 teaspoon ground cinnamon
    1/4 teaspoon ground ginger
    1/8 teaspoon salt
Dash ground nutmeg
      6 cups thinly sliced peeled pears
      1 tablespoon lemon juice
TOPPING:
    2/3 cup all-purpose flour
    1/3 cup packed brown sugar
    1/3 cup cold butter *or* margarine

In a bowl, combine flour and salt; cut in shortening until crumbly. Sprinkle with water, 1 tablespoon at a time, tossing with a fork until dough can be formed into a ball. On a floured surface, roll out dough to fit a 9-in. pie pan. Flute edges. Combine filling ingredients; spoon into crust. Bake at 400° for 25 minutes. For topping, combine flour and brown sugar; cut in butter until crumbly. Sprinkle over filling. Bake 40 minutes longer. Cover edges with foil during the last 15 minutes to prevent over-browning if necessary. **Yield:** 6-8 servings.

Cranberry Orange Sundaes

(Pictured above and on front cover)

*I always keep a supply of cranberries in the freezer to cook up this refreshing sauce year-round.
—Rita Goshaw, South Milwaukee, Wisconsin*

      1 cup sugar
    2/3 cup water
      2 cups fresh *or* frozen cranberries
    2/3 cup orange juice
    1/2 teaspoon grated orange peel
    1/2 teaspoon vanilla extract
Vanilla ice cream
Additional orange peel, optional

In a saucepan over medium heat, bring sugar and water to a boil; cook for 5 minutes. Add cranberries, orange juice and peel. Return to a boil. Reduce heat; simmer for 8-10 minutes or until berries pop. Remove from the heat; stir in vanilla. Serve warm or chilled over ice cream. Garnish with orange peel if desired. The sauce can also be served over angel food or pound cake. **Yield:** 2 cups sauce.

♥ ♥ ♥

'I Wish I Had That Recipe...'

AFTER RELISHING a dish someone has served you, the ultimate compliment is to ask for the recipe. Ruth Aldridge of Durant, Mississippi suggests that "someone" could just as well be a restaurant.

"I can't forget the luscious Chocolate Chip Pecan Pie I enjoyed at The Redbud Inn in Kosciusko, Mississippi," writes Ruth. "I hope *Taste of Home* can help me get the recipe—I'd like to try making it at home for a holiday dessert."

Proprietor Maggie Garrett tells us she's been operating The Redbud Inn tea and lunch room in a lovely old Victorian home for 14 years. Recently she opened a bed-and-breakfast besides.

Adds Maggie, "Chocolate Chip Pecan Pie is a treat we've been serving for many years. We have customers who never vary their dessert order from this pie. Many people order it topped with a scoop of vanilla ice cream."

You'll find The Redbud Inn at 121 North Wells, Kosciusko MS 39090; 1-601/289-5086. Lunch and dessert are served Monday-Saturday, 11:30 a.m. to 1:30 p.m.; dinners on Saturday 6:30 to 9 p.m. and other evenings by reservation.

Chocolate Chip Pecan Pie

    4 eggs
    1 cup sugar
    1 cup light corn syrup
    1 teaspoon vanilla extract
1/2 cup butter *or* margarine, melted
    1 cup chopped pecans
1/2 cup semisweet chocolate chips
    1 unbaked pastry shell (10 inches)
Vanilla ice cream, optional

In a mixing bowl, beat eggs, sugar, corn syrup and vanilla. Add butter and mix well. Stir in pecans and chocolate chips. Pour into pie shell. Bake at 350° for 50-55 minutes or until set. Serve with ice cream if desired. **Yield:** 10-12 servings.

♥ ♥ ♥

Blueberry Apple Crisp

When our family's together—almost 30 of us—we can consume a lot of desserts! This is one we especially enjoy. —Harriet Stichler, Milford, Indiana

    4 cups sliced peeled tart apples
    2 cups fresh *or* frozen blueberries
    2 tablespoons brown sugar
    1 cup all-purpose flour, *divided*
3/4 cup sugar
    1 teaspoon baking powder
1/2 teaspoon salt
1/2 teaspoon ground cinnamon
1/4 teaspoon ground nutmeg
    1 egg, beaten
1/2 cup butter *or* margarine, melted
Whipped cream, optional

Place the apples in a greased 11-in. x 7-in. x 2-in. baking dish. Top with blueberries. Combine brown sugar and 2 tablespoons flour; sprinkle over fruit. Combine sugar, baking powder, salt, cinnamon, nutmeg and remaining flour. Stir in the egg with a fork until mixture is crumbly. Sprinkle over fruit; drizzle with butter. Bake at 350° for 55-60 minutes or until apples are tender. Serve warm; top with whipped cream if desired. **Yield:** 12 servings.

♥ ♥ ♥

Harvest Upside-Down Cake

Shortly after I ended my professional baking career, I was feeling a little homesick for the old familiar trade, so I entered a local recipe contest. This recipe won top honors in the dessert category. What a thrill! —Bill Cowan, Hanover, Ontario

1/4 cup raisins
1/2 cup boiling water
1/4 cup shortening
2/3 cup packed brown sugar
    1 egg
1/2 cup milk
    1 tablespoon dark molasses
    1 teaspoon vanilla extract
1-1/4 cups cake flour
    2 teaspoons baking powder
    2 teaspoons ground cinnamon
1/4 teaspoon salt
TOPPING:
1/4 cup butter *or* margarine, melted
1/2 cup packed brown sugar
    2 tablespoons corn syrup
    2 tablespoons coarsely chopped walnuts
  12 maraschino cherries, quartered
    2 cups sliced peeled tart apples

In a small bowl, soak raisins in water for 10 minutes. Drain and set aside. Meanwhile, in a mixing bowl, cream shortening and brown sugar. Add egg, milk, molasses and vanilla; beat on high for 1 minute. Combine flour, baking powder, cinnamon and salt; gradually add to creamed mixture, beating until smooth. Pour butter into a greased 8-in. square baking pan; sprinkle with brown sugar. Drizzle with corn syrup; sprinkle with walnuts, raisins and cherries. Arrange apples on top, overlapping slices. Spoon batter over apples. Bake at 350° for 45-50 minutes or until apples are tender or a toothpick inserted near the center comes out clean. Run knife around edges of cake; immediately invert onto a serving plate. **Yield:** 9 servings.

Pumpkin Gingersnap Dessert

I like to dazzle family and guests with this dessert's distinctive gingersnap crust, spicy creamy pumpkin layer and praline topping.
—Sue Mackey
Galesburg, Illinois

1-1/2 cups finely crushed gingersnaps
    (about 32 cookies)
  1/4 cup butter *or* margarine, melted
  1/2 teaspoon ground cinnamon
  1/4 teaspoon ground nutmeg
FILLING:
    2 packages (3.4 ounces *each*) instant vanilla
    pudding mix
1-1/3 cups cold milk
    1 can (16 ounces) solid-pack pumpkin
1-1/2 teaspoons ground cinnamon
  1/2 teaspoon *each* ground ginger, cloves and
    nutmeg
    2 cups whipped topping
TOPPING:
1-1/2 cups evaporated milk
    1 cup packed brown sugar
    1 cup chopped pecans
    2 teaspoons vanilla extract

Combine the first four ingredients; press onto the bottom of a greased 13-in. x 9-in. x 2-in. baking pan. Bake at 350° for 8 minutes; cool completely. For filling, beat pudding mixes and milk in a mixing bowl. Add pumpkin, cinnamon, ginger, cloves and nutmeg; mix well. Fold in whipped topping. Pour over crust. Chill for at least 4 hours. For topping, in a saucepan, bring milk and sugar to a boil over low heat. Cook and stir for 6-8 minutes or until mixture thickens. Remove from the heat; stir in pecans and vanilla. Cool to room temperature. Cut dessert into squares; drizzle with topping. **Yield:** 16 servings.

Stars and Stripes Parfaits

(Pictured above)

Bright berries make this rice pudding perfectly patriotic. It's sure to add "spark" to any Fourth of July gathering. —Mrs. Fred Stacy, Big Rock, Virginia

  2 cups cooked rice
  1 cup milk
  1 cup whipping cream
1/4 cup sugar
  2 egg yolks, beaten
  1 tablespoon butter *or* margarine
  1 teaspoon vanilla extract
  1 cup fresh *or* frozen blueberries
  1 cup fresh *or* frozen raspberries *or* sliced
    strawberries
**Whipped cream and toasted sliced almonds,
optional**

In a saucepan, combine rice, milk, cream and sugar; simmer, uncovered, for 20 minutes, stirring frequently. Remove from the heat. Stir a small amount into egg yolks; return all to the pan. Bring to a gentle boil; cook and stir for 2 minutes. Remove from the heat; stir in butter and vanilla. Cool. Spoon half of the blueberries into five parfait or dessert glasses. Top with half of the pudding mixture and half of the raspberries. Repeat layers. Top with whipped cream and almonds if desired. **Yield:** 5 servings.

CRAZY ABOUT CUPCAKES? It's easy to grab a tasty treat when you have Cupcake Cones, Chocolate-Bottom Mini Cupcakes and Lemon Cream Cupcakes (shown above, clockwise from upper left) on hand.

Chocolate-Bottom Mini Cupcakes

(Pictured above)

These freeze very well. I like to keep a batch on hand for drop-in guests or when I'm too busy to bake.
—Bertille Cooper, St. Inigoes, Maryland

  1 package (8 ounces) cream cheese, softened
  1 egg
  1/3 cup sugar
  1/8 teaspoon salt
  1 cup (6 ounces) semisweet chocolate chips
BATTER:
  1 cup water
  1/3 cup vegetable oil
  1 tablespoon vinegar
  1 teaspoon vanilla extract
1-1/2 cups all-purpose flour
  1 cup sugar
  1/4 cup baking cocoa
  1 teaspoon baking soda
  1 teaspoon salt

In a mixing bowl, beat cream cheese, egg, sugar and salt until smooth. Stir in chocolate chips; set aside. For batter, combine water, oil, vinegar and vanilla in another mixing bowl. Combine remaining ingredients; add to the liquid mixture and beat well (the bat-

ter will be thin). Spoon about 2 teaspoons of batter into greased or paper-lined miniature muffin cups. Top with about 1 teaspoon of cream cheese mixture. Bake at 350° for 18-23 minutes or until a toothpick inserted in chocolate portion comes out clean. Cool for 10 minutes; remove to wire racks to cool completely. **Yield:** 6 dozen.

— 🍮 🍮 🍮 —

Cupcake Cones

(Pictured above)

Children love this treat, which is not as messy as a piece of cake. It's a fun and different way to prepare cupcakes. —Mina Dyck, Boissevain, Manitoba

  1/3 cup butter *or* margarine, softened
  1/2 cup creamy peanut butter
1-1/2 cups packed brown sugar
  2 eggs
  1 teaspoon vanilla extract
  2 cups all-purpose flour
2-1/2 teaspoons baking powder
  1/2 teaspoon salt
  3/4 cup milk
Cake ice cream cones (about 3 inches tall)
Frosting of your choice
Sprinkles *or* chopped peanuts, optional

In a mixing bowl, cream butter, peanut butter and brown sugar. Beat in eggs and vanilla. Combine dry ingredients; add to creamed mixture alternately with milk. Place ice cream cones in muffin cups. Spoon about 3 tablespoons batter into each cone, filling to 3/4 in. from the top. Bake at 350° for 25-30 minutes or until a toothpick inserted near the center comes out clean. Frost and decorate as desired. **Yield:** about 2 dozen.

— 🥄 🥄 🥄 —

Lemon Cream Cupcakes

(Pictured at left)

Just thinking of these delicate cupcakes makes me hungry! I'm sure your family will love them as much as mine does. —Ruth Ann Stelfox, Raymond, Alberta

1 cup butter *or* margarine, softened
2 cups sugar
3 eggs
2 teaspoons grated lemon peel
1 teaspoon vanilla extract
3-1/2 cups all-purpose flour
2 teaspoons baking powder
1 teaspoon baking soda
1/2 teaspoon salt
2 cups (16 ounces) sour cream
FROSTING:
3 tablespoons butter *or* margarine, softened
2-1/4 cups confectioners' sugar
2 tablespoons lemon juice
3/4 teaspoon vanilla extract
1/4 teaspoon grated lemon peel
1 to 2 tablespoons milk

In a mixing bowl, cream butter and sugar. Beat in eggs, one at a time. Add lemon peel and vanilla; mix well. Combine dry ingredients; add to creamed mixture alternately with sour cream (batter will be thick). Fill greased or paper-lined muffin cups with 1/4 cup of batter. Bake at 350° for 25-30 minutes or until a toothpick inserted near the center comes out clean. Cool for 10 minutes; remove to wire racks to cool completely. For the frosting, cream butter and sugar in a small mixing bowl. Add lemon juice, vanilla, lemon peel and milk; beat until smooth. Frost cupcakes. **Yield:** about 2-1/2 dozen.

— 🥄 🥄 🥄 —

Chocolate Chip Cupcakes

These crowd-pleasing cupcakes are quick, moist and yummy. —Paula Zsiray, Logan, Utah

1 package (18-1/2 ounces) yellow cake mix
1 package (3.4 ounces) instant vanilla pudding mix

1 cup water
1/2 cup vegetable oil
4 eggs
1 cup (6 ounces) miniature semisweet chocolate chips
1 can (16 ounces) chocolate *or* vanilla frosting
Additional miniature semisweet chocolate chips

In a mixing bowl, combine cake and pudding mixes, water, oil and eggs; beat on low speed for 30 seconds. Beat on medium for 4 minutes. Stir in chocolate chips. Fill greased or paper-lined muffin cups with 1/4 cup batter. Bake at 375° for 18-22 minutes or until a toothpick inserted near the center comes out clean. Cool for 10 minutes; remove to wire racks to cool completely. Frost. Decorate with additional chips. **Yield:** 2-1/2 dozen.

— 🥄 🥄 🥄 —

Blueberry Sauce Supreme

Planting blueberries started out as a retirement project for my wife and me. Now it's a full-time business. Every day we enjoy blueberries in a variety of foods. —Clarence Scrivner, Hartsburg, Missouri

1/2 cup sugar
1/4 cup orange juice concentrate
2 tablespoons cornstarch
3 cups fresh *or* frozen blueberries

In a saucepan, combine sugar, orange juice concentrate and cornstarch; stir until smooth. Add blueberries and bring to a boil. Boil for 2 minutes, stirring constantly. Use as a topping for pound cake, pancakes or waffles. **Yield:** 2-1/4 cups.

— 🥄 🥄 🥄 —

Chocolate Peppermint Pie

This delightful dessert will satisfy a chocolate lover's craving. It's quite simple as well. —Kristine Dorazio
Chepachet, Rhode Island

1 quart chocolate-chocolate chip ice cream, softened
1 chocolate cookie crust (9 inches)
1 package (6 ounces) chocolate-covered peppermint candies
1 cup whipping cream, *divided*

Spoon ice cream into crust. Freeze until firm, about 2 hours. Meanwhile, in a small saucepan, heat the candies with 3-4 tablespoons of cream; stir until smooth. Cool. Whip the remaining cream; spoon over ice cream. Drizzle with some of the chocolate-peppermint sauce; pass the remaining sauce. **Yield:** 6-8 servings.

Zucchini Cupcakes

(Pictured above)

I asked my grandmother for this recipe after trying these irresistible spice cupcakes at her house. I love their creamy caramel frosting. They're such a scrumptious dessert you actually forget you're eating your vegetables, too!
—Virginia Breitmeyer
Craftsbury, Vermont

    3 eggs
1-1/3 cups sugar
  1/2 cup vegetable oil
  1/2 cup orange juice
    1 teaspoon almond extract
2-1/2 cups all-purpose flour
    2 teaspoons ground cinnamon
    2 teaspoons baking powder
    1 teaspoon baking soda
    1 teaspoon salt
  1/2 teaspoon ground cloves
1-1/2 cups shredded zucchini
CARAMEL FROSTING:
    1 cup packed brown sugar
  1/2 cup butter *or* margarine
  1/4 cup milk
    1 teaspoon vanilla extract
1-1/2 to 2 cups confectioners' sugar

In a mixing bowl, beat eggs, sugar, oil, orange juice and extract. Combine dry ingredients; add to the egg mixture and mix well. Add zucchini and mix well. Fill greased or paper-lined muffin cups two-thirds full. Bake at 350° for 20-25 minutes or until cupcakes test done. Cool for 10 minutes; remove to a wire rack to cool completely. For frosting, combine brown sugar, butter and milk in a saucepan; bring to a boil over medium heat. Cook and stir for 2 minutes. Remove from the heat; stir in vanil-

la. Cool to lukewarm. Gradually beat in confectioners' sugar until the frosting reaches desired spreading consistency. Frost cupcakes. **Yield:** 1-1/2 to 2 dozen.

— 🍷 🍷 🍷 —

Pear Cranberry Crisp

It's a pleasure to combine the tart cranberries we grow with sweet pears in this lovely crisp. —*Dot Angley Carver, Massachusetts*

    6 cups sliced peeled pears
    1 cup fresh *or* frozen cranberries
  1/2 cup sugar
    2 tablespoons all-purpose flour
  1/2 teaspoon ground cinnamon
  1/2 teaspoon ground ginger
  1/4 teaspoon ground nutmeg
  1/8 teaspoon ground cloves
TOPPING:
    1 cup all-purpose flour
  2/3 cup packed brown sugar
  1/2 cup old-fashioned oats
  1/4 teaspoon salt
  1/2 cup cold butter *or* margarine
Whipped cream and fresh mint, optional

Combine the first eight ingredients; mix well. Pour into a greased 9-in. square baking pan. For topping, combine flour, brown sugar, oats and salt; cut in butter until crumbly. Sprinkle over fruit. Bake at 350° for 50-60 minutes or until pears are tender. Garnish with whipped cream and mint if desired. **Yield:** 6-8 servings.

— 🍷 🍷 🍷 —

Very Blueberry Cake

We grow our own blueberries, pick all summer and freeze them to use later. This extra-special recipe comes from my mother. —*Roberta Strohmaier Lebanon, New Jersey*

  1/2 cup butter *or* margarine, softened
  1/2 cup shortening
1-1/2 cups sugar
    4 eggs
    1 teaspoon vanilla extract
    1 teaspoon almond extract
    3 cups all-purpose flour
  1/2 teaspoon baking powder
FILLING:
    1 tablespoon all-purpose flour
    2 teaspoons cornstarch
    1 teaspoon quick-cooking tapioca
    4 cups fresh *or* frozen blueberries, *divided*
    1 teaspoon grated lemon peel

GLAZE:
>   1 cup confectioners' sugar
>   1 to 2 tablespoons milk
>   1 teaspoon lemon juice

In a mixing bowl, cream butter, shortening and sugar. Beat in eggs, one at a time. Add extracts. Combine flour and baking powder; add to creamed mixture and mix well. Spread two-thirds of the batter in a greased 15-in. x 10-in. x 1-in. baking pan. For filling, combine flour, cornstarch and tapioca in a large bowl. Add 1/2 cup of blueberries; mash with a fork and stir well. Add lemon peel and remaining berries; toss to coat. Pour evenly over batter in pan. Drop remaining batter by rounded tablespoonfuls over filling. Bake at 350° for 40 minutes or until golden brown. Combine glaze ingredients; drizzle over warm cake. **Yield:** 20 servings.

— 🍷 🍷 🍷 —

Sugarless Apple Pie

The natural goodness of fresh apples comes through in this delightful dessert. It's an old-fashioned treat everyone can savor.
                                                       —Arlene Taylor
                                                       Lacey, Washington

✓   This tasty dish uses less sugar, salt and fat. Recipe includes *Diabetic Exchanges.*

>   6 cups sliced peeled tart apples
>   (about 4 large)
>   1/3 cup apple juice concentrate
>   2 tablespoons quick-cooking tapioca
>   1 teaspoon ground cinnamon
>   1 unbaked pastry shell (9 inches)
>   1/4 cup finely chopped walnuts

In a large bowl, combine the first four ingredients; let stand for 15 minutes. Stir and pour into pastry shell. Sprinkle with nuts. Bake at 425° for 15 minutes. Reduce heat to 350°; bake 40-50 minutes longer or until apples are tender. Cover edges with foil during the last 15 minutes to prevent over-browning if necessary. **Yield:** 8 servings. **Diabetic Exchanges:** One serving equals 1-1/2 fat, 1 starch, 1 fruit; also, 195 calories, 63 mg sodium, 5 mg cholesterol, 32 gm carbohydrate, 2 gm protein, 8 gm fat.

— 🍷 🍷 🍷 —

Sesame Pound Cake

This seed-studded cake has a pleasant crunch. It's wonderful garnished with fresh fruit.
                                 —Jane Finney, East Grand Forks, Minnesota

>   1 cup butter (no substitutes), softened
>   1 cup sugar

>   4 eggs
>   1/2 cup milk
>   1 teaspoon vanilla extract
>   1 teaspoon grated lemon peel
>   1/3 cup sesame seeds, toasted, *divided*
>   2 cups all-purpose flour
>   1 teaspoon baking powder
>   1/2 teaspoon salt
> **Fresh fruit, optional**

In a mixing bowl, cream butter and sugar. Add eggs, one at a time, beating well after each addition. Combine milk, vanilla and lemon peel; set aside. Set 1 tablespoon of sesame seeds aside. Combine remaining sesame seeds with flour, baking powder and salt. Add dry ingredients to creamed mixture alternately with milk mixture; mix well. Pour into a greased and floured 9-in. x 5-in. x 3-in. loaf pan. Sprinkle with reserved sesame seeds. Bake at 325° for 60-70 minutes or until a toothpick inserted near the center comes out clean. Cool in pan for 10 minutes; remove to a wire rack to cool completely. Serve with fruit if desired. **Yield:** 8-10 servings.

— 🍷 🍷 🍷 —

Peaches 'n' Cream Dessert

Since finding this recipe in the 1970's, I've used it several times each summer. It's fabulous with the peaches grown in our area.
                                                       —Margery Bryan
                                                       Royal City, Washington

>   2 cups all-purpose flour
>   1 teaspoon salt
>   3/4 cup shortening
>   1 egg
>   3 tablespoons cold water
> **FILLING:**
>   1 cup sugar
>   1/3 cup all-purpose flour
>   5 medium fresh peaches, peeled and sliced
>   1 cup whipping cream
>   1/2 teaspoon ground cinnamon

In a large bowl, combine flour and salt; cut in shortening until the mixture resembles coarse crumbs. Whisk egg and water together; sprinkle over flour mixture and toss. Form dough into a ball; roll out on a lightly floured surface to a 13-in. x 9-in. rectangle. Place in an ungreased 13-in. x 9-in. x 2-in. baking pan. For filling, combine sugar and flour; toss with the peaches. Pour into the crust. Pour cream over peaches; sprinkle with cinnamon. Bake at 425° for 20 minutes. Reduce heat to 350°; bake 25 minutes longer or until peaches are tender. Let stand 25 minutes before serving. Refrigerate any leftovers. **Yield:** 12 servings.

Potluck Pleasers

Whether you're planning a menu for 10 or 100, you'll appreciate these large-quantity recipes. They come from experienced cooks, so they're guaranteed to satisfy your hungry crowd.

COOKING FOR A CROWD. Clockwise from upper left: Broccoli-Cheddar Casserole (p. 162), Tangy Barbecue Sandwiches (p. 164), Potluck Eggs Benedict (p. 161), Hot Curried Fruit (p. 161) and Crunchy Tossed Salad (p. 166).

a tent of foil. Bake at 325° for 4-1/2 to 5 hours or until a meat thermometer reads 185°, brushing with oil occasionally. Remove all stuffing. **Yield:** 10-12 servings (11 cups stuffing). **Editor's Note:** Stuffing may be baked separately in a greased 2-qt. casserole. Cover and bake at 325° for 1 hour; uncover and bake for 10 minutes.

Chicken in Cream Sauce

For a stick-to-the-ribs main course, reach for this recipe. Its down-home flavor makes it irresistible.
—*Clara Pennock, Nashville, Michigan*

  30 **bone-in chicken breast halves**
 2/3 **cup cooking oil**
   6 **cups water, *divided***
   6 **cups chicken broth**
   2 **cups chopped onion**
   3 **tablespoons Worcestershire sauce**
   1 **tablespoon salt**
   2 **teaspoons pepper**
 1-1/4 **cups all-purpose flour**
   6 **cups half-and-half cream**
Hot cooked rice

Brown the chicken in oil. Meanwhile, in a large Dutch oven, combine 5 cups water, chicken broth, onion, Worcestershire sauce, salt and pepper; bring to a boil over medium heat. Combine flour and remaining water until smooth; stir into broth mixture. Bring to a boil; cook and stir for 2 minutes or until thickened. Remove from the heat and stir in cream. Arrange chicken breasts in five greased 13-in. x 9-in. x 2-in. baking pans; pour about 3-1/2 cups sauce over the chicken in each pan. Cover and bake at 350° for 40-45 minutes or until the chicken juices run clear. Serve over rice. **Yield:** 30 servings.

Apple Dumplings

Coming from a family of 10 children, I've certainly learned how to cook for a crowd. This recipe is an easy dessert that feeds a bunch!
—*Jeanne Wade*
Icard, North Carolina

   3 **tubes (12 ounces *each*) refrigerated buttermilk biscuits**
  15 **medium apples, peeled, cored and halved**
   2 **cups sugar**
   2 **cups water**
   1 **cup butter *or* margarine, melted**

Turkey with Rye Dressing

(Pictured above)

My husband created the recipe for this tempting turkey and delectable dressing. It's a feast that seems like Thanksgiving whenever we enjoy it. He gets lots of recipe requests for this memorable main dish.
—*Joan Vernon, Riverton, Utah*

   1 **pound day-old light rye bread, cubed**
 1/2 **pound day-old dark rye bread, cubed**
 1-1/2 **cups chopped onion**
   2 **large tart apples, peeled and chopped**
   1 **cup chopped celery**
   4 **garlic cloves, minced**
 1/2 **cup butter *or* margarine**
 3/4 **cup chopped salted mixed nuts**
   2 **tablespoons dried parsley flakes**
   2 **teaspoons salt**
   2 **teaspoons dried thyme**
 1-1/2 **teaspoons rubbed sage**
 3/4 **teaspoon dried rosemary, crushed**
 1/2 **teaspoon pepper**
 1/4 **teaspoon ground nutmeg**
   3 **to 3-1/2 cups chicken broth**
   1 **turkey (12 to 14 pounds)**
   2 **tablespoons vegetable oil**

Toss bread cubes in a large bowl. In a skillet, saute onion, apples, celery and garlic in butter until apples and vegetables are tender; add to bread. Add nuts, seasonings and enough broth to moisten. Just before baking, stuff the turkey. Skewer openings; tie drumsticks together. Place on a rack in a roasting pan. Brush with some of the oil. Cover lightly with

2 teaspoons vanilla extract
1/2 teaspoon ground cinnamon

Flatten biscuits with your hand. Wrap each biscuit around an apple half; place seam side down in two greased 13-in. x 9-in. x 2-in. baking dishes. Combine sugar, water, butter and vanilla; pour about 1-2/3 cups into each pan. Sprinkle cinnamon over dumplings. Bake, uncovered, at 350° for 35-40 minutes or until golden brown and apples are tender. Serve immediately. **Yield:** 30 servings.

— 🍷 🍷 🍷 —

Dressing for a Crowd

When I'm planning a holiday meal for a crowd, this recipe is sure to be on the menu. It's a tried-and-true church supper dish. —Sue Norem, Ellsworth, Iowa

  5 loaves (1 pound *each*) day-old white bread, cubed
  5 pounds pork sausage, cooked and drained *or* 5 pounds giblets, cooked and chopped
2-1/2 cups chopped celery
  1/2 cup finely chopped onion
  2 pounds butter *or* margarine
3-3/4 to 4-1/2 cups chicken broth, *divided*
  1 tablespoon salt
  2 teaspoons rubbed sage
1-1/2 teaspoons pepper
  1 teaspoon dried thyme
  1 teaspoon celery salt
  1 teaspoon poultry seasoning
  1 teaspoon seasoned salt

Toss the bread cubes and sausage; set aside. In a saucepan over medium heat, saute celery and onion in butter until tender. Remove from the heat. Stir in 3-3/4 cups broth and seasonings; mix well. Pour over bread mixture; mix well. Add desired amount of remaining broth. Spoon into four greased 3-qt. baking dishes. Cover and bake at 325° for 1-1/4 hours. Uncover and bake 15 minutes longer or until heated through. **Yield:** 48 servings.

— 🍷 🍷 🍷 —

Tropical Punch

Bananas give this festive punch a deliciously different twist. It's a great refreshing beverage to take to church potlucks in summer. —Ruth Seitz, Columbus Junction, Iowa

  3 cups water
3/4 cup sugar
  3 large ripe bananas
  1 can (46 ounces) pineapple juice, chilled

1-1/2 cups orange juice
  1/4 cup lemon juice
    1 bottle (2 liters) ginger ale, chilled

Place water, sugar and bananas in a blender; cover and process until smooth and sugar is dissolved. Pour into a large bowl; stir in remaining ingredients. Serve immediately. **Yield:** 40 (1/2-cup) servings.

— 🍷 🍷 🍷 —

Apple-Cranberry Relish

(Pictured below)

This fresh ruby-colored relish is sweet and tangy, and the apples and celery give it a terrific crunch. At our house, it's a holiday menu mainstay since it's so pleasant with poultry and pork. —Edith McFarland, Willits, California

  2 medium navel oranges
  2 bags (12 ounces *each*) fresh *or* frozen cranberries
  2 medium apples, peeled and cut into chunks
  2 celery ribs, cut into chunks
  3 cups sugar

Grate peel of oranges and set aside. Peel and discard white membrane. Separate orange into sections and place half in a food processor or blender. Add half of the cranberries, apples and celery. Process until coarsely chopped. Transfer to a bowl; repeat with remaining oranges, cranberries, apples and celery. Stir in sugar and reserved orange peel. Cover and refrigerate overnight. **Yield:** 16 servings (8 cups).

Feather-Light Doughnuts

(Pictured below)

When I was growing up, our farm family always had an abundance of mashed potatoes at the supper table. We loved to use leftovers in these fluffy doughnuts.
—Darlene Alexander, Nekoosa, Wisconsin

2 packages (1/4 ounce *each*) active dry yeast
1-1/2 cups warm milk (110° to 115°)
1 cup cold mashed potatoes
1-1/2 cups sugar, *divided*
1/2 cup vegetable oil
2 teaspoons salt
2 teaspoons vanilla extract
1/2 teaspoon baking soda
1/2 teaspoon baking powder
2 eggs
5-1/2 to 6 cups all-purpose flour
1/2 teaspoon ground cinnamon
Cooking oil for deep-fat frying

In a large mixing bowl, dissolve yeast in warm milk. Add potatoes, 1/2 cup sugar, oil, salt, vanilla, baking soda, baking powder and eggs; mix well. Add enough of the flour to form a soft dough. Place in a greased bowl, turning once to grease top. Cover and let rise in a warm place until doubled, about 1 hour. Punch dough down; roll out on a floured surface to 1/2-in. thickness. Cut with a 3-in. doughnut cutter. Place on greased baking sheets; cover and let rise until almost doubled, about 45 minutes. Meanwhile, combine the cinnamon and remaining sugar; set aside. Heat oil in an electric skillet or deep-fat fryer to 350°; fry doughnuts until golden on both sides. Drain on paper towels; roll in cinnamon-sugar while still warm. **Yield:** about 2-1/2 dozen.

French Toast for 90

People are sometimes shocked when I say I'll bring French toast to feed a crowd. But this oven-baked version, which is prepared the night before, couldn't be easier. —*Kathleen Hall, Lakeview, Oregon*

9 unsliced loaves (1 pound *each*) day-old French bread
9 dozen eggs
2-1/2 gallons milk
2 cups sugar
1 cup vanilla extract
2 tablespoons salt
1 pound butter *or* margarine, melted
Confectioners' sugar

Cut bread into 3/4-in. slices and arrange in 18 greased 13-in. x 9-in. x 2-in. baking dishes. Beat eggs; add milk, sugar, vanilla and salt. Mix well. Pour about 3 cups over bread in each pan. Cover and chill 8 hours or overnight. Remove from refrigerator 30 minutes before baking. Brush with butter. Bake, uncovered, at 350° for 55-65 minutes or until a knife inserted near the center comes out clean. Let stand 5 minutes. Dust with confectioners' sugar. **Yield:** 90 servings (2 slices each).

— 🍵 🍵 🍵 —

Hash Brown Casserole

Whenever I serve these rich, cheesy potatoes, people always go back for seconds. This casserole is a snap to fix using quick convenient packaged ingredients.
—Susan Auten, Douglasville, Georgia

2 cans (10-3/4 ounces *each*) condensed cream of potato soup, undiluted
1 cup (8 ounces) sour cream
1/2 teaspoon garlic salt
1 package (2 pounds) frozen cubed hash brown potatoes
2 cups (8 ounces) shredded cheddar cheese
1/2 cup grated Parmesan cheese

In a large bowl, combine the soup, sour cream and garlic salt. Add potatoes and cheddar cheese; mix well. Pour into a greased 13-in. x 9-in. x 2-in. baking dish. Top with Parmesan cheese. Bake, uncovered, at 350° for 55-60 minutes or until potatoes are tender. **Yield:** 12-16 servings.

— 🍵 🍵 🍵 —

Christmas Party Pinwheels

The refreshing flavor of ranch dressing and crisp vegetables makes these pinwheels a pleasure to serve.
—Janis Plourde, Smooth Rock Falls, Ontario

2 packages (8 ounces *each*) cream cheese,
   softened
1 package (.4 ounce) ranch salad
   dressing mix
1/2 cup minced sweet red pepper
1/2 cup minced celery
1/4 cup sliced green onions
1/4 cup sliced stuffed olives
3 to 4 flour tortillas (10 inches)

In a mixing bowl, beat cream cheese and dressing
mix until smooth. Add red pepper, celery, onions
and olives; mix well. Spread about 3/4 cup on each
tortilla. Roll up tightly; wrap in plastic wrap. Refrigerate for at least 2 hours. Slice into 1/2-in.
pieces. **Yield:** 15-20 servings.

— ❦ ❦ ❦ —

Vanilla Fruit Salad

*I often serve this fruit salad as a side dish with a vari-
ety of main courses. But it has a nice sweet taste, which
also makes it perfect for dessert.*
                    —*Geraldine Grisdale, Mt. Pleasant, Michigan*

5 cans (20 ounces *each*) pineapple chunks
   in juice
1 can (8 ounces) pineapple chunks in juice
4 packages (5.1 ounces *each*) instant vanilla
   pudding mix
8 cans (15 ounces *each*) mandarin oranges,
   drained
10 medium red apples, chopped

Drain pineapple, reserving juice. Add water to
juice to make 6 cups. Place pudding mixes in a
large bowl; stir in pineapple juice until thickened,
about 4-6 minutes. Fold in pineapple, oranges
and apples. Pour about 8 cups each into four 13-
in. x 9-in. x 2-in. pans that have been coated with
nonstick cooking spray. Refrigerate. **Yield:** 64 (1/2-
cup) servings.

— ❦ ❦ ❦ —

Hot Curried Fruit

(Pictured on page 156)

*This soothing side dish is made with a blend of handy
canned fruits.*
                    —*Elizabeth Hunter
                    Prosperity, South Carolina*

1 can (29 ounces) apricot halves, drained
1 can (29 ounces) pear halves, drained
1 can (29 ounces) peach halves, drained
1 can (20 ounces) pineapple chunks, drained
3/4 cup golden raisins
1/4 cup butter *or* margarine

1/2 cup packed brown sugar
1 teaspoon curry powder

In a 2-1/2-qt. casserole, combine fruit and raisins.
Melt butter in a small saucepan; stir in brown sugar and curry powder. Cook and stir over low heat
until sugar is dissolved. Pour over fruit mixture; mix
gently. Cover and bake at 400° for 30 minutes or
until heated through. **Yield:** 10-12 servings.

Potluck Eggs Benedict

(Pictured above)

*Asparagus spears give this hearty breakfast dish big
springtime flavor. It's super served over warm fluffy
biscuits.*   —*Pauline vanBreemen, Franklin, Indiana*

1 pound fresh asparagus, trimmed
3/4 cup butter *or* margarine
3/4 cup all-purpose flour
4 cups milk
1 can (14-1/2 ounces) chicken broth
1 pound cubed fully cooked ham
1 cup (4 ounces) shredded cheddar cheese
8 hard-cooked eggs, quartered
1/2 teaspoon salt
1/8 teaspoon cayenne pepper
10 to 12 biscuits, warmed

Cut asparagus into 1/2-in. pieces. Cook in a small
amount of boiling water until tender, about 5
minutes; drain. Set aside to cool. Melt butter in a
saucepan; stir in flour until smooth. Add milk and
broth; bring to a boil. Cook and stir for 2 minutes.
Add ham and cheese; stir until the cheese melts.
Add eggs, salt, cayenne and asparagus; heat
though. Serve over biscuits. **Yield:** 10-12 servings.

8 cups chopped fresh broccoli
1 cup finely chopped onion
3/4 cup butter *or* margarine
12 eggs
2 cups whipping cream
2 cups (8 ounces) shredded cheddar cheese, *divided*
2 teaspoons salt
1 teaspoon pepper

In a skillet over medium heat, saute broccoli and onion in butter until crisp-tender, about 5 minutes; set aside. In a bowl, beat eggs. Add cream and 1-3/4 cups of cheese; mix well. Stir in the broccoli mixture, salt and pepper. Pour into a greased 3-qt. baking dish; set in a larger pan filled with 1 in. of hot water. Bake, uncovered, at 350° for 45-50 minutes or until a knife inserted near the center comes out clean. Sprinkle with remaining cheese. Let stand 10 minutes before serving. **Yield:** 12-16 servings.

Stuffed Pasta Shells

(Pictured above)

These savory shells never fail to make a big impression, even though the recipe is very easy. One or two of these shells makes a great individual serving at a potluck, so a single batch goes a long way.
—Jena Coffey, St. Louis, Missouri

4 cups (16 ounces) shredded mozzarella cheese
1 carton (15 ounces) ricotta cheese
1 package (10 ounces) frozen chopped spinach, thawed and drained
1 package (12 ounces) jumbo pasta shells, cooked and drained
1 jar (28 ounces) spaghetti sauce

Combine cheeses and spinach; stuff into shells. Arrange in a greased 13-in. x 9-in. x 2-in. baking dish. Pour spaghetti sauce over the shells. Cover and bake at 350° for 30 minutes or until heated through. **Yield:** 12-14 servings.

Broccoli-Cheddar Casserole

(Pictured on page 156)

We're lucky to have fresh fruits and vegetables year-round. I put bountiful Arizona broccoli to great use in this rich side dish. Even those who don't care for broccoli finish off big helpings. —Carol Strickland
Yuma, Arizona

Fruited Spinach Salad

I had a similar salad in a restaurant and thought it was great, so I came up with this recipe to prepare at home. I love the way the light, sweet dressing tops the refreshing salad ingredients. —Kate Reynolds
Seattle, Washington

1 can (11 ounces) mandarin oranges
1/4 cup olive *or* vegetable oil
3 tablespoons raspberry jam *or* spreadable fruit
1 tablespoon red wine vinegar
1 package (10 ounces) fresh spinach, torn
1 medium red apple, chopped
1 cup chopped pecans, toasted

Drain oranges, reserving 1/2 cup juice. In a jar with tight-fitting lid, combine oil, jam, vinegar and reserved juice; shake well. In a large salad bowl, toss oranges, spinach, apple and pecans. Serve with the dressing. **Yield:** 6-8 servings.

Yogurt Herb Bread

Slices from these high, savory loaves always seem to vanish quickly from a buffet. An enticing combination of herbs makes a distinctive flavor folks rave about.
—Carol Forcum, Marion, Illinois

✓ This tasty dish uses less sugar, salt and fat. Recipe includes *Diabetic Exchanges.*

5-1/2 to 6-1/2 cups all-purpose flour
    2 packages (1/4 ounce *each*) active dry yeast
    2 tablespoons sugar
    2 teaspoons salt
    1 cup water
    1 cup (8 ounces) plain yogurt
    3 tablespoons vegetable oil
    1 teaspoon dill weed
  1/2 teaspoon dried chives
  1/4 teaspoon *each* dried oregano, thyme and basil

In a large mixing bowl, combine 2-1/2 cups flour, yeast, sugar and salt. In a small saucepan, heat water and yogurt to 120°-130°. Add to flour mixture; mix well. Add oil, herbs and enough of the remaining flour to form a stiff dough. Turn onto a floured surface; knead until smooth and elastic, about 6-8 minutes. Place in a greased bowl, turning once to grease top. Cover and let rise in a warm place until doubled, about 1 hour. Punch dough down; shape into two loaves. Place in two greased 8-in. x 4-in. x 2-in. loaf pans. Cover and let rise until doubled, about 1 hour. Bake at 375° for 35-40 minutes or until golden brown. Remove from pans to cool on wire racks. **Yield:** 2 loaves (32 slices). **Diabetic Exchanges:** One slice (prepared with low-fat yogurt) equals 1-1/2 starch; also, 113 calories, 139 mg sodium, trace cholesterol, 21 gm carbohydrate, 3 gm protein, 2 gm fat.

— 🍷 🍷 🍷 —

Spaghetti for 100

A club I belong to used this main dish for a fund-raising dinner. One man came 50 miles because he'd had the dinner the year before and liked it so much!
    —Marilyn Monroe, Lansing, Michigan

    6 pounds ground beef
    2 cups chopped onion
  16 garlic cloves, minced
  12 cans (29 ounces *each*) tomato sauce
    4 cans (18 ounces *each*) tomato paste
1/4 cup salt
    3 tablespoons sugar
    2 tablespoons *each* Italian seasoning, dried basil and oregano
  13 pounds spaghetti, cooked and drained

In a large stockpot, brown beef, onion and garlic; drain. Add tomato sauce and paste, salt, sugar and seasonings; bring to a boil. Reduce heat; cover and simmer for 2-3 hours, stirring occasionally. Serve over spaghetti. **Yield:** 100 servings (about 50 cups sauce).

Peanut Butter Baskets

(Pictured below)

Rich, buttery cookies become more delightful still topped with peanut butter cups and candy. I use appropriately colored decorations to match occasions at any time of the year. —Darlene Markel
    Sublimity, Oregon

  30 green gumdrops
  3/4 cup creamy peanut butter
  1/2 cup shortening
  3/4 cup sugar, *divided*
  1/2 cup packed brown sugar
    1 egg
    2 tablespoons milk
    1 teaspoon vanilla extract
1-1/3 cups all-purpose flour
  1/2 teaspoon baking soda
  1/2 teaspoon salt
  30 miniature peanut butter cups, halved
  60 cake decorator candy flowers

Flatten the gumdrops; cut into small leaf shapes and set aside. In a mixing bowl, cream the peanut butter, shortening, 1/2 cup sugar and brown sugar. Add the egg, milk and vanilla; mix well. Combine the flour, baking soda and salt; add to the creamed mixture and mix well. Shape into 1-in. balls. Roll in remaining sugar; place on ungreased baking sheets. Bake at 350° for 10-12 minutes or until lightly browned. Remove from the oven and immediately lightly press one peanut butter cup, cut side down, into each cookie to form a basket. Press a candy flower onto cookie so it appears as if a flower is coming out of the basket; press gumdrop leaves next to flowers. Cool on wire racks. **Yield:** about 5 dozen.

That Good Salad

(Pictured below)

When a friend shared this recipe, it had a fancy French name. Our children just say, "Mom, please make 'that good salad'." Now our friends request it for potluck dinners. —Betty Lamb, Orem, Utah

- 3/4 cup vegetable oil
- 1/4 cup fresh lemon juice
- 2 garlic cloves, minced
- 1/2 teaspoon salt
- 1/2 teaspoon pepper
- 2 bunches (1 pound *each*) romaine, torn
- 2 cups chopped tomatoes
- 1 cup (4 ounces) shredded Swiss cheese
- 2/3 cup slivered almonds, toasted, optional
- 1/2 cup grated Parmesan cheese
- 8 bacon strips, cooked and crumbled
- 1 cup Caesar salad croutons

In a jar with tight-fitting lid, combine oil, lemon juice, garlic, salt and pepper; cover and shake well. Chill. In a bowl, toss romaine, tomatoes, Swiss cheese, almonds if desired, Parmesan cheese and bacon. Shake dressing; pour over salad and toss. Add croutons and serve immediately. **Yield:** 14 servings.

Tangy Barbecue Sandwiches

(Pictured on page 156)

Since I prepare the beef for these robust sandwiches in the slow cooker, it's easy to fix a meal for a hungry bunch. I never come home with leftovers.
—Debbi Smith, Crossett, Arkansas

- 3 cups chopped celery
- 1 cup chopped onion
- 1 cup ketchup
- 1 cup barbecue sauce
- 1 cup water
- 2 tablespoons vinegar
- 2 tablespoons Worcestershire sauce
- 2 tablespoons brown sugar
- 1 teaspoon chili powder
- 1 teaspoon salt
- 1/2 teaspoon pepper
- 1/2 teaspoon garlic powder
- 1 boneless chuck roast (3 to 4 pounds), trimmed
- 14 to 18 hamburger buns, split

In a slow cooker, combine the first 12 ingredients; mix well. Add roast. Cover and cook on high for 1 hour. Reduce heat to low and cook 7-8 hours longer or until meat is tender. Remove roast; cool. Shred meat and return to sauce; heat through. Using a slotted spoon, fill each bun with about 1/2 cup of meat mixture. **Yield:** 14-18 servings.

— 🍴 🍴 🍴 —

French Salad Dressing

We used this dressing at a drive-in I worked at and sold a lot of salads. It's a popular topper for all kinds of lettuce. —Jane Barta, St. Thomas, North Dakota

- 1-1/2 cups vegetable oil
- 1 cup ketchup
- 3/4 cup sugar
- 1/2 cup vinegar
- 1 small onion, chopped
- 1 teaspoon lemon juice
- 1 teaspoon paprika
- 1/2 teaspoon salt

In a blender or food processor, blend all ingredients until smooth. Store in the refrigerator. **Yield:** about 3-1/3 cups.

— 🍴 🍴 🍴 —

Chocolate Chip Cookie Bars

These mouth-watering bars are often requested at church dinners I help organize. They're tasty and easy to serve. —Barbara Witte, Irving, Texas

- 2 cups butter *or* margarine, softened
- 1-1/2 cups sugar
- 1-1/2 cups packed brown sugar
- 4 eggs
- 2 teaspoons vanilla extract
- 1 teaspoon water
- 4-1/2 cups all-purpose flour

2 teaspoons baking soda
1-1/2 teaspoons salt
  3 cups (18 ounces) semisweet chocolate chips
  1 cup chopped walnuts

In a large mixing bowl, cream butter and sugars. Add eggs, vanilla and water; beat until smooth. Combine flour, baking soda and salt; gradually add to creamed mixture and mix well. Fold in chocolate chips and nuts. Press into three greased 15-in. x 10-in. x 1-in. baking pans. Bake at 375° for 15-18 minutes or until golden brown. **Yield:** 8 dozen.

Ham Salad Sandwiches

Sweet pickles give these sandwiches a bold flavor that's hard to beat. They're excellent for a ladies' luncheon. —Pat Keuther, Denver, Colorado

  4 pounds fully cooked ham *or* ring bologna, coarsely ground
  3 cups chopped sweet pickles
  2 cups mayonnaise *or* salad dressing
  1 jar (2 ounces) diced pimientos, drained
100 slices of bread
Lettuce leaves, optional

Combine ham, pickles, mayonnaise and pimientos; mix well. Spoon 1/4 cup onto 50 slices of bread; top with lettuce if desired and remaining bread. **Yield:** 50 servings.

Zesty Slaw

I assure this will be the hit of the salad table at any gathering. It's crisp and colorful with a snappy dressing. —Ramona Hook Wysong, Paducah, Kentucky

  8 quarts shredded cabbage
  8 quarts shredded red cabbage
2-1/2 cups grated carrots
  3 cups mayonnaise
  1 cup (8 ounces) sour cream
1/2 cup grated onion
1/2 cup chopped fresh parsley
1/2 cup cider *or* red wine vinegar
  3 tablespoons Dijon mustard
  2 tablespoons celery seed
  2 teaspoons salt
  2 teaspoons pepper

Toss cabbage and carrots. Combine remaining ingredients until smooth; pour over cabbage mixture and toss to coat. Cover and refrigerate for several hours. **Yield:** about 85 servings (3/4 cup each).

Berry Big Pie

(Pictured above)

This giant pie's crust is so easy, and we have lots of berries that grow on our small acreage. With a dessert this size, everyone can enjoy a luscious piece. —Janelle Seward, Ontario, Oregon

  4 cups all-purpose flour
  1 tablespoon sugar
  2 teaspoons salt
1-3/4 cup cold shortening
1/2 cup cold water
  1 egg
  1 tablespoon vinegar
FILLING:
  8 cups fresh *or* frozen blackberries*
  2 cups sugar
1/2 cup all-purpose flour
Half-and-half cream

In a large bowl, combine flour, sugar and salt; cut in shortening until the mixture resembles coarse crumbs. In a bowl, combine water, egg and vinegar; stir into flour mixture just until moistened. Form into a roll. Cover and refrigerate for 1 hour. On a floured surface, roll two-thirds of the dough into an 18-in. x 14-in. rectangle. Carefully place onto the bottom and up the sides of a 13-in. x 9-in. x 2-in. glass baking dish. Combine the berries, sugar and flour; pour into crust. Roll out the remaining dough and make lattice strips; place over the filling. Brush pastry with cream. Bake at 400° for 15 minutes; reduce heat to 350°. Bake about 1 hour longer or until bubbly. Cool completely. Store in the refrigerator. **Yield:** 12-16 servings. ***Editor's Note:** If using frozen berries, do not thaw.

Dinner in a Dish

(Pictured above)

I haven't found anyone yet who can resist this saucy beef casserole topped with mashed potatoes. The frozen peas and canned tomatoes add color and make a helping or two a complete meal. —Betty Sitzman
Wray, Colorado

    2 pounds ground beef
    1 medium onion, chopped
    2 teaspoons beef bouillon granules
    2 cans (14-1/2 ounces *each*) diced
        tomatoes, undrained
    3 cups frozen peas
  2/3 cup ketchup
  1/4 cup chopped fresh parsley
    2 tablespoons all-purpose flour
    2 teaspoons dried marjoram
    1 teaspoon salt
  1/2 teaspoon pepper
    6 cups hot mashed potatoes (prepared with
        milk and butter)
    2 eggs

In a saucepan over medium heat, brown beef and onion; drain. Add the next nine ingredients; mix well. Bring to a boil; cook and stir for 2 minutes. Pour into an ungreased shallow 3-qt. baking dish. Combine potatoes and eggs; mix well. Drop by 1/2 cupfuls onto the beef mixture. Bake, uncovered, at 350° for 35-40 minutes or until bubbly and potatoes are lightly browned. **Yield:** 12 servings.

Crunchy Tossed Salad

(Pictured on page 156)

Count on compliments, not leftovers, when you share this fun, crunchy salad at your next gathering. It's so easy to toss together, and someone always asks for the recipe. —Deborah Weisberger
Mullett Lake, Michigan

  1/2 cup vegetable oil
  1/4 cup sugar
    2 tablespoons vinegar
    1 teaspoon salt
  1/4 teaspoon pepper
    1 large head iceberg lettuce, sliced
    6 bacon strips, cooked and crumbled
  1/3 cup sliced almonds, toasted
  1/4 cup sesame seeds, toasted
    4 green onions, sliced
  3/4 cup chow mein noodles

In a jar with a tight-fitting lid, combine oil, sugar, vinegar, salt and pepper; shake well. Chill for 1 hour. Just before serving, combine lettuce, bacon, almonds, sesame seeds and onions in a large bowl; add dressing and toss. Top with chow mein noodles. **Yield:** 12 servings.

———— 🍴 🍴 🍴 ————

Chicken Rice Salad

For a summer luncheon, this light, colorful salad is a treat. The crunchy celery, green pepper and almonds along with refreshing oranges and pineapple make this a chicken salad folks can't wait to dig into.
—Bernadine Stine, Roanoke, Indiana

    5 cups cubed cooked chicken
    3 cups cooked rice
1-1/2 cups diced green pepper
1-1/2 cups sliced celery
    1 can (20 ounces) pineapple tidbits, drained
  3/4 cup mayonnaise
    4 teaspoons orange juice
    2 teaspoons vinegar
    1 teaspoon salt
  1/2 teaspoon ground ginger
  1/4 teaspoon garlic salt
    1 can (15 ounces) mandarin oranges,
        drained
    1 cup slivered almonds, toasted

In a large bowl, combine the first five ingredients. In a small bowl, combine the mayonnaise, orange juice, vinegar, salt, ginger and garlic salt. Pour over salad and toss. Refrigerate. Just before serving, fold in the oranges and almonds. **Yield:** 12 servings.

Fluffy Lemonade Gelatin

I first tasted this light salad at a family reunion, and it went so well with the other foods on that buffet.
—Claire Darby, New Castle, Delaware

- **5 packages (3 ounces *each*) lemon gelatin**
- **6 cups boiling water**
- **1 can (12 ounces) frozen lemonade concentrate**
- **1 carton (12 ounces) frozen whipped topping, thawed**

Dissolve gelatin in boiling water; stir in lemonade until dissolved. Chill until partially set. Fold in whipped topping. Pour into a 13-in. x 9-in. x 2-in. dish. Chill until firm. **Yield:** 20-24 servings.

— 🥄 🥄 🥄 —

Overnight Salad

For a make-ahead salad with a refreshing lemon dressing that's a real crowd-pleaser, try this recipe. My daughter has made it often for family gatherings.
—Gladys Serafine, Southbury, Connecticut

- **2 bags (10 ounces *each*) fresh spinach, torn**
- **8 hard-cooked eggs, sliced**
- **1 pound bacon, cooked and crumbled**
- **1/2 pound fresh mushrooms, sliced**
- **2 large bunches romaine, torn**
- **3/4 cup chopped red onion**
- **2 cups (16 ounces) sour cream**
- **2 cups mayonnaise**
- **1/2 cup lemon juice**
- **1 teaspoon salt**
- **1/4 teaspoon pepper**
- **1/2 cup shredded cheddar cheese**
- **1 package (10 ounces) frozen peas, thawed**

In two 5-qt. bowls, layer spinach, eggs, bacon, mushrooms, romaine and onion. Combine sour cream, mayonnaise, lemon juice, salt and pepper; spread evenly over salads. Sprinkle with cheese. Chill for 12-24 hours. Just before serving, add peas and toss. **Yield:** 50 servings (about 1 cup each).

— 🥄 🥄 🥄 —

Yogurt Yeast Rolls

(Pictured at right)

People tend to snap up these fluffy, golden rolls in a hurry whenever I take them to a potluck. It's a nice contribution since rolls are easy to transport and one batch goes a long way.
—Carol Forcum
Marion, Illinois

✓ This tasty dish uses less sugar, salt and fat. Recipe includes _Diabetic Exchanges_.

- **1-1/2 cups whole wheat flour**
- **3-1/4 cups all-purpose flour, *divided***
- **2 packages (1/4 ounce *each*) active dry yeast**
- **2 teaspoons salt**
- **1/2 teaspoon baking soda**
- **1-1/2 cups (12 ounces) plain yogurt**
- **1/2 cup water**
- **3 tablespoons butter *or* margarine**
- **2 tablespoons honey**

In a mixing bowl, combine whole wheat flour, 1/2 cup all-purpose flour, yeast, salt and baking soda. In a saucepan over low heat, heat yogurt, water, butter and honey to 120°-130°. Pour over dry ingredients; blend well. Beat on medium speed for 3 minutes. Add enough remaining all-purpose flour to form a soft dough. Turn onto a floured surface; knead until smooth and elastic, about 6-8 minutes. Place in a greased bowl, turning once to grease top. Cover and let rise in a warm place until doubled, about 1 hour. Punch dough down; divide into 24 pieces. Roll each piece into a 9-in. rope. To form S-shaped rolls, coil each end of rope toward center in opposite directions. Place 3 in. apart on greased baking sheets. Cover and let rise until doubled, about 30 minutes. Bake at 400° for 15 minutes or until golden brown. Spray tops with nonstick cooking spray while warm. Cool on wire racks. **Yield:** 2 dozen. **Diabetic Exchanges:** One roll (prepared with margarine and nonfat yogurt) equals 1 starch, 1/2 fat; also, 98 calories, 231 mg sodium, 31 mg cholesterol, 18 gm carbohydrate, 3 gm protein, 2 gm fat.

Beef Burritos

(Pictured below)

Living in Arizona, we enjoy all sorts of foods with Southwestern flair, such as these beef-stuffed tortillas. The recipe is easy to make and easy to serve— folks can assemble their own burritos with their choice of garnishes. —Amy Martin, Waddell, Arizona

> 2 **chuck pot roasts (2-1/2 to 3 pounds *each*)**
> 2 **tablespoons cooking oil**
> 1 **cup water**
> 1 **large onion, chopped**
> 4 **garlic cloves, minced**
> 2 **teaspoons dried oregano**
> 2 **teaspoons salt**
> 1 **teaspoon pepper**
> 1 **can (28 ounces) diced tomatoes, undrained**
> 2 **cans (4 ounces *each*) chopped green chilies**
> 2 **tablespoons all-purpose flour**
> 1/4 **cup cold water**
> 4 to 6 **drops hot pepper sauce**
> 18 **flour tortillas (8 inches), warmed**
> **Shredded cheddar cheese, sour cream and salsa**

In a Dutch oven over medium heat, brown roasts in oil; drain. Add water, onion, garlic, oregano, salt and pepper; bring to a boil. Reduce heat; cover and simmer for 2 to 2-1/2 hours or until meat is tender. Remove roasts; cool. Remove meat from the bone and cut into bite-size pieces. Skim fat from pan juices. Add tomatoes and chilies; mix well. Add meat; bring to a boil. Reduce heat; simmer, un-covered, for 30 minutes. Combine flour and cold water; mix well. Stir into beef mixture. Cook over medium heat, stirring constantly, until thickened and bubbly. Add hot pepper sauce. Spoon down the center of tortillas; fold top and bottom of tortilla over filling and roll up. Serve with cheese, sour cream and salsa. **Yield:** 18 servings.

— 🍵 🍵 🍵 —

Cranberry Punch

Tingle taste buds with a rosy colored punch that suits the season. I discovered this recipe while working at a restaurant. —Elaine Schlender
Clintonville, Wisconsin

> 3 **pints honey**
> 3 **quarts hot tea**
> 4 **bottles (48 ounces *each*) cranberry juice**
> 1 **gallon orange juice**
> 3 **pints lemon juice**
> 4 **bottles (2 liters *each*) grapefruit-lime soda, chilled**

Dissolve honey in tea. Cool. Add cranberry, orange and lemon juices; chill. Just before serving, add soda. **Yield:** 90-95 servings (about 1/2 cup each).

— 🍵 🍵 🍵 —

Triple Treat Torte

A peanutty crust and three deliciously different creamy layers form a tempting treat you'll be proud to share. —Inez Orsburn, De Motte, Indiana

> 1/2 **cup cold butter *or* margarine**
> 1 **cup all-purpose flour**
> 2/3 **cup finely chopped dry roasted peanuts**
> **FILLING:**
> 1 **cup confectioners' sugar**
> 1 **package (8 ounces) cream cheese, softened**
> 1/2 **cup creamy peanut butter**
> 1 **carton (8 ounces) frozen whipped topping, thawed, *divided***
> **TOPPING:**
> 1 **package (3.9 ounces) instant chocolate pudding mix**
> 1 **package (3.4 ounces) instant vanilla pudding mix**
> 2-3/4 **cups cold milk**
> **Grated semisweet chocolate, optional**

Cut butter into flour until crumbly; stir in peanuts. Press onto the bottom of a greased 13-in. x 9-in. x 2-in. baking dish. Bake at 350° for 16-20 minutes or until golden brown. Cool completely. For filling,

beat sugar, cream cheese and peanut butter in a mixing bowl until smooth. Fold in 1 cup whipped topping. Spread over crust. In another mixing bowl, combine pudding mixes and milk; beat on low speed for 2 minutes. Spread over filling. Top with remaining whipped topping. Sprinkle with chocolate if desired. Cover and refrigerate 4 hours or overnight. **Yield:** 20-24 servings.

─── 🥄 🥄 🥄 ───

Hash Brown Bake

The first time I prepared this creamy potato dish for a church dinner, it got raves. I appreciate its make-ahead convenience. I hope you try it soon.
—Dorothy Byrom, Overland Park, Kansas

>   7 cups water
>   2 packages (32 ounces *each)* frozen cubed Southern-style hash brown potatoes
>   2 packages (8 ounces *each*) cream cheese, softened
>   4 eggs
>   2 teaspoons minced chives
> 1-1/4 teaspoons salt
>   1/2 teaspoon pepper
>   1/4 cup dry bread crumbs
>   1/4 cup grated Parmesan cheese
>   3 tablespoons butter *or* margarine, melted

In a Dutch oven, bring water and potatoes to a boil. Reduce heat; cover and simmer until potatoes are tender, about 12 minutes. Drain. Place potatoes in a mixing bowl; beat on low just until mashed. Add cream cheese, eggs, chives, salt and pepper; mix well. Divide potato mixture between two greased 2-qt. baking dishes. Combine the bread crumbs, Parmesan cheese and butter; sprinkle over potatoes. Cover and refrigerate overnight. Remove from the refrigerator 30 minutes before baking. Bake, uncovered, at 350° for 50-60 minutes or until top is browned and potatoes are heated through. **Yield:** 24 servings.

─── 🥄 🥄 🥄 ───

Cinnamon Chocolate Cake

(Pictured above right)

The best thing about this cake is how good it tastes. The next best thing is I can prepare it in about 45 minutes, since it gets frosted while still warm. I've even dashed home from work at lunch, baked this dessert and returned with it for an afternoon celebration.
—Rosemary Woodrow, Sparks, Nevada

>   2 cups all-purpose flour
>   2 cups sugar

> 1-1/2 teaspoons ground cinnamon
>   1/4 teaspoon salt
>   1 cup water
>   1/2 cup vegetable oil
>   1/2 cup butter *or* margarine
>   1/4 cup baking cocoa
>   2 eggs
>   1/2 cup buttermilk
>   1 teaspoon vanilla extract
>   1 teaspoon baking soda
> **FROSTING:**
>   1/2 cup butter *or* margarine
>   1/3 cup whipping cream
>   1/4 cup baking cocoa
> 1-1/2 teaspoons ground cinnamon
>   3 cups confectioners' sugar
>   1 teaspoon vanilla extract
>   1 cup finely chopped walnuts

In a mixing bowl, combine the first four ingredients. In a saucepan, combine the water, oil, butter and cocoa; bring to a boil over medium heat. Pour over dry ingredients; mix well. Add eggs, buttermilk, vanilla and baking soda; mix well. Pour into a greased and floured 15-in. x 10-in. x 1-in. baking pan. Bake at 375° for 15-20 minutes or until a toothpick inserted near the center comes out clean. Meanwhile, for frosting, combine butter, cream, cocoa and cinnamon in a saucepan. Cook and stir over medium heat until butter is melted and mixture is heated through. Remove from the heat; beat in sugar and vanilla until smooth. Stir in walnuts. Carefully spread over hot cake. Cool completely. **Yield:** 24-30 servings.

remaining cheese. Let stand for 15 minutes before serving. Garnish with peppers if desired. **Yield:** 12-15 servings.

— 🍵 🍵 🍵 —

Chicken Ham Supreme

This easy yet impressive main dish never fails to generate recipe requests. —Ki Humphreville
Lancaster, Pennsylvania

    4 cups (32 ounces) sour cream
    1/2 cup lemon juice
    4 teaspoons Worcestershire sauce
    4 teaspoons *each* celery salt, garlic salt and
        paprika
    1 teaspoon pepper
    24 boneless skinless chicken breast halves
        (3/4 to 1 inch thick)
    24 thin slices fully cooked ham
    4-1/2 cups dry bread crumbs
    1-1/2 cups butter *or* margarine, melted, *divided*

Combine sour cream, lemon juice, Worcestershire sauce and seasonings; add chicken. Refrigerate overnight. Remove chicken and discard marinade. Place one ham slice on each chicken breast; fold in half, enclosing ham. Secure with toothpicks if desired. Roll in bread crumbs; place in three greased 13-in. x 9-in. x 2-in. baking dishes. Pour about 1/4 cup butter over each dish. Cover and bake at 350° for 30 minutes. Uncover; baste with remaining butter. Bake 15-20 minutes longer or until juices run clear. Remove toothpicks. **Yield:** 24 servings.

— 🍵 🍵 🍵 —

Frosted Brownies

Here's my best brownie recipe—it makes a nice big batch. With a rich chocolaty frosting, these chewy bars are sure to become a favorite in your family.
—Edna Hoffman, Hebron, Indiana

    1 cup plus 2 tablespoons butter *or*
        margarine, softened
    4 cups sugar
    8 eggs
    2 cups all-purpose flour
    1-1/4 cups baking cocoa
    1 teaspoon salt
    2 teaspoons vanilla extract
    2 cups chopped nuts
FROSTING:
    1/4 cup butter *or* margarine, softened
    2-1/2 cups confectioners' sugar
    2 tablespoons baking cocoa

Mexican Corn Casserole

(Pictured above)

This satisfying side dish resembles an old-fashioned spoon bread with zip. My family and friends agree this recipe really dresses up plain corn. It's a convenient dish to transport to a potluck.
—Laura Kadlec, Maiden Rock, Wisconsin

    4 eggs
    1 can (15-1/4 ounces) whole kernel corn,
        drained
    1 can (14-3/4 ounces) cream-style corn
    1-1/2 cups cornmeal
    1-1/4 cups buttermilk
    1 cup butter *or* margarine, melted
    2 cans (4 ounces *each*) chopped green
        chilies
    2 medium onions, chopped
    1 teaspoon baking soda
    3 cups (12 ounces) shredded cheddar
        cheese, *divided*
**Jalapeno pepper and sweet red pepper rings,
    optional**

Beat eggs in a large bowl; add the next eight ingredients and mix well. Stir in 2 cups of cheese. Pour into a greased 13-in. x 9-in. x 2-in. baking dish. Bake, uncovered, at 325° for 1 hour. Top with

1/4 cup milk
2 teaspoons vanilla extract

In a mixing bowl, cream butter and sugar. Add eggs, one at a time, beating well after each. Combine flour, cocoa and salt; add to creamed mixture. Stir in vanilla and nuts. Spread the batter into two greased 13-in. x 9-in. x 2-in. baking pans. Bake at 325° for 25-30 minutes. Cool. In a mixing bowl, cream butter. Combine sugar and cocoa; add to butter. Add milk and vanilla; beat until fluffy. Frost brownies. **Yield:** 5 dozen.

🍴 🍴 🍴

Chicken Church Casserole

This is a stick-to-your-ribs comforting casserole that's a favorite at church luncheons. —*Charlotte Pizio*
Bryn Mawr, Pennsylvania

20 cups cubed cooked chicken
1 package (2 pounds) elbow macaroni, cooked and drained
6 jars (6 ounces *each*) sliced mushrooms, drained
2 jars (4 ounces *each*) diced pimientos, drained
2 large green peppers, chopped
2 large onions, chopped
4 cans (10-3/4 ounces *each*) condensed cream of celery soup, undiluted
4 cans (10-3/4 ounces *each*) condensed cream of mushroom soup, undiluted
2 pounds process American cheese, cubed
1-1/3 cups milk
4 teaspoons dried basil
2 teaspoons lemon-pepper seasoning
2 cups crushed cornflakes
1/4 cup butter *or* margarine, melted

Combine chicken, macaroni, mushrooms, pimientos, peppers and onions. In a large bowl, combine soups, cheese, milk, basil and lemon pepper; add to chicken mixture. Pour about 12 cups each into four greased 13-in. x 9-in. x 2-in. baking pans. Cover and refrigerate overnight. Remove from refrigerator 30 minutes before baking. Combine cornflakes and butter; sprinkle over casseroles. Cover and bake at 350° for 45 minutes. Uncover and bake 15-20 minutes longer or until bubbly. **Yield:** 45-50 servings (about 1 cup each).

🍴 🍴 🍴

Spicy Rice Pilaf

(Pictured above right)

I found this recipe back in the 1950's and have made some minor adjustments over the years to update the flavor. In summer, I like to serve the pilaf over slices of red ripe tomatoes. —*Cynthia Gobeli, Norton, Ohio*

1/2 cup chopped onion
2 tablespoons olive *or* vegetable oil
2 cups chicken broth
1/4 cup dry lentils, rinsed
1 can (16 ounces) kidney beans, rinsed and drained
1 cup salsa
1 cup uncooked long grain rice
1 cup frozen corn
1 jar (2 ounces) diced pimientos, drained
1 teaspoon chili powder

In a saucepan over medium heat, saute onion in oil until tender. Add broth and lentils; bring to a boil. Reduce heat; cover and simmer for 15 minutes. Stir in remaining ingredients; bring to a boil. Reduce heat; cover and simmer 20-25 minutes longer or until lentils and rice are tender. **Yield:** 12 servings.

Proven Potluck Tip

Here's a handy way to serve deviled eggs. Put them in paper cupcake liners and set them in muffin tins. The eggs stay upright and neat and won't slide around on people's plates.

Cooking for One or Two

These perfectly portioned meals—featuring an array of main dishes, side dishes, desserts and more—may not yield large amounts. But they're brimming with flavor!

— 🍴 🍴 🍴 —

IDEAL QUANTITIES. Clockwise from upper left: Three-Cheese Grilled Cheese, Potato Salad for One and Chocolate Pudding Mix (p. 175); Oven-Barbecued Chicken, Baked Beans for Two and Sour Cream Biscuits (p. 183); Fish in Foil, Clam Chowder for One and Green Beans with Mushrooms (p. 177); Lazy Lasagna, Cheese Bread and Little Chocolate Cake (p. 181).

Singling Out Good Food

TAKE A BREAK from addressing holiday greeting cards and treat yourself to a delectable lunch for one that gives a whole new meaning to "fast food".

An assortment of cheese, tomato and onion makes Three-Cheese Grilled Cheese, a traditional favorite, even more colorful and tasty. It's a quick lunch or main dish on busy days.

Just because you're cooking for one doesn't mean you have to settle for prepared foods, like store-bought potato salad. Potato Salad for One is perfectly portioned and made with everyday ingredients found in your own pantry or refrigerator.

For a chocolaty snack without a lot of leftovers, Chocolate Pudding Mix is both economical and convenient. With this easy-to-prepare mix in your pantry, you can whip up dessert in a matter of minutes.

You'll find more singular sensations on the following four pages.

— ❦ ❦ ❦ —

Three-Cheese Grilled Cheese

I once taught an adult program called Eating Smart for Seniors. For that class, I developed many recipes for one or two people that were simple to prepare and used common ingredients.
—Terri Brown
Delavan, Wisconsin

       2 slices wheat, rye *or* sourdough bread
       2 tablespoons softened cream cheese
   Butter *or* margarine
       2 slices white cheese (brick, Monterey
          Jack *or* Swiss)
       2 slices yellow cheese (cheddar, pepper
          or taco)
   Red onion and tomato slices

Spread each slice of bread with cream cheese on one side and butter on the other. Layer white cheese, yellow cheese, onion and tomato on the cream cheese side of one slice. Top with the other slice of bread, cream cheese side down. Grill 2-3 minutes on each side or until golden brown. Remove from the heat; cover until cheese melts. **Yield:** 1 serving.

— ❦ ❦ ❦ —

Potato Salad for One

When I became a widower, I took to heart the challenge of learning to cook just for myself. I now have a growing collection of wonderful single-serving recipes. This potato salad is delicious and a snap to prepare for even the newest cook.
—Ray Klinge
Tulsa, Oklahoma

     1/4 cup mayonnaise *or* salad dressing
       2 tablespoons chopped celery
       1 tablespoon chopped onion
       1 tablespoon pickle relish, drained
   1-1/2 teaspoons diced pimientos, drained
       1 teaspoon Dijon mustard
     1/2 teaspoon cider vinegar
   Salt and pepper to taste
       1 medium baking potato, cooked, peeled
          and cubed

In a small bowl, combine the mayonnaise, celery, onion, relish, pimientos, mustard, vinegar, salt and pepper; mix well. Add potato and toss to coat. Chill for 1 hour. **Yield:** 1 serving.

— ❦ ❦ ❦ —

Chocolate Pudding Mix

By keeping a batch of this mix on hand. I can easily make pudding just for myself. Plus, it's relatively low in fat. Everyone who tries this creamy concoction prefers it to any pre-made packaged pudding.
—Lois Miller, New Paris, Indiana

   PUDDING MIX:
       1 cup nonfat dry milk powder
     2/3 cup sugar
       6 tablespoons cornstarch
     1/3 cup baking cocoa
     1/4 teaspoon salt
   PUDDING:
     1/2 cup water
     1/4 cup Pudding Mix (above)
       2 teaspoons butter *or* margarine
     1/4 teaspoon almond *or* vanilla extract
   Whipped topping and baking cocoa, optional

Combine pudding mix ingredients; store in an airtight container or resealable plastic bag. **Yield:** 1-3/4 cups mix (7 batches of pudding). **To make pudding:** Combine water and mix in a small saucepan; bring to a boil over medium heat, stirring occasionally. Cook and stir for 2 minutes. Remove from the heat; stir in butter and extract. Pour into a serving dish. Serve warm or chilled; top with whipped topping and sprinkle with cocoa if desired. **Yield:** 1 serving.

WHY GO OUT when you can prepare a scrumptious single-serving spread in a snap? By staying in, you can cook what you like and not worry whether you'll enjoy it…you can serve as much as you want *when* you want…and you always eat in good company!

But do you think cooking a satisfying supper for one is too much fuss? These three foods from fellow cooks will surely change your mind.

If you really want to keep kitchen mess to a minimum, try this one-of-a-kind Fish in Foil recipe. Cooked this way, fish stays moist and picks up wonderful flavor from the other ingredients. Plus, there are no dishes to wash!

You don't have to go clamming to enjoy homemade chowder. Clam Chowder for One gets a head start with canned clams. The ingredients quickly combine for fresh soup in no time. And there aren't any leftovers!

Green Beans with Mushrooms is a nice addition to all of your favorite meals. The combination of flavors is unbeatable.

— 🥤 🥤 🥤 —

Fish in Foil

This fish recipe is a favorite of folks here at our summer guest ranch. Family and friends also like the fact that it's nutritious as well as flavorful. —Bill Davis
Casper, Wyoming

✓ This tasty dish uses less sugar, salt and fat. Recipe includes *Diabetic Exchanges.*

> 1 halibut steak (6 ounces)
> 4 medium mushrooms
> 2 cherry tomatoes, halved
> 2 lemon slices
> 1/2 medium green pepper, sliced
> 1/4 cup Mountain Dew
> Crushed pepper

Place fish in the center of a 20-in. x 14-in. piece of heavy-duty foil. Place mushrooms, tomatoes, lemon and green pepper around fish. Fold edges of foil up; pour soda over fish. Fold foil to seal tightly. Bake at 375° for 20-25 minutes or until fish flakes easily with a fork. Open foil carefully to allow steam to escape. Sprinkle with pepper. **Yield:** 1 serving. **Diabetic Exchanges:** One serving (prepared with diet Mountain Dew) equals 4 very lean meat, 1-1/2 vegetable; also, 205 calories, 95 mg sodium, 49 mg cholesterol, 8 gm carbohydrate, 34 gm protein, 4 gm fat.

— 🥤 🥤 🥤 —

Clam Chowder for One

If you love the classic clam chowders served in many restaurants, I know you'll enjoy this recipe. It tastes better than any other versions I've tried. You'll be delighted with this soup's easy preparation.
—Donna Smith, Victor, New York

> 1/2 cup cubed peeled potato
> 1/4 cup chopped onion
> 1/8 teaspoon salt
> Pinch pepper
> 1/2 cup water
> 1 can (6-1/2 ounces) chopped clams, drained
> 2/3 cup milk
> 1 tablespoon butter *or* margarine
> 1 bacon strip, cooked and crumbled
> Chopped fresh parsley, optional

In a small saucepan, cook potato, onion, salt and pepper in water until vegetables are tender (do not drain). Add clams, milk, butter and bacon; heat through (do not boil). Sprinkle with parsley if desired. **Yield:** 1 serving.

— 🥤 🥤 🥤 —

Green Beans with Mushrooms

I made this satisfying side dish often when I was single. Now I prepare it for my family. By adding fresh mushrooms, onion, butter and a little pepper, you can easily dress up ordinary green beans.
—Denise Albers, Belleville, Illinois

✓ This tasty dish uses less sugar, salt and fat. Recipe includes *Diabetic Exchanges.*

> 3/4 cup cut fresh green beans (2-inch pieces)
> 2 tablespoons chopped onion
> 2 teaspoons butter *or* margarine
> 1/4 cup sliced fresh mushrooms
> Pepper to taste

In a saucepan, cook beans in water for 6-8 minutes or until tender. In a skillet, saute onion in butter until tender. Add mushrooms; cook and stir for 1 minute. Drain beans; add the mushroom mixture and pepper. **Yield:** 1 serving. **Diabetic Exchanges:** One serving (prepared with margarine) equals 1-1/2 vegetable, 1-1/2 fat; also, 105 calories, 96 mg sodium, 0 cholesterol, 9 gm carbohydrate, 2 gm protein, 8 gm fat.

Fantastic Fish

Try marinating fish fillets in lemon juice and salt for 15 minutes before grilling or baking. It makes the flesh firmer and easier to handle and gives the fish a fresh taste.

WHEN DINING ALONE in the morning, you don't have to settle for a boring bowl of cereal or an ordinary piece of toast. Three cooks show how easy it is to treat yourself to a singularly super breakfast with little fuss!

Chopped tomato and everyday seasonings add life to a simple scrambled egg in the Egg and Tomato Scramble recipe.

Most pancake recipes make a batch big enough for a crowd. But Pancakes for One is perfectly portioned. So now whenever you have a taste for pancakes, it's easy to make just a few.

Apple Lemon Puff is a sweet treat you're sure to reach for around the clock.

One bite and you'll agree that the foods featured here may not be big, but they're still brimming with delightful flavor.

Egg and Tomato Scramble

My mother used to make this for me when I was a girl. I think of her every time I prepare it these days.
—Ilva Jasica, St. Joseph, Michigan

✓ This tasty dish uses less sugar, salt and fat. Recipe includes *Diabetic Exchanges.*

  1 plum tomato, peeled and chopped
  1 teaspoon chopped fresh basil *or* 1/4
     teaspoon dried basil
  1 egg *or* egg substitute equivalent
  1 teaspoon water
  1 garlic clove, minced
  1 teaspoon olive *or* vegetable oil, optional
Salt and pepper to taste, optional
  1 slice bread, toasted
Additional fresh basil, optional

In a small bowl, combine the tomato and basil; set aside. In another bowl, beat egg, water and garlic. Heat oil if desired in a small nonstick skillet; add the egg mixture. Cook and stir gently until egg is nearly set. Add tomato mixture and salt and pepper if desired. Cook and stir until egg is completely set and tomato is heated through. Serve with toast. Garnish with basil if desired. **Yield:** 1 serving. **Diabetic Exchanges:** One serving (prepared with egg substitute and without oil and salt) equals 1 starch, 1 meat; also, 152 calories, 289 mg sodium, 1 mg cholesterol, 20 gm carbohydrate, 11 gm protein, 4 gm fat.

Egg-cellent Idea

To check whether an egg has been hard-cooked, spin it like a top. If it spins on its end, it's cooked. If it turns on its side, the egg is raw.

Pancakes for One

This recipe originally served six, which was perfect when our children were younger. As they grew up and left home, I scaled down the recipe. You can easily adjust the number of servings to suit your needs.
—Ann Schenk, Winnett, Montana

1/2 cup all-purpose flour
  2 teaspoons wheat germ
1/4 teaspoon baking soda
1/4 teaspoon baking powder
1/4 teaspoon salt
  1 egg
1/2 cup buttermilk
1-1/2 teaspoons vegetable oil
Butter and maple syrup

In a bowl, combine flour, wheat germ, baking soda, baking powder and salt. In another bowl, beat egg; add buttermilk and oil. Stir into dry ingredients just until blended. Pour batter by 1/3 cupfuls onto a lightly greased hot griddle; turn when bubbles form on top of pancakes. Cook until the second side is golden brown. Serve with butter and syrup.
Yield: 1 serving (3 pancakes).

Apple Lemon Puff

(Not pictured)

I like to prepare this as a special morning treat for myself. But it also makes a light, refreshing dessert. I think you'll agree it's worth the little extra effort. Why not share this recipe with friends? *—Doris Heath*
Bryson City, North Carolina

1-1/2 teaspoons butter *or* margarine
  1 small apple, peeled, cored and cut into
     rings
  6 teaspoons sugar, *divided*
  1 egg, *separated*
1/2 teaspoon grated lemon peel
1/4 teaspoon vanilla extract
1/2 teaspoon all-purpose flour

In a skillet over medium heat, melt butter. Add apple rings; sprinkle with 2 teaspoons of sugar. Cook until tender, turning once. In a mixing bowl, beat the egg yolk, lemon peel and vanilla for 1 minute. In another mixing bowl, beat the egg white until stiff peaks form; fold in flour and remaining sugar. Fold into egg yolk mixture. Place apple rings in a greased 2-cup baking dish. Spread egg mixture on top. Bake at 350° for 15-18 minutes or until golden brown and set. Invert onto a serving plate.
Yield: 1 serving.

Cooking for 'Just the Two of Us'

ARE YOU SKEPTICAL that recipes designed to serve only two can have as much flavor as those that feed a bunch? You'll quickly change your mind after tasting these featured foods.

If you love lasagna but hate the thought of leftovers, reach for Lazy Lasagna. The recipe makes two hearty servings and calls for prepared spaghetti sauce. So, it's a great one-pot meal on hectic days.

Cheese Bread dresses up plain bread for a flavorful oven-fresh sensation.

Little Chocolate Cake is just the right size when cooking for a few people. Plus, it's topped with an irresistible fudgy frosting.

The following four pages present more delightful dishes for two.

— 🍺 🍺 🍺 —

Lazy Lasagna

Lasagna may seem like more work than it's worth to some people. But one day when I had a craving for it, I devised this simple recipe. —*Carol Mead*
Los Alamos, New Mexico

   1 **cup spaghetti sauce**
 1/2 **cup cottage cheese**
 3/4 **cup shredded mozzarella cheese**
1-1/2 **cups cooked wide noodles**
   2 **tablespoons grated Parmesan cheese**

Warm the spaghetti sauce; stir in cottage cheese and mozzarella. Fold in the noodles. Pour into two greased 2-cup casseroles. Sprinkle with Parmesan cheese. Bake, uncovered, at 375° for 20 minutes or until bubbly. **Yield:** 2 servings.

— 🍺 🍺 🍺 —

Cheese Bread

Nothing tastes better with lasagna than warm bread. This recipe makes just enough for my husband, Dan, and me, but it can be easily doubled to feed a crowd. It has a nice garlic flavor. —*Cookie Curci-Wright*
San Jose, California

 1 **Italian-style roll (6 inches)**
 1 **tablespoon butter** *or* **margarine, melted**
 1 **garlic clove, minced**
 1 **tablespoon grated Parmesan cheese**

Cut roll in half lengthwise. Combine butter, garlic and cheese; spread on the cut sides of roll. Broil 4 in. from the heat for 2-3 minutes, or microwave on high for 20-30 seconds, or until cheese melts. **Yield:** 2 servings.

— 🍺 🍺 🍺 —

Little Chocolate Cake

A small chocolate cake can be just as good as a large one. Plus, none of it goes to waste. Husband Loren and I love its terrific from-scratch taste and rich chocolate frosting. —*Paula Anderson*
Springfield, Illinois

   2 **squares (1 ounce** *each***) unsweetened chocolate**
 1/2 **cup boiling water**
   1 **cup sugar**
 1/4 **cup shortening**
   1 **egg**
 1/2 **teaspoon vanilla extract**
   1 **cup all-purpose flour**
 1/2 **teaspoon baking soda**
 1/2 **teaspoon salt**
 1/4 **cup sour milk***
FROSTING:
1-1/2 **cups sugar**
 1/3 **cup milk**
   2 **squares (1 ounce** *each***) unsweetened chocolate, melted**
   2 **tablespoons shortening**
   1 **tablespoon light corn syrup**
 1/4 **teaspoon salt**
   2 **tablespoons butter** *or* **margarine**
   1 **teaspoon vanilla extract**

In a mixing bowl, stir chocolate and water until blended. Cool. Add the sugar, shortening, egg and vanilla; mix well. Combine flour, baking soda and salt; gradually add to the chocolate mixture alternately with sour milk. Pour into a greased 8-in. square baking pan. Bake at 350° for 30-35 minutes or until a toothpick inserted in the center comes out clean. Cool completely. For frosting, combine the first six ingredients in a saucepan; bring to a boil. Boil for 1-1/2 minutes; remove from the heat. Set pan in a larger pan of ice water. Beat for 1 minute. Add butter and vanilla. Beat 10 minutes longer or until frosting is desired spreading consistency. Frost cake. **Yield:** 4 servings. ***Editor's Note:** To sour milk, place 1 teaspoon white vinegar in a measuring cup; add milk to equal 1/4 cup.

IT'S SAID that "good things come in twos"…but finding recipes that serve two isn't easy. Three cooks share their favorite recipes that together make up a sensational spread you "two" will surely enjoy!

You can pop Oven-Barbecued Chicken in the oven, forget about it and enjoy its wonderful aroma as it bakes.

Baked Beans for Two gets a convenient head start with canned pork and beans. They'll quickly disappear from the table.

Add a small batch of tender Sour Cream Biscuits to this or any meal. You and your dinner companion will appreciate the change from ordinary bread.

Topped with whipped cream, Lemon Pudding Cake is an irresistible end to the meal.

— 🍴 🍴 🍴 —

Oven-Barbecued Chicken

With our children grown and gone, adapting recipes to suit just husband Rodney and me is a new hobby. We enjoy this easy-to-assemble chicken. —Eldora Yoder
Versailles, Missouri

    3 **bone-in chicken breast halves (about 1-1/2 pounds)**
    1 **small onion, sliced**
    1 **bottle (12 ounces) chili sauce**
    1 **can (8 ounces) tomato sauce**
    1 **tablespoon Worcestershire sauce**
1/2 **teaspoon dried oregano**
Pepper to taste

Brown chicken on all sides in a skillet coated with nonstick cooking spray. Transfer to a greased 11-in. x 7-in. x 2-in. baking dish; top with onion. Combine chili sauce, tomato sauce, Worcestershire sauce and oregano; pour over chicken. Sprinkle with pepper. Bake, uncovered, at 350° for 45 minutes or until meat juices run clear. **Yield:** 2-3 servings.

— 🍴 🍴 🍴 —

Baked Beans for Two

A few additional ingredients dress up canned beans. This recipe can be easily doubled. —Eldora Yoder

    1 **can (16 ounces) pork and beans**
    3 **tablespoons ketchup**
    2 **tablespoons chopped onion**
    2 to 3 **teaspoons brown sugar**
    2 to 3 **teaspoons honey**
    1 **teaspoon prepared mustard**
1/2 **teaspoon Worcestershire sauce**
1/8 **teaspoon prepared horseradish**

Combine all ingredients in an ungreased 1-qt. baking dish. Bake, uncovered, at 350° for 30-40 minutes. **Yield:** 2 servings.

— 🍴 🍴 🍴 —

Sour Cream Biscuits

Biscuit recipes that feed a few are hard to come by. I couldn't wait to try these. —Nell Jones
Smyrna, Georgia

    1 **cup self-rising flour***
1/4 **teaspoon baking soda**
3/4 **cup sour cream**
    2 **teaspoons vegetable oil**

In a bowl, combine flour and baking soda. Add sour cream and oil; stir just until moistened. Turn onto a floured surface; knead 4-6 times. Roll out to 3/4-in. thickness; cut with a 2-1/2-in. biscuit cutter. Place on a greased baking sheet. Lightly spray tops with nonstick cooking spray. Bake at 425° for 10-12 minutes or until golden brown. **Yield:** 4 biscuits. ***Editor's Note:** As a substitute for self-rising flour, place 1-1/2 teaspoons baking powder and 1/2 teaspoon salt in a measuring cup. Add all-purpose flour to equal 1 cup.

— 🍴 🍴 🍴 —

Lemon Pudding Cake

(Not pictured)

My husband, Lloyd, loves this cake since it tastes like lemon meringue pie. It's little fuss and makes just enough for the two of us. —Dawn Fagerstrom
Warren, Minnesota

    1 **egg,** *separated*
1/2 **cup sugar**
1/3 **cup milk**
    2 **tablespoons all-purpose flour**
    2 **tablespoons lemon juice**
    1 **teaspoon grated lemon peel**
1/8 **teaspoon salt**
Whipped cream, optional

In a mixing bowl, beat egg yolk. Add sugar, milk, flour, lemon juice, peel and salt; beat until smooth. Beat egg white until stiff peaks form; gently fold into lemon mixture. Pour into two ungreased 6-oz. custard cups (cups will be very full). Place the cups in an 8-in. square baking pan. Pour boiling water into pan to a depth of 1 in. Bake at 325° for 40-45 minutes or until a knife inserted near the center comes out clean and top is golden. Serve with whipped cream if desired. **Yield:** 2 servings.

THE HOLIDAY SEASON seems to begin earlier every year. Before the inevitable hustle and bustle sets in, slow the pace and savor every mouth-watering morsel of this down-home meal.

This recipe for Elegant Pork Chops is so easy. It has wonderful old-fashioned flavor without the fuss or mess. Plus, the chops stay very moist.

The aroma of Apple-Stuffed Squash baking in the oven is unbeatable.

With cranberries and whipped topping, Frozen Cranberry Salad is perfect for meals throughout the year.

For a simple and tasty alternative to bread stuffing, try Cracker Dressing. Your dining companion will likely be surprised to hear of its unique ingredients.

— 🥄 🥄 🥄 —

Elegant Pork Chops

Cooking in small quantities doesn't have to be dull. As a widow, I enjoy cooking these chops for myself or inviting a friend to dine with me. —Nila Towler
Baird, Texas

- 2 **pork loin chops (about 1 inch thick)**
- 1 **tablespoon cooking oil**
- 1 **can (10-3/4 ounces) condensed cream of mushroom soup, undiluted**
- 3/4 **cup milk**
- 3/4 **cup uncooked instant rice**
- 1/8 **teaspoon onion powder**
- 1/8 **teaspoon garlic powder**
Dash **pepper**

In a skillet over medium heat, brown pork chops in oil; set aside. In an ungreased 8-in. square baking dish, combine soup, milk, rice and seasonings; mix well. Top with pork chops. Cover and bake at 350° for 45 minutes or until meat is tender. Uncover and bake 5 minutes longer. Let stand for 10 minutes before serving. **Yield:** 2 servings.

— 🥄 🥄 🥄 —

Apple-Stuffed Squash

Apple and raisins pair nicely with acorn squash.
—Nila Towler

- 1 **medium acorn squash, halved**
- 1/4 **teaspoon salt**
- 1 **medium tart apple, thinly sliced**
- 1 **tablespoon raisins**
- 2 **tablespoons butter *or* margarine**
- 2 **tablespoons brown sugar**
- 1/2 **teaspoon ground cinnamon**
- 1/4 **teaspoon ground nutmeg**

Sprinkle squash with salt. In a skillet, saute apple slices and raisins in butter until apples are tender.

Add sugar, cinnamon and nutmeg. Spoon into the squash halves; place in a baking dish. Bake, uncovered, at 350° for 45-55 minutes or until squash is tender. **Yield:** 2 servings.

— 🥄 🥄 🥄 —

Frozen Cranberry Salad

I often double this recipe to have extra individual salads on hand for anytime snacking. —Rita Goshaw
South Milwaukee, Wisconsin

- 1 **cup fresh *or* frozen cranberries**
- 1/4 **cup sugar**
- 1 **can (8 ounces) crushed pineapple, drained**
- 1/2 **cup whipped topping**
Chopped pecans
Additional cranberries and fresh mint, optional

In a food processor or blender, process cranberries, sugar and pineapple until cranberries are finely chopped. Pour into a bowl; let stand for 10 minutes. Fold in whipped topping. Spoon into four foil muffin cups; sprinkle with pecans. Freeze. Remove from the freezer 15 minutes before serving. Garnish with cranberries and mint if desired. **Yield:** 4 servings.

— 🥄 🥄 🥄 —

Cracker Dressing
(Not pictured)

I've been making this colorful, nicely seasoned stuffing since the 1960's. Its old-fashioned flavor has certainly—and deliciously—stood the test of time.
—Jan Woodruff, Chandler, Arizona

- 1/2 **cup chopped celery**
- 1/2 **cup chopped onion**
- 2 **tablespoons butter *or* margarine**
- 1 **egg**
- 2/3 **cup milk**
- 1 **tablespoon minced fresh parsley**
- 1/2 **teaspoon rubbed sage**
- 1/4 **teaspoon dried thyme**
- 1/4 **teaspoon salt**
Dash **pepper**
- 2 **cups coarsely crushed saltines (about 27 crackers)**

In a skillet over medium heat, saute celery and onion in butter until tender. In a bowl, combine egg, milk, parsley, sage, thyme, salt and pepper. Add crackers and celery mixture; toss lightly. Place in a greased 1-qt. baking dish. Bake, uncovered, at 350° for 25-30 minutes or until browned. **Yield:** 2 servings.

'My Mom's Best Meal'

Six cooks recall special times when they prepare the same meals for which their moms are fondly remembered.

MEMORABLE MEALS include, clockwise from upper left: Down-Home Cooking (p. 200), Cherished Family Recipes (p. 192), Italian-Style Meal (p. 204) and Sunday Supper Standby (p. 188).

Mom dressed up Sunday suppers for guests with roasted chicken and all the fixin's.

By Sandra Melnychenko, Grandview, Manitoba

MY MOM has a reputation among our family and friends for being an excellent cook and baker. It comes as naturally to her as it did to my grandma.

Looking back, I'm sure cooking for four children wasn't easy, but Mom (Peggy Chapman, above) always had something delicious for us to eat. I give her lots of credit now that I have to plan tasty menus and prepare appealing recipes for my own husband and four children. Sometimes it can be a real challenge!

All the years I lived at home, we'd look forward to having company for Sunday supper. It was my job to set the table with our best china. Mom felt it was important for everything to be just right. She believed in treating guests like royalty.

One dish Mom often served was Roasted Chicken and Potatoes with dressing. I can still recall the wonderful aroma of this dish as it cooked. We couldn't wait for Mom to announce that dinner was ready.

Along with the chicken, Mom would make comforting Cheesy Turnips and Carrots. I'm convinced it's the best way to eat these vegetables. Our company must have felt the same way, because the serving bowl was usually empty at the end of the meal! It was a rare occasion when there were any leftovers.

Mom would round out the meal with her tender Parkerhouse Rolls. I've yet to meet a person who can eat just one.

But the best part, as far as we kids were concerned, was the Old-Fashioned Rice Pudding. Its country-style flavor appeals to everyone.

Why not make a special supper for your family by serving my mom's best meal?

PICTURED AT LEFT: Roasted Chicken and Potatoes, Parkerhouse Rolls, Cheesy Turnips and Carrots and Old-Fashioned Rice Pudding (recipes are on the next page).

or until potatoes are tender and a meat thermometer reads 180°-185°. Thicken pan drippings for gravy if desired. **Yield:** 4-6 servings.

— 🥄 🥄 🥄 —

Cheesy Turnips and Carrots

Mild-tasting turnips and carrots are wonderfully enhanced by ginger, onion and a mouth-watering creamy cheese sauce in this super side dish. The serving bowl is always empty at the end of the meal.

      3 cups diced peeled turnips
      2 cups sliced carrots
  1/4 teaspoon ground ginger
  3/4 cup water
      1 teaspoon salt, *divided*
  1/2 cup chopped onion
  1/2 cup diced celery
      3 tablespoons butter *or* margarine
      3 tablespoons all-purpose flour
  1/4 teaspoon pepper
1-1/2 cups milk
      1 cup (4 ounces) shredded cheddar cheese

In a saucepan, combine the turnips, carrots, ginger, water and 1/2 teaspoon salt. Cover and cook over medium-high heat for 10-15 minutes or until vegetables are tender; drain and reserve liquid. Set vegetables aside. In a skillet, saute onion and celery in butter until tender; stir in flour, pepper and remaining salt. Add milk and reserved vegetable liquid; bring to a boil. Cook and stir until thickened and bubbly. Stir in cheese until melted; stir in vegetables and heat through. **Yield:** 4-6 servings.

Roasted Chicken and Potatoes

(Also pictured on front cover)

My mom's tender roasted chicken with potatoes and sage dressing is even more delicious than its aroma while baking. My children now enjoy this main dish as much as I did when I was young.

      1 cup chopped celery
      1 medium onion, chopped
  1/2 cup butter *or* margarine
      2 tablespoons poultry seasoning
  1/2 teaspoon rubbed sage
      8 cups cubed day-old white bread
  1/2 cup chicken broth
      1 roasting chicken (5 to 6 pounds)
  1/2 teaspoon paprika
  1/4 teaspoon salt
Pinch pepper
      6 medium baking potatoes, peeled and
        quartered

In a skillet, saute celery and onion in butter until tender, about 5 minutes. Add poultry seasoning and sage. Place the bread cubes in a large bowl. Stir in celery mixture and chicken broth; mix lightly. Just before baking, stuff the chicken. Place on a rack in a roasting pan; tie the drumsticks together. Combine paprika, salt and pepper; rub over chicken. Bake, uncovered, at 350° for 1-1/2 hours, basting every 30 minutes. Place the potatoes around chicken; cover and bake 1-1/2 hours longer

pans and cool on wire racks. **Yield:** 2-1/2 dozen.
Diabetic Exchanges: One roll (prepared with skim milk and without butter) equals 1-1/2 starch; also, 108 calories, 220 mg sodium, 7 mg cholesterol, 21 gm carbohydrate, 3 gm protein, 1 gm fat.

— 🍷 🍷 🍷 —

Old-Fashioned Rice Pudding

This comforting dessert is a wonderful way to end any meal. As a girl, I always waited eagerly for the first heavenly bite. Today, my husband likes to top his with a scoop of ice cream.

✓ This tasty dish uses less sugar, salt and fat. Recipe includes *Diabetic Exchanges.*

**3-1/2 cups milk
1/2 cup uncooked long grain rice
1/3 cup sugar
1/2 teaspoon salt, optional
1/2 cup raisins
1 teaspoon vanilla extract
Ground cinnamon, optional**

In a saucepan, combine milk, rice, sugar and salt if desired; bring to a boil over medium heat, stirring constantly. Pour into a greased 1-1/2-qt. baking dish. Cover and bake at 325° for 45 minutes, stirring every 15 minutes. Add raisins and vanilla; cover and bake for 15 minutes. Sprinkle with cinnamon if desired. Serve warm or chilled. Store in the refrigerator. **Yield:** about 6 servings. **Diabetic Exchanges:** One 1/2-cup serving (prepared with skim milk and without salt) equals 1 starch, 1 fruit, 1/2 skim milk; also, 177 calories, 83 mg sodium, 3 mg cholesterol, 37 gm carbohydrate, 7 gm protein, trace fat.

Parkerhouse Rolls

Mom is especially well-known for the delectable things she bakes, like these moist, golden rolls. When that basket comes around the table, we all automatically take two—one is just never enough.

✓ This tasty dish uses less sugar, salt and fat. Recipe includes *Diabetic Exchanges.*

**1 package (1/4 ounce) active dry yeast
6 tablespoons plus 1 teaspoon sugar, *divided*
1 cup warm water (110° to 115°), *divided*
1 cup warm milk (110° to 115°)
1 tablespoon salt
5-1/2 to 6 cups all-purpose flour
1 egg
2 tablespoons plus 2 teaspoons vegetable oil
3 tablespoons butter *or* margarine, melted, optional**

In a mixing bowl, dissolve yeast and 1 teaspoon sugar in 1/2 cup water; let stand for 10 minutes. Add milk, salt and the remaining sugar and water. Gradually add 2 cups flour; beat until smooth. Beat in egg and oil. Stir in enough of the remaining flour to make a soft dough. Turn onto a floured board; knead until smooth and elastic, about 6-8 minutes. Place in a greased bowl, turning once to grease top. Cover and let rise in a warm place until doubled, about 1 hour. Punch dough down. Divide in half; roll each half on a floured board to 1/3- or 1/2-in. thickness. Cut with a floured 2-1/2-in. round cutter. Brush with butter if desired. Using the dull edge of a table knife, make an off-center crease in each roll. Fold along crease so the large half is on top. Press along folded edge. Place 2-3 in. apart on greased baking sheets. Cover and let rise until doubled, about 30 minutes. Bake at 375° for 15-20 minutes or until golden brown. Remove from

Busy teacher and mom inspired many future cooks with valuable lessons in the kitchen.

By Mildred Sherrer, Bay City, Texas

WHETHER she followed a recipe or just combined a "pinch of this and that", my mom had a way of making everything taste delicious.

Mom (Lillian Herman, above) enjoyed spending every spare moment in the kitchen. She'd either try new recipes she received from others or create her own magical dishes. She especially loved cooking big meals.

But since our immediate family was small—just my parents and me—she often invited other family and friends for dinner. They were always happy to receive an invitation!

Although she worked full-time as a teacher, Mom still managed to plan and prepare scrumptious meals during the week as well as on the weekends. The meal I share with you here is one I fondly remember.

One dish that always brought Mom compliments was her Brunswick Stew. Some of our friends still say it's the best they ever tasted.

The perfect side dish to go with that stew was Texas Spoon Bread. Father and I couldn't wait to dig in. Made with home-canned beets, Mom's Pickled Beets made a tangy and colorful part of the meal.

We made sure to save room for a big helping of Lemon Bread Pudding. This wonderful old-fashioned dessert was even more special topped with the delightful lemon sauce.

I'm grateful I was able to learn by working with Mom in the kitchen. She not only inspired me to create fabulous foods for my family, she even taught my three sons to cook. I'm proud to share these cherished family recipes with you.

<hr />

PICTURED AT LEFT: Brunswick Stew, Texas Spoon Bread, Mom's Pickled Beets and Lemon Bread Pudding (recipes are on the next page).

Brunswick Stew

Like a thick hearty soup, this stew is packed with tender chicken and an eye-catching combination of vegetables. I could never wait patiently to eat when Mother had this stew on the stove.

1 broiler/fryer chicken (3 to 4 pounds), cut up
1 cup water
4 medium potatoes, peeled and cubed
1 can (15 ounces) lima beans, rinsed and drained
2 medium onions, sliced
1 teaspoon salt
1/2 teaspoon pepper
Dash cayenne pepper
1 can (15-1/4 ounces) corn, drained
1 can (14-1/2 ounces) diced tomatoes, undrained
1/4 cup butter *or* margarine
1/2 cup dry bread crumbs

Place the chicken and water in a Dutch oven; bring to a boil. Reduce heat; cover and simmer for 1-1/2 to 2 hours or until chicken is tender. Remove chicken and debone; cube chicken and return to broth. Add potatoes, beans, onions and seasonings. Simmer for 30 minutes or until potatoes are tender. Stir in remaining ingredients. Simmer, uncovered, for 10 minutes or until slightly thickened. **Yield:** 6 servings.

Texas Spoon Bread

This Southern dish has appealing down-home flavor. A sizable serving topped with butter is a treat. When I was growing up, Mother baked it to go with soups and stews. I always thought her spoon bread was the best.

3 cups milk
1 cup yellow cornmeal
1 tablespoon butter *or* margarine
1 teaspoon sugar
1 teaspoon salt
1/4 teaspoon baking powder
3 eggs, *separated*

In a saucepan, scald the milk (heat to 180°); stir in cornmeal. Reduce heat; simmer for 5 minutes, stirring constantly. Remove from the heat; stir in butter, sugar, salt and baking powder. In a small bowl, beat egg yolks. Gradually stir a small amount of the hot mixture into yolks; return all to pan and mix well. In a mixing bowl, beat egg whites until soft peaks form. Fold egg whites into hot mixture until well blended. Pour into a greased 8-in. square baking dish. Bake at 350° for 40-45 minutes or until well puffed. Use a spoon to serve. **Yield:** 6 servings.

Mom's Pickled Beets

Zesty and fresh-tasting, these bright, beautiful beet slices add spark to any meal. My mouth still begins to water when I think of how wonderful they tasted when Mother prepared them.

3/4 cup sugar
3/4 cup vinegar
3/4 cup water
1-1/2 teaspoons salt
3/4 to 1 teaspoon pepper
1 large onion, thinly sliced
2 cans (13-1/4 ounces *each*) sliced beets, undrained
Sliced green onions, optional

In a saucepan, combine the first six ingredients; bring to a boil. Reduce heat; cover and simmer for 5 minutes. Remove from the heat; add beets. Let stand at room temperature for 1 hour. Cover and chill for 6 hours or overnight. Garnish with green onions if desired. **Yield:** 6 servings.

Lemon Bread Pudding

Sweet raisins and a smooth hot lemon sauce make this bread pudding extra special. Even today, I get requests for the recipe from people who tasted this traditional dessert years ago.

3 slices day-old bread, cubed
3/4 cup raisins
2 cups milk
1/2 cup sugar
2 tablespoons butter *or* margarine
1/4 teaspoon salt
2 eggs
1 teaspoon vanilla extract

LEMON SAUCE:
3/4 cup sugar
2 tablespoons cornstarch
1 cup water
3 tablespoons lemon juice
2 teaspoons grated lemon peel
1 tablespoon butter *or* margarine

Toss bread and raisins in an ungreased 1-1/2-qt. baking dish. In a saucepan, combine milk, sugar, butter and salt; cook and stir until butter melts. Remove from the heat. Whisk eggs and vanilla in a small bowl; gradually stir in a small amount of the hot mixture. Return all to the pan and mix well. Pour over bread and raisins. Set the dish in a larger baking pan; add 1 in. of hot water. Bake, uncovered, at 350° for 50-60 minutes or until a knife inserted near the center comes out clean. For sauce, combine the sugar and cornstarch in a saucepan. Stir in water until smooth; bring to a boil over medium heat. Boil for 1-2 minutes, stirring constantly. Remove from the heat; stir in lemon juice, peel and butter until butter melts. Serve over warm or cold pudding. Refrigerate any leftovers. **Yield:** 6 servings.

*With her flair for
Southwestern fare,
Mom brought
everyday dinners
to life.*

By Jerri Moror, Rio Rancho, New Mexico

MY MOTHER (Lupe Mirabal, above) had the daily challenge of preparing economical foods that could feed a family of 10 *and* that would appeal to all of our different palates.

But she managed to make every meal terrific, even though she also had to meet the needs of our father, who's diabetic.

Being a nutritionist and fixing foods suitable for Father's diet, Mom was a very careful cook and measured everything she added.

Since she has lived her whole life in New Mexico, Mom relies on Southwestern-style recipes. Her Chicken Tortilla Bake has been my favorite for years. She made this casserole often when I was growing up.

Using ingredients she had on hand, Mom developed her more mild version of Spanish Rice. It's a colorful side dish that pairs perfectly with the chicken or any other meat.

Lots of hearty and refreshing ingredients go into the Southwestern Salad. After our family said grace, we kids would quickly reach for this fun salad.

Even if Mom made a big batch of her special Anise Cutout Cookies for dessert, they'd be gone before she knew it.

There was plenty of work to be done in the kitchen to keep us all well-fed. I'm grateful for the cooking skills I learned from her.

We still love going home for Mom's meals. And now I use her recipes for my husband and three young children. I look forward to the day when I can pass these recipes on to our own children and grandchildren!

PICTURED AT LEFT: Chicken Tortilla Bake, Spanish Rice, Southwestern Salad and Anise Cutout Cookies (recipes are on the next page).

Spanish Rice

We were always glad to see a big bowl of this festive rice on the table. The carrots, peas and tomatoes make it so pretty. This versatile side dish goes great with any meat or Mexican meal.

✓ This tasty dish uses less sugar, salt and fat. Recipe includes *Diabetic Exchanges.*

> 1 cup uncooked long grain rice
> 2 tablespoons cooking oil
> 1 small onion, chopped
> 1 garlic clove, minced
> 1/2 teaspoon salt, optional
> 2 large tomatoes, peeled and chopped
> 1 cup water
> 1 cup chicken broth
> 1/3 cup frozen peas, thawed
> 1/3 cup diced cooked carrots

In a large skillet over medium heat, saute rice in hot oil until lightly browned. Add the onion, garlic and salt if desired; cook over low heat until onion is tender. Add tomatoes; cook over medium heat until softened. Add water; cover and simmer until water is absorbed. Stir in broth, peas and carrots; cover and simmer until liquid is absorbed and rice is tender, about 10 minutes. **Yield:** 6 servings. **Diabetic Exchanges:** One 3/4-cup serving (prepared with low-sodium broth and without salt) equals 2 starch, 1 fat; also, 185 calories, 40 mg sodium, 1 mg cholesterol, 31 gm carbohydrate, 4 gm protein, 5 gm fat.

Chicken Tortilla Bake

Mother frequently made this comforting casserole when I was growing up. Our family would scrape the pan clean. Chicken, cheese and zippy green chilies are a mouth-watering mix.

> 3 cups shredded cooked chicken
> 2 cans (4 ounces *each*) chopped green chilies
> 1 cup chicken broth
> 1 can (10-3/4 ounces) condensed cream of mushroom soup, undiluted
> 1 can (10-3/4 ounces) condensed cream of chicken soup, undiluted
> 1 small onion, finely chopped
> 12 corn tortillas
> 2 cups (8 ounces) shredded cheddar cheese, *divided*

In a bowl, combine the chicken, chilies, broth, soups and onion; set aside. Warm tortillas according to package directions. Layer half of the tortillas on the bottom of a greased 13-in. x 9-in. x 2-in. baking pan, cutting to fit pan if desired. Top with half of the chicken mixture and half of the cheese. Repeat layers. Bake, uncovered, at 350° for 30 minutes. **Yield:** 6-8 servings.

Southwestern Salad

You get an explosion of Southwestern flavor in every bite of this deliciously different salad. It's a favorite for kids of all ages since it mixes beans and cheese, tasty vegetables and crisp corn chips.

```
2-1/2  cups corn chips
  1/2  head iceberg lettuce, torn
    1  cup (4 ounces) shredded Mexican or
         cheddar cheese
    1  can (15 ounces) pinto beans, rinsed and
         drained
    1  small tomato, seeded and diced
  1/4 to 1/2 cup salad dressing of your choice
    2  tablespoons sliced green onions
    1 to 2 tablespoons chopped green chilies
    1  small avocado, peeled and sliced
```

In a serving bowl or platter, toss chips, lettuce, cheese, beans, tomato, salad dressing, onions and chilies. Top with avocado. Serve immediately. **Yield:** 6-8 servings.

— 🥄 🥄 🥄 —

Anise Cutout Cookies

Mother prepared these soft cookies for holidays and special-occasion meals. My seven siblings and I gob-

bled them up as fast as she made them. I still can't re-sist the cinnamon-sugar coating.

```
  2  cups shortening
  1  cup sugar
  2  eggs
  2  teaspoons aniseed
  6  cups all-purpose flour
  1  tablespoon baking powder
  1  teaspoon salt
1/4  cup apple juice
1/2  cup sugar
  1  teaspoon ground cinnamon
```

In a mixing bowl, cream shortening and sugar until fluffy; add eggs and aniseed. Combine flour, baking powder and salt; add to the creamed mixture. Add apple juice and mix well. On a floured surface, knead until well blended, about 4-5 minutes. Roll dough to 1/2-in. thickness; cut into 2-in. shapes. Place on greased baking sheets. Bake at 375° for 12-16 minutes or until lightly browned. Combine sugar and cinnamon; roll cookies in the mixture while still warm. Cool on wire racks. **Yield:** about 5 dozen.

Lively dinnertime discussions paired perfectly with Mom's delicious down-home cooking.

By Michelle Beran, Claflin, Kansas

I HAVE fond memories of always enjoying dinner at home when I was growing up. There was fun conversation between my parents, two sisters, brother and me…and Mom served delectable food.

Mom (Linda Engemann, above) worked hard as a schoolteacher. So during her busy weeks, she often prepared casseroles ahead or had dinner simmering in the slow cooker.

The meal that's still my favorite starts with Mom's Meat Loaf. Mom frequently fixed this main dish on the weekend when she had time to put something in the oven. It's tender and flavorful with a tangy topping we love.

Cheesy Potato Bake is an excellent, hearty side dish that goes perfectly with meat loaf. Of course, we loved these potatoes so much Mom served them with a variety of main courses.

A summertime staple on Mom's table is her Cucumbers with Dressing. Now my own family asks me to prepare this dish for our meals together.

Dessert is out of the ordinary and has wonderful old-fashioned goodness. Purple Plum Pie is one of Mom's specialties. A big slice of this sweet-tart pie still takes me back to those carefree days at home.

I gained kitchen confidence helping Mom. And she's inspired me to make dinners for my own family special by presenting great food and having good conversation. There are 16 around Mom's table these days, and dinner there is still a treat!

PICTURED AT LEFT: Mom's Meat Loaf, Cheesy Potato Bake, Cucumbers with Dressing and Purple Plum Pie (recipes are on the next page).

Mom's Meat Loaf

Mom made this scrumptious main dish frequently when I was growing up. When I first met my husband, he wasn't fond of meat loaf. This is the first meal I prepared for him, and now he requests it often.

        2 eggs
    3/4 cup milk
    2/3 cup finely crushed saltines
    1/2 cup chopped onion
        1 teaspoon salt
    1/2 teaspoon rubbed sage
Dash pepper
1-1/2 pounds lean ground beef
        1 cup ketchup
    1/2 cup packed brown sugar
        1 teaspoon Worcestershire sauce

In a large bowl, beat the eggs. Add milk, saltines, onion, salt, sage and pepper. Add beef and mix well. Shape into an 8-1/2-in. x 4-1/2-in. loaf in an ungreased shallow baking pan. Combine remaining ingredients; spread 3/4 cup over meat loaf. Bake at 350° for 60-65 minutes or until no pink remains; drain. Let stand 10 minutes before slicing. Serve with remaining sauce. **Yield:** 6-8 servings.

Cucumbers with Dressing

It wouldn't be summer if Mom didn't make lots of these creamy cucumbers. Just a few simple ingredients—mayonnaise, sugar, vinegar and salt—dress up slices of this crisp garden vegetable.

        1 cup mayonnaise
    1/4 cup sugar
    1/4 cup vinegar
    1/4 teaspoon salt
        4 cups sliced cucumbers

In a bowl, combine mayonnaise, sugar, vinegar and salt. Add cucumbers; stir to coat. Cover and refrigerate for 2 hours. **Yield:** 6-8 servings.

Cues for Storing Cukes

Store whole cucumbers, unwashed, in a plastic bag in the refrigerator for up to 10 days. Cut cucumbers can be wrapped and refrigerated for up to 5 days.

Cheesy Potato Bake

This saucy side dish satisfies even hearty appetites. It's easy to fix since there's no need to peel the potatoes. The mild, comforting flavor goes nicely with any meat—I especially like it with meat loaf.

4 large unpeeled baking potatoes
1/4 cup butter *or* margarine
1 tablespoon grated onion
1 teaspoon salt
1/2 teaspoon dried thyme
1/8 teaspoon pepper
1 cup (4 ounces) shredded cheddar cheese
1 tablespoon chopped fresh parsley

Thinly slice the potatoes and place in a greased shallow 2-qt. baking dish. In a small saucepan, heat butter, onion, salt, thyme and pepper until the butter is melted. Drizzle over potatoes. Cover and bake at 425° for 45 minutes or until tender. Sprinkle with cheese and parsley. Bake, uncovered, 15 minutes longer or until the cheese melts. **Yield:** 6-8 servings.

—— 🥄 🥄 🥄 ——

Purple Plum Pie

I can never resist a tart, tempting slice of this beautiful pie. It's a down-home dessert that makes any meal special. This pie is a terrific way to put bountiful summer plums to use.

4 cups sliced fresh plums (about 1-1/2 pounds)
1/2 cup sugar
1/4 cup all-purpose flour
1/4 teaspoon salt
1/4 teaspoon ground cinnamon
1 tablespoon lemon juice

1 unbaked deep-dish pastry shell (9 inches)
TOPPING:
1/2 cup sugar
1/2 cup all-purpose flour
1/4 teaspoon ground cinnamon
1/4 teaspoon ground nutmeg
3 tablespoons cold butter *or* margarine

In a bowl, combine the first six ingredients; pour into the pastry shell. For topping, combine sugar, flour, cinnamon and nutmeg in a small bowl; cut in butter until the mixture resembles coarse crumbs. Sprinkle over filling. Bake at 375° for 50-60 minutes or until bubbly and golden brown. Cover edges of crust with foil during the last 20 minutes to prevent overbrowning. Cool on a wire rack. **Yield:** 8 servings.

Purchasing Plums

Select plums that are free of blemishes like cracks, soft spots and brown discoloration. The skin's light gray cast is natural and doesn't affect quality.

Mom's kitchen produced Italian meals seasoned with lots of flavor and memories.

·By Cookie Curci-Wright, San Jose, California

WHEN I look back on growing up in my family's house during the 1940's, one room comes most quickly to mind—Mom's kitchen.

Despite its size, this tiny room is where Mom (Sarah Curci, above) spent most of her time. That made it the heart of our home, especially during the cooler winter months.

One of the meals I remember best centers around Mom's Special Chicken Soup. The aroma of it simmering on the stove gave us a feeling of love that still remains.

Whenever I caught a cold, Mom always reached for this recipe, not the medicine cabinet. This soup was the perfect remedy. Even today, all I have to do is sip a steaming bowl of this soup and my cares melt away. My husband enjoys each spoonful as much as I do.

Mom is also known for her Cheesy Italian Bread. The crispy slices have a nice cheese taste and a heavenly aroma. This bread accompanied many meals while I was growing up.

A pretty side dish is Sweet Red Pepper Salad. Garlic, olive oil and oregano give this salad a bold flavor to match its bright color. It also tastes great on top of toasted bread slices.

A traditional cookie for us and many other Italian families, Memorable Biscotti have a toasty texture and delicate flavor that make them perfect for dunking.

I still fondly recall the mouth-watering food and the warmth and comfort of Mom's cozy kitchen. Hopefully this old-fashioned meal will help you create some memories of your own!

PICTURED AT LEFT: Mom's Special Chicken Soup, Cheesy Italian Bread, Sweet Red Pepper Salad and Memorable Biscotti (recipes are on the next page).

Mom's Special Chicken Soup

Nothing is more comforting than this chicken soup. I am convinced a single bowl can soothe anything from the common cold to a stressful day. My mother made it often for our family when I was growing up. Now I fix it for my husband, Dan, and me.

✓ This tasty dish uses less sugar, salt and fat. Recipe includes *Diabetic Exchanges.*

>   1 broiler-fryer chicken (3-1/2 to 4 pounds)
>   3 quarts water
>   1 medium onion, quartered
>   4 celery ribs
>   2 chicken bouillon cubes
>   2 parsley sprigs
>   1 garlic clove
> 2-1/2 teaspoons salt, optional
>   1/2 cup thinly sliced carrots
>   1/2 cup chopped fresh parsley
>   3 cups cooked rice

Place chicken and water in a large kettle or Dutch oven; bring to a boil. Reduce heat; add onion, celery, bouillon, parsley sprigs, garlic and salt if desired. Cover and simmer until the chicken is tender, about 1 hour. Remove chicken; allow to cool. Strain and reserve broth; discard vegetables. Add carrots to broth and simmer until tender, about 15 minutes. Debone chicken and cut into cubes. Add chicken and chopped parsley to the broth; heat through. Ladle into bowls; add rice to each bowl. **Yield:** 14 servings (3-1/2 quarts). **Diabetic Exchanges:** One 1-cup serving (prepared with low-sodium bouillon and without salt) equals 1-1/2

meat, 1 starch; also, 184 calories, 41 mg sodium, 44 mg cholesterol, 13 gm carbohydrate, 15 gm protein, 7 gm fat.

———— 🛒 🛒 🛒 ————

Cheesy Italian Bread

This crusty bread is as big a treat today as it was when Mom made it back when I was growing up. It goes so well with an Italian meal or alongside a big bowl of soup.

✓ This tasty dish uses less sugar, salt and fat. Recipe includes *Diabetic Exchanges.*

>   1 package (1/4 ounce) active dry yeast
> 1-1/4 cups warm water (110° to 115°)
>   2 tablespoons sugar
>   1 teaspoon salt
>   1 teaspoon garlic salt
>   1/2 cup grated Romano cheese
>   3 to 3-1/2 cups all-purpose flour
> **Cornmeal**

In a mixing bowl, dissolve yeast in water. Add sugar, salt, garlic salt, cheese and 2 cups of flour; beat until smooth. Add enough remaining flour to form a soft dough. Turn onto a floured surface; knead until smooth and elastic, about 6-8 minutes. Place in a greased bowl, turning once to grease top. Cover and let rise in a warm place until doubled, about 1 hour. Punch dough down; divide in half. Shape each half into a 14-in. loaf. Place on an ungreased baking sheet that has been sprinkled with cornmeal. Cover and let rise until doubled, about 45 minutes. Brush loaves with water. Make three

diagonal slashes about 1/2 in. deep with a very sharp knife in each loaf. Fill a 13-in. x 9-in. x 2-in. baking pan with 1 in. of hot water and place on the bottom oven rack. Preheat to 400°. Bake loaves for 20-25 minutes. Remove to wire racks. **Yield:** 2 loaves (16 slices each). **Diabetic Exchanges:** One slice equals 1 starch; also, 60 calories, 102 mg sodium, 2 mg cholesterol, 11 gm carbohydrate, 2 gm protein, 1 gm fat.

Sweet Red Pepper Salad

The garlic, oregano and olive oil give this salad a true Italian taste that just can't be beat. We've eaten it as a side dish or piled high on garlic toast as an appetizer or snack.

     6 medium sweet red peppers
 1/2 cup olive *or* vegetable oil
 1/4 cup chopped fresh parsley
     2 to 3 garlic cloves, minced
 1/2 teaspoon dried oregano
 1/4 teaspoon salt
Lettuce leaves, optional

Place whole peppers on a broiler pan; broil 4 in. from the heat until skins blister, about 2-3 minutes. With tongs, rotate the peppers slightly. Continue broiling and rotating until all sides are blistered and blackened. Immediately place peppers in a brown paper bag. Close bag and let stand for 15-20 minutes. Peel off the charred skin and discard. Remove the stem and seeds. Cut peppers into 1/4-in.-wide strips. In a shallow container, combine the oil, parsley, garlic, oregano and salt. Add peppers and toss. Cover and chill for 3-4 hours. Serve on lettuce if desired. **Yield:** 6 servings. **Editor's Note:** The salad may also be spooned onto toasted garlic bread and served as an appetizer.

Memorable Biscotti

The enticing aroma of anise filled the kitchen and wafted through the house as Mom baked these traditional cookies when I was a girl. Mom always kept a big glass jar filled so we had a supply of these crisp cookies on hand.

    1 cup butter (no substitutes), softened
    1 cup sugar
    3 eggs
    1 teaspoon vanilla extract
    1 teaspoon anise extract
    3 cups all-purpose flour
    1 tablespoon baking powder
 1/2 teaspoon salt
    1 cup chopped almonds

In a mixing bowl, cream butter and sugar. Beat in the eggs, one at a time. Stir in extracts. Combine flour, baking powder and salt; add to creamed mixture. Stir in almonds. Line a baking sheet with foil and grease the foil. Divide dough in half. On the foil, form dough into two 11-in. x 3-in. rectangles. Bake at 300° for 35 minutes or until golden brown and firm to the touch. Remove from the oven; increase temperature to 325°. Using the foil, lift the rectangles onto wire racks; cool completely. Place on a cutting board; cut diagonally with a serrated knife into 3/4-in. slices. Place with cut side down on ungreased baking sheets. Bake for 10 minutes. Turn over; bake 10 minutes longer. Cool completely on wire racks. Store in an airtight container. **Yield:** about 2-1/2 dozen.

Great food and good company made her birthday celebrations extra special.

By Lisa Andis, Morristown, Indiana

MY MOM (Sue Wortman, above) always prepared our favorite foods on our birthdays and invited our grandparents to celebrate with us.

On my birthday, November 7, I would request her Broiled Pork Chops. These juicy tender chops are made with a tangy barbecue sauce that's more zippy than sweet. Chili powder gives it a nice kick that makes these chops deliciously unique.

A comforting side dish that's perfect with the pork chops is Creamed Beans and Potatoes. I'd help myself to several servings.

Hawaiian Salad makes a cool, crisp addition to this meal. With just a few ingredients, it's very simple to make. I love the refreshing tropical flavor.

The best part, of course, is the German Chocolate Birthday Cake. As a girl, I preferred the coconut-pecan frosting—partly because I like coconut and partly because my brother doesn't care for it. That assured he wouldn't be eating much of "my" cake!

Even though Mom helped Dad with the family business, she still found time to cook from scratch. She learned from her mother and encouraged me in the kitchen.

These days, Mom still makes dinner on our birthdays. But now she's cooking for a crowd with Dad, my brother and me and our spouses, all the grandkids and my two grandmothers.

We've agreed to compromise on the cake. Mom frosts half in plain frosting and half with the coconut-pecan. The whole meal tastes just as good as I remember!

— 🍴 🍴 🍴 —

PICTURED AT LEFT: Broiled Pork Chops, Creamed Beans and Potatoes, Hawaiian Salad and German Chocolate Birthday Cake (recipes are on the next page).

Broiled Pork Chops

These zippy, tender chops are one of my mother's specialties. She's been making them for years. I still request this delightful main dish when our family gets together to celebrate birthdays and other occasions.

- 3/4 cup ketchup
- 3/4 cup water
- 2 tablespoons vinegar
- 1 tablespoon Worcestershire sauce
- 2 teaspoons brown sugar
- 1 teaspoon salt
- 1/2 teaspoon paprika
- 1/2 teaspoon chili powder
- 1/8 teaspoon pepper
- 6 pork loin chops (3/4 inch thick)

In a saucepan, combine the first nine ingredients; bring to a boil. Reduce heat; simmer for 5 minutes, stirring occasionally. Set aside half of the sauce. Place the pork chops on broiling pan rack. Broil about 4 in. from the heat for 4 minutes on each side. Brush with remaining sauce. Continue broiling, turning and basting occasionally, for 3-4 minutes or until juices run clear. Serve with reserved sauce. **Yield:** 6 servings.

Creamed Beans and Potatoes

This soothing side dish is so much nicer than plain potatoes and peas. Mother relied on hearty down-home recipes such as this one. Now I also make it for my own family.

- 4 medium red potatoes, cut into wedges
- 1 package (10 ounces) frozen beans *or* peas
- 2 tablespoons butter *or* margarine
- 2 tablespoons all-purpose flour
- 1/2 teaspoon salt
- 1/8 teaspoon pepper
- 1 cup milk

Place the potatoes in a saucepan; cover with water and cook until tender, about 10 minutes. Cook the beans according to package directions. Meanwhile, melt the butter in a saucepan; stir in flour, salt and pepper until smooth. Gradually add milk. Bring to a boil; boil for 1 minute. Drain potatoes and beans; place in a serving bowl. Add sauce and stir to coat. **Yield:** 6 servings.

— 🍴 🍴 🍴 —

Hawaiian Salad

To add a refreshing spark to any meal, try this tempting salad with tropical flair. A few simple ingredients are easily combined for a memorable salad. We always empty the bowl.

- 1 can (8 ounces) pineapple tidbits
- 6 to 8 cups torn salad greens
- 1 cup (4 ounces) shredded cheddar cheese
- 1/2 cup mayonnaise *or* salad dressing
- 1 tablespoon sugar

Drain pineapple, reserving 1 tablespoon juice. In a large bowl, combine greens, pineapple and cheese. In a small bowl, combine mayonnaise, sugar and reserved pineapple juice; mix well. Pour over salad; toss to coat. Serve immediately. **Yield:** 6 servings.

⌣ ⌣ ⌣

German Chocolate Birthday Cake

This moist, flavorful cake was the traditional birthday cake at our house when I was growing up. Everyone requested it. I especially like it topped with sweet coconut-pecan frosting.

> 1 **package (4 ounces) German sweet chocolate**
> 1/2 **cup water**
> 1 **cup butter *or* margarine, softened**
> 2 **cups sugar**
> 4 **eggs, *separated***
> 1 **teaspoon vanilla extract**
> 2-1/2 **cups cake flour**
> 1 **teaspoon baking soda**
> 1/2 **teaspoon salt**
> 1 **cup buttermilk**
> **COCONUT-PECAN FROSTING:**
> 1 **cup evaporated milk**
> 1 **cup sugar**
> 3 **egg yolks, lightly beaten**
> 1/2 **cup butter *or* margarine**
> 1 **teaspoon vanilla extract**
> 1-1/3 **cups flaked coconut**
> 1 **cup chopped pecans**

In a saucepan over low heat, stir chocolate and water until chocolate is melted. Cool. In a mixing bowl, cream butter and sugar. Add egg yolks, one at a time, beating well after each addition. Add chocolate mixture and vanilla; mix well. Combine flour, baking soda and salt; add alternately with buttermilk to creamed mixture. In another mixing bowl, beat egg whites until stiff peaks form; fold into batter. Line a greased 13-in. x 9-in. x 2-in. baking pan with waxed paper. Grease and flour the paper. Spread batter evenly in pan. Bake at 350° for 50-55 minutes or until a toothpick inserted near the center comes out clean. Cool in pan for 10 minutes; invert onto a wire rack to cool completely. Remove waxed paper. For frosting, combine milk, sugar, egg yolks, butter and vanilla in a saucepan; cook and stir over medium heat until thickened. Remove from the heat; stir in coconut and pecans. Beat until frosting is cool and reaches desired spreading consistency. Place cake on a serving platter; spread frosting over top and sides. **Yield:** 12-15 servings.

Reusable Wrappers

Save the paper wrapping from sticks of butter or margarine and store them in the freezer. When a recipe calls for a greased pan, rub the pan with one of the wrappings.

Editors' Meals

Taste of Home magazine is edited by 1,000 cooks across North America. On the following pages, you'll "meet" some of those editors who share a family-favorite meal.

CREATIVE COOKING. Clockwise from upper left: Easter Table Traditions (p. 218), A Pilgrim's Presentation (p. 234), Great Outdoor Grilling (p. 226) and Memorable Christmas Menu (p. 214).

A "late bloomer" in the kitchen, this enthusiastic cook makes up for lost time with a memorable Christmas menu.

By Dorothy Pritchett, Wills Point, Texas

BEFORE I became a first-time bride at 48, I had a challenging career in administrative nursing. I was lucky to have any time to *eat*, much less cook.

I worked in a number of hospitals across the Southwest and later joined the faculty at St. Mary's Hospital in Enid, Oklahoma.

In 1970, I married Charlie, a retired GI who has a farm background like me. To get me started with home cooking, my sisters gave me some of their favorite recipes and several cookbooks.

Charlie encouraged me from the start. He's a jolly man who's always snooping around when I'm cooking to see if there's something for him to sample!

Things have changed a lot in the years since I first started cooking. Now I collect recipes and enjoy trying different dishes. The five recipes I'm sharing are some I've served to the enthusiastic appreciation of Charlie and our guests at Christmas.

A pretty golden color, Pork Roast with Fruit Sauce is made with apple juice, apple jelly, apricots and a Christmasy hint of cardamom.

For holiday fare, I dress up red potatoes with a perky lemon sauce and minced fresh parsley to present as Lemon Parsley Potatoes.

Creamed Celery and Peas sounds unusual, but it's delicious—everyone asks for "seconds" and copies of the recipe whenever I serve this side dish.

Seasoned with nutmeg and brown sugar for just the right sweetness, Whipped Squash is so simple.

I clipped the Cherry Almond Mousse Pie recipe from a brochure some time ago, smacking my lips as I read the ingredients. How can you go wrong with chocolate, almonds, maraschino cherries, whipped cream, cream cheese and pudding?

I hope you'll find my merry menu to your liking at Christmas and throughout the year!

PICTURED AT LEFT: Pork Roast with Fruit Sauce, Creamed Celery and Peas, Whipped Squash, Lemon Parsley Potatoes and Cherry Almond Mousse Pie (recipes are on the next page).

Pork Roast with Fruit Sauce

A tender, savory pork roast gets dressed up for the holidays in a tangy apricot sauce. It's a wonderful old-fashioned dish that's a family favorite. It looks so pretty on the table.

> 1 pork loin roast with bone (3 to 4 pounds)
> 1 jar (10 ounces) apple jelly
> 1 cup apple juice
> 1/2 teaspoon ground cardamom
> 3/4 cup chopped dried apricots
> 1 tablespoon cornstarch
> 2 tablespoons water

Place roast on a rack in a shallow roasting pan. Bake, uncovered, at 350° for 1-1/2 hours. In a saucepan, combine apple jelly, apple juice and cardamom; cook and stir over medium heat until smooth and heated through. Set aside 1/2 cup. Brush some of the remaining sauce over roast; bake 40-60 minutes longer or until a meat thermometer reads 160°-170°, brushing with sauce every 20 minutes. Transfer roast to a serving platter and keep warm. Pour pan drippings into a saucepan. Add apricots and reserved fruit sauce; cook over medium heat until softened, about 5 minutes. Combine the cornstarch and water until smooth; add to apricot mixture. Bring to a boil, stirring constantly; cook 2 minutes. Serve with roast. **Yield:** 10-12 servings.

Lemon Parsley Potatoes

(Pictured on page 214)

For a simply delicious side dish, I often prepare these potatoes. I like the fact that there are few ingredients and they take such little time to prepare.

> 3 pounds small red potatoes, quartered
> 1/2 cup butter *or* margarine, melted
> 3 tablespoons lemon juice
> 3 tablespoons minced fresh parsley

Cook potatoes in boiling salted water until tender, about 15 minutes; drain. Combine butter, lemon juice and parsley; pour over the potatoes and stir gently to coat. **Yield:** 10-12 servings.

Whipped Squash

(Pictured on page 214)

This is an excellent way to serve one of winter's most delicious vegetables—butternut squash. Its rich flavor and golden harvest color really come through.

✓ This tasty dish uses less sugar, salt and fat. Recipe includes *Diabetic Exchanges.*

> 1 butternut squash (about 2-1/2 pounds), peeled, seeded and cubed

1/4 teaspoon salt, optional
2 tablespoons butter *or* margarine
1 tablespoon brown sugar
1/8 to 1/4 teaspoon ground nutmeg

In a saucepan over medium heat, cook squash in boiling salted water until tender, about 20 minutes. Drain; transfer to a mixing bowl. Add butter, brown sugar, nutmeg and salt if desired; beat until smooth. **Yield:** 6 servings. **Diabetic Exchanges:** One 1/2-cup serving (prepared with margarine and without salt) equals 1 starch, 1/2 fat; also, 86 calories, 37 mg sodium, 0 cholesterol, 14 gm carbohydrate, 1 gm protein, 4 gm fat.

Creamed Celery and Peas

This special side dish never fails to have people returning to the table for more. Celery and almonds provide great crunch. It tastes impressive, but it's very simple to prepare.

1/3 cup water
2 cups sliced celery
1 package (10 ounces) frozen peas
1/2 cup sour cream
1/2 teaspoon dried rosemary, crushed
1/4 teaspoon salt
Dash garlic salt
1 tablespoon chopped pimientos, drained
1/4 cup slivered almonds, toasted

In a saucepan over medium heat, bring water to a boil. Add celery; cover and cook for 8 minutes. Add peas; return to a boil. Cover and cook for 2-3 minutes or until vegetables are tender; drain. In a small bowl, combine sour cream, rosemary, salt and garlic salt; mix well. Toss vegetables with pimientos; place in a serving bowl. Top with sour cream mixture. Sprinkle with almonds. **Yield:** 6 servings.

Cherry Almond Mousse Pie

Holidays are a perfect time to treat your family and guests to a luscious pie with chocolate, cherries and nuts in a creamy vanilla mousse. It's a sweet yet light dessert.

1 can (14 ounces) sweetened condensed milk, *divided*
1 square (1 ounce) unsweetened chocolate
1/2 teaspoon almond extract, *divided*
1 pastry shell (9 inches), baked
1 jar (10 ounces) maraschino cherries, drained
1 package (8 ounces) cream cheese, softened
1 cup cold water
1 package (3.4 ounces) instant vanilla pudding mix
1 cup whipping cream, whipped
1/2 cup chopped toasted almonds
Chocolate curls, optional

In a saucepan over low heat, cook and stir 1/2 cup milk and chocolate until the chocolate is melted and mixture is thickened, about 4-5 minutes. Stir in 1/4 teaspoon extract. Pour into pastry shell; set aside. Reserve eight whole cherries for garnish. Chop the remaining cherries; set aside. In a mixing bowl, beat the cream cheese until light. Gradually beat in water and remaining milk. Add the pudding mix and remaining extract; mix well. Fold in whipped cream. Stir in chopped cherries and almonds. Pour over pie. Chill for 4 hours or until set. Garnish with whole cherries and chocolate curls if desired. **Yield:** 8-10 servings.

A devout veteran of kitchen and congregation serves up a delightful meal full of spring's flavors to brighten your Easter table.

By Ellen Benninger, Stoneboro, Pennsylvania

AS a minister's wife, my top priority is "food for the spirit". But I also believe there is a blessing in sharing delicious home-cooked food.

I've been cooking since I was 7 years old. My mother was bedridden for 18 years. As a child, I stood at her bedside while she told me each ingredient to add to whatever we were making. How patiently she taught me—and she was so cheerful.

It's no surprise then that one of the things I like to do best is run to the kitchen and make something good—whether it's supper for husband Jack and myself, a dish for a school function or a dinner for family, friends or visiting evangelists and missionaries.

The four favorite foods I share here are perfect for any spring gathering, especially Easter.

Ham Balls—baked in a sweet, tangy sauce—seem to please and satisfy most everyone who tastes them. I've served them often on Sundays after church.

I devised my Springtime Potato Salad by putting together two similar recipes from friends from past churches. I think of those kind folks when I stir in this salad's tasty creamy dressing.

My first taste of the Apricot Gelatin Salad was at a friend's birthday celebration. As soon as I tried this light fluffy salad, I knew I had to get the recipe.

I've tasted different versions of Pickled Eggs and Beets, often finding the eggs quite sour. I've found this simple recipe is not too puckery.

Our son says that of the many types of pie I've made, he likes my Perfect Rhubarb Pie best. A spring treat, this pie is just sweet enough and just tart enough to be perfect.

Like many of you, I never tire of trying new foods. Yet, there are some dishes I go back to time and again, remembering just how good they are. That's truly the case with this can't-miss menu.

— 🍴 🍴 🍴 —

PICTURED AT LEFT: Ham Balls, Springtime Potato Salad, Pickled Eggs and Beets, Apricot Gelatin Salad and Perfect Rhubarb Pie (recipes are on the next page).

1 can (13-1/4 ounces) sliced beets
1/2 cup sugar
1/4 cup vinegar
1/2 cinnamon stick
6 whole cloves, optional
8 hard-cooked eggs, shelled

Drain beets, reserving juice; set beets aside. Add enough water to juice to measure 3/4 cup; place in a saucepan. Add sugar, vinegar, cinnamon stick and cloves if desired; bring to a boil. Remove from the heat. Place eggs in a bowl; top with beets. Pour liquid over all. Cover and chill for 4 hours or overnight. Remove the cinnamon stick and cloves before serving. **Yield:** 8 servings.

Ham Balls

This tasty main dish, pairing ham and pork, is a wonderful way to use up leftover Easter ham. Covered with a savory brown sugar sauce, these ham balls are hard to resist.

  1 pound ground pork
  1 pound ground fully cooked ham
  2 eggs
  3/4 cup milk
  2/3 cup crushed Shredded Wheat cereal
SAUCE:
1-1/2 cups packed brown sugar
  2/3 cup water
  1/3 cup vinegar
  3/4 teaspoon ground mustard

In a bowl, combine the pork, ham, eggs, milk and cereal; mix well. Shape into 1-1/2-in. to 2-in. balls; place in a greased 13-in. x 9-in. x 2-in. baking dish. In a saucepan, combine sauce ingredients; bring to a boil over medium heat. Reduce heat; simmer, uncovered, for 4 minutes. Pour over the ham balls. Bake, uncovered, at 350° for 60-70 minutes or until browned. **Yield:** 8 servings.

— 🏺 🏺 🏺 —

Pickled Eggs and Beets

(Pictured on page 218)

This is a popular dish, especially at Eastertime when hard-cooked eggs are abundant.

Springtime Potato Salad

Traditional potato salad gets fun flavor from sweet pickles and a hearty crunch from celery and radishes in this recipe. I'm especially fond of the creamy dressing.

  6 cups diced peeled cooked potatoes
  4 hard-cooked eggs, chopped
1/2 cup chopped celery
1/2 cup chopped sweet pickles
1/3 cup chopped onion
1/3 cup chopped radishes
1/2 cup mayonnaise
  3 tablespoons sugar
  1 tablespoon vinegar
  1 tablespoon milk
1-1/2 teaspoons prepared mustard
1/2 teaspoon salt
Paprika, optional

In a bowl, combine potatoes, eggs, celery, pickles, onion and radishes. In another bowl, combine mayonnaise, sugar, vinegar, milk, mustard and salt; mix well. Pour over potato mixture; stir to coat. Cover and refrigerate. Sprinkle with paprika before serving if desired. **Yield:** 8-10 servings.

Apricot Gelatin Salad

I serve this smooth, fluffy salad all year for special meals, but it's so pleasant around Eastertime with its pretty color and fruity flavor. The apricot pieces are an unexpected treat.

     1 package (6 ounces) apricot *or* orange
       gelatin
     2 cups boiling water
     1 can (20 ounces) crushed pineapple
     1 package (8 ounces) cream cheese, softened
     1 can (15 ounces) apricot halves, drained and
       chopped
   1/2 cup chopped walnuts
     1 carton (8 ounces) frozen whipped
       topping, thawed
Additional chopped walnuts, optional

In a bowl, dissolve gelatin in water. Drain pineapple, reserving juice. Add pineapple to gelatin and set aside. In a mixing bowl, beat cream cheese and pineapple juice until smooth. Stir in gelatin mixture; chill until partially set, stirring occasionally. Stir in apricots and walnuts. Fold in whipped topping. Pour into a 13-in. x 9-in. x 2-in. dish. Sprinkle with walnuts if desired. Chill until firm. **Yield:** 12-16 servings.

Perfect Rhubarb Pie

Nothing hides the tangy rhubarb in this lovely pie, which has just the right balance of sweet and tart. Serving this dessert is a nice way to celebrate the end of winter!

     4 cups sliced fresh rhubarb
     4 cups boiling water
 1-1/2 cups sugar
     3 tablespoons all-purpose flour
     1 teaspoon quick-cooking tapioca
     1 egg
     2 teaspoons cold water
Pastry for double-crust pie (9 inches)
     1 tablespoon butter *or* margarine

Place rhubarb in a colander and pour water over it; set aside. In a bowl, combine sugar, flour and tapioca; mix well. Drain rhubarb; add to sugar mixture and toss to coat. Let stand for 15 minutes. Beat egg and water; add to rhubarb mixture and mix well. Line a 9-in. pie plate with bottom pastry. Add filling. Dot with butter. Cover with remaining pastry; flute edges. Cut slits in top crust. Bake at 400° for 15 minutes. Reduce heat to 350°; bake 40-50 minutes longer or until crust is golden brown and filling is bubbly. **Yield:** 8 servings.

Pieplant Pointers

To preserve the pleasing crisp texture of raw rhubarb, wrap it tightly and store in the refrigerator for up to 1 week. One pound of rhubarb equals 3 to 4 cups of sliced fruit.

From her cozy Heartland kitchen, this busy rural cook turns out satisfying family meals and tempting baked treats.

By Pat Habiger, Spearville, Kansas

FOR ME, the country is truly the place to be. Both my husband, Melvin, and I grew up on farms in this area and were raised on basic country cooking.

The dishes I prepare in our farmhouse kitchen in southwest Kansas reflect the down-home foods our mothers served to us while we were kids. When our three grown children come for dinner on birthdays, holidays or just to be together, the meal they most often request is this one.

Steak Roll-Ups is an entree that's both distinctive and old-fashioned. When I first saw the recipe in a cookbook many years ago, I knew I had to try it. I wasn't disappointed—these hearty, saucy meat rolls make attractive servings, and the stuffing can take the place of potatoes.

My Glazed Carrot Coins appeal to kids. First endorsed by our children years ago, this slightly sweet preparation now receives "thumbs up" from our granddaughter.

Each time I bite into a Golden Knot, I say, "These are the most mouth-watering, soft and buttery rolls I've ever tasted!" And everyone agrees.

Layered Pudding Dessert is an old-time treat with a refreshing combination of fruit and pudding.

When not cooking for the family, I enjoy baking breads and cookies for my co-workers to snack on at the bank where I work.

Besides farming, Melvin teaches math and chemistry at a nearby high school. When something is needed for a bake sale or covered-dish dinner, he has plenty of suggestions for yummy items I can make.

About 15 years ago, on a lark, I entered my first recipe contest and won a prize. I've participated in quite a few others since then.

I hope you bring a little bit of country to your table tonight with this well-loved down-home dinner.

PICTURED AT LEFT: Steak Roll-Ups, Golden Knots, Glazed Carrot Coins and Layered Pudding Dessert (recipes are on the next page).

1/3 cup on each piece of steak; roll up and fasten with a toothpick. Roll in flour. In a large skillet, brown roll-ups in oil. Combine soup, water and browning sauce if desired; pour over the roll-ups. Cover and simmer for 2 hours or until meat is tender, turning occasionally. Remove toothpicks before serving. **Yield:** 6 servings.

Golden Knots

No matter how you form these tender, golden rolls, it's hard to eat just one. My husband's aunt gave me this treasured recipe.

    2 packages (1/4 ounce *each*) active dry yeast
    1 cup plus 2 tablespoons sugar, *divided*
1-1/2 cups warm water (110° to 115°), *divided*
    1 cup milk
 1/2 cup butter *or* margarine
    2 eggs
    2 teaspoons salt
8-1/2 to 9 cups all-purpose flour
Melted butter *or* margarine

In a large mixing bowl, dissolve yeast and 2 tablespoons of sugar in 1/2 cup of water. In a saucepan, heat the milk, butter and remaining water to 110°-115°; add to yeast mixture. Add eggs, salt, 5 cups flour and the remaining sugar; beat until smooth. Add enough of the remaining flour to form a soft dough. Turn onto a floured surface; knead until

Steak Roll-Ups

My family tells me these hearty stuffed beef rolls with a creamy sauce "taste like home". They're attractive enough to serve for a special dinner but economical and easy to prepare.

1-1/2 pounds boneless round steak
  1/4 cup chopped onion
  1/4 cup butter *or* margarine, melted
    2 cups fresh bread cubes
  1/2 cup chopped celery
    1 tablespoon dried parsley flakes
  1/2 teaspoon salt
  1/2 teaspoon poultry seasoning
  1/4 teaspoon pepper
    1 cup all-purpose flour
    2 tablespoons cooking oil
    1 can (10-3/4 ounces) condensed cream of
      mushroom soup, undiluted
1-1/3 cups water
  3/4 teaspoon browning sauce, optional

Pound steak to 1/3-in. thickness. Cut into six pieces. Combine the next eight ingredients; mix well. Place

smooth and elastic, about 6-8 minutes. Place in a greased bowl, turning once to grease top. Cover and let rise in a warm place until doubled, about 1 hour. Punch dough down. Divide into thirds; roll each portion into a 14-in. roll. Divide each roll into 14 pieces. Roll pieces into 9-in. ropes and tie into knots. Place the rolls 2 in. apart on greased baking sheets. Cover and let rise until doubled, about 30 minutes. Bake at 350° for 15-20 minutes or until golden brown. Brush with melted butter. **Yield:** 3-1/2 dozen.

Glazed Carrot Coins

When I pull fresh carrots from the garden, my mouth waters just thinking about how this simple recipe enhances their flavor with brown sugar and a hint of lemon.

  12 **medium carrots, cut into 1-inch pieces**
 1/2 **cup packed brown sugar**
   3 **tablespoons butter *or* margarine**
   1 **tablespoon grated lemon peel**
 1/4 **teaspoon vanilla extract**

In a saucepan, cook carrots in a small amount of water until crisp-tender; drain. Remove and keep warm. In the same pan, heat brown sugar and butter until bubbly. Stir in lemon peel. Return carrots to pan; cook and stir over low heat for 10-15 minutes or until glazed. Remove from the heat; stir in vanilla. **Yield:** 6 servings.

Layered Pudding Dessert

This fluffy, fruity refrigerated treat continues to hold its own against new dessert recipes I try.

   1 **cup crushed vanilla wafers, *divided***
   1 **package (3 ounces) cook-and-serve vanilla pudding mix**
   2 **medium ripe bananas, *divided***
   1 **package (3 ounces) strawberry gelatin**
   1 **cup whipped topping**

Spread half of the crushed wafers in the bottom of a greased 8-in. square pan. Prepare pudding mix according to package directions; spoon hot pudding over crumbs. Slice one banana; place over pudding. Top with remaining crumbs. Chill for 1 hour. Meanwhile, prepare gelatin according to package directions; chill for 30 minutes or until partially set. Pour over crumbs. Slice the remaining banana and place over gelatin. Spread whipped topping over all. Chill for 2 hours. **Yield:** 9 servings.

Banana Basics

To ripen bananas, keep them uncovered at room temperature. To speed the process, place bananas in a brown paper bag with an apple.

The great outdoors supplants the kitchen for this rural cook as she grills a delectable supper. Even the kids pitch in with preparation of her summertime menu.

By Denise Nebel, Wayland, Iowa

WHEN I was younger, I didn't spend much time in the kitchen. Before my husband, Keith, and I were married, Mother gave me a "crash course" on fixing the basics so I'd be able to put a hearty meal on the table. Now I've come to enjoy cooking.

Keith and I raise hogs, cattle and about 60,000 turkeys a year. So it shouldn't be a surprise that turkey stars in our favorite summer meal.

The Grilled Turkey Tenderloin is my scaled-down version of a crowd-pleasing recipe that's used for grilled turkey sandwiches at the Iowa State Fair. At home, I usually serve it sliced rather than on a bun.

For the Potato Pockets, our sons, Trace and Zeke, often help me put the potatoes and other vegetables into foil packets. They think it's great fun to put the cheese on top of this simple medley just before serving and see how fast it melts.

Cool, old-fashioned Orange Tapioca Salad is a colorful addition to the meal. The children love it, and it appeals to adults as well because it's not too sweet.

We also grow berries, which star in my Strawberry Lemonade. Glasses of this refreshing summery punch add fruity flavor to any warm-weather meal. The sweet strawberry taste is accented by a little tartness from the lemon.

For dessert, I've found I can't go wrong with Triple Fudge Brownies. Chock-full of chocolate chips, these yummy bars use cake and pudding mixes, so they're convenient and uncomplicated to mix and bake.

With crops to tend to, in addition to our livestock and the boys' activities, my schedule is always full. I prefer flavorful foods without a lot of fuss. We don't have too many gourmet meals, just down-home delicious foods like these!

PICTURED AT LEFT: Potato Pockets (on the grill), Grilled Turkey Tenderloin, Orange Tapioca Salad, Triple Fudge Brownies and Strawberry Lemonade (recipes are on the next page).

Grilled Turkey Tenderloin

When they taste my grilled specialty, guests say, "This turkey melts in your mouth—and the flavor is fantastic!" The recipe includes a tangy marinade that was developed for our turkey producers' booth at the state fair.

✓ This tasty dish uses less sugar, salt and fat. Recipe includes *Diabetic Exchanges.*

> **1/4 cup soy sauce**
> **1/4 cup vegetable oil**
> **1/4 cup apple juice**
> **2 tablespoons lemon juice**
> **2 tablespoons dried minced onion**
> **1 teaspoon vanilla extract**
> **1/4 teaspoon ground ginger**
> **Dash *each* garlic powder and pepper**
> **2 turkey breast tenderloins (1/2 pound *each*)**

In a large resealable plastic bag or shallow glass dish, combine the soy sauce, oil, apple juice, lemon juice, onion, vanilla, ginger, garlic powder and pepper. Add turkey; seal or cover and refrigerate for at least 2 hours. Discard marinade. Grill turkey, covered, over medium coals for 8-10 minutes on each side or until juices run clear. **Yield:** 4 servings. **Diabetic Exchanges:** One serving (prepared with light soy sauce) equals 4 lean meat, 1 vegetable, 1/2 fat; also, 284 calories, 558 mg sodium, 82 mg cholesterol, 6 gm carbohydrate, 31 gm protein, 14 gm fat.

Potato Pockets

Our young sons like to help me assemble potatoes, carrots and onion into foil packages that we can grill alongside the turkey. Just before serving, we top the steaming medley of vegetables with a sprinkling of cheese.

✓ This tasty dish uses less sugar, salt and fat. Recipe includes *Diabetic Exchanges.*

> **4 medium potatoes, julienned**
> **3 medium carrots, julienned**
> **1/3 cup chopped red onion**
> **2 tablespoons butter *or* margarine**
> **1/2 teaspoon salt, optional**
> **1/8 teaspoon pepper**
> **1/2 cup shredded Parmesan *or* cheddar cheese**

Divide the potatoes, carrots and onion equally between four pieces of heavy-duty aluminum foil (about 18 in. x 12 in.). Top with butter; sprinkle with salt if desired and pepper. Bring opposite short ends of foil together over vegetables and fold down several times. Fold unsealed ends toward vegetables and crimp tightly. Grill, covered, over medium coals for 20-30 minutes or until potatoes are tender. Remove from grill. Carefuly open foil and sprinkle with cheese; reseal for 5 minutes or until the cheese melts. **Yield:** 4 servings. **Diabetic Exchanges:** One serving (prepared with margarine and low-fat cheddar cheese and without salt) equals 1-1/2 starch, 1 vegetable; also, 238 calories, 92 mg sodium, 10 mg cholesterol, 33 gm carbohydrate, 8 gm protein, 9 gm fat.

Orange Tapioca Salad

Fresh, fruity flavor makes this pretty salad popular with all ages. Our whole family really digs into its fluffy goodness. I can put it together in the morning or even the night before and pop it in the fridge until suppertime.

- **3 cups water**
- **1 package (3 ounces) orange gelatin**
- **1 package (3.4 ounces) instant vanilla pudding mix**
- **1 package (3 ounces) tapioca pudding mix**
- **1 can (15 ounces) mandarin oranges, drained**
- **1 can (8 ounces) crushed pineapple, drained**
- **1 carton (8 ounces) frozen whipped topping, thawed**

In a saucepan, bring water to a boil. Whisk in gelatin and pudding mixes. Return to a boil, stirring constantly; boil for 1 minute. Remove from the heat and cool completely. Fold in oranges, pineapple and whipped topping. Spoon into a serving bowl. Cover and chill at least 2 hours. **Yield:** 12-14 servings.

— 🍷 🍷 🍷 —

Strawberry Lemonade

(Pictured on page 226)

Keith is always happy to see me coming with a jug of this quenching beverage and a snack for a break when he's busy around the farm.

- **3 cups cold water**
- **1 quart fresh strawberries**

- **3/4 cup sugar**
- **3/4 cup lemon juice**
- **2 cups cold club soda**
- **Lemon slices, optional**

Place water, strawberries and sugar in a blender; cover and blend until smooth. Stir in lemon juice. Blend in soda; serve immediately. Garnish with lemon if desired. **Yield:** 8 servings (2 quarts).

Triple Fudge Brownies

When you're in a hurry to make dessert, here's a "mix of mixes" that's so convenient and quick. The result is a big pan of very rich, fudgy brownies. Friends who ask me for the recipe are amazed that it's so easy.

- **1 package (3.9 ounces) instant chocolate pudding mix**
- **1 package (18-1/4 ounces) chocolate cake mix**
- **2 cups (12 ounces) semisweet chocolate chips**
- **Confectioners' sugar**
- **Vanilla ice cream, optional**

Prepare pudding according to package directions. Whisk in cake mix. Stir in chocolate chips. Pour into a greased 15-in. x 10-in. x 1-in. baking pan. Bake at 350° for 30-35 minutes or until the top springs back when lightly touched. Dust with confectioners' sugar. Serve with ice cream if desired. **Yield:** 4 dozen.

Skills learned on a Western ranch serve this transplanted cook well when she rings the dinner bell for a delectable meal.

By Marie Hoyer, Hodgenville, Kentucky

FOR SOMEONE like me who loves to garden and cook, there's no better season than summer. My husband, Lee, and I enjoy entertaining and sharing our homegrown produce in a casual meal.

We're Montana transplants who have taken root in Kentucky. On our ranch, we barbecued often. I found the recipe for Ribs with Plum Sauce years ago when I had an abundance of plums and had made all the jams, jelly and syrup I needed.

A tasty accompaniment, Creamy Potato Sticks also goes well with just about any meat. The ingredients can be assembled ahead of time, and you can substitute different types of cream soups for variety.

Garden-fresh Broccoli Tomato Salad says "summer" from the first sight of its bright color to its just-picked taste. The combination of red tomatoes with the green broccoli is beautiful.

For dessert, Zucchini Cake is easy to make and not too sweet. The recipe yields a big pan, perfect for a party or potluck. And it's also a good way to use up some of an abundant zucchini crop.

As a ranch wife, I made my own baked goods, churned butter, prepared *big* meals and collected recipes for using all of the milk, cream, eggs and other abundant foods we produced.

I also learned how to preserve produce from our large garden and the wild grapes, chokecherries and serviceberries we picked on the hillsides.

Family gatherings, haying, shipping cattle and calf branding provided many opportunities to feed people. We could always squeeze an extra chair around the table!

That's changed now, but we still enjoy sharing home-cooked meals like this one.

PICTURED AT LEFT: Ribs with Plum Sauce, Creamy Potato Sticks, Broccoli Tomato Salad and Zucchini Cake (recipes are on the next page).

Ribs with Plum Sauce

I found the recipe for this tangy-sweet basting sauce when a surplus of plums sent me searching for new ideas to use all the fruit. In summer, I like to finish the ribs on the grill, brushing on the sauce, after first baking them in the oven.

    5 to 6 pounds pork spareribs
    3/4 cup soy sauce
    3/4 cup plum jam *or* apricot preserves
    3/4 cup honey
    2 to 3 garlic cloves, minced

Cut ribs into serving-size pieces; place with bone side down on a rack in a shallow roasting pan. Cover and bake at 350° for 1 hour or until ribs are tender; drain. Combine remaining ingredients; brush some of the sauce over ribs. Bake at 350° or grill over medium coals, uncovered, for 30 minutes, brushing occasionally with sauce. **Yield:** 6 servings.

— ☕ ☕ ☕ —

Creamy Potato Sticks

This homey potato side dish harks back to my ranch kitchen in Montana, where my husband and I raised four sons and a daughter. Hearty eaters, they always spooned up big servings of this casserole. Cutting the potatoes into sticks is a nice change.

    1/4 cup all-purpose flour
    1/2 teaspoon salt
    1-1/2 cups milk
      1 can (10-3/4 ounces) condensed cream of
        celery soup, undiluted
    1/2 pound process American cheese, cubed
      5 to 6 large baking potatoes, peeled
      1 cup chopped onion
    Paprika

In a saucepan, combine flour and salt; gradually whisk in milk until smooth. Bring to a boil; cook and stir for 2 minutes. Remove from the heat; whisk in soup and cheese until smooth. Set aside. Cut potatoes into 4-in. x 1/2-in. x 1/2-in. sticks; place in a greased 13-in. x 9-in. x 2-in. baking dish. Sprinkle with onion. Top with cheese sauce. Bake, uncovered, at 350° for 55-60 minutes or until potatoes are tender. Sprinkle with paprika. **Yield:** 6 servings.

— ☕ ☕ ☕ —

Broccoli Tomato Salad

Garden-fresh tomatoes and broccoli brighten this summertime salad with distinctive flavor and eye-catching color. My homemade dressing mixes up in a jiffy and complements the vegetables.

✓ This tasty dish uses less sugar, salt and fat. Recipe includes *Diabetic Exchanges*.

- 1 **large bunch broccoli, separated into florets**
- 2 **large tomatoes, cut into wedges**
- 3/4 **cup sliced fresh mushrooms**
- 2 **green onions, sliced**

DRESSING:
- 3/4 **cup olive *or* vegetable oil**
- 1/3 **cup tarragon *or* cider vinegar**
- 2 **tablespoons water**
- 1 **teaspoon lemon juice**
- 1 **teaspoon sugar**
- 1 **teaspoon salt, optional**
- 3/4 **teaspoon dried thyme**
- 1 **garlic clove, minced**
- 1/2 **teaspoon celery seed**
- 1/4 **teaspoon Italian seasoning**
- 1/4 **teaspoon lemon-pepper seasoning**
- 1/4 **teaspoon paprika**
- 1/4 **teaspoon ground mustard**

Cook broccoli in a small amount of water for 5 minutes or until crisp-tender. Rinse with cold water and drain. Place in a large bowl; add tomatoes, mushrooms and onions. Combine dressing ingredients in a jar with a tight-fitting lid; shake well. Pour over salad; toss gently. Cover and chill for 1 hour. Serve with a slotted spoon. **Yield:** 6-8 servings. **Diabetic Exchanges:** One 1-cup serving (prepared without salt) equals 2 fat, 1-1/2 vegetable; also, 130 calories, 32 mg sodium, 0 cholesterol, 8 gm carbohydrate, 3 gm protein, 11 gm fat.

Zucchini Cake

What gardener doesn't have extra zucchini? When it's abundant, I shred and freeze plenty so I have it on hand to bake this moist sheet cake all year long. The cream cheese frosting is yummy, and the big panful always goes fast.

- 2-1/2 **cups all-purpose flour**
- 2 **cups sugar**
- 1-1/2 **teaspoons ground cinnamon**
- 1 **teaspoon salt**
- 1/2 **teaspoon baking powder**
- 1/2 **teaspoon baking soda**
- 1 **cup vegetable oil**
- 4 **eggs**
- 2 **cups shredded zucchini**
- 1/2 **cup chopped walnuts, optional**

FROSTING:
- 1 **package (3 ounces) cream cheese, softened**
- 1/4 **cup butter *or* margarine, softened**
- 1 **tablespoon milk**
- 1 **teaspoon vanilla extract**
- 2 **cups confectioners' sugar**

Additional chopped walnuts, optional

In a mixing bowl, combine flour, sugar, cinnamon, salt, baking powder and baking soda. Combine oil and eggs; add to dry ingredients and mix well. Add zucchini; stir until thoroughly combined. Fold in walnuts if desired. Pour into a greased 13-in. x 9-in. x 2-in. baking pan. Bake at 350° for 35-40 minutes or until a toothpick inserted near the center comes out clean. Cool. For frosting, in a small mixing bowl, beat cream cheese, butter, milk and vanilla until smooth. Add confectioners' sugar and mix well. Frost cake. Sprinkle with nuts if desired. Store in the refrigerator. **Yield:** 20-24 servings.

This proud Pilgrim descendant freshens family's traditional Thanksgiving feast by adding a bit of this and that.

By Keri Scofield Lawson, Fullerton, California

THANKSGIVING is my favorite holiday because I am related to five famous Pilgrims who came over to Plymouth, Massachusetts on the *Mayflower*!

This rich heritage colors every aspect of planning and preparation for our holiday dinner. I make the meal using foods that combine tradition with a twist for personal taste.

My Turkey with Sausage-Pecan Stuffing is always "gobbled up" quickly. I came up with the stuffing several years ago. Starting out with a box of herb stuffing mix, I'd thrown in a bit of this and that—pork sausage, plump golden raisins and some pecans from our backyard tree. When everyone raved that it was fabulous, I quickly wrote down the recipe.

Complementing our turkey, Apple-Cran-Pear Sauce evolved because I find cranberries alone a bit tart.

My father particularly loves Creamy Herbed Vegetables. I begin with a basic white sauce or "roux", then add seasonings and vegetables.

To Grandmother's and Mom's basic recipe for Sweet Potato Casserole, I put in more cinnamon and spices, plus maple syrup, brown sugar and dried apricots. It just wouldn't be Thanksgiving without it.

Desserts are the crowning glory of our feast. Along with serving the pumpkin and mince pies, I surprised everyone a few years ago with Chocolate Truffle Pie. By popular demand, it, too, has become an annual treat.

There is no other day on our calendar like Thanksgiving just to celebrate being together with our families, loved ones and friends.

In my Pilgrim ancestors' spirit, we continue to celebrate the many blessings of our rich land, its bountiful harvests, our dear families and precious freedoms.

🍴 🍴 🍴

PICTURED AT LEFT: Turkey with Sausage-Pecan Stuffing, Creamy Herbed Vegetables, Apple-Cran-Pear Sauce, Sweet Potato Casserole and Chocolate Truffle Pie (recipes are on the next page).

Turkey with Sausage-Pecan Stuffing

The combination of sweet, savory, crunchy and spicy ingredients makes a fabulous turkey stuffing that's become a tradition at our Thanksgiving dinner. Left-over stuffing could be a meal in itself.

- 4 medium onions
- 1 pound bulk pork sausage
- 2 packages (6 ounces *each*) herb stuffing mix
- 1 package (15 ounces) golden raisins
- 1 cup pecan halves
- 6 celery ribs, diced
- 1/4 teaspoon *each* dried basil, oregano, curry powder, caraway seeds, poultry seasoning, garlic powder, salt and pepper
- 2-1/2 cups chicken broth
- 1 turkey (12 to 14 pounds)

Melted shortening

Slice two of the onions; set aside. Chop the remaining onions. In a large skillet, brown sausage and chopped onions. Add herb packet from stuffing mixes. Stir in raisins, pecans, celery and seasonings; simmer for 10 minutes. Add stuffing mixes and broth; mix well. Cook and stir for about 5 minutes. Place reserved onions inside turkey. Add 6-7 cups stuffing. (Place remaining stuffing in a greased 1-1/2-qt. baking dish; refrigerate.) Skewer openings; tie drumsticks together. Place on a rack in a roasting pan. Bake, uncovered, at 325° for 4 to 4-1/2 hours or until a meat thermometer reads 185°, basting often with shortening. (Cover and bake reserved stuffing for 1 hour; uncover and bake 10 minutes more.) When the turkey begins to brown, baste if needed and cover lightly with foil. **Yield:** 12-14 servings (12 cups stuffing). **Editor's Note:**

Stuffing may be prepared as directed and baked separately in a 3-qt. baking dish. Cover and bake at 325° for 1 hour; uncover and bake 10 minutes longer or until lightly browned.

Creamy Herbed Vegetables

We pass this dish to Dad first, since he likes the herbed cream sauce so much. He rates it tops among all the "trimmings" served for the turkey dinner when our gang of more than 20 gathers to celebrate.

- 1/4 cup butter *or* margarine
- 1/4 cup all-purpose flour
- 2 cups half-and-half cream
- 1/4 cup chicken broth
- 1/2 teaspoon *each* rubbed sage, dried thyme, parsley flakes, garlic powder, salt and pepper
- 1/2 teaspoon dried rosemary, crushed
- 1 jar (16 ounces) pearl onions, drained
- 1 package (16 ounces) frozen peas
- 1 package (14 ounces) frozen baby carrots

Melt butter in a large saucepan; stir in flour until smooth. Gradually add cream, broth and seasonings. Bring to a boil, stirring constantly until thickened and bubbly. Add onions, peas and carrots. Cover and simmer for 30 minutes, stirring occasionally. **Yield:** 12-14 servings.

— ▼ ▼ ▼ —

Apple-Cran-Pear Sauce

(Pictured on page 234)

This pretty pink sauce is a nice change from typical cranberry relish. Apple pie filling and canned pears add just the right amount of sweetness.

2 packages (12 ounces *each*) fresh *or* frozen
   cranberries
2 quarts water
1 can (21 ounces) apple pie filling
2 cans (15-1/4 ounces *each*) sliced pears,
   drained
1/2 cup sugar
1/2 cup unsweetened applesauce
1 tablespoon butter *or* margarine
1 tablespoon grated lemon peel

In a large saucepan, cook cranberries and water
over medium-high heat until berries pop, about 10
minutes, stirring occasionally. Drain. Add remaining ingredients. Cook, uncovered, over medium
heat until the mixture boils. Reduce heat; cover
and simmer for 30 minutes, stirring occasionally.
Serve warm or cold. **Yield:** 12-14 servings.

Sweet Potato Casserole

*It wouldn't be Thanksgiving without that versatile root
vegetable—the sweet potato. Building on traditional
recipes used by my mother and grandmother, I've
added maple syrup, brown sugar, dried apricots and
more spices to update this holiday casserole.*

1 can (2 pounds 8 ounces) cut sweet
   potatoes, drained
1 can (8 ounces) crushed pineapple, drained
1/2 cup maple syrup
1/2 cup pecan halves
1/4 cup sliced dried apricots
1/4 cup packed brown sugar
1 tablespoon butter *or* margarine, melted
1 teaspoon ground cinnamon
1 teaspoon pumpkin pie spice
1/4 teaspoon salt

Place sweet potatoes in an ungreased 1-1/2-qt. baking dish. Combine remaining ingredients; pour over
potatoes. Bake, uncovered, at 350° for 45 minutes
or until heated through. **Yield:** 8-10 servings.

Chocolate Truffle Pie

*I discovered a fast recipe for a delectable chocolate
mousse some years ago and thought it might make a
good filling for a pie. Chocolate lovers in our family
endorse this delectable dessert, saying it "melts in
your mouth"!*

2 cups (12 ounces) semisweet chocolate
   chips
1-1/2 cups whipping cream, *divided*
1/4 cup confectioners' sugar
1 tablespoon vanilla extract
1 chocolate cookie crust (8 *or* 9 inches)
Whipped cream and chocolate-covered
   peppermint candies, optional

In a microwave-safe dish, combine chocolate chips
and 1/2 cup cream; cook on high for 1-2 minutes,
stirring every 30 seconds until smooth. Cool to
room temperature. Stir in sugar and vanilla; set
aside. In a small mixing bowl, beat remaining
cream until soft peaks form. Beat in chocolate mixture on high, one-third at a time; mix well. Spoon
into crust. Refrigerate for at least 3 hours. Garnish
with whipped cream and candies if desired. **Yield:**
8-10 servings.

Meals in Minutes

Mix and match these recipes to make countless meals that go from start to finish in less than 30 minutes.

TIMELESS TREASURES. Clockwise from upper left: Classic Comfort Foods (p. 250), Chicken Dinner (p. 242), Hearty Sandwich Supper (p. 248) and Simple Stir-Fry (p. 244).

Round up the Family For Ham Rolls!

AFTER SPENDING hours in the kitchen baking holiday breads, muffins and fruitcakes, you deserve to give yourself a precious present...time to relax!

So when your family starts calling for dinner, reach for the complete-meal menu featured here. It's made up of favorite recipes shared by three great cooks and combined in our test kitchen.

Best of all, you can have everything ready to serve in only half an hour. The fabulous flavor will be just the nourishment you need before heading back to the kitchen for the next marathon session of baking!

Apricot Ham Rolls, from Carolyn Hannay of Antioch, Tennessee, are both speedy and special. "This is the kind of hearty dish we 10 kids would devour after doing chores on our parents' farm," Carolyn recalls. "Mom always had lots of hungry mouths to appreciate her good food. When I'm short on cooking time, I rely on this tasty recipe."

Broccoli Stir-Fry is a great way to dress up a nutritious vegetable. Reports Susan Davis of Vernon Hills, Illinois, "As a wife and mother who also works full-time, I'm pleased to pass along this easy recipe to other busy cooks. Broccoli stir-fried with lemon pepper makes a mouth-watering side dish."

Microwave Cherry Crisp uses a time-saving method to produce a treat with old-fashioned flavor, says Debra Morello of Edwards, California. She assures, "It tastes just like the old-time 'crisp' with half the fuss and mess. For a little variety, you can substitute other fruit pie fillings—including apple, blueberry and peach —for the cherry pie filling."

Apricot Ham Rolls

1-2/3 cups apricot nectar, *divided*
   1 tablespoon Dijon mustard
1/2 teaspoon salt
   1 cup uncooked instant rice
   2 tablespoons minced fresh parsley
   8 thin slices fully cooked ham
   2 tablespoons maple syrup

In a saucepan over medium heat, combine 1-1/3 cups apricot nectar, mustard and salt; bring to a boil. Stir in rice. Remove from the heat; cover and let stand for 6-8 minutes or until the liquid is absorbed. Add parsley and fluff with fork. Place about 1/4 cup of rice mixture on each slice of ham. Overlap two opposite corners of ham over rice mixture; secure with a toothpick. In a large skillet over medium-high heat, combine syrup and remaining nectar; bring to a boil. Add ham rolls; reduce heat. Cover and simmer for about 5 minutes or until heated through, basting occasionally with the sauce. Remove the toothpicks before serving. **Yield:** 4 servings.

Broccoli Stir-Fry

   3 cups fresh broccoli florets
1/4 cup butter *or* margarine
1-1/2 teaspoons lemon-pepper seasoning

In a skillet over medium-high heat, stir-fry broccoli in butter and lemon pepper until crisp-tender, about 2-3 minutes. **Yield:** 4 servings.

Microwave Cherry Crisp

   1 can (21 ounces) cherry pie filling
3/4 cup packed brown sugar
2/3 cup quick-cooking oats
1/3 cup all-purpose flour
1/4 cup cold butter *or* margarine
Vanilla ice cream, optional

Spoon pie filling into a greased 9-in. pie plate. In a bowl, combine brown sugar, oats and flour; cut in butter until crumbly. Sprinkle over filling. Microwave on high for 12-14 minutes. Serve warm with ice cream if desired. **Yield:** 4-6 servings.

Selecting and Storing Broccoli

When purchasing fresh broccoli, look for firm stalks with a deep green color and heads that are tightly packed. Stalks with wilted leaves and florets that are light green or yellow are past their prime. Fresh broccoli can be stored in a plastic bag in the refrigerator for up to 4 days. To store broccoli longer, blanche it and freeze for up to 1 year.

Folks Will Have Fun Dipping into Chicken Dinner

IF CABIN FEVER has struck at your house, invite friends over for a spur-of-the moment gathering. You can plan the party in short order with "fast foods".

The complete-meal menu here from three everyday cooks can be ready to serve in just 30 minutes.

Oven Chicken Fingers are tender, golden strips of breaded chicken with two tempting sauces for dipping. The recipe comes from Mary Peterson of Charlestown, Rhode Island.

Broccoli Noodle Side Dish is colorful and satisfying, relates Louise Saluti of Sandwich, Massachusetts.

Raspberry Mallow Pie is a delightful way to end a quick-to-fix meal. The recipe is shared by Judie Anglen of Riverton, Wyoming.

— ♟ ♟ ♟ —

Oven Chicken Fingers

  1 cup Italian bread crumbs
  2 tablespoons grated Parmesan cheese
  1 garlic clove, minced
1/4 cup vegetable oil
  6 boneless skinless chicken breast halves
CRANBERRY ORANGE SAUCE:
1/4 cup sugar
  2 teaspoons cornstarch
1/2 cup fresh *or* frozen cranberries
1/2 cup orange juice
1/4 cup water
HONEY MUSTARD SAUCE:
  2 tablespoons cornstarch
  1 cup water, *divided*
1/2 cup honey
1/4 cup prepared mustard

In a large resealable plastic bag, combine bread crumbs and Parmesan cheese; set aside. In a small bowl, combine garlic and oil. Flatten the chicken to 1/2-in. thickness; cut into 1-in.-wide strips. Dip strips in oil; place in bag with crumb mixture and toss to coat. Place on a greased baking sheet. Bake at 350° for 20 minutes or until golden brown. Meanwhile, combine the sugar and cornstarch in a saucepan. Add cranberries, orange juice and water; bring to a boil over medium heat, stirring constantly. Cook 2-3 minutes more, stirring to crush the berries. For honey mustard sauce, dissolve cornstarch in 1 tablespoon water in a saucepan. Add honey, mustard and remaining water; bring to a boil over medium heat. Boil for 1 minute, stirring constantly. Serve sauces with chicken for dipping. **Yield:** 6 servings.

— ♟ ♟ ♟ —

Broccoli Noodle Side Dish

✓ This tasty dish uses less sugar, salt and fat. Recipe includes *Diabetic Exchanges.*

  6 cups (8 ounces) uncooked wide noodles
  3 to 4 garlic cloves, minced
1/4 cup olive *or* vegetable oil
  4 cups broccoli florets (about 1 pound)
1/2 pound fresh mushrooms, thinly sliced
1/2 teaspoon dried thyme
1/4 teaspoon pepper
  1 teaspoon salt, optional

Cook the noodles according to package directions. Meanwhile, in a skillet, saute garlic in oil until tender. Add broccoli; saute for 4 minutes or until crisp-tender. Add mushrooms, thyme, pepper and salt if desired; saute for 2-3 minutes. Drain noodles and add to broccoli mixture. Stir gently over low heat until heated through. **Yield:** 8 servings. **Diabetic Exchanges:** One 1-cup serving (prepared without salt) equals 1-1/2 fat, 1 starch, 1 vegetable; also, 167 calories, 12 mg sodium, 23 mg cholesterol, 20 gm carbohydrate, 5 gm protein, 8 gm fat.

— ♟ ♟ ♟ —

Raspberry Mallow Pie

 35 large marshmallows
1/2 cup milk
  1 package (10 ounces) sweetened frozen raspberries, undrained
  1 carton (8 ounces) frozen whipped topping, thawed
  1 graham cracker crust (9 inches)

In a large microwave-safe bowl, combine marshmallows and milk. Cook on high for 1-2 minutes; stir until smooth. Stir in raspberries. Fold in the whipped topping. Pour into crust. Refrigerate or freeze. **Yield:** 6-8 servings. **Editor's Note:** This recipe was tested in a 700-watt microwave.

Stir-Fry Is Simple Way To Serve Supper

AFTER SPRING has "sprung" where you live, you can't wait to start enjoying the flavors of the season. There's no better way to do that than by serving foods that feature plenty of refreshing, colorful produce.

Here three country cooks share family-favorite recipes for delightful dishes showcasing peppers, peas and pineapple! Together, these foods create a complete-meal menu that goes from start to serving in 30 minutes or less.

With peppers, onion and celery, Curried Beef Stir-Fry is a flavorful eye-catching entree. "I created this hearty recipe myself and prepare it often when time is short," informs Karen Munn from St. Francois Xavier, Manitoba.

Dilly Pea Salad dresses up peas in a deliciously different way. "I got the recipe for this refreshing salad from my best friend when I was a young bride," relates Rita Applegate of La Mesa, California. "I've shared it with many people over the years."

Broiled Pineapple Dessert is a sweet and tangy treat that looks impressive but is very little fuss, assures Karen Owen of Rising Sun, Indiana. "Family and friends frequently request seconds of this fruity dessert."

— 🍶 🍶 🍶 —

Curried Beef Stir-Fry

3 tablespoons soy sauce
3 garlic cloves, minced
1 tablespoon minced fresh gingerroot *or* 1 teaspoon ground ginger
4 tablespoons vegetable oil, *divided*
1 pound boneless sirloin steak, cut into 1/8-inch strips
1 large onion, cut into 1-inch pieces
1 medium green pepper, cut into 1-inch pieces
1 medium sweet red pepper, cut into 1-inch pieces
2 large celery ribs, sliced
1 cup cold water
5 teaspoons cornstarch
1 to 2 teaspoons curry powder
Hot cooked rice *or* noodles

In a bowl, combine soy sauce, garlic, ginger and 2 tablespoons oil. Add beef; toss to coat. Cover and refrigerate for 15-20 minutes. In a large skillet or wok, heat remaining oil. Stir-fry beef over medium-high heat for 2-3 minutes. Remove beef and set aside. In the same skillet, stir-fry onion for 1 minute; add peppers and celery. Stir-fry for 2 minutes; return beef to the skillet. Combine water, cornstarch and curry until smooth; add to skillet. Bring to a boil and boil for 1 minute, stirring constantly. Serve over rice or noodles. **Yield:** 4 servings.

— 🍶 🍶 🍶 —

Dilly Pea Salad

✓ This tasty dish uses less sugar, salt and fat. Recipe includes *Diabetic Exchanges*.

1 cup (8 ounces) sour cream
4 teaspoons lemon juice
4 teaspoons sliced green onion
2 teaspoons sugar
1 teaspoon dill weed
1/2 teaspoon curry powder
1/2 teaspoon salt, optional
1/4 teaspoon pepper
2 packages (10 ounces *each*) frozen peas, thawed

In a medium bowl, combine the first eight ingredients. Add peas; toss. Chill until ready to serve. **Yield:** 6 servings. **Diabetic Exchanges:** One 1/2-cup serving (prepared with nonfat sour cream and without salt) equals 1-1/2 starch; also, 123 calories, 111 mg sodium, 3 mg cholesterol, 23 gm carbohydrate, 7 gm protein, trace fat.

— 🍶 🍶 🍶 —

Broiled Pineapple Dessert

4 pineapple slices
8 teaspoons brown sugar
2 tablespoons butter *or* margarine
4 slices pound cake
4 scoops vanilla ice cream
Ground cinnamon

Place pineapple slices on a broiler pan. Top each with 2 teaspoons brown sugar and 1-1/2 teaspoons butter. Broil 4 in. from the heat for 3-5 minutes or until the sugar is bubbly. Place each slice on a piece of pound cake; top with ice cream and sprinkle with cinnamon. Serve immediately. **Yield:** 4 servings.

Quick Cooking Will Keep Your Summer Kitchen Cool

EVEN FOLKS who love to cook may want to spend less time in the kitchen on warm, sunny days. Since fresh air builds appetites, a fast-to-fix, nutritious meal is especially appropriate.

The complete-meal menu here is made up of favorites from three great cooks and combined in our test kitchen. You can have everything ready to serve in just half an hour!

Meat Loaf Hamburgers are tender mellow-tasting burgers everyone will enjoy, assures Sandi Pichon of Slidell, Louisiana. "They're a nice alternative to plain ground beef patties and very popular whenever I serve them," she says.

Microwave German Potato Salad has big flavor for a quick salad. "The first time I tried this easy side dish I was so impressed I had to have the recipe," recalls Barbara Erdmann of West Allis, Wisconsin. "That's what happens to most people who taste it. It's a time-saver when I need a salad for a get-together."

Fruit-Topped Almond Cream is a light and refreshing dessert. The recipe comes from Donna Friedrich of Fishkill, New York. "It's delicious with berries, but it can be made all year using whatever fruit is available," Donna informs.

— 🦪 🦪 🦪 —

Meat Loaf Hamburgers

1-1/2 pounds ground beef
1 cup (8 ounces) sour cream
1-1/4 cups crushed cornflakes
1 tablespoon diced onion
1/2 to 1 teaspoon salt
1/8 teaspoon pepper
8 kaiser _or_ hamburger buns, split
Lettuce leaves
Tomato slices

In a large bowl, gently mix the first six ingredients; shape into eight patties. Grill, broil or pan-fry until the meat is no longer pink. Serve on buns with lettuce and tomato. **Yield:** 8 servings.

Hamburger Helper

Don't press hamburger patties with a spatula or other utensil while pan-frying them—this squeezes out the meat's flavorful juices.

— 🦪 🦪 🦪 —

Microwave German Potato Salad

2 pounds red potatoes, cooked and sliced
3 hard-cooked eggs, chopped
1/2 cup chopped onion
1/2 cup chopped celery
6 bacon strips, diced
2 tablespoons sugar
4 teaspoons all-purpose flour
2 tablespoons vinegar
1/2 teaspoon salt
1/8 teaspoon pepper
3/4 cup milk

In a large bowl, combine potatoes, eggs, onion and celery; set aside. Place the bacon in a microwave-safe bowl; cover with a paper towel and microwave on high for 2 minutes. Stir. Microwave 3-4 minutes longer or until the bacon is crisp, stirring after each minute. Remove bacon to paper towel to drain; reserve 2 tablespoons drippings. Stir sugar, flour, vinegar, salt and pepper into drippings until smooth; gradually add milk. Microwave on high for 5-6 minutes, stirring every 2 minutes, or until thickened. Pour over potato mixture; toss. Top with bacon. Serve immediately. **Yield:** 8 servings. **Editor's Note:** This recipe was tested in a 700-watt microwave.

— 🦪 🦪 🦪 —

Fruit-Topped Almond Cream

1 package (3.4 ounces) instant French vanilla pudding mix
2-1/2 cups cold milk
1 cup whipping cream
1/2 to 3/4 teaspoon almond extract
3 cups assorted fruit (strawberries, grapes, raspberries, blueberries, mandarin oranges)

In a large mixing bowl, combine pudding mix and milk. Beat on low speed for 2 minutes; set aside. In a small mixing bowl, beat cream and extract until stiff peaks form. Fold into the pudding. Spoon into a shallow 2-qt. serving dish. Chill. Top with fruit just before serving. **Yield:** 8 servings.

Hearty Sandwiches Are Sure to Please!

WHETHER you're working in the garden or relaxing in the shade, nice weather tempts even avid cooks to spend more time outdoors and less in the kitchen.

Fresh air builds appetites, so you'll surely need a fast-to-fix, nutritious meal that satisfies.

With the complete-meal menu here, you can sit down to eat in about 30 minutes!

"Honey-Mustard Chicken Sandwiches are home-made 'fast food' that's more delicious than the kind you go out to pick up," assures Christina Levrant of Bensalem, Pennsylvania. The special sauce has just the right amount of sweetness and tang.

Black 'n' White Bean Salad is a cool, hearty side dish Kay Ogden created after tasting a similar one in a restaurant. "It goes together in no time and complements most entrees," she reports from Grants Pass, Oregon.

Quick Banana Splits are a simple but special way to serve ice cream. The recipe comes from Doreen Stein of Ignace, Ontario.

— 🍶 🍶 🍶 —

Honey-Mustard Chicken Sandwiches

✓ This tasty dish uses less sugar, salt and fat. Recipe includes *Diabetic Exchanges.*

1/4 cup Dijon mustard
2 tablespoons honey
1 teaspoon dried oregano
1 teaspoon water
1/4 teaspoon garlic powder
1/8 to 1/4 teaspoon cayenne pepper
4 boneless skinless chicken breast halves (1 pound)
4 sandwich buns, split
8 thin tomato slices
1 cup shredded lettuce

In a bowl, combine the first six ingredients. Broil chicken 4 in. from the heat for 3 minutes on each side. Brush with mustard sauce. Broil 4-6 minutes longer or until juices run clear, basting and turning several times. Serve on buns with tomato and lettuce. **Yield:** 4 servings. **Diabetic Exchanges:** One serving (calculated without bun) equals 3 very lean meat, 1 starch; also, 185 calories, 438 mg sodium, 63 mg cholesterol, 13 gm carbohydrate, 24 gm protein, 4 gm fat.

Black 'n' White Bean Salad

✓ This tasty dish uses less sugar, salt and fat. Recipe includes *Diabetic Exchanges.*

1 can (15 ounces) black beans, rinsed and drained
1 can (15 ounces) white kidney beans, rinsed and drained
1/2 cup chopped cucumber
1/2 cup chopped sweet red pepper
1/4 cup chopped onion
1/4 cup minced fresh cilantro *or* parsley
1/3 cup cider *or* red wine vinegar
1/4 cup olive *or* vegetable oil
1/2 teaspoon salt, optional
1/4 teaspoon garlic powder
1/8 teaspoon pepper
Lettuce leaves, optional

In a large bowl, combine the first six ingredients. In a small bowl, whisk vinegar, oil and seasonings. Pour over bean mixture and toss to coat. Cover and refrigerate until serving. Using a slotted spoon, serve over lettuce if desired. **Yield:** 4-6 servings. **Diabetic Exchanges:** One 1/2-cup serving (prepared without salt) equals 1-1/2 starch, 1 vegetable, 1 fat; also, 187 calories, 219 mg sodium, 0 cholesterol, 26 gm carbohydrate, 9 gm protein, 5 gm fat.

— 🍶 🍶 🍶 —

Quick Banana Splits

2 medium bananas
1 pint vanilla ice cream
Chocolate syrup *or* ice cream topping
Chopped nuts
Maraschino cherries

Slice bananas into four dessert dishes. Top each with 1/2 cup of ice cream. Drizzle with chocolate syrup. Sprinkle with nuts; top with cherries. **Yield:** 4 servings.

Honey of a Hint

To easily remove honey from a measuring spoon, first coat the spoon with nonstick cooking spray.

Classic Comfort Foods Will Warm the Spirit This Fall

WHEN cooler days signal the start of the busy pre-holiday season, even dedicated cooks can't always spend as much time in the kitchen.

The fast-to-fix meal here is from three super cooks, combined in our test kitchen. You can have everything ready to serve in just 30 minutes!

Tangy Beef Stroganoff, from Rita Farmer of Houston, Texas, is a rich, comforting main dish that tastes like you were in the kitchen all day.

"Now that I'm retired, I'm busy taking computer classes and helping out at church," relates Rita. "When I want to treat my daughter and her family to a meal, this dish is quick and delicious."

Crumb-Topped Brussels Sprouts get a tasty Parmesan cheese topping in the recipe sent by Ruth Peterson of Jenison, Michigan.

Says Mary Brenneman of Tavistock, Ontario, "Microwave Chocolate Cake is a wonderfully versatile cake I've made many times."

— 🥄 🥄 🥄 —

Tangy Beef Stroganoff

       1 pound sirloin steak
     1/4 cup butter *or* margarine
       8 ounces fresh mushrooms, sliced
     1/2 cup sliced onion
       1 garlic clove, minced
       2 tablespoons all-purpose flour
       1 cup water
       1 tablespoon lemon juice
       1 tablespoon cider *or* red wine vinegar
       2 teaspoons beef bouillon granules
     1/2 teaspoon salt
     1/4 teaspoon pepper
       1 cup (8 ounces) sour cream
Hot cooked noodles
Chopped fresh parsley and paprika, optional

Cut beef into 1/8-in.-thick strips. In a large skillet over medium-high heat, cook beef in butter until no longer pink. Remove with a slotted spoon and keep warm. In the pan juices, cook mushrooms, onion and garlic until tender; stir in flour. Add water, lemon juice, vinegar, bouillon, salt and pepper; bring to a boil. Cook and stir for 2 minutes. Stir in sour cream and beef; heat through but do not boil. Serve over noodles. Garnish with parsley and paprika if desired. **Yield:** 4 servings.

Crumb-Topped Brussels Sprouts

1-1/2 pounds fresh *or* frozen brussels sprouts
       3 tablespoons butter *or* margarine, melted
     1/4 cup Italian-seasoned dry bread crumbs
       2 tablespoons grated Parmesan cheese

In a saucepan, cook brussels sprouts in salted water until crisp-tender, about 8-10 minutes; drain. Place in an ungreased shallow 1-1/2-qt. baking dish. Drizzle with 2 tablespoons butter. Combine remaining butter, bread crumbs and Parmesan cheese; sprinkle over brussels sprouts. Cover and bake at 325° for 10 minutes. Uncover and bake 10 minutes longer. **Yield:** 4-6 servings.

— 🥄 🥄 🥄 —

Microwave Chocolate Cake

1-1/2 cups all-purpose flour
       1 cup sugar
       3 tablespoons baking cocoa
       1 teaspoon baking soda
     1/4 teaspoon salt
       1 cup cold water
     1/3 cup vegetable oil
       1 tablespoon vinegar
       1 teaspoon vanilla extract
CHOCOLATE SAUCE:
       1 cup sugar
       3 tablespoons cornstarch
       2 tablespoons baking cocoa
       1 cup boiling water
Dash salt
       1 tablespoon butter *or* margarine
       1 teaspoon vanilla extract

In a bowl, combine the first five ingredients. Stir in water, oil, vinegar and vanilla until well blended. Pour into an ungreased 8-in. square microwave-safe dish. Microwave on high for 6-8 minutes, turning dish every 2 minutes, or until a toothpick inserted near the center comes out clean. In a 1-qt. microwave-safe bowl, combine sugar, cornstarch and cocoa. Stir in water and salt. Microwave on high for 2-3 minutes, stirring occasionally, or until mixture boils. Microwave 1 minute more. Stir in butter and vanilla. Spoon over pieces of warm cake. **Yield:** 9 servings. **Editor's Note:** This recipe was tested in a 700-watt microwave.

Enjoy Seasonal Meals in Minutes... Year-Round!

The 12 time-saving menus on the following pages were created by the Taste of Home staff with your hectic schedule in mind. These meals will keep you satisfied the whole year through.

IF YOU THINK serving a complete meal in minutes to your family means popping a frozen pizza in the oven or assembling a simple sandwich, the 12 meals (36 recipes in all) on the following pages will have you eagerly heading back to the kitchen!

Each and every recipe was created and kitchen-tested just for you by the staff of *Taste of Home*, so you can serve your family savory, well-rounded meals even on the busiest days. Each meal takes 30 minutes or less to prepare—and was planned with a specific season in mind.

Ring in the New Year with good food and cheer by presenting holiday guests "Herbed Sirloin", "Easy Au Gratin Potatoes" and "Raspberry Chocolate Trifle" (recipes on pages 254 and 255).

When you want to head outdoors for some summer fun, your picnic basket will be brimming with tender "Broiled Chicken Sandwiches", refreshing "Two-Bean Salad" and chocolaty "Rocky Road Pizza" (recipes on pages 264 and 265).

And to truly capture the fabulous flavors of fall, reach for hearty "Harvest Pork Chops", satisfying "Skillet Ranch Vegetables" and delectable "Honey-Nut Apples" (recipes on pages 272 and 273).

With the 36 mouth-watering recipes on the next few pages, the possibilities for year-round fast, flavorful foods are endless.

EACH MONTH'S COVERED in this chapter with meals that include, clockwise from upper left: Heart-Felt Favorites (pages 256 and 257), Thanksgiving Feast (pages 274 and 275), Good Morning, Sunshine! (pages 262 and 263) and Quick-and-Easy Cookout Cuisine (pages 268 and 269).

New Year Cheer

WHAT BETTER WAY to greet Father Time than with this fantastic feast? A robust mushroom-onion sauce enhances the flavor of specially seasoned Herbed Sirloin. You'll agree the cheesy Easy Au Gratin Potatoes go perfectly with all your favorite main meals. And for the time being, you'll want to toss aside those New Year resolutions and relish every bite of Raspberry Chocolate Trifle!

Herbed Sirloin

There's no reason to head outdoors to serve up sizzling steak. One skillet's all you need to brown the meat, cook the vegetables and make the accompanying marvelous mustard sauce. With such fantastic flavor, you just may prepare steak this way no matter what time of year!

1-1/2 to 2 pounds boneless top sirloin (1 inch thick)
2 tablespoons cooking oil
1 small onion, sliced
2 cups sliced fresh mushrooms
1/2 cup beef broth
2 teaspoons Dijon mustard
1 teaspoon Worcestershire sauce
1/2 teaspoon dried thyme
1/4 teaspoon garlic powder

Cut steak into four serving-size pieces; brown in a large skillet in oil for 5 minutes on each side. Add onion and mushrooms. Cook until vegetables are tender and the meat has reached desired doneness, stirring occasionally. Remove meat to a platter and keep warm. Combine the broth, mustard, Worcestershire sauce, thyme and garlic powder; stir into vegetables. Bring to a boil. Reduce heat; simmer for 2-3 minutes. Spoon over meat. **Yield:** 4 servings.

Easy Au Gratin Potatoes

One taste of this classic dish and you'll never buy a store-bought box of au gratin potatoes again! Thinly sliced "spuds" cook up tender in no time. Your family will request this recipe many times over.

3/4 cup half-and-half cream
1/2 cup milk
1/2 teaspoon salt
1/4 teaspoon garlic powder
3 medium potatoes, peeled and thinly sliced
1 cup seasoned salad croutons, *divided*
1/8 teaspoon pepper
1/2 cup shredded cheddar cheese

In a medium saucepan, bring cream, milk, salt and garlic powder to a boil. Add potatoes; reduce heat. Cover and simmer for 10-15 minutes or until the potatoes are tender. Coarsely crush 1/4 cup of croutons. Remove potatoes from the heat; stir in the crushed croutons and pepper. Pour into a greased 1-1/2-qt. baking dish. Sprinkle with the cheese and remaining croutons. Bake, uncovered, at 400° for 5-6 minutes or until the cheese is melted. **Yield:** 4 servings.

Raspberry Chocolate Trifle

"Elegant but easy" perfectly describes this rich and creamy trifle. Prepared pound cake, frozen berries and instant pudding combine to create one mouth-watering masterpiece that is great for both weekday dinners or special-occasion suppers. For a little variety, substitute angel food cake or another variety of fruit and preserves.

1 package (3.9 ounces) instant chocolate pudding mix
2 cups cold milk
1 loaf (10-3/4 ounces) frozen pound cake, thawed
2 cups fresh *or* frozen raspberries, thawed
1 cup raspberry preserves
Whipped topping
Additional raspberries, optional

Mix pudding and milk according to package directions; chill. Cut cake into 1-in. cubes; place half in a 2-qt. glass bowl. Gently stir together raspberries and preserves; spoon half over cake. Pour half of the pudding over raspberries. Cover with remaining cake cubes. Layer with remaining berries and pudding. Chill until ready to serve. Garnish with whipped topping and raspberries if desired. **Yield:** 4-6 servings.

Heart-Felt Favorites

THERE'S NO NEED to wait until Valentine's Day to shower your family with love and a breakfast that comes straight from the heart! Topped with a succulent cherry sauce, light and fluffy Sweetheart Pancakes will be gobbled up in no time. A comforting casserole like Sausage Granola Squares is guaranteed to please, while a refreshing Morning Fruit Shake blends the fantastic flavors of an assortment of tantalizing fruits. What better way to show your loved ones you care than by getting their days off to a nutritious start?

Sweetheart Pancakes

Hot-off-the-griddle goodies are always a welcome sight on the table...morning, noon and night. Instead of serving these palate-pleasing pancakes with ordinary maple syrup, make this extraordinary cherry sauce. You'll be thanked mmm-many times over!

1-3/4 cups all-purpose flour
   2 tablespoons sugar
   2 teaspoons baking powder
1/2 teaspoon salt
   2 eggs
1-1/2 cups milk
   3 tablespoons vegetable oil
1/2 teaspoon lemon juice
CHERRY SAUCE:
   1 can (21 ounces) cherry pie filling
1/2 to 3/4 teaspoon almond extract
1/8 to 1/4 teaspoon ground nutmeg
Whipped cream in a can

In a bowl, combine the flour, sugar, baking powder and salt. In another bowl, beat the eggs; add milk, oil and lemon juice. Stir into dry ingredients just until moistened. Pour batter by 1/3 cupfuls onto a lightly greased hot griddle; turn when bubbles form on top of pancakes. Cook until the second side is golden brown. For cherry sauce, combine pie filling, extract and nutmeg in a medium saucepan. Cook, stirring occasionally, until heated through. To serve as shown in the photo, stack pancakes on serving plates and make a heart outline with whipped cream; spoon cherry sauce into heart. **Yield:** 4 servings (12 pancakes).

Sausage Granola Squares

No morning meal would be complete without a meaty side dish. With a trio of ingredients, these homemade sausage squares couldn't be easier...or more down-home delicious. Plus, they're oven-baked instead of pan-fried, for less mess and greater convenience.

1/2 pound bulk pork sausage
3/4 cup granola cereal with fruit and nuts
   1 egg, lightly beaten

Combine all ingredients; pat into a greased shallow 2-cup baking dish. Bake, uncovered, at 375° for 20 minutes or until browned. **Yield:** 4 servings.

☕ ☕ ☕

Morning Fruit Shake

In addition to offering an assortment of juices and milk, why not serve this cool beverage filled with your family's favorite fruit flavors? Your thirsty clan will savor it so much, you'll be asked to make it from sunrise to sundown!

✓ This tasty dish uses less sugar, salt and fat. Recipe includes *Diabetic Exchanges*.

1 cup cranberry juice
2 medium ripe bananas, sliced
**2 cartons (8 ounces *each*) raspberry yogurt
or flavor of choice**
1 tablespoon confectioners' sugar, optional
Few drops red food coloring, optional
Mint leaves, optional

In a blender, combine all ingredients; blend at medium speed until smooth. Garnish with mint if desired. Serve immediately. **Yield:** 4 servings. **Diabetic Exchanges:** One 3/4-cup serving (prepared with sugar-free raspberry yogurt and without confectioners' sugar) equals 1 fruit, 1 skim milk; also, 138 calories, 64 mg sodium, 0 cholesterol, 30 gm carbohydrate, 6 gm protein, trace fat.

Springtime Sensations

CELEBRATE SPRING with family and friends by serving this formal no-fuss dinner. Mustard Pork Medallions pop in the oven for a main dish in a flash. Dilly Asparagus, delicately topped with an easy-to-prepare cream cheese sauce, and your favorite dinner rolls make outstanding additions. For a fantastic finale, Rhubarb Sundaes are simply delicious.

— 🥄 🥄 🥄 —

Mustard Pork Medallions

Your famished family will be thrilled when you call them to the dinner table with the irresistible aroma of these tasty pork medallions. Brushing the pork with mustard and coating it with seasoned dry bread crumbs before you bake it make the meat tender and juicy every time.

✓ This tasty dish uses less sugar, salt and fat. Recipe includes *Diabetic Exchanges.*

- **1/2 cup seasoned dry bread crumbs**
- **1/2 teaspoon dried thyme**
- **1/4 teaspoon garlic salt**
- **1/4 teaspoon onion powder**
- **1-1/4 pounds pork tenderloin**
- **1/4 cup Dijon mustard**
- **1 tablespoon butter *or* margarine, melted**

In a shallow bowl, combine the crumbs, thyme, garlic salt and onion powder; set aside. Cut tenderloin crosswise into 12 pieces and pound each piece to 1/4-in. thickness. Combine mustard and butter; brush on each side of pork, then coat with reserved crumb mixture. Place in a greased shallow baking pan. Bake, uncovered, at 425° for 10 minutes; turn and bake about 5 minutes more or until no longer pink. **Yield:** 4 servings. **Diabetic Exchanges:** One serving (prepared with margarine) equals 3 lean meat, 1 starch, 1/2 fat; also, 254 calories, 855 mg sodium, 53 mg cholesterol, 15 gm carbohydrate, 25 gm protein, 11 gm fat.

— 🥄 🥄 🥄 —

Dilly Asparagus

A sure sign of spring is a fresh crop of young asparagus. And this recipe superbly ushers in this wonderful

season. A delicate cheese sauce nicely complements tender stalks without being overwhelming.

- **1 cup water**
- **1/4 teaspoon salt**
- **1 pound fresh asparagus, trimmed**
- **1 package (3 ounces) cream cheese**
- **1/2 cup milk**
- **1/4 teaspoon dill weed**
- **1/8 teaspoon garlic salt**
- **1/8 teaspoon pepper**

In a large skillet, bring water and salt to a boil; add the asparagus. Cover and cook over medium heat until crisp-tender, about 6-8 minutes; drain.

Transfer to a serving platter and keep warm. In the same skillet over low heat, stir cream cheese and milk until smooth. Stir in dill, garlic salt and pepper. Pour over asparagus. **Yield:** 4 servings.

— 🍶 🍶 🍶 —

Rhubarb Sundaes

After one taste, your family will agree rhubarb never tasted so good! The sweet sauce will disappear so fast when you serve it over ice cream that you might want to keep some on hand to serve over pancakes, waffles...even French toast.

> **2 cups chopped fresh *or* frozen rhubarb**
> **1/4 cup water**
> **1/3 cup sugar**
> **1/4 teaspoon ground cinnamon**
> **1/2 teaspoon honey**
> **Vanilla ice cream**
> **Chopped walnuts, optional**

In a saucepan, bring rhubarb, water, sugar and cinnamon to a boil. Reduce heat; simmer, uncovered, for 8-10 minutes or until rhubarb is tender and the sauce has reached desired consistency. Remove from the heat; stir in honey. Serve warm over ice cream. Sprinkle with nuts if desired. **Yield:** 4 servings (1 cup sauce).

Rainy-Day Dinner

IF APRIL SHOWERS won't go away and you're stuck inside the house all day, treat your restless family to this one-of-a-kind menu that you can take from start to finish at a moment's notice. Folks will surely fall for flaky Oven-Fried Fish…hook, line and sinker! Lemon Rice adds a subtle citrus taste to the table, and creative Raspberry Almond Rounds dress up refrigerated biscuit dough in a snap.

— 🍴 🍴 🍴 —

Oven-Fried Fish

When you're looking for a fast, flavorful meal, look no further than fish! Parmesan cheese and special seasonings add a bit of Italian flair to these fillets. Not only is this recipe low in fat, it's delicious as well. So it's sure to please everyone in the family.

✓ This tasty dish uses less sugar, salt and fat. Recipe includes *Diabetic Exchanges.*

1-1/2 **pounds frozen cod** *or* **haddock fillets, thawed**
   2 **tablespoons butter** *or* **margarine, melted**
 1/2 **cup crushed wheat crackers** *or* **seasoned dry bread crumbs**
   2 **tablespoons grated Parmesan cheese**
   1 **tablespoon dried parsley flakes**
 1/2 **teaspoon Italian seasoning**

Cut fish into serving-size pieces; place in a greased 13-in. x 9-in. x 2-in. baking dish. Brush with butter. Combine the remaining ingredients; sprinkle over fish. Bake, uncovered, at 425° for 10-15 minutes or until the fish flakes easily with a fork. **Yield:** 4 servings. **Diabetic Exchanges:** One serving (prepared with margarine and bread crumbs) equals 4 very lean meat, 1 starch, 1 fat; also, 261 calories, 753 mg sodium, 78 mg cholesterol, 15 gm carbohydrate, 30 gm protein, 9 gm fat.

— 🍴 🍴 🍴 —

Lemon Rice

This easy recipe pleasantly proves you can dress up regular rice with a few simple additions. Best of all, it can simmer while you're preparing the rest of the meal. These delicately lemon-flavored grains go nicely with fish.

   1 **cup water**
   1 **cup chicken broth**
   2 **tablespoons lemon juice**
   2 **teaspoons butter** *or* **margarine**
   1 **cup uncooked long grain rice**
 1/4 **teaspoon dried basil**
 1/8 **to 1/4 teaspoon grated lemon peel**
 1/4 **teaspoon lemon-pepper seasoning**

In a medium saucepan, bring water, broth, lemon juice and butter to a boil. Stir in the rice, basil and lemon peel. Reduce heat; cover and simmer for 20 minutes. Let stand 5 minutes or until the water is

absorbed. Before serving, sprinkle with lemon pepper. **Yield:** 4 servings.

⚡ ⚡ ⚡

Raspberry Almond Rounds

Folks will find these nutty raspberry rounds so enticing you may not want to divulge that the "secret" to their success begins with refrigerated biscuit dough! These sweet treats bake up in a hurry, so they're great to serve when unexpected company drops in.

2 tablespoons butter *or* margarine, melted

1 tube (7-1/2 ounces) refrigerated buttermilk
   biscuits, separated into 10 biscuits
2 tablespoons sugar
1/4 cup raspberry preserves
2 tablespoons slivered almonds

Brush butter on both sides of biscuits. Place on a greased baking sheet or in a greased 9-in. round baking pan; sprinkle with sugar. Make an indentation in the center of each biscuit; fill with 1 teaspoon preserves. Sprinkle almonds on top. Bake at 425° for 9-11 minutes or until golden brown. **Yield:** 4-6 servings.

Good Morning, Sunshine!

SET A PRETTY TABLE and present your family with some tasty down-home cooking. It's guaranteed to make an ordinary day extra-special. Served beside a fresh fruit garnish, Calico Scrambled Eggs satisfy any hungry appetite. And fun-filled Sausage Breadsticks will appeal to kids of all ages. For a unique dessert, impress breakfast guests with easy Tropical Banana Compote...they'll certainly savor the old-fashioned flavor.

— 🍴 🍴 🍴 —

Calico Scrambled Eggs

When you're short on time and scrambling to get a meal on the table, this recipe is "eggs-actly" what you need. There's a short ingredient list, and cooking is kept to a minimum. Plus, with green pepper and tomato, it's colorful.

    1/2 cup chopped green pepper
    1/4 cup chopped onion
      1 tablespoon butter *or* margarine
      8 eggs
    1/4 cup milk
    1/8 to 1/4 teaspoon dill weed
    1/8 to 1/4 teaspoon salt
    1/8 to 1/4 teaspoon pepper
    1/2 cup chopped fresh tomato

In a 12-in. nonstick skillet, saute green pepper and onion in butter until tender. Remove and set aside. In a medium bowl, beat eggs with milk, dill, salt and pepper. Pour into the skillet; cook and stir gently over medium heat until eggs are nearly set. Add pepper mixture and tomato; cook and stir until heated through and the eggs are completely set. **Yield:** 4 servings.

— 🍴 🍴 🍴 —

Sausage Breadsticks

Bring out the kid in everyone by preparing pigs-in-a-blanket with sausage links and refrigerated breadsticks. This fun and festive finger food is a unique addition to a breakfast buffet. Or make a heaping plateful for a snack.

      1 tube (11 ounces) refrigerated
        breadstick dough
      8 smoked sausage links *or* hot dogs

Separate the dough into eight strips; unroll and wrap one strip around each sausage. Place on an ungreased baking sheet. Bake at 350° for 15-17 minutes or until golden brown. Serve warm. **Yield:** 4 servings. **Editor's Note:** You may use refrigerated crescent rolls in place of the breadsticks. Just roll up a sausage in each triangle and follow the package directions for baking temperature and time.

Tropical Banana Compote

Don't limit your use of bananas to the cereal bowl. Instead, send your family's taste buds on a "trip" to the tropics with this special speedy dessert. Bananas are available in every season...so this is bound to become a favorite all year-round.

3 medium firm bananas
1/4 cup orange juice
2 tablespoons butter *or* margarine
3 tablespoons brown sugar
2 tablespoons flaked coconut, toasted
Maraschino cherries *or* strawberries, optional

Cut bananas in half lengthwise, then cut crosswise into quarters. Arrange in a greased 11-in. x 7-in. x 2-in. baking dish. In a saucepan, combine orange juice, butter and brown sugar; cook and stir until sugar is dissolved and butter is melted. Pour over the bananas. Bake, uncovered, at 350° for 10-12 minutes. Spoon into individual serving dishes; sprinkle with coconut. Garnish with cherries or strawberries if desired. **Yield:** 4 servings.

Exciting Outdoor Eating

IT'S TIME to invite family and friends to a potluck in the park. And don't forget the picnic basket brimming with summertime treats! A platterful of tender Broiled Chicken Sandwiches is a great way to greet your hungry guests. For a cool complement to the meal, dish up some extraordinary Two-Bean Salad. Then add a new twist to traditional dessert with melt-in-your-mouth Rocky Road Pizza. With great food and good company, everyone will be sad to see the day come to an end. But you can always plan a repeat performance next weekend!

Broiled Chicken Sandwiches

No one will be able to resist these sandwiches, with tender chicken strips tucked into a lightly toasted bun. And in place of traditional mayonnaise or mustard, it features a creamy herbed cheese spread.

- 1 **package (3 ounces) cream cheese, softened**
- 2 **tablespoons butter *or* margarine, softened**
- 1/2 **teaspoon lemon-pepper seasoning, *divided***
- 1/4 **teaspoon dried basil**
- 1/8 **teaspoon garlic salt**
- 1 **tablespoon vegetable oil**
- 1 **tablespoon lemon juice**
- 3 **to 4 boneless skinless chicken breast halves**
- 4 **French *or* Italian sandwich rolls, split**
- 1 **small red onion, sliced**

Lettuce leaves

In a small mixing bowl, beat cream cheese, butter, 1/4 teaspoon of lemon pepper, basil and garlic salt until smooth; set aside. Combine oil, lemon juice and remaining lemon pepper. Cut chicken into 1/2-in.-wide strips; brush with lemon juice mixture. Broil chicken 4 in. from the heat for 5 minutes on each side or until juices run clear. Place rolls with cut side up on broiler pan; broil for 1-2 minutes or until light golden brown; spread with the cream cheese mixture. Layer chicken, onion and lettuce over cream cheese. Replace roll tops. **Yield:** 4 servings.

Two-Bean Salad

This simple salad uses frozen and canned beans and prepared salad dressing...so it is extra easy. Assemble this dish and then chill it to have the fabulous flavors blend as you fix the rest of your meal. It's a one-dish delicacy that goes well with many entrees.

- 1 **package (10 ounces) frozen cut green beans, thawed**
- 1 **can (15 ounces) garbanzo beans, rinsed and drained**
- 1/3 **cup Caesar salad dressing**
- 1/4 **cup sliced green onions**
- 1/4 **teaspoon garlic salt**

1/8 teaspoon lemon-pepper seasoning

Combine all ingredients in a large bowl. Cover and chill until ready to serve. **Yield:** 4 servings.

Rocky Road Pizza

Looking for a new, interesting dessert to offer your hungry clan? Chocolate lovers will relish this palate-pleasing pizza that cleverly captures the flavor of rocky road ice cream. Folks will have a hard time eating just one slice!

Pastry for a single-crust pie
  3/4 cup semisweet chocolate chips
  1/2 cup miniature marshmallows
  1/4 cup salted peanuts

Roll pastry into a 9-in. circle; place on a lightly greased baking sheet. Prick with a fork. Bake at 450° for 8-10 minutes or until light brown. Sprinkle with chocolate chips; return to the oven for 1-2 minutes or until chocolate is softened. Spread chocolate out to within 1/2 in. of edges. Sprinkle with marshmallows; return to the oven for 1-2 minutes or until marshmallows puff slightly and are golden brown. Sprinkle with peanuts. Cool. **Yield:** 6-8 servings.

Bountiful Summer Buffet

SUMMERTIME'S in full swing. So why not easily capture the season's terrific tastes with these finger-lickin'-good foods? Pepper Patties tastefully combine colorful peppers, hearty ground beef and tender pasta. Turn your fresh sweet corn into a succulent delight with Spicy Corn Spread. Caramel sauce enhances the natural sweetness of fruits in Strawberry Kiwi Dessert.

🍴 🍴 🍴

Pepper Patties

Bring the season's taste inside by fixing skillet-fried beef burgers and colorful peppers. The serving suggestions are many—present them on a bed of hot cooked noodles for a hearty dinner, alone for a lighter meal or on bread as an open-faced sandwich.

 2 tablespoons soy sauce
 1/4 teaspoon garlic powder
 1/4 teaspoon pepper
 1 pound ground beef
 1 teaspoon cooking oil
 1 small onion, sliced
 1 small green pepper, julienned
 1 small sweet red pepper, julienned
Hot cooked noodles, optional

In a medium bowl, combine soy sauce, garlic powder and pepper; place 1 tablespoon in a large skillet and set aside. Add beef to remaining soy sauce mixture; mix well. Shape into four 1/2-in.-thick patties. Add oil to the skillet; heat on medium. Add onion and peppers; cook and stir for 3-4 minutes or until crisp-tender. Remove and set aside. Add patties to skillet; cook for 3 minutes on each side or until beef is no longer pink. Top patties with peppers and onion; heat through. Serve over noodles if desired. **Yield:** 4 servings.

🍴 🍴 🍴

Spicy Corn Spread

This specially seasoned spread won't only add "kick" to corn on the cob, it'll "zip up" zucchini or any other cooked vegetables. If you like, you can adapt the recipe to suit your family's tastes by adjusting the amount of chili powder.

 1/4 cup butter *or* margarine, softened
 1/2 teaspoon dried parsley flakes
 1/4 teaspoon chili powder
 1/4 teaspoon salt
Hot cooked corn on the cob

In a small bowl, combine the butter, parsley, chili powder and salt until smooth. Spread on hot ears of corn. Refrigerate any leftovers. **Yield:** 4 servings.

Strawberry Kiwi Dessert

In the heat of summer, folks will look forward to a light dessert like this. The season's finest fruits are slightly sweetened with caramel, orange juice and honey. Serve this fruity finale alone or as a topping on other favorite desserts.

   3 cups halved fresh strawberries
   2 kiwifruit, peeled and sliced
   2 tablespoons caramel ice cream topping
   1 tablespoon orange juice
   2 to 3 tablespoons honey roasted
      almonds *or* toasted almonds

Place fruit in a serving bowl. Combine caramel topping and orange juice; drizzle over fruit. Sprinkle with nuts. **Yield:** 4 servings. **Editor's Note:** May also be served over angel food cake, pound cake or ice cream.

Quick-and-Easy Cookout Cuisine

WHEN WARM WEATHER comes your way, it's time to fire up the grill for an old-fashioned country-style barbecue. Nothing says "Summer!" quite like sizzling juicy Mushroom Cheeseburgers. Busy cooks will appreciate that kitchen mess is kept to a minimum with Grilled Parmesan Potatoes. Ruby-red homegrown "maters" make Italian Tomato Salad an extra-special addition.

Mushroom Cheeseburgers

Instead of topping juicy cheeseburgers with sauteed mushrooms, include some savory 'shrooms in the meat mixture for a new twist! Folks will be pleasantly surprised with these deluxe sandwiches...bite after bite.

- **1 pound ground beef**
- **1/4 cup chopped canned mushrooms**
- **1/4 cup finely chopped onion**
- **1 teaspoon dried oregano**
- **1/2 teaspoon salt**
- **1/2 teaspoon pepper**
- **4 slices process American cheese**
- **4 hamburger buns, split**

Lettuce leaves, optional

In a medium bowl, combine the beef, mushrooms, onion, oregano, salt and pepper; mix well. Shape into four patties. Grill burgers, uncovered, over medium-hot coals for 5-6 minutes on each side or until no longer pink. Top each burger with a slice of cheese. Serve on buns with lettuce if desired. **Yield:** 4 servings.

Grilled Parmesan Potatoes

Take a break from usual baked potatoes—and keep the oven cool in the meantime—by cooking these spectacular "spuds" on the grill. Since there's no need to boil the potatoes ahead of time, this tasty, no-fuss favorite is sure to become a timeless classic in your recipe collection.

✓ This tasty dish uses less sugar, salt and fat. Recipe includes *Diabetic Exchanges.*

- **1 pound small red potatoes**
- **1/4 cup chopped green onions**
- **2 teaspoons vegetable oil**
- **1 tablespoon grated Parmesan cheese**
- **1 teaspoon dried oregano**
- **1/2 teaspoon garlic salt**
- **1/4 teaspoon pepper**

Cut potatoes into 1/2-in. cubes; place in a medium bowl. Add onions and oil; toss to coat. Place in the center of a large piece of heavy-duty aluminum foil (about 18 in. x 12 in.). Combine Parmesan cheese, oregano, garlic salt and pepper; sprinkle over potato mixture. Fold foil into a pouch and seal tightly. Grill, uncoverd, over medium-hot coals for 18-20 minutes or until potatoes are tender. Open foil

carefully to allow steam to escape. **Yield:** 4 servings. **Diabetic Exchanges:** One serving equals 1 starch, 1/2 fat; also, 104 calories, 200 mg sodium, 1 mg cholesterol, 16 gm carbohydrate, 3 gm protein, 3 gm fat.

🍸 🍸 🍸

Italian Tomato Salad

When sharing your bumper crop of tomatoes with friends, be sure to send along a copy of this extra-easy recipe. The light oil-and-vinegar dressing and subtle seasonings let the wonderful flavors of just-picked tomatoes and crisp cucumbers come through.

   2 medium tomatoes, sliced
1/2 medium cucumber, sliced
   1 small red onion, thinly sliced
1/4 cup vegetable oil
   2 tablespoons cider *or* red wine vinegar
   2 tablespoons chopped fresh basil *or* 2 teaspoons dried basil
1/4 teaspoon salt
1/8 teaspoon pepper

Layer tomatoes, cucumber and onion in a large salad bowl. Combine oil, vinegar, basil, salt and pepper; drizzle over vegetables. Cover and refrigerate until ready to serve. **Yield:** 4 servings.

Finger-Licking-Good Fixin's

WITH the warm autumn sun shining on a cool, crisp day, round up relatives and friends for a spur-of-the-moment outing featuring all-time favorite foods. Because it's skillet-fried, traditional Picnic Chicken couldn't be easier to assemble. You can use the last of your garden's bounty in Citrus Tossed Salad. And don't forget to pass a basket brimming with slightly sweet Cinnamon Biscuits.

— 🧺 🧺 🧺 —

Picnic Chicken

Whether you're gathering for a picnic in the park or a get-together in the backyard, this pan-fried chicken is the perfect entree. It's moist inside, crispy outside...and goes from skillet to table in no time!

>   4 boneless skinless chicken breast halves
>   1 cup dry bread crumbs
>   1/2 teaspoon dried parsley flakes
>   1/2 teaspoon garlic salt
>   1/4 teaspoon pepper
>   1/4 teaspoon paprika
>   1/8 teaspoon dried thyme
>   1 egg, lightly beaten
>   1 tablespoon cooking oil
>   1 tablespoon butter *or* margarine

Pound chicken to 1/4-in. thickness. In a shallow bowl, combine bread crumbs and seasonings. Dip chicken in egg, then in the crumb mixture. In a skillet, brown the chicken in oil and butter over medium heat for 3-5 minutes on each side or until juices run clear. **Yield:** 4 servings.

— 🧺 🧺 🧺 —

Citrus Tossed Salad

Reach for this recipe when you want a nicely tangy change of pace from ordinary salads. Everyday ingredients come together in a delightful dressing that enhances the greens, vegetables, oranges and walnuts.

>   3 tablespoons olive *or* vegetable oil
>   2 teaspoons orange juice
>   1/2 teaspoon sugar
>   1/2 teaspoon honey
>   1/2 teaspoon Dijon mustard
>   1/2 teaspoon lemon juice
>   1/8 teaspoon grated orange peel
>   1/8 teaspoon salt
>   1/8 teaspoon pepper
> Dash onion powder
>   6 cups torn romaine *or* other greens
>   1/2 cup *each* sliced fresh mushrooms,
>   sweet red pepper and red onion
>   1/2 cup mandarin oranges
>   1/4 cup chopped walnuts, optional

In a jar with a tight-fitting lid, combine the first 10 ingredients and shake well. In a large salad bowl, combine lettuce, vegetables, oranges and walnuts

if desired. Just before serving, add dressing and toss to coat. **Yield:** 4 servings.

———— 🏆 🏆 🏆 ————

Cinnamon Biscuits

These oven-fresh biscuits will disappear from your table as quickly as it took to prepare them! But you can easily whip up another batch. Serve them with fried chicken, at breakfast or as a savory snack.

2 cups all-purpose flour
1 tablespoon baking powder
2 teaspoons sugar
1/2 teaspoon salt
1/4 teaspoon ground cinnamon
1/4 cup cold butter *or* margarine
1 cup milk
Melted butter *or* margarine
Cinnamon-sugar

In a bowl, combine dry ingredients; cut in butter until crumbly. Stir in milk just until moistened. Drop by 1/4 cupfuls onto a greased baking sheet. Brush with melted butter and sprinkle with cinnamon-sugar. Bake at 450° for 10-12 minutes or until lightly browned. Serve warm. **Yield:** about 1 dozen.

Festive Fall Fare

COUNTRY COOKS know that cool autumn air calls for plenty of flavorful family-style suppers. Folks will find the aroma of stick-to-the-ribs Harvest Pork Chops irresistible, while Skillet Ranch Vegetables splendidly showcase the last of your garden's goodness. Then head to the orchard and select some of fall's finest fruit for sweet Honey-Nut Apples.

Harvest Pork Chops

Cooks agree the very best recipes are fast, flavorful and versatile! These tender pork chops are quickly browned, then popped into the oven. For a casual dinner, present each guest with an individual packet. Or unwrap the chops and present on a pretty platter.

    1/2 teaspoon salt
    1/4 teaspoon pepper
    1/4 teaspoon paprika
    1/4 teaspoon rubbed sage
    1/4 teaspoon dried thyme
      4 boneless loin pork chops (1/2 inch thick)
      1 tablespoon cooking oil
      1 small onion, sliced

Combine salt, pepper, paprika, sage and thyme; sprinkle over both sides of pork chops. In a skillet, brown chops in oil for 1-2 minutes on each side. Place each chop in the center of a large piece of heavy-duty aluminum foil (about 12 in. x 9 in.). Top with onion slices. Seal foil tightly; place pouches on a baking sheet. Bake at 450° for 25 minutes or until meat is no longer pink. Open foil carefully to allow steam to escape. **Yield:** 4 servings.

Skillet Ranch Vegetables

Celebrate the last garden harvest with this satisfying side dish. Simply cook carrots, squash and zucchini in oil that's been spiced up with ranch dressing mix. You'll be able to dish out hot and hearty helpings in minutes!

      1 tablespoon cooking oil
      1 envelope buttermilk ranch salad
        dressing mix
      2 medium carrots, thinly sliced
      2 medium yellow squash, sliced
      2 medium zucchini, sliced

In a skillet, combine the oil and salad dressing mix. Add carrots; cook over medium heat for 4-5 minutes or until crisp-tender. Add squash and zucchini; cook 4-5 minutes longer or until all of the vegetables are tender. Remove with a slotted spoon to serving dish. **Yield:** 4 servings.

Honey-Nut Apples

When apples are ripe for the picking, you're bound to get many requests for this tempting treat. It's a fun, festive way to bring a fall feel to your table.

2 tablespoons butter *or* margarine
2 tablespoons brown sugar
1/8 teaspoon ground cinnamon

3 large baking apples, thickly sliced
1/4 cup chopped walnuts
1 tablespoon honey

Melt butter in a large skillet over medium heat. Stir in brown sugar and cinnamon. Add apples and walnuts. Cook, stirring occasionally, for 8-10 minutes or until tender. Remove from the heat and drizzle with honey. Serve warm. **Yield:** 4 servings.

Thanksgiving Feast

THIS TIMELESS traditional fare means you don't have to wait for a holiday to bring a festive touch to your table. Turkey with Cranberry Sauce features a succulent tangy topping for the tender meat. Looking for some speedy side dishes? Walnut Stuffing Balls are fresh from the oven in no time...while Carrot Saute goes from stove to table in minutes. The meal is complete served with sweet apple cider.

Turkey with Cranberry Sauce

You'll hear rave reviews when fantastic fowl stars as the flavorful fare on your weekday menu. Cooking the turkey in butter and oil locks in the succulent juices. And what's turkey without cranberries? This tangy sauce is served right on top!

> 2 turkey breast tenderloins (1 to 1-1/2 pounds)
> 1/2 teaspoon poultry seasoning
> 1 tablespoon cooking oil
> 1 tablespoon butter *or* margarine
> 1 cup whole-berry cranberry sauce
> 3 tablespoons apple jelly
> 3/4 teaspoon Dijon mustard
> 1/4 teaspoon ground allspice

Cut tenderloins crosswise in half. Slice each half lengthwise in half, but do not cut all the way through. Open and flatten each piece. Sprinkle both sides with poultry seasoning. In a large skillet over medium-high heat, cook turkey in oil and butter for 3-4 minutes on each side. Reduce heat to medium-low; cover and cook for 12-15 minutes or until juices run clear. Remove turkey to a platter and keep warm. Add cranberry sauce, jelly, mustard and allspice to skillet; simmer for 2-3 minutes. Spoon over turkey. **Yield:** 4 servings.

Walnut Stuffing Balls

Don't forget the stuffing even though you're not preparing a whole turkey. Your family will be happy to see these perfectly portioned stuffing balls on their plates ...and you will be delighted to know they take just minutes to put together and bake.

> 1/3 cup *each* chopped celery, green pepper and onion
> 1/3 cup chopped walnuts
> 2 tablespoons butter *or* margarine
> 1 egg
> 3 cups herb-seasoned stuffing croutons
> 1/2 cup chicken broth
> 1/4 teaspoon salt
> 1/4 teaspoon pepper

In a saucepan, saute celery, green pepper, onion and walnuts in butter until vegetables are tender;

cool slightly. In a bowl, beat the egg. Add croutons, broth, salt, pepper and vegetable mixture; mix well. Shape into 12 balls, 1/4 cup each; place on a greased baking sheet. Bake at 375° for 20 minutes or until heated through. **Yield:** 4 servings.

—— 🍷 🍷 🍷 ——

Carrot Saute

Every cook knows delicious carrots don't need to be disguised with lots of seasonings. Simply saute them, then sprinkle with some fresh chives and garlic salt.

> 3 cups sliced *or* baby carrots
> 1 tablespoon finely chopped onion
> 1 to 2 tablespoons butter *or* margarine
> 2 tablespoons chopped chives
> 1/8 teaspoon garlic salt

In a medium skillet, saute carrots and onion in butter for 4 minutes; reduce heat. Cover and cook for 8-10 minutes or until carrots are tender. Toss with chives and garlic salt. **Yield:** 4 servings.

Yummy Yuletide Treats

WHEN THE FAMILY gathers for an old-fashioned tree-trimming party, serve up newfound favorites like saucy Stroganoff Meatballs. No one will be able to eat just one! With four simply satisfying ingredients, Holiday Pasta Toss will become a much-requested recipe year-round. And for dessert, why not dip into chocolaty Peppermint Fondue with an assortment of store-bought or homemade cookies?

— 🍴 🍴 🍴 —

Stroganoff Meatballs

For even quicker preparation, make these meatballs ahead of time and freeze. Then thaw, combine with the creamy sauce and warm in a chafing dish.

      1 egg
  1/2 cup dry bread crumbs
  1/4 cup milk
      1 tablespoon dried minced onion
      1 tablespoon dried parsley flakes
  1/4 teaspoon garlic salt
  1/4 teaspoon pepper
      1 pound ground beef
SAUCE:
      1 can (10-3/4 ounces) condensed cream of
        mushroom soup, undiluted
  1/2 cup sour cream
      2 tablespoons chili sauce
  1/4 teaspoon dried oregano
  1/4 teaspoon pepper
  1/8 teaspoon garlic salt

In a large bowl, beat the egg; add the next six ingredients. Add the beef and mix well. Shape into 1-in. balls; place on ungreased baking sheets. Bake, uncovered, at 450° for 12-15 minutes or until no longer pink. Drain on paper towels; place meatballs in a serving dish and keep warm. Combine all of the sauce ingredients in a medium saucepan; cook and stir until well blended and heated through. Spoon over meatballs. **Yield:** 4 servings.

Perfect Pasta

Your pasta will turn out wonderfully every time if you cook it, uncovered, at a fast boil. Also, be sure to stir it frequently as it cooks.

— 🍴 🍴 🍴 —

Holiday Pasta Toss

This recipe uses frozen spinach, so it's always in season. Plus, you can add other produce if you'd like. It's great month after month.

      2 cups uncooked spiral pasta
  1/4 to 1/3 cup Italian salad dressing
      1 package (10 ounces) frozen chopped
        spinach, thawed and drained
      1 teaspoon poppy seeds, optional

In a large saucepan, cook the pasta according to package directions; drain. In the same pan, heat dressing and spinach over medium heat. Return pasta to pan and toss to coat. Sprinkle with poppy seeds if desired. **Yield:** 4 servings.

— 🛷 🛷 🛷 —

Peppermint Fondue

When your festive meal is over, continue the celebration by gathering around the fondue pot. Everyone will enjoy dipping cookies into this chocolaty concoction...but they'll have an even better time gobbling up the fabulous results!

**12 ounces chocolate-covered peppermint
patties, coarsely chopped**
1/4 cup milk
Butter cookies

In a medium saucepan over low heat, melt peppermint patties with milk, stirring frequently. Serve warm, using the cookies for dipping. **Yield:** 1 cup sauce.

Meals on a Budget

These budget-minded meals deliciously prove you don't have to sacrifice taste or quality to feed your family for just pennies a person.

ECONOMICAL ENTREES. Clockwise from upper left: Chicken Confetti, Dilled Zucchini and Orange Whip (p. 284); Country-Fried Steak, Chive Carrots and Dilly Mashed Potatoes (p. 282); After Thanksgiving Salad, Quick Corn Chowder and Popovers (p. 290); Tuna Mushroom Casserole, Snap Salad and Vanilla Wafer Cookies (p. 288).

Feed Your Family for 99¢ a Plate!

IF THE HOLIDAYS stretch your family budget, here's a penny-pinching meal you will love. This frugal yet flavorful feast is from three cooks who estimate the total cost at just 99¢ per setting (including two rolls).

Hearty Bean Soup is convenient to simmer all day in a slow cooker, says Alice Schnoor of Arion, Iowa.

Cornmeal Rolls, from Carol Forcum of Marion, Illinois, are golden and have a subtle cornmeal flavor.

Hot Water Gingerbread is a moist, old-fashioned dessert from country cook Marjorie Green of South Haven, Michigan.

Hearty Bean Soup

- **3 cups chopped parsnips**
- **2 cups chopped carrots**
- **1 cup chopped onion**
- **1-1/2 cups dry great northern beans**
- **5 cups water**
- **1-1/2 pounds smoked ham hocks *or* ham shanks**
- **2 garlic cloves, minced**
- **2 teaspoons salt**
- **1/2 teaspoon pepper**
- **1/8 to 1/4 teaspoon hot pepper sauce**

In a 5-qt. slow cooker, place parsnips, carrots and onion. Top with beans. Add water, ham, garlic, salt, pepper and hot pepper sauce. Cover and cook on high for 6-7 hours or until beans are tender. Remove meat and bones when cool enough to handle. Cut meat into bite-size pieces and return to slow cooker; heat through. **Yield:** 6 servings.

Cornmeal Rolls

(Also pictured on front cover)

- **2-1/4 cups warm water (110° to 115°), *divided***
- **1/3 cup cornmeal**
- **1/4 cup sugar**
- **3 tablespoons vegetable oil**
- **2 teaspoons salt**
- **2 packages (1/4 ounce *each*) active dry yeast**
- **2 eggs**
- **5 to 5-1/2 cups all-purpose flour**
- **Melted butter *or* margarine**
- **Additional cornmeal**

In a saucepan, combine 1-3/4 cups water, cornmeal, sugar, oil and salt. Cook and stir over medium heat until mixture boils, about 10 minutes. Cool at room temperature to 120°-130°. Place in a mixing bowl. Dissolve yeast in remaining water; add to cornmeal mixture. Add eggs and mix well. Add enough flour to make a soft dough. Turn onto a floured board; knead until smooth and elastic, about 6-8 minutes. Place in a greased bowl, turning once to grease top. Cover and let rise in a warm place until doubled, about 45-60 minutes. Punch

dough down. Shape into 24 balls. Place on greased baking sheets; brush with butter and sprinkle with cornmeal. Let rise, uncovered, until doubled, about 30 minutes. Bake at 375° for 18-20 minutes or until golden brown. Immediately remove from baking sheet; serve warm. **Yield:** 2 dozen.

Hot Water Gingerbread

    1 cup all-purpose flour
1/2 cup sugar
    1 teaspoon salt
    1 teaspoon ground ginger
1/2 teaspoon baking soda
    1 egg
1/2 cup molasses
1/2 cup hot water
    1 tablespoon butter *or* margarine, softened
TOPPING:
    2 tablespoons sugar
    2 teaspoons ground cinnamon
Whipped topping

Combine flour, sugar, salt, ginger and baking soda; set aside. In a mixing bowl, beat egg, molasses, water and butter until smooth. Gradually add dry ingredients; beat for 1 minute. Pour into a greased 8-in. square baking pan. Combine the sugar and cinnamon; sprinkle evenly over gingerbread. Bake at 350° for 25 minutes or until a toothpick inserted near the center comes out clean. Cool completely before cutting. Top each square with whipped topping. **Yield:** 9 servings.

Feed Your Family for $1.29 a Plate!

WHY NOT welcome family and friends to a casual supper featuring a country meat-and-potatoes meal? Three creative cooks show how entertaining can be simple and satisfying as well as economical. They estimate this meat-and-potatoes meal at just $1.29 per setting!

Country Fried Steak is a favorite of Betty Claycomb and her husband, Harold, who live in Alverton, Pennsylvania. It's easy to make and so delicious.

Chive Carrots have such rich garden-fresh flavor, you'd never guess how inexpensive this dish is to prepare. Wills Point, Texas cook Dorothy Pritchett says garlic gives them great flavor.

In Spencerport, New York, Theresa Evans recalls her grandmother making Dilly Mashed Potatoes for her over the past 24 years. You'll agree they're perfect anytime.

Country-Fried Steak

1/2 cup all-purpose flour
1/2 teaspoon salt
1/2 teaspoon pepper
3/4 cup buttermilk
1 cup crushed saltines
4 cube steaks (1 pound)
3 tablespoons cooking oil
1 can (10-3/4 ounces) condensed cream of mushroom soup, undiluted
1 cup milk

In a plastic bag or bowl, combine flour, salt and pepper. Place buttermilk in a shallow bowl. Place saltine crumbs in a plastic bag or bowl. Coat steaks with flour mixture, then dip into buttermilk and coat with crumbs. In a large skillet over medium-high heat, cook steaks in hot oil for 2-3 minutes on each side or until golden and cooked to desired doneness. Remove and keep warm. Add soup and milk to skillet; bring to a boil, stirring to loosen browned bits from pan. Serve gravy with steaks. **Yield:** 4 servings.

Chive Carrots

✓ This tasty dish uses less sugar, salt and fat. Recipe includes *Diabetic Exchanges.*

1 pound carrots, cut into 2-inch julienne strips
1 garlic clove, minced
1 tablespoon cooking oil
1 tablespoon butter *or* margarine
2 tablespoons minced fresh chives *or* parsley

In a large skillet, saute the carrots and garlic in oil and butter for 3 minutes. Reduce heat; cover and cook for 10 minutes or until carrots are crisp-ten-

der. Sprinkle with chives or parsley. Serve immediately. **Yield:** 4 servings. **Diabetic Exchanges:** One 1/2-cup serving (prepared with margarine) equals 2 vegetable, 1 fat; also, 106 calories, 64 mg sodium, 0 cholesterol, 12 gm carbohydrate, 1 gm protein, 6 gm fat.

1/4 cup milk
1/4 cup sour cream
1/2 to 3/4 teaspoon dill weed
1/2 to 3/4 teaspoon salt
1/4 teaspoon pepper

Cook potatoes in boiling water until tender; drain. Mash with remaining ingredients. **Yield:** 4 servings.

Dilly Mashed Potatoes

2 pounds potatoes, peeled and cubed
2 tablespoons butter *or* margarine, softened

Magical Marmalade

For fast and flavorful glazed carrots, toss 1 pound cooked carrots with 2 tablespoons orange marmalade.

Feed Your Family for $1.33 a Plate!

TWO TERRIFIC COOKS show that it *is* possible to eat a well-balanced meal without breaking the bank. They estimate that the frugal yet flavorful meal featured here costs just $1.33 per setting!

Chicken Confetti is hearty and delicious with a fresh-tasting sauce. "Before our children grew up and started out on their own, this was a real favorite around our house," remembers Sundra Lewis of Bogalusa, Louisiana.

"Now when the kids come home and bring friends, this main dish is the most requested. No one can resist the tender chicken simmering in a savory homemade tomato sauce. This dish is a definite budget-stretcher."

Sundra also shares her recipe for Dilled Zucchini. "These super squash couldn't be easier to prepare, and their mild flavor goes so well with the chicken," she relates. "I often rely on this side dish when I have a bumper crop of zucchini to use up."

From Winnsboro, Texas, Dorothy Collins sends the recipe for Orange Whip. "It's a wonderfully light and refreshing dessert," she assures.

— 🍴 🍴 🍴 —

Chicken Confetti

- 1 **broiler-fryer chicken (3 pounds), cut up**
- 1 **teaspoon salt,** *divided*
- 1/4 **teaspoon pepper**
- 2 **tablespoons cooking oil**
- 1 **medium onion, chopped**
- 1 **garlic clove, minced**
- 2 **cans (14-1/2 ounces** *each***) diced tomatoes, undrained**
- 1 **can (8 ounces) tomato sauce**
- 1 **can (6 ounces) tomato paste**
- 1-1/2 **teaspoons dried basil**
- 1 **package (7 ounces) spaghetti, cooked and drained**

Sprinkle chicken with 1/2 teaspoon salt and pepper. In a large skillet over medium heat, brown chicken in oil. Remove chicken and set aside. Reserve 1 tablespoon drippings in skillet; add onion and garlic. Saute until tender. Add tomatoes, sauce, paste, basil and remaining salt; bring to a boil. Return chicken to skillet. Reduce heat; cover and simmer for 60-70 minutes or until meat is tender. Serve over spaghetti. **Yield:** 6 servings.

— 🍴 🍴 🍴 —

Dilled Zucchini

✓ This tasty dish uses less sugar, salt and fat. Recipe includes *Diabetic Exchanges*.

3 medium zucchini, halved lengthwise

1 tablespoon butter *or* **margarine, melted**
1/4 teaspoon dill weed
Salt and pepper to taste, optional

Place zucchini in a skillet and cover with water; bring to a boil over medium heat. Cook until tender, about 12-14 minutes. Drain; brush with butter. Sprinkle with dill and salt and pepper if desired. **Yield:** 6 servings. **Diabetic Exchanges:** One serving (prepared with margarine and without salt) equals 1/2 vegetable, 1/2 fat; also, 28 calories, 25 mg sodium, 0 cholesterol, 2 gm carbohydrate, 1 gm protein, 2 gm fat.

Orange Whip

1 envelope unflavored gelatin
1/3 cup sugar
1/8 teaspoon salt
1-3/4 cups hot orange juice (150°)
3/4 cup whipped topping

In a mixing bowl, combine gelatin, sugar and salt; add orange juice and stir until gelatin dissolves. Chill until slightly thickened, about 1-1/2 hours. Beat on low speed until light and fluffy. Spoon into dessert dishes; chill until firm. Top with a dollop of whipped topping. **Yield:** 6 servings.

Feed Your Family for $1.30 a Plate!

EATING light—yet still satisfying—meals during warmer months means a break for your pocketbook. Here, three terrific cooks show how easy it is to put together a tempting low-budget menu for just $1.30 a setting (including two muffins per person) that's sure to please the whole family.

Roast Beef and Potato Salad comes from Joanna Lonnecker of Omaha, Nebraska. "This hearty salad is a favorite of the 'meat-and-potatoes' members of our family," shares Joanna. "I like to serve it as a light main course throughout the year."

Cornmeal Cheese Muffins are preferred over a pan of plain corn bread at the Dallas, Oregon home of Sherri Gentry. "They're moist, tasty and favored by everyone who samples them," she says.

"Banana Custard Pudding is an easy dessert you can whip up anytime your family requests it," declares Hazel Fritchie of Palestine, Illinois. "So be sure to keep this recipe and its ingredients on hand."

Roast Beef and Potato Salad

   2 cups cubed cooked roast beef
   2 cups cubed peeled potatoes, cooked
1/2 cup chopped green pepper
1/2 cup thinly sliced celery
1/4 cup chopped onion
   2 tablespoons chopped pimientos
1/3 cup vegetable oil
   2 to 3 tablespoons vinegar
   2 teaspoons prepared horseradish
1/2 teaspoon salt
1/8 teaspoon pepper
Lettuce leaves
   2 tablespoons chopped fresh parsley

In a large bowl, combine beef, potatoes, green pepper, celery, onion and pimientos. Combine the next five ingredients; mix well. Pour over beef mixture and toss to coat. Cover and refrigerate for at least 1 hour. Serve on lettuce; sprinkle with parsley. **Yield:** 4 servings.

Cornmeal Cheese Muffins

1-1/2 cups all-purpose flour
  1/2 cup yellow cornmeal
  1/4 cup sugar
    1 tablespoon baking powder
  3/4 teaspoon salt
  1/2 cup small-curd cottage cheese
  3/4 cup milk
  1/4 cup vegetable oil
    1 egg
  1/2 cup shredded cheddar cheese
  1/2 teaspoon dried thyme

In a mixing bowl, combine flour, cornmeal, sugar, baking powder and salt. In another bowl, mash cot-

tage cheese with a fork; add milk, oil and egg. Add to dry ingredients; stir just until moistened. Fold in cheddar cheese and thyme. Fill greased or paper-lined muffin cups three-fourths full. Bake at 400° for 20-25 minutes or until golden brown. Cool in pan 5 minutes before removing to a wire rack. **Yield:** 1 dozen.

———— 🍵 🍵 🍵 ————

Banana Custard Pudding

1/2 cup sugar
1 tablespoon cornstarch

1/8 teaspoon salt
1-1/2 cups milk
3 egg yolks, beaten
1 teaspoon vanilla extract
1 medium firm banana, sliced
Fresh mint, optional

In a saucepan, combine sugar, cornstarch and salt. Gradually add milk; cook and stir over medium heat until mixture comes to a boil. Cook and stir 2 minutes longer. Stir a small amount into the egg yolks; return all to pan. Cook and stir until thickened. Remove from the heat; stir in vanilla. Chill for 1 hour. Just before serving, fold in banana. Garnish with mint if desired. **Yield:** 4 servings.

Feed Your Family for 89¢ a Plate!

EATING "cent-sibly" is simple, especially when you rely on a family-favorite casserole, refreshing salad and easy-to-make cookies.

The frugal yet flavorful meal here costs just *89¢* per setting.

Tuna Mushroom Casserole is a rich-tasting main dish. The recipe was sent by Connie Moore of Medway, Ohio, who relates, "I usually serve this casserole when I'm short on time and we need something hearty and comforting."

Snap Salad comes from Rick Leeser of Medford, Oregon. "This colorful, refreshing salad is a snap to make and is enjoyable with any meal," he says. Crisp cucumbers really star in this zippy marinated medley.

Vanilla Wafer Cookies are an irresistible treat, comments Edith Mac Beath of Gaines, Pennsylvania. They're a wonderful way to round out a penny-pinching menu.

Tuna Mushroom Casserole

- 1 **package (12 ounces) wide noodles, cooked and drained**
- 2 **cans (6 ounces *each*) tuna, drained**
- 1 **can (4 ounces) mushroom stems and pieces, drained**
- 1 **can (10-3/4 ounces) condensed cream of mushroom soup, undiluted**
- 1-1/3 **cups milk**
- 1/2 **teaspoon salt**
- 1/4 **teaspoon pepper**
- 1/2 **cup crushed saltines**
- 3 **tablespoons butter *or* margarine, melted**
Paprika, tomato slices and fresh thyme, optional

In a large bowl, combine noodles, tuna and mushrooms. Combine the soup, milk, salt and pepper; pour over noodle mixture and mix well. Pour into a greased 2-1/2-qt. baking dish. Combine saltines and butter; sprinkle over noodles. Bake, uncovered, at 350° for 35-45 minutes or until heated through. If desired, sprinkle with paprika and garnish with tomato and thyme. **Yield:** 6 servings.

Snap Salad

- 2 **medium cucumbers, halved and thinly sliced**
- 2 **medium carrots, julienned**
- 1/4 **cup diced onion**
- 2 **tablespoons raisins**
- 3/4 **cup water**
- 1/4 **cup vinegar**
- 2 **tablespoons sugar**
- 1/2 **teaspoon salt**
- 1/4 **teaspoon pepper**
- 1/4 **teaspoon paprika**

In a large bowl, combine cucumbers, carrots, onion and raisins. Combine the remaining ingredients; pour over the cucumber mixture. Cover and refrigerate for at least 6 hours. Serve with a slotted spoon. **Yield:** 6 servings.

———— 🥄 🥄 🥄 ————

Vanilla Wafer Cookies

1/2 cup butter (no substitutes), softened
1 cup sugar
1 egg
1 tablespoon vanilla extract
1-1/3 cups all-purpose flour
3/4 teaspoon baking powder
1/4 teaspoon salt

In a mixing bowl, cream butter and sugar. Beat in egg and vanilla. Combine dry ingredients; add to creamed mixture and mix well. Drop by teaspoonfuls 2 in. apart onto ungreased baking sheets. Bake at 350° for 12-15 minutes or until edges are golden brown. Remove to a wire rack to cool. **Yield:** about 3-1/2 dozen.

Feed Your Family for 87¢ a Plate!

IF YOU'RE pinching your pennies for future holiday purchases, you don't have to forgo flavorful foods. Three terrific cooks share their recipes for a filling—yet frugal—meal with an estimated total cost of just 87¢ per setting.

After Thanksgiving Salad is a delightful and unexpected way to use leftover turkey. "This hearty salad is so delicious and pretty," remarks Betty Peel of Milford, Ohio.

Quick Corn Chowder is recommended by Diane Brewster of Highland, New York. "When my husband and I decided I'd stay home with our new baby, his salary had to be stretched pretty thin," Diane recalls. "I became an expert at preparing meals with more 'sense' than dollars! This is a favorite."

Popovers make even an inexpensive meal fun and special. The recipe comes from Lourdes Dewick of Fort Lauderdale, Florida.

After Thanksgiving Salad

3-1/2 cups diced cooked turkey
    4 celery ribs, sliced
    4 green onions, sliced
  1/2 cup chopped pecans, toasted
  1/2 cup chopped sweet red pepper
  1/2 cup mayonnaise
    1 tablespoon lemon juice
  1/4 teaspoon dill weed *or* dried tarragon
  1/4 teaspoon salt
  1/8 teaspoon pepper
Lettuce leaves, optional

In a large bowl, combine turkey, celery, onions, pecans and red pepper. Combine mayonnaise, lemon juice, dill, salt and pepper; stir into turkey mixture. Refrigerate until serving. Serve on lettuce if desired. **Yield:** 6 servings.

Quick Corn Chowder

    1 bacon strip, diced

    1 medium onion, diced
    1 can (14-1/2 ounces) chicken broth
    2 cups water
    2 large potatoes, peeled and diced
  1/2 teaspoon salt
  1/4 teaspoon pepper
    1 can (15 ounces) whole kernel corn, drained
    1 cup milk, *divided*
  1/4 cup all-purpose flour
Chopped fresh parsley, optional

In a 3-qt. saucepan, cook bacon until crisp; remove to paper towel to drain. Saute onion in drippings until tender. Add broth, water and potatoes; bring

to a boil. Reduce heat; cover and simmer for 15 minutes or until potatoes are tender. Add salt and pepper; mix well. Add corn and 3/4 cup milk. Combine flour and remaining milk until smooth; add to soup. Bring to a boil; cook and stir for 2 minutes. Garnish with bacon and parsley if desired. **Yield:** 6 servings.

Popovers

1 tablespoon shortening
2 eggs
1 cup milk
1 tablespoon butter *or* margarine, melted
1 cup all-purpose flour
1/2 teaspoon salt

Using 1/2 of teaspoon shortening for each cup, grease the bottom and sides of six 6-oz. custard cups or the cups of a popover pan. Place custard cups on a 15-in. x 10-in. x 1-in. baking pan; set aside. In a mixing bowl, beat eggs; blend in milk and butter. Beat in flour and salt until smooth (do not overbeat). Fill cups half full. Bake at 450° for 15 minutes. Reduce heat to 350°; bake 30 minutes longer or until very firm. Remove from the oven and prick each popover to allow steam to escape. Serve immediately. **Yield:** 6 servings.

Getting in the Theme of Things

These fun and festive meals—
featuring theme-related menus,
decorating ideas and activities—
will make your get-togethers
extra special.

PARTY PLANS. Clockwise from upper left: Main-land Luau (p. 298), "Dino-mite" Birthday Party (p. 302), Christmas Tea (p. 294) and Romantic Holiday Supper (p. 296).

'Hats on' for Christmas Tea, pastor's plan proved a treat for hardworking church women.

By Rev. David Bostedt, Zephyrhills, Florida

Last Christmas, my wife, Jo, and I hosted a traditional English high tea at our Victorian home for the ladies' society at the small rural Wisconsin church where I served as minister.

We wanted to do something a bit different to thank this dedicated group, and my interest in the Victorian era inspired our holiday party theme.

Formal invitations asked each woman to wear a hat. The ladies showed up in a variety—pillboxes, fur-lined hats, country bonnets and knit stocking caps. Later, everyone voted for the best, most antique, most humorous…and the "I wouldn't be caught dead in that hat" hat!

Unfamiliar with the idea of a formal tea, the women were curious at first. I encouraged everyone to relax and enjoy as I explained its history.

A traditional high tea includes three courses, the first being finger sandwiches. While Jo kept everyone's teacup full, I served as the "butler", delivering Festive Tea Sandwiches stuffed with chicken and a seasonal spread, along with Cheery Tomato Bites, featuring a cool, creamy do-ahead filling.

Pretty glass luncheon sets (picked up at local auctions and garage sales) and Victorian-style ornaments we'd made as favors were perfect table decorations. Sherbet glasses holding votive candles made sparkling centerpieces.

For the second course, we served Gingerbread Scones, which are delicious spread with blackberry cream cheese.

Then we played Victorian parlor games, which had us giggling.

The wonderful aroma of Steamed Cranberry Pudding wafted as we presented the grand finale. Savoring its fruity flavor, several of the ladies reminisced about their mothers' puddings.

As we concluded with a gift exchange and singing of English carols, Jo and I felt we'd created a memorable afternoon for a group of ladies who fill the days of others with special blessings.

Maybe you'll want to "pour" some of our Victorian format into planning a similar gathering. Your guests will likely say "hats off to you" for a fancy but fun-filled holiday party.

Festive Tea Sandwiches

These delicate sandwiches were the memorable first course at our Victorian tea. A mayonnaise, pecan and cranberry spread complements the chicken.

- 1/2 cup mayonnaise
- 1/3 cup chopped fresh *or* frozen cranberries
- 2 tablespoons chopped pecans
- 1/4 teaspoon salt
- 1/8 teaspoon pepper
- 16 slices bread, crusts removed
- 16 to 24 thin slices cooked chicken
- 8 lettuce leaves

Combine the first five ingredients; spread on one side of each slice of bread. Layer half the slices with chicken and lettuce. Top with remaining bread. Cut into quarters or decorative shapes. **Yield:** 8 servings. **Editor's Note:** Chive butter may be used in place of the cranberry mayonnaise. Beat 1/2 cup softened butter or margarine, 1/2 teaspoon of lemon juice and 1/8 teaspoon of pepper until fluffy; stir in 2 tablespoons minced chives.

— ☕ ☕ ☕ —

Cheery Tomato Bites

Cherry tomatoes may be small, but these are full of great flavor. Plus, they add color to any table.

- 2 pints cherry tomatoes
- 1 package (8 ounces) cream cheese, softened
- 6 bacon strips, cooked and crumbled
- 1/4 cup minced green onions
- 1/4 cup minced fresh parsley
- 1/4 teaspoon Worcestershire sauce

Cut a thin slice off the top of each tomato. Scoop out and discard pulp. Invert the tomatoes on a paper towel to drain. Meanwhile, combine remaining ingredients in a small bowl; mix well. Spoon into tomatoes. Refrigerate until serving. **Yield:** about 4 dozen.

— ☕ ☕ ☕ —

Gingerbread Scones

These festive moist scones are a scrumptious treat with tea or coffee.

- 2 cups all-purpose flour
- 3 tablespoons brown sugar
- 2 teaspoons baking powder
- 1 teaspoon ground ginger
- 1/2 teaspoon baking soda
- 1/2 teaspoon salt
- 1/2 teaspoon ground cinnamon
- 1/4 cup cold butter *or* margarine
- 1/3 cup molasses
- 1/4 cup milk
- 1 egg, *separated*

Sugar

In a large bowl, combine flour, brown sugar, baking powder, ginger, baking soda, salt and cinnamon. Cut in butter until mixture resembles coarse crumbs. In a small bowl, combine the molasses, milk and egg yolk until smooth; stir into the flour mixture just until moistened. Turn onto a floured surface; knead gently 6-8 times. Pat into an 8-in. circle; cut into 12 wedges and place 1 in. apart on a greased baking sheet. Beat egg white until frothy; brush over scones. Sprinkle with sugar. Bake at 400° for 12-15 minutes or until golden brown. Serve warm. **Yield:** 1 dozen.

— ☕ ☕ ☕ —

Steamed Cranberry Pudding

This fruity molded pudding brought back memories for many whose mothers and grandmothers prepared similar delicacies.

- 1/2 cup shortening
- 2/3 cup sugar
- 2 eggs
- 2 tablespoons molasses
- 1-2/3 cups all-purpose flour
- 3/4 teaspoon baking soda
- 1/2 teaspoon ground cinnamon
- 1/4 teaspoon ground nutmeg
- 1/4 teaspoon salt
- 2-1/2 cups chopped fresh *or* frozen cranberries

HARD SAUCE:
- 1 cup sugar
- 1/2 cup butter *or* margarine
- 1/2 cup half-and-half cream
- 1/2 teaspoon vanilla extract

In a mixing bowl, cream shortening and sugar; beat in eggs and molasses. Combine dry ingredients; stir into creamed mixture and mix well. Fold in the cranberries. Pour into a well-greased and floured 6-cup heatproof mold. Cover tightly with a double layer of foil. Place on a rack in a deep kettle. Fill kettle with boiling water to a depth of 1 in.; cover kettle and boil gently. Replace water as needed. Steam about 3 hours or until a toothpick inserted near the center comes out clean. Let stand 10 minutes before unmolding. Let pudding cool 30 minutes before slicing. For hard sauce, combine sugar, butter and cream in a saucepan; cook and stir over medium heat until smooth. Remove from the heat; stir in vanilla. Serve pudding and sauce warm. **Yield:** 8-10 servings.

Heartfelt sentiments take shape in memorable fare for romantic holiday supper.

By Kay Curtis, Guthrie, Oklahoma

Thanking my one-and-only valentine for 17 wonderful years of marriage was the heartfelt motivation for a colorful theme meal I planned to surprise my dear husband, Dan.

The table was covered with a white lace cloth overlaying a red one, and I intertwined wide red ribbon among the candlesticks. Heart sticker strips made an easy trim for our napkins.

I even became part of the decor that evening, wearing a white lacy dress, red beads, and a red and white apron with a heart pocket.

"You look like a valentine!" Dan commented appreciatively as I brought on the food. (We chose to include our four children in our romantic meal—even though when we lit the candles and dimmed the lights, they volunteered to leave!)

Chili in a Bread Bowl made a big hit with everyone. I baked the tasty bread "bowl" in a heart-shaped pan, and after spooning out the chili, I cut the bread into pieces for all of us.

We drank pretty Sparkling Berry Punch. For a special garnish in Dan's glass, I froze a heart-shaped ice cube in a cookie cutter.

Red-Hot Molded Hearts were an easy addition to the meal. Individual servings made in molds carried out the shape and color motif.

Topping off our theme supper was my Cherry Meringue Dessert. Dan hesitated to cut into it because he thought it looked so pretty. But the meringue heart held a cream cheese filling topped with cherries that proved to be irresistible.

It was a delightful meal! Besides my husband's appreciation, I experienced an extra blessing when our teenage daughter longingly expressed her desire to someday fix a valentine meal like this for *her* husband. I look forward to the day when she calls home to tell me about it!

Meanwhile, you may want to surprise someone special with these ideas on February 14 or another sweet day.

Chili in a Bread Bowl

For a simple, speedy recipe, this chili has the rich flavor of one that has simmered a lot longer. Set on the table in the unique heart-shaped bread bowl, it's an especially "hearty" main dish.

> 1 pound ground beef
> 1 cup chopped onion
> 1 can (16 ounces) kidney beans, rinsed and drained
> 1 can (15 ounces) tomato sauce
> 1 can (14-1/2 ounces) diced tomatoes, undrained
> 1 tablespoon chili powder
> 1/2 teaspoon garlic powder

BREAD BOWL:

> 1 tablespoon cornmeal
> 2/3 cup water
> 1/4 cup butter *or* margarine
> 1 cup all-purpose flour
> 1/4 cup grated Parmesan cheese
> 2 teaspoons baking powder
> 4 eggs

In a saucepan, brown beef with onion; drain. Add the next five ingredients; simmer, uncovered, for 20 minutes. Grease a 9-in. heart-shaped or round baking pan; sprinkle with cornmeal and set aside. In a saucepan over medium heat, bring water and butter to a boil. Add flour, Parmesan and baking powder; stir until a smooth ball forms. Remove from the heat; beat in eggs, one at a time. Continue beating until mixture is smooth and shiny. Spread into prepared pan, building up edges slightly. Bake at 425° for 25-30 minutes or until the center is firm and puffed and edges are golden brown. Make a shallow slit in the center to allow steam to escape. Cool for 5 minutes before removing to a serving plate. Fill with chili; serve immediately. **Yield:** 6 servings. **Editor's Note:** Chili recipe makes more than will fit in the bread bowl.

—— 🥄 🥄 🥄 ——

Sparkling Berry Punch

This thirst-quenching beverage really rounded out our Valentine's Day dinner. But I've found it makes a colorful addition to any special occasion no matter what time of year.

> 6 cups cranberry juice, chilled
> 2 cans (12 ounces *each*) ginger ale, chilled
> 1/4 teaspoon almond extract

Combine all ingredients in a punch bowl or pitcher. Serve immediately on ice. **Yield:** about 2 quarts.

Red-Hot Molded Hearts

This cool salad gets a bit of "warmth" from melted cinnamon candies. Stirred into strawberry gelatin, the applesauce picks up a rosy hue and molds wonderfully.

> 1/4 cup red-hot candies
> 1 cup boiling water
> 1 package (3 ounces) strawberry gelatin
> 2-1/2 cups applesauce

In a bowl, dissolve candies in water. Stir in gelatin until dissolved. Fold in applesauce. Pour into 12 oiled 1/3-cup individual molds, a 4-cup heart-shaped mold or a 1-qt. bowl. Chill overnight. **Yield:** 10-12 servings.

—— 🥄 🥄 🥄 ——

Cherry Meringue Dessert

Who can resist luscious cherries floating over a rich creamy layer tucked inside a crispy shell? This tempting dessert looks almost too good to eat, but don't let that stop you—it's sure to impress your sweetheart.

> 3 egg whites
> 1/4 teaspoon cream of tartar
> 3/4 cup sugar

FILLING:

> 1 package (3 ounces) cream cheese, softened
> 1/4 cup confectioners' sugar
> 1/2 teaspoon vanilla extract
> 1 cup whipping cream, whipped
> 1 can (21 ounces) cherry pie filling

In a mixing bowl, beat egg whites until foamy. Add cream of tartar; beat until soft peaks form. Gradually add sugar, 1 tablespoon at a time, beating until very stiff peaks form. Cover a baking sheet with foil or parchment paper. Spoon meringue onto foil. Using the back of a spoon, form meringue into a 9-in. heart shape, building up the edges slightly. Bake at 275° for 1-1/2 hours. Turn oven off and do not open door. Let cool in oven for 1 hour. Remove from the oven; cool completely. In a mixing bowl, beat cream cheese, sugar and vanilla until smooth. Fold in whipped cream until mixture is well blended. To serve, place heart on a serving platter; fill with cream cheese mixture and top with pie filling. **Yield:** 6 servings.

Delectable Disguise

If you need to "hide" vegetables in your chili from fussy eaters, puree them in a blender or food processor first.

Flavors savored on Hawaiian trips inspired her to host a 'Mainland Luau'.

By Mary Gaylord, Balsam Lake, Wisconsin

Aloha! Welcome to my Mainland Luau. A lifelong interest in Hawaii and several trips to the islands encouraged me to share some delightful island delicacies with friends back home.

More than 60 years ago, I began corresponding with a pen pal in Oahu. She visited me in 1951, and I made my first trip to see her in 1959, flying 9 hours on a prop plane from Los Angeles. My stay included a whole new world of culinary delights.

Since then, I've returned to Hawaii six times and have attended several luaus. My party menu was based on island recipes I've collected and "dabbled" with in my kitchen.

Arriving guests were greeted with an artificial lei and a kiss on the cheek from my daughter. We both wore colorful muumuus, and I played my old favorite Don Ho record for background music.

Brightly patterned sheets made pretty tablecloths, and plenty of flowers (mostly artificial) helped set the mood.

At a luau meal, the central attraction is the kalua pig, wrapped in banana leaves and roasted in an outdoor pit. I've adapted the recipe for the kitchen, and my tender Hawaiian Pork Roast falls apart just like a kalua pig. You can garnish the platter with artificial or edible flowers to go along with the theme (those are edible orchids in the photo above).

Crunchy Asparagus Medley features fresh asparagus with toasted almonds, celery and water chestnuts.

Tropical Sweet Potatoes is my version of those usually cooked with the luau pig. This dish can be fixed a day or two ahead—a big help for this 80-year-old hostess.

In addition, guests sampled fresh pineapple, smoked salmon with onions and tomatoes plus poi—a traditional Hawaiian staple made of crushed taro roots.

Everyone loved my Macadamia Nut Cookies, which I served with coconut pudding and Kona coffee for dessert.

Entertaining Hawaiian-style was something I had longed to do, and it stirred such precious memories. Perhaps the spirit of "aloha" will bid you to try my Hawaiian feast!

Hawaiian Pork Roast

Preparing a pork roast with bananas, liquid smoke and soy sauce produces a wonderfully tender meat with flavor that recalls the specialty I so enjoyed at Hawaiian luaus.

> 1 boneless pork shoulder roast (3 to 4 pounds), trimmed
> 4 teaspoons liquid smoke
> 4 teaspoons soy sauce
> 2 unpeeled ripe bananas
> 1/2 cup water

Place the roast on a 22-in. x 18-in. piece of heavy-duty foil; sprinkle with liquid smoke and soy sauce. Wash bananas and place at the base of each side of roast. Pull sides of foil up around roast; add water. Seal foil tightly; wrap again with another large piece of foil. Place in a shallow baking pan; refrigerate overnight, turning several times. Place foil-wrapped meat in a roasting pan. Bake at 400° for 1 hour. Reduce heat to 325°; continue baking for 3-1/2 hours. Drain; discard bananas and liquid. Shred meat with a fork. **Yield:** 8-10 servings. **Editor's Note:** Escarole and edible orchids were used to garnish the serving platter shown in the photo. If you use flowers, make sure they are edible and have not been chemically treated; wash thoroughly and pat dry before using.

— ♣ ♣ ♣ —

Crunchy Asparagus Medley

This savory side dish made a special appearance at our Hawaiian dinner. But I've also been known to prepare it with different foods on other occasions.

> 1-1/2 pounds fresh asparagus, cut into 2-inch pieces
> 1 cup thinly sliced celery
> 2 cans (8 ounces *each*) sliced water chestnuts, drained
> 1/4 cup slivered almonds, toasted
> 2 tablespoons soy sauce
> 2 tablespoons butter *or* margarine

In a large saucepan, cook the asparagus and celery in a small amount of water for 5-6 minutes or until crisp-tender; drain. Stir in the water chestnuts, almonds, soy sauce and butter; heat through. **Yield:** 8-10 servings.

— ♣ ♣ ♣ —

Tropical Sweet Potatoes

Sweet potatoes take on a tropical twist with crushed pineapple mixed in. I add a crumb topping, which bakes to a pretty golden color, and a fresh pineapple garnish. This festive dish would also make a nice addition to a traditional Thanksgiving dinner.

> 4 large sweet potatoes (3-1/2 pounds)
> 1 can (8 ounces) crushed pineapple, undrained
> 6 tablespoons butter *or* margarine, melted, *divided*
> 3/4 teaspoon salt
> Pinch pepper
> 1/2 cup crushed saltines
> 2 tablespoons brown sugar
> Pinch cloves

In a large saucepan, cover sweet potatoes with water; bring to a boil. Reduce heat; cover and simmer for 30 minutes or until tender. Drain and cool. Peel the potatoes and place in a mixing bowl; mash. Add the pineapple, 2 tablespoons butter, salt and pepper; mix well. Transfer to a greased 2-qt. baking dish. Combine saltines, brown sugar, cloves and remaining butter; sprinkle over potatoes. Bake, uncovered, at 375° for 30 minutes. **Yield:** 8-10 servings.

— ♣ ♣ ♣ —

Macadamia Nut Cookies

These rich cookies—full of Hawaiian macadamia nuts and chocolate chips—make a delectable ending for my festive Mainland Luau menu.

> 1 cup butter *or* margarine, softened
> 3/4 cup sugar
> 3/4 cup packed brown sugar
> 2 eggs
> 1 teaspoon vanilla extract
> 2-1/4 cups all-purpose flour
> 1 teaspoon baking soda
> 1 teaspoon salt
> 2 jars (3-1/2 ounces *each*) macadamia nuts, chopped
> 2 cups (12 ounces) semisweet chocolate chips
> 1 cup (6 ounces) vanilla baking chips

In a mixing bowl, cream butter and sugars. Add eggs and vanilla; beat on medium speed for 2 minutes. Combine flour, baking soda and salt; add to creamed mixture and beat for 2 minutes. Stir in nuts and chips. Cover and refrigerate several hours or overnight. Drop by tablespoonfuls 2 in. apart onto ungreased baking sheets. Bake at 375° for 10-12 minutes or until golden brown. Cool on pans for 1 minute before removing to wire racks; cool completely. **Yield:** about 6 dozen. **Editor's Note:** 2 cups of chopped almonds may be substituted for the macadamia nuts.

Clever country women milked black-and-white motif to put guests in the party 'moo-d'.

By Teresa Stutzman, Adair, Oklahoma

My friend Carol Troyer and I, both married to dairy farmers, picked a familiar theme for my husband Curt's birthday party—and we milked it for all it was worth!

We asked guests to dress in black and white. The two of us wore look-alike cow dresses we'd bought at a craft fair we'd attended together.

Carol and I both have cow dinnerware and collect cow accessories, so pooling resources for the party was a lot of fun. We set the table with Holstein-patterned place mats, plates, glasses, napkins and salt and pepper shakers.

A miniature milk can filled with black and white flowers was the centerpiece. Barn-shaped wooden place card holders and cowbell favors (made from upside-down flowerpots) waited at each place.

The menu was planned around some of our favorite dairy recipes. When the guests arrived, we poured Brown Cow Punch.

The delicious beverage calls for chocolate milk and coffee ice cream. It was a nice change from typical fruit punches.

Guests also nibbled on Cattleman's Spread, a flavorful dried beef spread featuring cream cheese and sour cream.

Creamy Hash Brown Casserole tasted great with the steaks we grilled. Green salad, homemade creamed corn and rolls rounded out the main course.

Later, everyone raved over Homemade Ice Cream topped with chocolate sauce (served with birthday cake). This wonderful ice cream recipe came from Carol's mother-in-law and is her husband Earl's favorite dessert.

It was such an udderly fun evening that we partied until the cows came home! Moo! Moo!

You needn't wait for a birthday to try our recipes. Why not plan a "Bovie Day" gathering soon simply to celebrate the delicious dairy foods we're so proud to produce?

Brown Cow Punch

When we came across this recipe, we knew it would be perfect for our theme party. The chocolate milk made everyone feel like a kid again!

2 quarts chocolate milk
1/4 teaspoon almond extract
1/2 gallon coffee ice cream*

In a punch bowl, combine milk and extract. Add ice cream by scoopfuls and allow to float on top of punch. Or scoop ice cream into glasses; combine milk and extract, then pour over ice cream. **Yield:** 3 quarts. ***Editor's Note:** If coffee ice cream is unavailable, dissolve 2 teaspoons instant coffee granules in 2 teaspoons hot water and stir into vanilla ice cream.

—— 🍺 🍺 🍺 ——

Cattleman's Spread

Fit for a dairy farmer's birthday, this appetizer was perfect for our theme dinner. The spread is "beefed up" with dairy products, and pecans give it a pleasant crunch.

1 cup chopped pecans
2 tablespoons butter *or* margarine
2 packages (8 ounces *each*) cream cheese, softened
1 cup (8 ounces) sour cream
1/2 teaspoon garlic powder
2 packages (2-1/2 ounces *each*) dried beef, chopped
4 teaspoons diced onion
Crackers and breadsticks

In a skillet, saute pecans in butter until golden; set aside. In a mixing bowl, beat cream cheese until smooth. Add sour cream and garlic powder; mix well. Stir in beef and onion. Spread into a greased 8-in. square baking dish. Top with the pecans. Bake, uncovered, at 350° for 20 minutes or until heated through. Serve with crackers and breadsticks. **Yield:** 3-1/2 cups.

—— 🍺 🍺 🍺 ——

Creamy Hash Brown Casserole

This versatile side dish was dairy-good with the steaks we grilled and is delicious with other meats as well. A creamy cheese sauce and crunchy topping make this casserole popular for family dinners and potlucks.

1 package (32 ounces) frozen Southern-style hash brown potatoes, thawed

1 pound process American cheese, cubed
1 can (10-3/4 ounces) condensed cream of chicken soup, undiluted
2 cups (16 ounces) sour cream
3/4 cup butter *or* margarine, melted, *divided*
3 tablespoons chopped onion
1/4 teaspoon paprika
2 cups cornflakes, slightly crushed
Fresh savory, optional

In a large bowl, combine hash browns, cheese, soup, sour cream, 1/2 cup butter and onion. Spread into a greased 13-in. x 9-in. x 2-in. baking dish. Sprinkle with paprika. Combine cornflakes and remaining butter; sprinkle on top. Bake, uncovered, at 350° for 50-60 minutes or until heated through. Garnish with savory if desired. **Yield:** 8-10 servings.

—— 🍺 🍺 🍺 ——

Homemade Ice Cream

Take it from us dairy farmers, this old-fashioned ice cream is marvelous! It's made from a treasured recipe passed down in the Troyer family and was a big hit at our "black-and-white" birthday party.

8 cups milk, *divided*
6 eggs, *separated*
3 cups sugar, *divided*
3 tablespoons cornstarch
1/4 teaspoon salt
2 teaspoons vanilla extract
2 cups whipping cream
Maraschino cherries, optional

In a large saucepan, bring 6 cups milk to a boil over medium heat. Remove from the heat and set aside. In a mixing bowl, beat egg yolks; add remaining milk and mix well. Combine 2 cups sugar, cornstarch and salt; gradually add to egg mixture. Add to hot milk and bring to a boil. Cook and stir for 2 minutes or until slightly thickened. Pour into a clean mixing bowl; set aside. Beat egg whites until soft peaks form; gradually add remaining sugar, beating well after each addition. Beat until stiff peaks form. Fold into warm milk mixture. Beat in vanilla and cream until well mixed. Refrigerate at least 5 hours or overnight. Freeze in an ice cream freezer according to manufacturer's directions. Garnish with cherries if desired. **Yield:** 3-1/2 quarts.

"Ripening" Homemade Ice Cream

To fully develop the flavor and texture of homemade ice cream, it should be stored in the freezer for at least 4 hours after being prepared.

Colorful creatures and kid-pleasing menu made for dino-mite birthday party.

By Robin Werner, Brush Prairie, Washington

Dinosaurs once again roamed the earth (at least around our house!) during our preschool son's birthday party.

As the children arrived, I took each of their pictures with the Greet-a-saurus, a big purple beast I'd made from a refrigerator box. (Later, we enclosed those photos in thank-you notes.)

Waiting for everyone to arrive, the kids colored a giant Paint-a-saurus. Then we played Extinction. In this Jurassic rendition of musical chairs, we used pictures of dinosaurs instead of chairs. The child who was "out" got to pick one dinosaur to become extinct.

Next the kids reveled in the Stegosaurus Stomp, jumping on balloons to pop them, and Bust-a-Boulder, hitting prehistoric pinatas I made by stuffing paper bags with candy and prizes.

On the table, candy dinosaur dots and candy pebbles were scattered among palm trees "grown" from bathroom tissue rolls wrapped with paper twist and stuffed with fronds cut from green tissue.

Lunch featured dinosaur-shaped canteens filled with Caveman Cooler, Padysaurus Pizza Pockets, Dinosaur Eggs and Giant Dinosaur Cookies.

After present-opening, the kids settled down to watch *Land Before Time*, a cute dinosaur movie. Each child was sent home with a dinosaur goody bag.

Before the ideas fossilize, I'm sharing them in case you want to call out the beasts for some party fun.

— 🦖 🦖 🦖 —

Caveman Cooler

I appreciated this easy-to-make punch when preparing for my son's party. Our guests liked its slightly tart flavor.

- 1 quart cranberry juice
- 1 quart ginger ale
- 1 cup tropical punch-flavored soft drink
- 1 cup orange juice

Chill all ingredients; combine in a punch bowl just before serving. **Yield:** 10-14 servings (2-1/2 quarts).

Padysaurus Pizza Pockets

Stuffed with a pizza-style filling, these special sandwiches surprise you with a burst of flavor in every bite. They were popular with the preschool set at our son's dinosaur theme birthday party...but adults will love them, too!

> **3 to 3-1/4 cups all-purpose flour**
> **1 package (1/4 ounce) active dry yeast**
> **1 tablespoon sugar**
> **1 teaspoon salt**
> **1 cup warm water (120° to 130°)**
> **1 tablespoon butter *or* margarine, melted**
> **1 can (8 ounces) pizza sauce**
> **12 slices pepperoni**
> **1 package (2-1/2 ounces) thinly sliced fully cooked pastrami, chopped**
> **1 package (2-1/2 ounces) thinly sliced fully cooked ham, chopped**
> **3/4 cup shredded mozzarella cheese**
> **1 egg, beaten**

In a mixing bowl, combine 2-1/4 cups flour, yeast, sugar and salt. Add water and butter; mix well. Add enough remaining flour to form a soft dough. Turn onto a floured surface; knead for 4 minutes. Roll dough into a 14-in. x 10-in. rectangle. Cut with a 3-in. round cookie cutter. Reroll scraps to cut a total of 24 circles. Place 1 teaspoon pizza sauce and a slice of pepperoni in center of 12 circles. Combine pastrami, ham and cheese; place equal amounts over pepperoni. Top with 1/2 teaspoon of pizza sauce if desired. (Save remaining sauce for another use or use for dipping.) Cover with remaining dough circles; pinch edges or press with a fork to seal. Place on greased baking sheets. Brush with egg. Bake at 400° for 20-25 minutes or until browned. **Yield:** 12 servings.

— 🝙 🝙 🝙 —

Dinosaur Eggs

The mold I'd used to make Jell-O treats at Easter inspired me to include these unusual and fun green "dinosaur eggs" on the party menu. Instant pudding and cinnamon give the eggs a creamy look with speckles.

> **2 packages (6 ounces *each*) lime gelatin**
> **2-1/2 cups boiling water**
> **1/2 teaspoon ground cinnamon**
> **1 cup cold milk**
> **1 package (3.4 ounces) instant vanilla pudding mix**
> **Alfalfa sprouts, optional**

In a large bowl, dissolve gelatin in boiling water; let stand at room temperature for 30 minutes. Stir in the cinnamon. In a large measuring cup with a spout, beat milk and pudding mix until blended, about 1 minute. Quickly whisk into the gelatin until smooth. Pour into a 13-in. x 9-in. x 2-in. pan coated with nonstick cooking spray. Refrigerate for 3 hours or until firm. Cut into ovals or use an egg-shaped cookie cutter. Serve over alfalfa sprouts if desired. **Yield:** 12-14 servings. **Editor's Note:** For eggs like those shown in the photo, use a Jell-O Jigglers egg mold and the following directions. Coat the inside and rim of each egg mold with nonstick cooking spray. Securely close each egg mold. Place mold, fill side up, on a tray. After whisking pudding mixture into gelatin, immediately pour it into the mold through fill holes just to the top of the egg shape. Refrigerate for 3 hours or until firm. To unmold eggs, slide a dull flat knife between eggs. Gently pry between each egg (do not pull on the handle). Turn mold over and shake gently to remove eggs. This recipe will make 12 eggs.

— 🝙 🝙 🝙 —

Giant Dinosaur Cookies

Decorated sugar cookies delighted the dinosaur lovers at our party. I had a lot of fun frosting the shapes and decorating them with mini-chocolate chip "eyes" and colorful candy spots to give them character.

> **1 cup butter *or* margarine, softened**
> **1 cup sugar**
> **1 egg**
> **1 teaspoon vanilla extract**
> **3 cups all-purpose flour**
> **2 teaspoons baking powder**
> **Food coloring, optional**
> **1 can (16 ounces) vanilla frosting**
> **Miniature *or* regular semisweet chocolate chips**
> **Sliced gumdrops *or* small decorating candies**

In a mixing bowl, cream butter and sugar. Add egg and vanilla; mix well. Combine flour and baking powder; add to creamed mixture, 1 cup at a time, mixing well after each addition (dough will be very stiff). Divide into two balls; roll each ball directly on an ungreased baking sheet to 1/4-in. thickness. Cut cookies with a dinosaur cookie cutter, leaving at least 1 in. between cookies. Remove excess dough and reroll scraps if desired. Bake at 400° for 7-9 minutes for small cookies and 10-12 minutes for large cookies or until lightly browned around the edges. Cool 1-2 minutes before removing to wire racks. Add food coloring to frosting if desired. Frost the cookies. Decorate with chocolate chips for eyes and candies for spots. **Yield:** about 2 dozen 4-inch cookies or 1 dozen 8-inch cookies.

Quilter patterns luncheon menu and table setting to please stitching pals.

By Grace Yaskovic, Branchville, New Jersey

I'm an avid quilter, and so are many of my friends. When I hosted a luncheon for them, our favorite hobby proved to be the perfect theme.

My guests felt right at home when they saw the colorful table…and my theme-related menu had everyone in stitches!

Decorating was a snap because I used "material" I had on hand. The table was covered with an old-fashioned calico pieced quilt, and I used two baskets to create the centerpiece.

A smaller one with a plastic protector inside was filled with bright fresh flowers. This was nestled into a larger basket overflowing with pieces of fabric, scissors, patterns, pins, needles, thread and other quilting items.

I bought some pretty little notepads edged with quilting designs for favors, setting one at each place.

For the meal, I turned to some tried-and-true recipes from my files but renamed and decorated them especially for this gathering of handcrafters.

I knew I wouldn't run "afowl" serving a chicken salad I liked. For this occasion, I named it Flock of Geese Chicken Salad, after a popular quilt design. Everyone commented on this festive salad's great flavor.

My Patchwork Veggie Pizza resembled a sampler when I arranged assorted finely chopped vegetables to create mini "quilt squares" on top of the rectangular crescent-roll crust.

Our lunch also included soup, potato salad, iced tea, hot tea and coffee.

For dessert, Quilted Sugar Cookies were a crafty success. I piped on patterns with a decorating tube of frosting to make an eye-catching sampler of confections. These treats made for sweet munching as we continued to catch up on each other's news and chat about quilts we were working on.

Easy as it was, the theme turned lunch with friends into a memorable party for the congenial group. If you like quilting or other handcrafts, why not thread your materials, tools and menu into a casual social gathering like I did? It was such a satisfying project!

— 🎏 🎏 🎏 —

Flock of Geese Chicken Salad

Named for a time-honored quilt pattern, this salad flies high with a combination of chicken, red grapes, crisp celery and crunchy cashews. Its pleasant, creamy dressing is deliciously simple to make.

> **8 boneless skinless chicken breast halves (about 2 pounds), cooked and cubed**
> **2 cups seedless red grapes, halved**
> **2 cups salted cashew halves**
> **2 celery ribs, sliced**
> **3/4 cup mayonnaise**
> **1/2 cup sour cream**
> **1 tablespoon tarragon *or* white wine vinegar**
> **Lettuce leaves, optional**

In a large bowl, combine the first four ingredients; set aside. In a small bowl, combine mayonnaise, sour cream and vinegar; mix well. Pour over chicken mixture; toss to coat. Cover and refrigerate for at least 1 hour. Serve in a lettuce-lined bowl if desired. **Yield:** 12 servings.

— 🎏 🎏 🎏 —

Patchwork Veggie Pizza

Decorating one of my favorite appetizers to serve an avid group of quilters turned out to be such fun! I arranged the colorful vegetable toppings into a savory sampler for my luncheon guests to snack on.

✓ This tasty dish uses less sugar, salt and fat. Recipe includes *Diabetic Exchanges.*

> **2 tubes (8 ounces *each*) refrigerated crescent rolls**
> **1 package (8 ounces) cream cheese, softened**
> **1/4 cup Italian salad dressing**
> **1 cup chopped broccoli**
> **1 cup chopped carrots**
> **1 cup chopped cucumbers**
> **1 cup chopped tomato**

Unroll crescent dough and place on an ungreased baking sheet; press seams together to form a 15-in. x 12-in. rectangle. Bake at 375° for 11-13 minutes or until golden brown; cool completely. Combine cream cheese and salad dressing; spread over crust to within 1 in. of edge. With a knife, mark off 20 squares. Fill each square with one vegetable to make a patchwork design or the quilt pattern of your choice. Refrigerate or serve immediately. **Yield:** 20 servings. **Diabetic Exchanges:** One serving (prepared with reduced-fat crescent rolls and fat-free cream cheese and salad dressing) equals 1 vegetable, 1/2 starch, 1/2 fat; also, 98 calories, 274 mg sodium, 1 mg cholesterol, 12 gm carbohydrate, 4 gm protein, 4 gm fat.

— 🎏 🎏 🎏 —

Quilted Sugar Cookies

Piped-on frosting made my cookies into vivid mini-quilt blocks for a sweet ending to the theme luncheon. My friends appreciated the fact that even the food reflected our mutual love of quilting.

> **3/4 cup butter *or* margarine, softened**
> **1/3 cup confectioners' sugar**
> **2 tablespoons sugar**
> **1 egg**
> **1-1/2 cups all-purpose flour**
> **1/2 cup vanilla frosting and food coloring *or* decorator's icing**

In a mixing bowl, cream butter and sugars. Add egg; mix well. Add flour; mix well. Cover and chill for at least 1 hour. Line a 15-in. x 10-in. x 1-in. baking pan with heavy-duty foil. Press dough onto the bottom of pan. Score dough with a sharp knife to make 2-in. x 2-in. squares (discard scraps or reroll and bake as directed). Bake at 325° for 16-18 minutes or until set (cookies will not brown). Carefully lift cookies out of pan using foil. Cut into squares; cool. Mix frosting with food coloring to make desired colors or use decorator's icing. Decorate cookies with quilt patterns. **Yield:** about 3 dozen.

Sensational Sugar Tips

Sugar will last almost indefinitely if stored in an airtight container in a cool dry place.

One pound of granulated sugar is equal to 2-1/4 cups.

Make your own colored sugar by putting granulated sugar in a resealable plastic bag with a few drops of food coloring. Knead the sugar in the bag to disperse the color. Add a few more drops and repeat the process for a darker color.

General Recipe Index

This handy index lists every recipe by food category and/or major ingredient, so you can easily locate recipes.

Issue-by-Issue Index

Do you have a favorite dish from a specific Taste of Home issue but can't recall the recipe's actual name? You'll easily find it in this categorized listing of recipes by issue.

Diabetic Recipes Index

Refer to this index when you're looking for a recipe that uses less sugar, salt and fat and that includes Diabetic Exchanges. These good-for-you recipes are conveniently marked with this ✓ throughout the book.

The Cook's Quick Reference

From the *Taste of Home* Test Kitchens

Substitutions & Equivalents

Cooking Terms

Guide to Cooking with Popular Herbs

Substitutions & Equivalents

Equivalent Measures

3 teaspoons	=	1 tablespoon	16 tablespoons	=	1 cup
4 tablespoons	=	1/4 cup	2 cups	=	1 pint
5-1/3 tablespoons	=	1/3 cup	4 cups	=	1 quart
8 tablespoons	=	1/2 cup	4 quarts	=	1 gallon

Food Equivalents

Grains

Macaroni	1 cup (3-1/2 ounces) uncooked	=	2-1/2 cups cooked
Noodles, Medium	3 cups (4 ounces) uncooked	=	4 cups cooked
Popcorn	1/3 to 1/2 cup unpopped	=	8 cups popped
Rice, Long Grain	1 cup uncooked	=	3 cups cooked
Rice, Quick-Cooking	1 cup uncooked	=	2 cups cooked
Spaghetti	8 ounces uncooked	=	4 cups cooked

Crumbs

Bread	1 slice	=	3/4 cup soft crumbs, 1/4 cup fine dry crumbs
Graham Crackers	7 squares	=	1/2 cup finely crushed
Buttery Round Crackers	12 crackers	=	1/2 cup finely crushed
Saltine Crackers	14 crackers	=	1/2 cup finely crushed

Fruits

Bananas	1 medium	=	1/3 cup mashed
Lemons	1 medium	=	3 tablespoons juice, 2 teaspoons grated peel
Limes	1 medium	=	2 tablespoons juice, 1-1/2 teaspoons grated peel
Oranges	1 medium	=	1/4 to 1/3 cup juice, 4 teaspoons grated peel

Vegetables

Cabbage	1 head	=	5 cups shredded	Green Pepper	1 large	=	1 cup chopped
Carrots	1 pound	=	3 cups shredded	Mushrooms	1/2 pound	=	3 cups sliced
Celery	1 rib	=	1/2 cup chopped	Onions	1 medium	=	1/2 cup chopped
Corn	1 ear fresh	=	2/3 cup kernels	Potatoes	3 medium	=	2 cups cubed

Nuts

Almonds	1 pound	=	3 cups chopped	Pecan Halves	1 pound	=	4-1/2 cups chopped
Ground Nuts	3-3/4 ounces	=	1 cup	Walnuts	1 pound	=	3-3/4 cups chopped

Easy Substitutions

When you need...		Use...
Baking Powder	1 teaspoon	1/2 teaspoon cream of tartar + 1/4 teaspoon baking soda
Buttermilk	1 cup	1 tablespoon lemon juice *or* vinegar + enough milk to measure 1 cup (let stand 5 minutes before using)
Cornstarch	1 tablespoon	2 tablespoons all-purpose flour
Honey	1 cup	1-1/4 cups sugar + 1/4 cup additional liquid called for in recipe
Light Cream	1 cup	1 tablespoon melted butter + enough whole milk to measure 1 cup
Onion	1 small, chopped (1/3 cup)	1 teaspoon onion powder *or* 1 tablespoon dried minced onion
Tomato Juice	1 cup	1/2 cup tomato sauce + 1/2 cup water
Tomato Sauce	2 cups	3/4 cup tomato paste + 1 cup water
Unsweetened Chocolate	1 square (1 ounce)	3 tablespoons baking cocoa + 1 tablespoon shortening *or* oil
Whole Milk	1 cup	1/2 cup evaporated milk + 1/2 cup water

Cooking Terms

HERE'S a quick reference for some of the cooking terms used in *Taste of Home* recipes:

Baste—To moisten food with melted butter, pan drippings, marinades or other liquid to add more flavor and juiciness.

Beat—A rapid movement to combine ingredients using a fork, spoon, wire whisk or electric mixer.

Blend—To combine ingredients until *just* mixed.

Boil—To heat liquids until bubbles form that cannot be "stirred down". In the case of water, the temperature will reach 212°.

Bone—To remove all meat from the bone before cooking.

Cream—To beat ingredients together to a smooth consistency, usually in the case of butter and sugar for baking.

Dash—A small amount of seasoning, less than 1/8 teaspoon. If using a shaker, a dash would comprise a quick flip of the container.

Dredge—To coat foods with flour or other dry ingredients. Most often done with pot roasts and stew meat before browning.

Fold—To incorporate several ingredients by careful and gentle turning with a spatula. Used generally with beaten egg whites or whipped cream when mixing into the rest of the ingredients to keep the batter light.

Julienne—To cut foods into long thin strips much like matchsticks. Used most often for salads and stir-fry dishes.

Mince—To cut into very fine pieces. Used often for garlic or fresh herbs.

Parboil—To cook partially, usually used in the case of chicken, sausages and vegetables.

Partially set—Describes the consistency of gelatin after it has been chilled for a small amount of time. Mixture should resemble the consistency of egg whites.

Puree—To process foods to a smooth mixture. Can be prepared in an electric blender, food processor, food mill or sieve.

Saute—To fry quickly in a small amount of fat, stirring almost constantly. Most often done with onions, mushrooms and other chopped vegetables.

Score—To cut slits partway through the outer surface of foods. Often used with ham or flank steak.

Stir-Fry—To cook meats and/or vegetables with a constant stirring motion in a small amount of oil in a wok or skillet over high heat.

Guide to Cooking with Popular Herbs

HERB	APPETIZERS SALADS	BREADS/EGGS SAUCES/CHEESE	VEGETABLES PASTA	MEAT POULTRY	FISH SHELLFISH
BASIL	Green, Potato & Tomato Salads, Salad Dressings, Stewed Fruit	Breads, Fondue & Egg Dishes, Dips, Marinades, Sauces	Mushrooms, Tomatoes, Squash, Pasta, Bland Vegetables	Broiled, Roast Meat & Poultry Pies, Stews, Stuffing	Baked, Broiled & Poached Fish, Shellfish
BAY LEAF	Seafood Cocktail, Seafood Salad, Tomato Aspic, Stewed Fruit	Egg Dishes, Gravies, Marinades, Sauces	Dried Bean Dishes, Beets, Carrots, Onions, Potatoes, Rice, Squash	Corned Beef, Tongue Meat & Poultry Stews	Poached Fish, Shellfish, Fish Stews
CHIVES	Mixed Vegetable, Green, Potato & Tomato Salads, Salad Dressings	Egg & Cheese Dishes, Cream Cheese, Cottage Cheese, Gravies, Sauces	Hot Vegetables, Potatoes	Broiled Poultry, Poultry & Meat Pies, Stews, Casseroles	Baked Fish, Fish Casseroles, Fish Stews, Shellfish
DILL	Seafood Cocktail, Green, Potato & Tomato Salads, Salad Dressings	Breads, Egg & Cheese Dishes, Cream Cheese, Fish & Meat Sauces	Beans, Beets, Cabbage, Carrots, Cauliflower, Peas, Squash, Tomatoes	Beef, Veal Roasts, Lamb, Steaks, Chops, Stews, Roast & Creamed Poultry	Baked, Broiled, Poached & Stuffed Fish, Shellfish
GARLIC	All Salads, Salad Dressings	Fondue, Poultry Sauces, Fish & Meat Marinades	Beans, Eggplant, Potatoes, Rice, Tomatoes	Roast Meats, Meat & Poultry Pies, Hamburgers, Casseroles, Stews	Broiled Fish, Shellfish, Fish Stews, Casseroles
MARJORAM	Seafood Cocktail, Green, Poultry & Seafood Salads	Breads, Cheese Spreads, Egg & Cheese Dishes, Gravies, Sauces	Carrots, Eggplant, Peas, Onions, Potatoes, Dried Bean Dishes, Spinach	Roast Meats & Poultry, Meat & Poultry Pies, Stews & Casseroles	Baked, Broiled & Stuffed Fish, Shellfish
MUSTARD	Fresh Green Salads, Prepared Meat, Macaroni & Potato Salads, Salad Dressings	Biscuits, Egg & Cheese Dishes, Sauces	Baked Beans, Cabbage, Eggplant, Squash, Dried Beans, Mushrooms, Pasta	Chops, Steaks, Ham, Pork, Poultry, Cold Meats	Shellfish
OREGANO	Green, Poultry & Seafood Salads	Breads, Egg & Cheese Dishes, Meat, Poultry & Vegetable Sauces	Artichokes, Cabbage, Eggplant, Squash, Dried Beans, Mushrooms, Pasta	Broiled, Roast Meats, Meat & Poultry Pies, Stews, Casseroles	Baked, Broiled & Poached Fish, Shellfish
PARSLEY	Green, Potato, Seafood & Vegetable Salads	Biscuits, Breads, Egg & Cheese Dishes, Gravies, Sauces	Asparagus, Beets, Eggplant, Squash, Dried Beans, Mushrooms, Pasta	Meat Loaf, Meat & Poultry Pies, Stews & Casseroles, Stuffing	Fish Stews, Stuffed Fish
ROSEMARY	Fruit Cocktail, Fruit & Green Salads	Biscuits, Egg Dishes, Herb Butter, Cream Cheese, Marinades, Sauces	Beans, Broccoli, Peas, Cauliflower, Mushrooms, Baked Potatoes, Parsnips	Roast Meat, Poultry & Meat Pies, Stews & Casseroles, Stuffing	Stuffed Fish, Shellfish
SAGE		Breads, Fondue, Egg & Cheese Dishes, Spreads, Gravies, Sauces	Beans, Beets, Onions, Peas, Spinach, Squash, Tomatoes	Roast Meat, Poultry, Meat Loaf, Stews, Stuffing	Baked, Poached & Stuffed Fish
TARRAGON	Seafood Cocktail, Avocado Salads, Salad Dressings	Cheese Spreads, Marinades, Sauces, Egg Dishes	Asparagus, Beans, Beets, Carrots, Mushrooms, Peas, Squash, Spinach	Steaks, Poultry, Roast Meats, Casseroles & Stews	Baked, Broiled & Poached Fish, Shellfish
THYME	Seafood Cocktail, Green, Poultry, Seafood & Vegetable Salads	Biscuits, Breads, Egg & Cheese Dishes, Sauces, Spreads	Beets, Carrots, Mushrooms, Onions, Peas, Eggplant, Spinach, Potatoes	Roast Meat, Poultry & Meat Loaf, Meat & Poultry Pies, Stews & Casseroles	Baked, Broiled & Stuffed Fish, Shellfish, Fish Stews